Frommer's®

Tahiti & French Polynesia

2nd Edition

by Bill Goodwin

Here's what the critics say about Frommer's:

"Amazingly easy to use. Very portable, very complete."
—BOOKLIST

"Detailed, accurate, and easy-to-read information for all price ranges."
—GLAMOUR MAGAZINE

"Hotel information is close to encyclopedic."
—DES MOINES SUNDAY REGISTER

"Frommer's Guides have a way of giving you a real feel for a place."
—KNIGHT RIDDER NEWSPAPERS

WILEY

Wiley Publishing, Inc.

Published by:

WILEY PUBLISHING, INC.

111 River St.
Hoboken, NJ 07030-5774

ISBN 978-0-470-18988-7

Editor: Shelley W. Bance with Marc Nadeau
Production Editor: M. Faunette Johnston
Cartographer: Guy Ruggiero
Photo Editor: Richard Fox
Production by Wiley Indianapolis Composition Services

Front cover photo: Bora Bora: Pearl Beach Resort and Spa
Back cover photo: Outrigger canoe with sail and tourists off Bora Bora

CONTENTS

4 SUGGESTED ITINERARIES   87

5 TAHITI   97

6 MOOREA   142

8 RAIATEA & TAHAA 184

9 BORA BORA 199

10 MAUPITI 221

11 THE TUAMOTU ARCHIPELAGO 229

TAHITI & FRENCH POLYNESIA

CONTENTS

12 THE MARQUESAS ISLANDS 253

**APPENDIX A: FAST FACTS TAHITI &
FRENCH POLYNESIA** 286

APPENDIX B: USEFUL FRENCH TERMS & PHRASES 292

INDEX 300

LIST OF MAPS

ABOUT THE AUTHOR

Bill Goodwin began his writing career as an award-winning newspaper reporter and then served as legal counsel and speechwriter for two influential U.S. senators—Sam Nunn of Georgia and the late Sam Ervin of North Carolina. In 1977 he and a friend said goodbye to office life and sailed a 41-foot yacht from Annapolis, Maryland, through the Panama Canal to the Marquesas Islands, the Tuamotu Archipelago, and Tahiti. He left the boat in Papeete and, with girlfriend and backpack, explored Tahiti, Moorea, and the Society Islands for as long as the local immigration authorities would allow. He has returned for extended visits many times since, most devoted to researching and writing *Frommer's South Pacific*. He is also the author of *Frommer's Fiji* and, at home, *Frommer's Virginia*. Find out more at www.billgoodwin.com.

DEDICATION

To my father,
with love and grateful thanks for supporting
my being a writer rather than a lawyer

ACKNOWLEDGMENTS

I owe a debt of gratitude to many individuals and organizations for their assistance, information, and advice without which it would have been impossible to research and write this book. You will become acquainted with many of them in these pages, and it will be your good fortune if you meet them in the islands.

I am particularly grateful to Dany Panero, Céline Teihotaata Vaini Roloux, Al Keahi, Jonathan Reap, Carmen Estrada, and Leila Laille of Tahiti Tourisme, French Polynesia's terrific tourist information bureau.

My deep personal thanks go to Connie Haeder, Anne Simon, Curtis and Judy Moore, Suzanne McIntosh, Nancy Monseaux, and Max Parrish, who have tended the home front while I was away in the islands; to Bill and Donna Wilder, who introduced me to the intricacies of Tahiti and who once loaned me their home on Moorea; and to my sister, Jean Goodwin Santa Maria, who has consistently given much-needed moral support. I am truly blessed to have these wonderful folks in my life.

—Bill Goodwin

AN INVITATION TO THE READER

In researching this book, we discovered many wonderful places—hotels, restaurants, shops, and more. We're sure you'll find others. Please tell us about them, so we can share the information with your fellow travelers in upcoming editions. If you were disappointed with a recommendation, we'd love to know that, too. Please write to:

Frommer's Tahiti & French Polynesia, 2nd Edition
Wiley Publishing, Inc. • 111 River St. • Hoboken, NJ 07030-5774

AN ADDITIONAL NOTE

Please be advised that travel information is subject to change at any time—and this is especially true of prices. We therefore suggest that you write or call ahead for confirmation when making your travel plans. The authors, editors, and publisher cannot be held responsible for the experiences of readers while traveling. Your safety is important to us, however, so we encourage you to stay alert and be aware of your surroundings. Keep a close eye on cameras, purses, and wallets, all favorite targets of thieves and pickpockets.

FROMMER'S STAR RATINGS, ICONS & ABBREVIATIONS

Every hotel, restaurant, and attraction listing in this guide has been ranked for quality, value, service, amenities, and special features using a **star-rating system.** In country, state, and regional guides, we also rate towns and regions to help you narrow down your choices and budget your time accordingly. Hotels and restaurants are rated on a scale of zero (recommended) to three stars (exceptional). Attractions, shopping, nightlife, towns, and regions are rated according to the following scale: zero stars (recommended), one star (highly recommended), two stars (very highly recommended), and three stars (must-see).

In addition to the star-rating system, we also use **seven feature icons** that point you to the great deals, in-the-know advice and unique experiences that separate travelers from tourists. Throughout the book, look for:

Finds	Special finds—those places only insiders know about
Fun Facts	Fun facts—details that make travelers more informed and their trips more fun
Kids	Best bets for kids and advice for the whole family
Moments	Special moments—those experiences that memories are made of
Overrated	Places or experiences not worth your time or money
Tips	Insider tips—great ways to save time and money
Value	Great values—where to get the best deals

The following **abbreviations** are used for credit cards:

AE	American Express	DISC	Discover	V	Visa
DC	Diners Club	MC	MasterCard		

FROMMERS.COM

Now that you have this guidebook to help you plan a great trip, visit our website at **www.frommers.com** for additional travel information on more than 4,000 destinations. We update features regularly to give you instant access to the most current trip-planning information available. At Frommers.com, you'll find scoops on the best airfares, lodging rates, and car rental bargains. You can even book your travel online through our reliable travel booking partners. Other popular features include:

- Online updates of our most popular guidebooks
- Vacation sweepstakes and contest giveaways
- Newsletters highlighting the hottest travel trends
- Podcasts, interactive maps, and up-to-the-minute events listings
- Opinionated blog entries by Arthur Frommer himself
- Online travel message boards with featured travel discussions

What's New in Tahiti & French Polynesia

Tahiti and French Polynesia continue to develop at a rapid pace, with more resorts and restaurants being added and renovated. Here's a recap of the major changes since the first edition of this guide in 2007. Other recent developments are posted on the "Updates" page of my personal website, **www.billgoodwin.com**.

PLANNING YOUR TRIP Air Tahiti Nui (www.airtahitinui.com) has stopped flying between New York and Papeete during the Northern Hemisphere winter from November 2008 until April 2009, normally the slowest time of year on the route. The New York–Papeete flights now stop in Los Angeles. Air Tahiti Nui still flies between Papeete and Tokyo, but it has discontinued its service to Osaka in Japan.

Air New Zealand has stopped flying over its historic "Coral Route" between Tahiti, the Cook Islands, and Fiji. Inaugurated in the 1950s, it was the only east-west shortcut between Tahiti and Fiji via the Cooks. **Air Tahiti,** French Polynesia's domestic carrier, has taken over part of the route, flying between Tahiti and Rarotonga twice a week.

Air New Zealand and **Air Tahiti Nui** are code-sharing their routes between Los Angeles, Tahiti, and Auckland. Air New Zealand continues to fly its planes between Auckland and Papeete, but you will travel in Air Tahiti Nui aircraft between Papeete and Los Angeles. The changes mean that only Air Tahiti Nui and **Air France** fly their own planes between Los Angeles and Tahiti.

The *Tahitian Princess* (www.princess. com) will operate in Alaska rather than French Polynesia from June through September 2009, after which it will relocate to Asia.

The 170-passenger tall ship *Star Flyer* makes 7-, 10-, and 11-day cruises from Papeete through the Society and Tuamotu islands. It's operated by Star Clippers (© 800/442-0552; www.starclippers. com).

Silversea Cruises (© 800/722-9955; www.silversea.com) has announced plans to send its luxurious ship *Prince Albert II* to French Polynesia for 6 months in 2009, with the Marquesas and Austral islands among its expected ports of call. Named the *World Discoverer* before Silversea Cruises upgraded it, the *Prince Albert* now has such luxuries as a wine restaurant by Relais & Châteaux. One stop it is expected to make is at Le Taha'a Private Island & Spa, a Relais & Châteaux–affiliated resort.

The live-aboard dive boat *Tahiti Aggressor* (www.aggressor.com) has pulled out of French Polynesia and is now in Fiji.

The luxurious, 330-passenger *Paul Gauguin* (www.rssc.com) occasionally ventures from Papeete as far west as Fiji, spending 14 days in each direction with stops in French Polynesia, the Cook Islands, Tonga, and Fiji.

See chapter 3 for complete trip-planning information.

TAHITI In Papeete, the **Musée de la Perle Robert Wan (Robert Wan Pearl Museum)** has moved to boulevard Pomare at rue l'Arthémise, opposite the Eglise Evangélique. Admission is free.

The Sofitel Tahiti Resort has reverted to its former name, the **Sofitel Tahiti Maeva Beach Resort.** It's less confusing, since locals have always called it simply the "Maeva Beach."

The modern **Tahiti Airport Motel** (© 50.40.00; www.tahitiairportmotel. com) overlooks the runways of Tahiti-Faaa International Airport. Its 42 air-conditioned units are minimally decorated, but have TVs, phones, fridges, Wi-Fi, and private bathrooms.

Fare Suisse (© 42.00.30; www.fare suisse.com) is a four-room guesthouse on rue des Poilus Tahitiens in the Paofai neighborhood, within walking distance of the Papeete waterfront.

Backpackers can bunk in the two gender-segregated dorm rooms at **Teamo Hostel,** on rue du Pont-Neuf (© 42.00. 35; teamohostel@mail.pf), in a 126-year-old house about 6 blocks inland from the Moorea Ferry docks.

Among Tahiti's restaurants, **Auberge du Pacifique** and **Le Rubis** have closed. Auberge du Pacifique's building is now occupied by the family-oriented **Restaurant Blue Banana** (© 42.22.24), serving French and Italian cuisine.

L'O a la Bouche, on Passage Cardella, has switched from traditional French food to a fusion of cooking styles; it's expensive, but it's also the top restaurant downtown. At Marina Taina on the west coast, Casablanca Cocktail Restaurant is now **Casa Bianca,** offering Italian instead of Mediterranean fare. Even better at Marina Taina is the **Pink Coconut** (© 42.22.23), which has a gorgeous view of Moorea to accompany very good French and Tahitian fare.

See chapter 5 for complete information on Tahiti.

MOOREA The Jack Nicklaus–designed **Moorea Green Pearl Golf Course of Polynesia,** at Temae near the airport (© 56. 27.32; www.mooreagolf-resort.com), has French Polynesia's second course.

The **Sofitel Moorea Ia Ora Beach Resort,** formerly the Sofitel Moorea Beach Resort, has reopened after a year of extensive renovation. The resort's 1960s-vintage bungalows have been replaced by 80 versions that are more luxurious.

Moorea's dining options have broadened with the additions of **Rudy's** (© 56. 58.00), a steakhouse in Maharepa, and **La Petite Maison** (© 56.34.80), a French restaurant beside Cook's Bay in Pao Pao village.

The colonial-style **La Plantation** restaurant on Moorea's northwest coast has a new owner and now serves jambalaya and other dishes from Louisiana.

See chapter 6 for complete information on Moorea.

HUAHINE You may think you're staying at a tented safari camp in Kenya if you opt for the **Fare Ie** (© 60.63.77; www.tahiti safari.com). It has well-equipped tents perched beside a beach north of Fare, Huahine's main town, and near Parea, on the island's southern end.

Relais Mahana (www.relaismahana. com) has reopened after nearly US$4 million in renovations. **Patisserie Fare** has closed.

See chapter 7 for complete information on Huahine.

RAIATEA & TAHAA On Raiatea's west coast, **Hotel Mirimiri** has changed its name to **Raiatea Lodge Hotel** (www. raiateahotel.com) and reduced its room rates.

In Uturoa, **Restaurant Quai des Pecheurs** is now known as **Restaurant L'Espadon.** Frankly, I was unimpressed with the food.

See chapter 8 for complete information on Raiatea and Tahaa.

BORA BORA Among the superluxurious amenities at the **St. Regis Resort Bora Bora** (© **800/787-3447** or 60.78.88; www.stregis.com/borabora) is a 1210-sq.-m (13,000-sq.-ft.) spa on its own islet. The 100 superluxe guest quarters range from house-size bungalows to the Royal Estate, where Nicole Kidman and Keith Urban spent their honeymoon.

Also over-the-top is the **InterContinental Resort and Thalasso Spa Bora Bora** (© **800/327-0200** or 60.49.00; www.boraboraspa.intercontinental.com). The entire resort is the world's first to be air-conditioned using cold seawater pumped from 760m (2,500 ft.) down in the ocean. The saltwater is reheated for the Thalasso Spa's large swimming pool and unique treatments, some dispensed in rooms with glass floors set over water for fish viewing. The wedding chapel also is over the lagoon.

On the main island, the **Sofitel Bora Bora Marara Resort,** formerly the Sofitel Bora Bora Beach Resort, has reopened after being completely revamped. Its sister hotel, the Sofitel Bora Bora Motu, has changed its name to **Sofitel Bora Bora Motu Private Island** to reflect improvements during its own renovations. The **InterContinental Le Moana Resort Bora Bora** is back in business and much improved after a freak ocean swell did extensive damage in 2005 (no, it was not a tsunami).

La Matira Beach Restaurant (© **67.53. 79)** has taken over the lagoonside perch of the former Matira Bar and Restaurant, serving very good lunches and French fare for dinner.

Pirate's Bar and Restaurant has changed into **Restaurant St. James** (© **67.64.62),** offering both French and Continental fare. The lagoonside bar is a fine place for a sunset cocktail.

L'Appetisserie is now the **Aloe Cafe,** but little else has changed at my favorite breakfast spot. You can still check your e-mail and talk on Skype.

See chapter 9 for complete information on Bora Bora.

MAUPITI **Le Kuriri** (© **74.54.54** or 67.82.23; www.maupiti-kuriri.com) is now the top pension on Maupiti. On the ocean side of Motu Tiapaa, it's owned by Anne-Marie Badolle and Camille Marjorel, who gave up corporate life in France to sail around the world and then settle on Maupiti.

See chapter 10 for complete information on Maupiti.

THE TUAMOTU ARCHIPELAGO The charming **Relais Royal Tikehau** (© **96. 23.37;** www.royaltikehau.pf) has brought moderately priced accommodations to Tikehau atoll. Its four rooms and seven bungalows are on a small islet near the main island.

I no longer recommend **Panau Lagoon** and **Pension Hotu** on Tikihau.

See chapter 11 for complete information on the Tuamotu Archipelago.

The Best of Tahiti & French Polynesia

Tahiti and her sister islands in French Polynesia have conjured up romantic images of an earthly paradise since European sailors brought home tales of their tropical splendor and uninhibited people in the 1760s. My own love affair with these remote outposts doesn't go back quite that far, but when I did wash ashore in 1977, I quickly understood why they came to have such a reputation. In fact, I was so smitten that I stayed for 7 months, as long as the gendarmes would allow in those days.

You may wish to plan a longer trip yourself, for these are the most beautiful islands in the world—an opinion shared with many others, including the late James A. Michener. They are blessed with gorgeous beaches, and their lagoons allow for spectacular diving and snorkeling.

Then there are the Polynesian islanders who live here. Their fabled history has provided fodder for famous books and films, their storied culture inspires hedonistic dreams, and their big, infectious smiles add charm to any visit.

In this chapter, I point out the best of the best—not necessarily to pass qualitative judgment, but to help you choose among the surprisingly many options in the islands. They're listed here in the order in which they appear in the book.

For a preview of the islands, see "The Islands in Brief" in chapter 4.

1 THE MOST BEAUTIFUL ISLANDS

"In the South Seas," the poet Rupert Brooke wrote in 1914, "the Creator seems to have laid himself out to show what He can do." How right the poet was, for here lie some of the world's most dramatically beautiful islands. The best of the lot have jagged mountain peaks plunging into aquamarine lagoons.

Here are some that you see on travel posters and in brochures:

- **Moorea:** To my mind, Moorea is the most beautiful island in the world. Nothing compares with its saw-toothed ridges and the great dark-green hulk of Mount Rotui separating glorious Cook's and Opunohu bays. The view from Tahiti of Moorea's dinosaur-like skyline is unforgettable. See chapter 6.

- **Huahine:** Although Moorea and Bora Bora get most of the ink, Huahine is almost as gorgeous. Its bays are surrounded by mountains that almost rival Moorea's. But since it is off the well-beaten tourist track, it still retains an air of old Polynesia. Relatively unhurried by both tourists and the pressures of modern life, its residents still greet you with a big smile and have time to sit and chat. See chapter 7.

- **Bora Bora:** The late James Michener thought Bora Bora was the most beautiful island in the world. Although tourism has turned this gem into a sort of expensive South Seas Disneyland since Michener's day, development hasn't altered the incredible beauty of Bora

Bora's basaltic tombstone towering over a lagoon ranging in color from yellow to deep blue. See chapter 9.

- **Maupiti:** An unspoiled jewel, Maupiti is like nearby Bora Bora in miniature, but without any modern hotels or resorts. Like Bora Bora, its mountainous central island towers over a crystal-clear lagoon. See chapter 10.

- **Rangiroa, Tikehau, Manihi, & Fakarava:** These atolls are lumped together because they are equally beautiful. Each has a string of islets enclosing large lagoons, like giant lakes in the middle of the ocean. See chapter 11.

- **Ua Pou & Fatu Hiva:** The two most gorgeous of the Marquesas Islands, Ua Pou and Fatu Hiva both are high and mountainous, with cliffs and steep ridges outlining valleys descending to the edge of the sea. Ua Pou's mountain ridges are topped by stovepipe spires, while Virgin's Bay on Fatu Hiva is one of the world's most spectacularly beautiful yacht anchorages. See chapter 12.

2 THE BEST BEACHES

Because all but a few of the islands are surrounded by coral reefs, there are few surf beaches here. Most of those on Tahiti have heat-absorbing black volcanic sand. Except in the Marquesas, which are almost devoid of coral, most islands (and all but a few resorts) have bathtub-like lagoons that lap on white-coral sands draped by coconut palms. Here are a few that stand out from the many (the French word for "beach" being *plage*):

- **La Plage de Maui** (Tahiti): Bordering the southern shore of Tahiti Iti, the main island's peninsula, this strip of white sand is far and away the best beach on Tahiti. The lagoon is suitable for swimming, and there's an excellent snack bar beside the beach. See chapter 5.

- **Mareto Plage Publique** (Moorea): Although it isn't as picturesque as Moorea's Temae Plage Publique (see below), this beach between Cook's and Opunohu bays sits between a coconut grove and the lagoon. See chapter 6.

- **Temae Plage Publique** (Moorea): The northeastern coast of Moorea is fringed by a nearly uninterrupted stretch of white-sand beach that commands a glorious view: across a speckled lagoon to Tahiti, sitting on the horizon across the Sea of the Moon. See chapter 6.

- **Avea Beach** (Huahine): My favorite resort beach is at Relais Mahana, a small hotel on Auea Bay near Huahine's southern end. Trees grow along the white beach, which slopes into a lagoon deep enough for swimming at any tide. The resort's pier goes out to a giant coral head, a perfect and safe place to snorkel, and the lagoon here is protected from the trade winds, making it safe for sailing. See chapter 7.

- **Matira Beach** (Bora Bora): Beginning at the Hotel Bora Bora, this fine ribbon of sand stretches around skinny Matira Point, which forms the island's southern extremity, all the way to Club Med. The eastern side has views of the sister islands of Raiatea and Tahaa. See chapter 9.

- **Plage Tereia** (Maupiti): Like Matira Beach on Bora Bora, this white-sand beach wraps around a peninsula on Maupiti's main island. Unlike Matira, however, you'll likely have this one all to yourself, since there are no resorts on Maupiti. Almost as beautiful is the beach at the northern end of Motu Tiapaa, where you have a view of Maupiti's central mountain, and no one cares if you skinny-dip. See chapter 10.

• **Les Sables Rose/The Pink Sands** (Rangiroa): At a remote corner of Rangiroa's lagoon, the world's second largest, lies a gorgeous beach made up of pink sand. It's well worth the hour-long boat ride from Rangiroa's hotels. See chapter 11.

• **Motu Tuherahera** (Tikehau): The eastern half of Tikihau's main island is skirted by a beautiful stretch of white sand, much of it flanked by the atoll's pensions. See chapter 11.

3 THE BEST HONEYMOON RESORTS

Whether you're on your honeymoon or not, French Polynesia is a marvelous place for romantic escapes. After all, romance and the islands have gone hand-in-hand since the young women of Tahiti gave rousing, bare-breasted welcomes to the 18th-century European explorers.

Back in those days, everyone here lived in a proverbial little grass shack by the beach. The modern resorts have elevated that concept into luxurious guest bungalows, many built on stilts out over the lagoons. I've never stayed anywhere as romantic as these thatched-roof overwater units, most with glass panels in their floors for viewing fish swimming below. If their indoor luxuries aren't enough, you can climb down the steps leading from your front deck and go skinny-dipping in the warm waters below. The overwater bungalows help make French Polynesia—especially Bora Bora—one of the world's most famous honeymoon destinations. Naturally, they are the most expensive accommodations here.

One caveat is in order: Many overwater bungalows are relatively close together, meaning that your honeymooning next-door neighbors will be within earshot if not eyeshot. ("It can be like watching an X-rated video," a hotel manager once confessed, "but without the video.") Therefore, if you're seeking a high degree of privacy and seclusion, these won't necessarily be your best choice.

The top resorts are variations on the same theme: a beachside central complex with a restaurant, bar, and other public facilities flanked by individual guest bungalows in a coconut grove. From the shoreline, piers reach out to the overwater units. I point out the top resorts island-by-island in the paragraphs below, but please read the reviews in the chapters that follow before making your choice.

• **Tahiti:** Most visitors now consider Tahiti to be a way station to the other islands, but the **InterContinental Resort Tahiti** (p. 126) has overwater bungalows that face the dramatic outline of Moorea across the Sea of the Moon. Some of those at **Le Meridien Tahiti** (p. 128) also have this view.

• **Moorea:** The units at the **Club Bali Hai** (p. 158) are among the oldest—and the least expensive—overwater bungalows in the islands, but they enjoy an unparalleled view of the jagged mountains surrounding Cook's Bay. Some overwater units at the **Sofitel Moorea Ia Ora Beach Resort** (p. 158) actually face Tahiti across the Sea of the Moon, and they're built over Moorea's most colorful lagoon. The **Moorea Pearl Resort & Spa** (p. 158) has a few bungalows perched on the edge of the cliflike reef, making for superb snorkeling right off your front deck. You'll have more of these luxurious cabins at the **InterContinental Resort and Spa Moorea** (p. 161).

• **Huahine:** After a few days on Bora Bora, many couples today are opting to end their honeymoons by decompressing on

Huahine or Tahaa (see below). On Huahine, the American-owned **Te Tiare Beach Resort** (p. 179) is one of the smallest and most intimate retreats in French Polynesia. Its units have some of the largest decks of any overwater bungalows (one side is completely shaded by a thatched roof).

- **Tahaa:** The most charmingly Polynesian of all overwater units are at the **Le Taha'a Private Island & Spa** (p. 195), a luxurious resort on a small islet off Tahaa. Some of these have views of Bora Bora on the horizon.

- **Bora Bora:** This most famous—and crowded—of French Polynesia's honeymoon islands has several hundred overwater bungalows. Some at the superluxe **St. Regis Resort Bora Bora** (p. 213) have swimming pools set in their overwater decks. Not only does the **InterContinental Resort and Thalasso Spa Bora Bora** (p. 212) have overwater units for its guests, but three treatment rooms at its extraordinary spa also extend out over the lagoon (you can watch the fish through a glass floor panel while getting a massage). The **Bora Bora Nui Resort & Spa** (p. 210) has large, two-room overwater units, but only a few look out to tombstone-like Mount Otemanu, one of the most photographed scenes in the entire South Pacific. You will have that awesome view at the **Sofitel Bora Bora Motu**

Private Island (p. 213), most of whose bungalows directly face the tombstone mountain. Among the most private units are the garden units at the **Bora Bora Pearl Beach Resort** (p. 211); you can cavort to your heart's content in their wall-enclosed patios, which have sun decks and splash pools. The smaller but well-appointed overwater units at the friendly **Hotel Maitai Polynesia** (p. 214) are the least expensive on Bora Bora. You'll be up on a hillside rather than by the beach, but the three units at the inexpensive **Rohutu Fare Lodge** (p. 216) are the most suggestively decorated in French Polynesia.

- **Tuamotu Archipelago:** Out at the huge atoll of Rangiroa, the **Hotel Kia Ora** (p. 235) has bungalows over the world's second-largest lagoon. It also boasts beachside units with Jacuzzi pools set in their front porches. On the adjacent atoll, the **Tikehau Pearl Beach Resort** (p. 240) resides on its own small islet, affording more privacy than most other French Polynesian resorts. Some overwater bungalows actually sit over the riptides in a pass that lets the sea into the lagoon. Although its bungalows are all ashore, the charming **Relais Royal Tikehau** (p. 242) is a less expensive alternative. On Manihi atoll, units at the **Manihi Pearl Beach Resort** (p. 244) are cooled by the almost constantly blowing trade winds.

(Tips) Getting Hitched in the Islands

The islands are marvelous places for a honeymoon. Getting married in French Polynesia, however, is another matter, due to a required 30-day residency. That is, you have to stay here at least a month before you can get a marriage license. On the other hand, most resorts have romantic wedding packages including traditional ceremonies, often right on the beach, so many couples get legally hitched at home, and then go through it again here. Others come here to reaffirm their vows.

4 THE BEST FAMILY RESORTS

There are no Disney Worlds or other such attractions in the islands. As I point out in the "Family Travel" section in chapter 3 (p. 70), most tourism here is geared toward honeymooners and other couples. In fact, most resorts in French Polynesia are designed specifically for romance. Accordingly, most resorts house their guests in individual bungalows best occupied by two people. That's not to say that children won't have a fine time here, for more and more resorts are making provisions for families as well as honeymooners. Kids who like being around the water will enjoy themselves the most.

Here are a few family-friendly resorts:

*   **InterContinental Resort Tahiti** (Tahiti): Tahiti's best all-around resort has a few overwater bungalows, but most units are hotel rooms that interconnect, thus giving families who can afford them two or more units in which to roam. See p. 126.
*   **Radisson Plaza Resort Tahiti** (Tahiti): The lagoon off the black-sand beach at the Radisson Plaza is subject to dangerous riptides, but kids can play in the walk-in swimming pool. Parents who don't mind letting their youngsters bunk on the living-room sofa can sleep upstairs in a two-story "duplex" suite. The Radisson frequently offers special deals for families, such as letting kids stay and eat free. See p. 131.
*   **Club Bali Hai** (Moorea): Along with an awesome view of Cook's Bay, the Club Bali Hai has numerous units with kitchens, a benefit of the fact that about half of the units are timeshares. It lacks the organized activities of the InterContinental Resort & Spa Moorea (see below), but you will pay considerably less for a unit here. See p. 158.
*   **Bora Bora Lagoon Resort & Spa** (Bora Bora): This upscale resort on an islet off Bora Bora has a two-bedroom villa among its inventory, a plus for well-heeled families. See p. 160.
*   **Bora Bora Nui Resort & Spa** (Bora Bora): This large and swanky resort has a variety of accommodations, including hotel-style units that interconnect. See p. 210.
*   **Bora Bora Pearl Beach Resort** (Bora Bora): Families can opt for one of Pearl's beachside one-bedroom villas. See p. 211.
*   **Le Meridien Bora Bora** (Bora Bora): In my opinion, the top family resort in French Polynesia, this Meridien has units beside a shallow, man-made lagoon, a safe haven for children playing in the water. The youngsters can also both play and learn in the resort's award-wining sea turtle rescue and breeding program. See p. 212.
*   **St. Regis Resort Bora Bora** (Bora Bora): While most French Polynesian resorts take the view that you're here to get away from it all and thus don't need Internet access, the over-the-top St. Regis Bora Bora provides high-speed access even in its high-tech Hono Iti kids' club, where well-heeled youngsters can also play the latest video games. See p. 213.

5 THE BEST HISTORICAL & CULTURAL EXPERIENCES

The people of Tahiti and French Polynesia are justly proud of their ancient culture, as well as the unique modern history that sets them apart from all other Pacific Islanders.

Below are the best ways to learn about the people, their lifestyle, and their history.

- **La Maison de James Norman Hall/ James Norman Hall's Home** (Tahiti): The coauthor of *Mutiny on the Bounty* and other books set in the South Pacific lived most of his adult life on Tahiti. His family maintains his former home as a fascinating museum. See p. 105.

- **Marché Municipal/Municipal Market** (Tahiti): Papeete's large, teeming market is a wonderful place to examine tropical foodstuffs as well as to buy handicrafts. It's especially busy before dawn on Sunday. See p. 106.

- **Musée de Tahiti et Ses Isles/Museum of Tahiti and Her Islands** (Tahiti): This terrific lagoonside museum recounts the geology, history, culture, flora, and fauna of French Polynesia. It's worth a stop just for the outstanding view of Moorea from its coconut-grove setting. See p. 106.

- **Musée Gauguin/Gauguin Museum** (Tahiti): The great French painter Paul Gauguin lived and worked on Tahiti's south coast from 1891 until moving to Hiva Oa in the Marquesas Islands, where he died. This museum has a few of his original works, but is best at tracing his adventures in French Polynesia. See p. 107.

- **Tiki Theatre Village** (Moorea): Built to resemble a pre-European Tahitian village, this cultural center has demonstrations of handicrafts making and puts on a nightly dance show and feast. It's a bit commercial, and the staff isn't always fluent in English, but this is the only place in French Polynesia where one can sample the old ways. See p. 151.

- **Maeva** *Maraes* (Huahine): The ancient Tahitians gathered to worship their gods and hold other ceremonies at stone temples known as *maraes*. More than 40 of these structures have been restored near the village of Maeva and are a highlight of any visit to Huahine. See p. 174.

- **Taputapuatea** *Marae* (Raiatea): French Polynesia's largest and most important *marae* sits beside the lagoon on Raiatea. Archaeologists have uncovered bones apparently from human sacrifices from beneath its 45m-long (150-ft.) grand altar. See p. 187.

- **Tohua Papa Nui/Paul Gauguin Cultural Center** (Hiva Oa): This small museum recounts Paul Gauguin's last days on Hiva Oa, where he died in 1903. It's worth a visit to see the exact replicas of his original paintings executed by a team of French artists. See p. 276.

6 THE BEST OF THE OLD SOUTH SEAS

The islands are developing rapidly, with modern, fast-paced cities like Papeete replacing what were once sleepy backwater ports. But there are still remnants of the old South Seas days of coconut planters, beach bums, and missionaries.

- **Huahine:** Of the major French Polynesian islands, Huahine has been the least affected by tourism, and its residents are still likely to give you an unprompted Tahitian greeting, *"Ia orana!"* Agriculture is still king on Huahine, which

makes it the "Island of Fruits." There are ancient *maraes* (temples) to visit, and the only town, tiny **Fare,** is little more than a collection of Chinese shops fronting the island's wharf, which come to life when ships pull in. See chapter 7.

- **Tahaa:** With no towns and barely a village, Tahaa is still predominantly a vanilla-growing island—as sweet aromas will attest. One of French Polynesia's top resorts is on a small islet off

Tahaa, but otherwise this rugged little island takes you back to the way Moorea used to be. See chapter 8.

- **Maupiti:** Not long ago, residents of Maupiti voted down a proposal to build an upscale resort on their gorgeous little island, thus leaving it as a day trip from Bora Bora or as an unspoiled retreat for those who can do without maximum luxuries—or the English language. Maupiti looks like Bora Bora; locals boast that it's how Bora Bora used to be. See chapter 10.

- **The Tuamotu Archipelago:** Whether you choose to visit Rangiroa, Tikehau, Manihi, or Fakarava, you will find modern Polynesian life relatively undisturbed by modern ways, except for the many black-pearl farms in their lagoons. See chapter 11.

- **The Marquesas Islands:** Best visited on the cruise ship *Aranui 3,* the Marquesas hearken back to the early 19th century, when Herman Melville and others jumped off whaling ships and disappeared into the islands' haunting valleys. See chapter 12.

7 THE BEST DINING EXPERIENCES

Wherever the French go, fine food and wine are sure to follow, and French Polynesia is no exception. You will get good food everywhere here, but these are a few of the best places to sample fine fare.

- **Le Coco's** (Tahiti): On Tahiti's west coast, you'll have a fine view of Moorea from the patio at Le Coco's, specializing in light nouvelle cuisine. See p. 135.

- **Le Lotus** (Tahiti): The most romantic setting of any French Polynesian restaurant is in this overwater dining room at the InterContinental Resort Tahiti. The food is gourmet French and the service highly efficient and unobtrusive, but even if they weren't, the view of Moorea on a moonlit night would still make an evening here special. See p. 135.

- **Restaurant Pink Coconut** (Tahiti): Also with a spectacular view of Moorea from Marina Taina, the Pink Coconut is my favorite place for a romantic lunch. See p. 136.

- **Le Royal Tahitien Restaurant** (Tahiti): The food is very good and moderately priced at Hotel Le Royal Tahitien's dining room, which occupies a 1937 vintage building beside the black-sand beach in the Pirae suburb. See p. 137.

- **Le Belvédère** (Tahiti): The fondue isn't worth writing home about, but the spectacular view of Papeete and Moorea from high in the hills above the city is worth a postcard. See p. 138.

- **L'O a la Bouche** (Tahiti): Downtown Papeete's best fare is this stylish bistro emphasizing fusion cooking and fine wines. See p. 137.

- **Les Roulottes** (Tahiti): Dining in a parking lot is far from romantic, but the meal wagons on the Papeete waterfront after dark are the best food value in French Polynesia. The carnival-like scene itself is worth seeing. See p. 140.

- **Le Mahogany** (Moorea): After 30 years at the former Hotel Bali Hai, Chef François Courtien now works his magic at Le Mahogany, one of the best food values on Moorea. See p. 167.

- **Le Mayflower** (Moorea): Mainly locals in the know frequent this roadside restaurant, Moorea's best. The sauces are delightfully light, as are the prices for such good food. See p. 169.

- **Painapo (Pineapple) Beach** (Moorea): This beachside pavilion is my favorite place for an authentic Sunday buffet of traditional Tahitian food. It's one of French Polynesia's best values, too. See p. 170.

- **Bloody Mary's Restaurant & Bar** (Bora Bora): A fun evening at French Polynesia's most famous restaurant is a must-do when on Bora Bora. That's because Bloody Mary's provides the most unique and charming dining experience in the islands. Come early for a drink at the friendly bar, and then pick your fresh seafood from atop a huge tray of ice. After eating heavy French fare elsewhere for a few days, the sauceless fish from the grill will seem downright refreshing. See p. 218.

- **La Villa Mahana** (Bora Bora): Corsican chef Damien Rinaldi Dovio also provides relief from traditional French sauces at his romantic little restaurant, where he uses "exotic" spices to enliven fresh fish and beef dishes. See p. 219.

8 THE BEST ISLAND NIGHTS

Don't come to the islands expecting opera and ballet, or Las Vegas–style floor shows either. Other than pub-crawling to bars and nightclubs in Papeete, evening entertainment here consists primarily of feasts of island foods followed by traditional dancing—and whatever else you and your companion can concoct in these extraordinarily romantic islands.

Of course, the Tahitian hip-swinging traditional dances are world-famous. They are not as lewd and lascivious today as they were in the days before the missionaries arrived, but they still have plenty of suggestive movements to the primordial beat of drums; see "A Most Indecent Song & Dance" (p. 35).

Every hotel will have at least one dance show a week. The best are on Tahiti, especially the thrice-weekly performances at the InterContinental Resort Tahiti that feature one of the best troupes, the **Grande** Danse de Tahiti (p. 141). Also good are the Friday and Saturday evening shows at the **Captain Bligh Restaurant and Bar** (p. 119).

Moorea has one of the best shows at **Tiki Theatre Village,** where the dancers wear traditional costumes (p. 149). Among Moorea's hotels, the **InterContinental Resort and Spa Moorea** (p. 161) stages a spectacular beachside show on Saturday nights, and the **Club Bali Hai** (p. 171) has a free performance at 6pm on Wednesday, followed by an à la carte barbecue, making it also a very good value.

If you want to see the very best Tahitian dancing, come here in July during the annual *Heiva Nui* festival, when the top troupes compete on the Papeete waterfront. Plan early, since tickets can be hard to come by if you wait until the last minute. See the "French Polynesia Calendar of Events" (p. 48) for details.

9 THE BEST BUYS

Take some extra money along, for you'll likely spend it on black pearls, handicrafts, and tropical clothing.

See "Shopping," in chapter 5, for an overall discussion and the "Shopping" sections in the individual destination chapters for the best shops on the other islands.

- **Black Pearls:** Few people will escape French Polynesia without buying at least one black pearl. That's because the shallow, clear-water lagoons of the Tuamotu Archipelago are the world's largest producers of the beautiful dark orbs. The seemingly inexhaustible supply has resulted in fierce competition by vendors ranging from market stalls to high-end jewelry shops.

- **Handicrafts:** Although many of the items you will see in island souvenir shops are actually made in Asia, locally produced handicrafts are among the best buys. The most widespread are hats, mats, and baskets woven of pandanus leaves or other fibers, usually by women who have maintained this ancient art to a high degree. Woodcarvings are also popular, especially those from the Marquesas Islands. Many carvings in some large stores, however, tend to be produced for the tourist trade and often lack the imagery of

bygone days; some may also be machine-produced these days.

- **Tropical Clothing:** Colorful hand-screened, hand-blocked, and hand-dyed fabrics are very popular in the islands for making dresses or the wraparound skirt known as *pareu*. Many *pareus* are hand-painted, some almost works of art. Others are produced when heat-sensitive dyes are applied by hand to gauzelike cotton, which is then laid in the sun for several hours. Flowers, leaves, and other designs are placed on the fabric, and as the heat of the sun darkens and sets the dyes, the shadows from these objects leave their images behind on the finished product.

10 THE BEST DIVING & SNORKELING

All the islands have excellent scuba diving and snorkeling, and all but a few of the resorts have their own dive operations or can easily make arrangements with a local company.

The lagoons in French Polynesia are known less for colorful soft corals than for the wide variety of sea life they contain. Both the number and variety of colorful tropical fish are astounding. Stingrays and manta rays are prevalent, and some in the Society Island lagoons are quite friendly to humans, the result of having been hand-fed (you'll see them hanging around the waterside restaurants after dark, hoping for handouts).

Rare is the diver who doesn't encounter sharks here, though most will be of the relatively harmless reef varieties—blacktip, silvertip, whitetip, and gray. The most visited islands now have shark-feeding encounters (see "The Best Offbeat Travel Experiences" at the end of this chapter). Hammerheads and other large sharks live

outside the reef and in the passes leading into the lagoons.

Most dive sites are along or just outside the barrier reefs and within short boat rides of the resorts.

If you like to snorkel, you're in for a few treats, whether on a shark-feeding excursion with other tourists or just swimming off your hotel beach. In some cases, snorkelers can go out with scuba divers.

The best diving and snorkeling are at **Rangiroa, Tikehau, Manihi,** and **Fakarava** in the Tuamotu Archipelago, where the huge lagoons harbor an incredible variety of fish and sharks. Go to Rangiroa to see sharks; go to the others to see more fish than you ever imagined existed. See chapter 11.

The atolls are also home to heart-stopping "ride the rip" dives and snorkeling trips, on which you literally ride the tidal current through the passes into the lagoons. See "The Best Offbeat Travel Experiences," below.

Sailboats based on Tahiti and Moorea will take you out for a spin, or even to the late Marlon Brando's island of Tetiaroa, but the best sailing here is among the Leeward Islands of Raiatea, Tahaa, Bora Bora, and Huahine. Having arrived here originally via yacht from the East Coast of the United States, I can say without qualification that the sailing among the Leeward Islands is world-class.

French Polynesia's center for charter-yacht sailing is **Raiatea,** where rentals are available from several companies (including The Moorings, the outstanding American company).

Raiatea shares a lagoon with **Tahaa,** its rugged sister island. Tahaa is indented with long bays sheltering numerous picturesque anchorages, and you can sail completely around it without leaving the lagoon.

If you are reasonably skilled at "blue water" offshore sailing, both Bora Bora and Huahine are just 32km (20 miles) away, albeit in opposite directions. Most of the charter-boat companies will let you leave the boat in either Huahine or Bora Bora, so you won't have to beat back to Raiatea after your week or so of knocking around the islands.

Details are in "Seeing the Islands by Cruise Ship & Yacht," in chapter 3.

12 THE BEST OFFBEAT TRAVEL EXPERIENCES

Some cynics might say that a visit to French Polynesia itself is an offbeat experience, but there are three things to do here that are really unusual.

- **Getting Asked to Dance** (everywhere): I've seen so many traditional dance shows that I now stand by the rear door, ready to beat a quick escape before those lovely young women in grass skirts can grab my hand and force me to make a fool of myself trying to gyrate my hips up on the stage. It's part of the tourist experience at all resorts, and it's all in good fun.

- **Swimming with the Sharks** (Bora Bora): A key attraction in Bora Bora's magnificent lagoon is to snorkel with a guide, who actually feeds a school of sharks as they thrash around in a frenzy. I prefer to leave this one to the Discovery Channel. See p. 207.

- **Riding the Rip** (Rangiroa and Manihi): Divers and snorkelers will never forget the flying sensation as they ride the strong currents ripping through passes into the lagoons at Rangiroa and Manihi. See "Rangiroa" and "Manihi" in chapter 11.

Tahiti & French Polynesia in Depth

One of my editors once commented that I mention several bars and nightclubs in Papeete, French Polynesia's busy capital city, but not on Bora Bora, Moorea, and elsewhere. "Isn't there nightlife on the other islands?" she queried.

"No," I answered. "It's like this in French Polynesia: You get up in the morning, you look at an unbelievably beautiful island over breakfast, you play in the blue lagoon all day, you come back to your thatched-roof bungalow for a shower, and you have a fine French meal followed by a hip-swinging Tahitian dance show. It's all over by 9pm. If you don't know how to occupy yourselves between 9pm and midnight on your honeymoon, you need more than travel advice."

My reply may have been in jest, but many people do choose to honeymoon on these gorgeous islands, and for good reason. Married or not, these perpetually warm, languid specks of land on a vast ocean are the perfect places for passion—as I can vouch from personal experience!

Romance is inspired not only by the beauty of the islands but by the prevailing attitude here. You are likely to encounter women with bare breasts on the beaches, for these islands are French as well as Polynesian. Unlike other South Pacific island countries, where the preaching of puritanical 19th-century missionaries took deeper root, here you will discover a marvelous combination of French laissez faire and Tahitian *joie de vivre* born of a hedonistic Polynesian past.

Understanding that storied past, the culture and language of the marvelous people, and the fascinating flora and fauna will add an immeasurable richness to your visit. That's especially true of Tahiti, the first South Pacific island to be examined in detail by Europeans and historically the most significant island in the region.

The material in this chapter will give you an in-depth look at the islands. I strongly recommend you read it before beginning your own exploration of these most intriguing islands.

---

1 FRENCH POLYNESIA TODAY

One reason there is so little nightlife in the islands is that Polynesians traditionally go to bed early so they can get up with the sun. This lifestyle comes in handy on Tahiti, where they rise before the crack of dawn to make the 2-hour-plus commute to work in Papeete. That's right: While you're sleeping late on your honeymoon, many thousands of islanders are sitting in Tahiti's choking traffic.

Therein lies one of the paradoxes of French Polynesia today. On the one hand are the outer islands with their small populations, crystal-clear lagoons, and resorts designed with love (or at least sex) in mind. On the other are Papeete and its suburbs, a busy metropolitan area that—except for the phenomenal scenery surrounding it—could be on the French Riviera.

On another hand, wealthy French expatriates build luxury homes high into the hills overlooking the city, while many Tahitians live in homes of plywood and tin jammed into crowded neighborhoods. French Polynesia is governed by France, but about half of the local population consistently votes for politicians favoring independence from France.

Although those are the realities, they bear little resemblance to the fantasy world most of us experience while here. Instead, we're whisked away to resorts designed to make us forget our own realities back home, while barely seeing the real world around us here.

However, one thing we all do experience is the warmth and friendliness of the Polynesian people, which no amount of money, vehicles, or political bickering has managed to change.

GOVERNMENT

French Polynesia is a "community" within the French system of overseas territories. France sends a high commissioner from Paris and controls foreign affairs, defense, justice, internal security, and currency. French Polynesians have considerable autonomy over their internal affairs through a 49-member Assembly, which selects a president, the country's highest-ranking local official. The Assembly decides all issues that are not reserved for the metropolitan French government.

Local voters also cast ballots in French presidential elections and choose two elected deputies and two senators to the French parliament in Paris.

The city of Papeete and a few other communities have local police forces, but the French gendarmes control most law enforcement (they are as likely to be from Martinique as from Moorea).

Local politics breaks down generally into two camps: those who favor remaining under French control, but with increased local autonomy (that is, pro-autonomy), and those who seek complete independence from France (pro-independence). The two sides have swapped control of the local government several times in recent years, and the "musical chairs" may continue. Except for an occasional demonstration or labor stoppage, the instability has had little effect on visitors. See "Looking at the Past of Tahiti & French Polynesia," below.

THE ECONOMY

French Polynesia has only two significant industries: tourism and black pearls. More than 200,000 visitors arrive in the islands each year, making tourism the largest earner. Some US$150 million (£75 million) worth of pearls are exported annually, mostly to Japan. Vanilla, copra, coconut-oil cosmetics (you will see the *Monoi* brand everywhere), and an elixir made from the *noni* fruit are minor exports (most of the *noni* processed here is imported from Fiji). About 80% of all food consumed here is imported.

French Polynesia would be bankrupt were it not for more than 20€ billion (US$31 billion/£15.5 million) poured in by the government in Paris each year. That includes some 150€ million (US$233 million/£116 million) a year from an economic restructuring fund, set up after France closed its nuclear testing facility in 1996, to foster self-sufficiency by developing the local infrastructure. The fund has paid for public-works projects that have transformed the waterfronts in Papeete and on Raiatea, improved the roads, and built new schools, hospitals, and docks.

In addition, the local government set up highly favorable tax and investment laws that have spurred hotel construction. Bora Bora has most of the new properties, but islands such as Tahaa and Fakarava also have major resorts for the first time. The emphasis has been on the high end, however, which has done little to reduce the cost to visitors.

All this money translates into a high standard of living. The *minimum* wage here is more than US$1,500 (£750) a month plus benefits, compared to about

US$850 (£425), not including benefits in the U.S. Consequently, prices are high for everyone. If there is a saving grace for us visitors, it's the lack of both required tipping and a direct sales tax, which together can add 25% or more to your bill in Hawaii and elsewhere.

2 LOOKING AT THE PAST OF TAHITI & FRENCH POLYNESIA

The South Pacific Ocean came to Europe's attention during the latter half of the 18th century with the theory that an unknown southern land—a *terra australis incognita*—lay somewhere in the Southern Hemisphere. It must be there, the theory went, for otherwise the unbalanced earth would wobble off into space.

King George III of Great Britain took interest in the idea and, in 1764, sent Capt. John Byron (the poet's grandfather) to the Pacific in HMS *Dolphin*. Although Byron came home without discovering *terra australis incognita* (though he found some Tuamotu islands), King George immediately dispatched Capt. Samuel Wallis in the *Dolphin*.

Instead of a southern continent, Wallis discovered Tahiti. Surely he and his crew could hardly believe their eyes when they sailed into Matavai Bay in 1767 and were greeted by Tahitians in more than 500 canoes, many loaded with pigs, chickens, coconuts, fruit, and topless young women.

The latter, Wallis reported, "played a great many droll and wanton tricks" on his scurvy-ridden crew.

Less than a year later, the Tahitians similarly welcomed French explorer Louis Antoine de Bougainville. Although he stayed at Hitiaa, on Tahiti's east coast, for just 10 days, Bougainville was so enchanted by the Venus-like quality of Tahiti's women that he named their island New Cythère—after the Greek island of Cythera, associated with the goddess Aphrodite (Venus).

Bougainville took back to France a young Tahitian named Ahutoru, who became a sensation in Paris as living proof of Jean-Jacques Rousseau's theory that man was, at his best, a "noble savage." Indeed, Bougainville and Ahutoru contributed mightily to Tahiti's hedonistic image.

CAPTAIN COOK'S TOURS

After Wallis arrived back in England, the Lords of the Admiralty put a young

DATELINE

- **6th century A.D.** Polynesians arrive (estimated time).
- **1595** Alvaro de Mendaña discovers the Marquesas Islands.
- **1606** Pedro Fernández de Quirós sails through the Tuamotus.
- **1765** Searching for *terra australis incognita*, Capt. John Byron on HMS *Dolphin* finds some Tuamotu islands, but misses Tahiti.

- **1767** Also on HMS *Dolphin*, Capt. Samuel Wallis discovers Tahiti and claims it for King George III.
- **1768** French Capt. Antoine de Bougainville discovers Tahiti.
- **1769** Capt. James Cook arrives to observe the transit of Venus on the first of his three voyages of discovery.
- **1788** HMS *Bounty* under Capt. William Bligh arrives

and then takes breadfruit to the Caribbean.
- **1789** Lt. Fletcher Christian leads the mutiny on the *Bounty*.
- **1797** London Missionary Society emissaries arrive, looking for converts.
- **1827** Queen Pomare IV succeeds to the throne.
- **1837** Protestants deny French Catholic priests permission to land. Irate France demands full reparations.

(Fun Facts) Bougainville & Bougainvillea

The French explorer Antoine de Bougainville discovered several islands in Samoa and the Solomon Islands, of which the island of Bougainville—now part of Papua New Guinea—still bears his name. So does the bright tropical shrub known as bougainvillea.

lieutenant named James Cook in command of a converted collier and sent him to Tahiti. A product of the Age of Enlightenment, Cook was a master navigator, a mathematician, an astronomer, and a practical physician who became the first captain of any ship to prevent scurvy among his crewmen by feeding them fresh fruits and vegetables. His ostensible mission was to observe the transit of Venus—the planet, that is—across the sun, an astronomical event that would not occur again until 1874, but which, if measured from widely separated points on the globe, would enable scientists for the first time to determine longitude on the earth's surface. Cook's second, highly secret mission was to find the elusive southern continent.

Cook set up an observation point at the end of a sandy peninsula on Tahiti's north shore, a locale he appropriately named Point Venus. His measurements of Venus were somewhat less than useful, but his observations of Tahiti, made during a stay of 6 months, were of immense importance in understanding the "noble savages" who lived there.

Using Tahiti as a base, Cook went on to discover the Society Islands northwest of Tahiti and the Australs to the south, and then fully explored the coasts of New Zealand and eastern Australia. After nearly sinking his ship on the Great Barrier Reef, he left the South Pacific through the strait between Australia and Papua New Guinea, which he named for his ship, the *Endeavor*. He returned to London in 1771.

During two subsequent voyages, Cook discovered several other islands, among them what are now known as Fiji, the Cook Islands, Tonga, Niue, New Caledonia, and Norfolk Island. His ships were the first to sail below the Antarctic Circle. On his third voyage in 1778–79, he traveled to the Hawaiian Islands and explored the northwest coast of North America until ice in the Bering Strait turned him back. He returned to the Big Island of Hawaii, where, on February 14, 1779, he was killed during a petty skirmish with the islanders.

- **1838** Queen reluctantly signs ultimatum of French Adm. du Petit-Thouars.
- **1841** French traders trick Tahitian chiefs into asking for French protection. They later disavow it.
- **1842** Tahiti becomes a French protectorate. Herman Melville jumps ship, spends time in the *Calaboosa Beretane* (British jail). He later writes *Omoo* about his adventures.

- **1844–48** Tahitians wage guerrilla war against the French.
- **1847** Queen Pomare acquiesces to full French protection.
- **1862** Irish adventurer William Stewart starts a cotton plantation at Atimaono.
- **1865** The first 329 Chinese people arrive from Hong Kong to work Stewart's plantation, which fails. Most of the Chinese people stay.

- **1872** Pierre Loti (Julien Viaud) spends several months on Tahiti. His *The Marriage of Loti* is published 8 years later.
- **1877** Queen Pomare IV dies at age 64.
- **1880** King Pomare V abdicates in return for pensions for him, his family, and mistress. Tahiti becomes a French colony.

continues

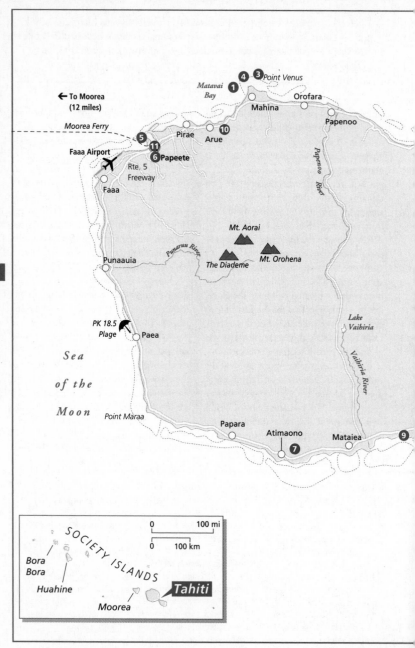

← To Moorea
(12 miles)

Moorea Ferry

Faaa Airport

Rte. 5
Freeway

Faaa

Matavai
Bay

4 3 Point Venus
1

Mahina

Orofara

Papenoo

Papenoo River

Pirae

5
11 6 Papeete

Arue 10

Punaauia

Punaruu River

Mt. Aorai

The Diademe Mt. Orohena

Lake
Vaihiria

Vaihiria River

PK 18.5
Plage Paea

Sea

of the

Moon Point Maraa

Papara

Atimaono 7

Mataiea

9

Bora
Bora

SOCIETY ISLANDS

Huahine

Moorea

Tahiti

0   100 mi
0   100 km

1 Capt Samuel Wallis discovers Tahiti in 1767

2 French Capt. Antoine de Bougainville lands at Hitiaa in 1767

3 Capt. James Cook observes transit of Venus in 1769

4 Capt. William Bligh arrives in the *Bounty* to collect breadfruit in 1788

5 First Christian missionaries arrive in 1797

6 Tahiti becomes a French protectorate in 1842

7 First Chinese laborers arrive to work cotton plantation at Atimaono in 1865

8 Robert Louis Stevenson spends two months at Tautira in 1888

9 Paul Gauguin arrives on Tahiti, moves to Papaeari in 1891

10 Charles Nordhoff and James Norman Hall publish *Mutiny on the Bounty* in 1935

11 Infamous Quinn's Bar closes in 1973

2 Hitiaa

Faaone

SOUTH PACIFIC OCEAN

Taravao

Taravao Plateau

Pueu

8 Tautira

Vaitepiha R.

Teohatu

Plage de Maui

Vairao

TAHITI ITI

Mt. Rooniu

Teahupoo

Airport

Beach

Ferry

Reef

0   5 mi

0   5 km

N

With the exception of the Hawaiians who smashed his skull, Captain Cook was revered throughout the Pacific. He treated the islanders fairly and respected their traditions. The Polynesian chiefs looked upon him as one of their own. Cook's Bay on Moorea bears his name. Elsewhere in the South Pacific is a Cooktown, a Cook Strait, any number of Captain Cook's Landing Places, and an entire island nation named for this giant of an explorer.

MUTINY ON THE BOUNTY

Based on reports by Cook and others about the abundance of breadfruit, a head-size, potato-like fruit that grows on trees throughout the islands, a group of West Indian planters asked King George III if he would be so kind as to transport the trees from Tahiti to Jamaica as a cheap source of food for the slaves. The king dispatched Capt. William Bligh, who had been one of Cook's navigators and was later in command of HMS *Bounty* in 1787. One of Bligh's officers was a former shipmate named Fletcher Christian.

Their story is one of history's great sea yarns.

The *Bounty* was late arriving in Tahiti, so Christian and the crew frolicked on Tahiti for 6 months, waiting for the next breadfruit season. Christian and some of the crew apparently enjoyed the island's women and easygoing lifestyle, for on the way home they staged a mutiny on April 28, 1789, off the Ha'apai islands in Tonga. Christian set Bligh and 18 of his loyal officers and crewmen adrift with a compass, a cask of water, and a few provisions. Bligh and his men miraculously rowed the *Bounty*'s longboat some 4,830km (3,000 miles) to the Dutch East Indies, where they hitched a ride back to England.

Meanwhile, Christian sailed the *Bounty* back to Tahiti, where he put ashore 25 other crew members who were loyal to Bligh. Christian, eight mutineers, their Tahitian wives, and six Tahitian men then disappeared.

The Royal Navy's HMS *Pandora* eventually rounded up the *Bounty* crewmen still on Tahiti and returned them to England. Three were hanged, four were acquitted, and three were convicted but pardoned.

In 1808, the captain of an American whaling ship happened upon remote Pitcairn Island, between Tahiti and South America, and was astonished when some mixed-race teenagers rowed out and greeted him not in Tahitian but in perfect English. They were the children of the mutineers, only one of whom was still alive. A handful of the mutineers' descendants live on Pitcairn to this day.

Bligh later collected more breadfruit on Tahiti, but his whole venture went for naught when the slaves on Jamaica insisted on rice.

> ## Fun Facts   Recovering the Bounty's Rudder
>
> Sunk by the mutineers in 1789, HMS *Bounty* remained in its watery grave until it was discovered by a *National Geographic* expedition in the 1950s. The *Bounty's* rudder is now on display at the Fiji Museum in Suva.

GUNS & WHISKEY

The *Bounty* mutineers hiding on Tahiti loaned themselves and their guns to rival chiefs, who for the first time were able to extend their control beyond their home valleys. With the mutineers' help, a chief named Pomare II came to control half of Tahiti and all of Moorea.

The U.S. ship that found the mutineers' retreat at Pitcairn was one of many whalers roaming the South Pacific in the early 1800s. Their ruffian crews made dens of iniquity of several South Pacific ports, including Papeete and Nuku Hiva in what is now French Polynesia. Many crewmen jumped ship and lived on the islands, some of them even casting their lots—and their guns—with rival chiefs during tribal wars. With their assistance, some chiefs were able to extend their power over entire islands or groups of islands.

Along with the whalers came traders in search of sandalwood, pearls, shells, and sea cucumbers (known as *bêches-de-mer),* which they traded for beads, cloth, whiskey, and

guns and then sold at high prices in China. Some established stores became the catalysts for Western-style towns. The merchants brought more guns and alcohol to people who had never used them before. They also put pressure on local leaders to coin money, which introduced a cash economy where none had existed before. Guns, alcohol, and money had far-reaching effects on the easygoing, communal traditions of the Pacific Islanders.

While the traders were building towns, other arrivals were turning the bush country into coconut and cotton plantations. With the native islanders disinclined to work, Chinese indentured laborers were brought to a cotton plantation in Tahiti in the 1860s. After it failed, some of the Chinese stayed and became farmers and merchants. Their descendants now form the merchant class of French Polynesia.

THE FATAL IMPACT

The European discoverers brought many changes to the islands, starting with iron, which the Tahitians had never seen. The

- **1977** France grants limited self-rule to French Polynesia.
- **1984** Local autonomy statute enacted by French parliament.
- **1992** France halts nuclear testing, hurting local economy.
- **1995** Conservative French Pres. Jacques Chirac permits six more underground nuclear explosions; antinuclear riots take place in Papeete; Japanese boycott Tahiti tourism.
- **1996** France halts nuclear testing, signs Treaty of Rarotonga (declaring South Pacific to be nuclear-free), and tells French Polynesia to start earning its own way.
- **1997** Spurred by economic restructuring funds from Paris, the first of several new hotels are built, and Papeete waterfront reconstruction begins.
- **1999** Local officials propose increased autonomy from France.
- **2001** Longtime pro-autonomy Gaston Flosse is reelected as president, continuing 20-year control of local government.
- **2004** French Polynesia becomes an overseas "collective" of France with new legislative assembly. Pro-independence leader Oscar Temaru is elected president by a narrow margin, holds office for 4

continues

> **(Fun Facts)** **First Novels**
>
> One deserter who jumped ship in the Marquesas Islands and later went to Tahiti, in the early 1820s, was Herman Melville. He returned to New England and wrote two books, *Typee* and *Omoo,* based on his South Pacific exploits. They were the start of his illustrious literary career.

Tahitians figured out right away that iron was much harder than stone and shells, and that they could swap pigs, breadfruit, bananas, and the affections of their young women for it. So many iron nails soon disappeared from the *Dolphin* that Wallis restricted his men to the ship out of fear it would fall apart in Matavai Bay. A rudimentary form of monetary economy was introduced to Polynesia for the first time, and the English word "money" entered the Tahitian language as *moni.*

Much more devastating European imports were diseases such as measles, influenza, pneumonia, and syphilis, to which the islanders had no resistance. Captain Cook estimated Tahiti's population at some 200,000 in 1769. By 1810, it had dropped to fewer than 8,000.

BRINGING THE WORD OF GOD

The reports of the islands by Cook and Bougainville may have brought word of noble savages living in paradise to some

people in Europe; to others, they heralded heathens to be rescued from hell. So while alcohol and diseases were destroying the islanders' bodies, a stream of missionaries arrived on the scene to save their souls.

The "opening" of the South Pacific coincided with a fundamentalist religious revival in England, and it wasn't long before the London Missionary Society (LMS) was on the scene in Tahiti. Its missionaries, who arrived in 1797, were the first Protestant missionaries to leave England for a foreign country. They chose Tahiti because there "the difficulties were least."

Polynesians, already believing in a supreme being at the head of a hierarchy of lesser gods, quickly converted to Christianity in large numbers. With the exception of Roman Catholic priests serving in the Marquesas Islands, the puritanical missionaries demanded the destruction of all tikis, the stylized statues representing ancestors, which they regarded as idols. With the exception of authentic Marquesan

months until no-confidence vote returns Flosse to power.
- **2005** Special elections on Tahiti and Moorea return Temaru to the presidency. He calls for independence from France over 15- to 20-year period.
- **2006** Votes of no confidence replace Temaru with Gaston Tong Sang, pro-autonomy mayor of Bora Bora.
- **2007** French Polynesia becomes an "overseas community" of France.
- **2008** Gaston Flosse is briefly returned to presidency in coalition with Temaru, who serves as assembly speaker, before Tong Sang is restored to power.

Sexy Skin

The United States isn't the only place where it's cool to have a tattoo. With their increasing interest in ancient Polynesian ways, many young Tahitian men and women are getting theirs—but not necessarily with modern electric needles.

The 18th-century explorers from Europe were amazed to find many Polynesians on Tahiti and throughout the South Pacific who were covered from face to ankle with a plethora of geometric and floral designs. In his journal, Capt. James Cook described in detail the excruciatingly painful tattoo procedure, in which natural dyes are hammered into the skin by hand. The repetitive tapping of the mallet gave rise to the Tahitian word *tatau,* which became "tattoo" in English.

Members of the opposite sex rejected anyone with plain skin, which may explain why members of Cook's crew were so willing to endure the torture to get theirs. At any rate, thus began the tradition of the tattooed sailor.

Appalled at the sexual aspects of tattoos, the missionaries stamped out the practice on Tahiti in the early 1800s. Although the art continued in the remote Marquesas and in Samoa, by 1890 there were no tattooed natives left in the Society Islands.

When a British anthropologist undertook a study of tattooing in 1900, the only specimen he could find was on the skin of a Tahitian sailor, who died in England in 1816. Before he was buried, an art-loving physician removed his hide and donated it to the Royal College of Surgeons.

carvings, most tikis carved for the tourist souvenir trade today resemble those of New Zealand, where the more liberal Anglican missionaries were less demanding.

The missionaries in French Polynesia also insisted that most heathen temples (known as *maraes*) be abandoned. Many have now been restored, however, and can be visited.

THE TRICKED QUEEN

The Protestant missionaries enjoyed a monopoly until the first Roman Catholic priests arrived from France in the 1830s. The Protestants immediately saw a threat, and in 1836 they engineered the interlopers' expulsion by Queen Pomare IV, the illegitimate daughter of Pomare II, who had succeeded her father's throne.

When word of this outrage reached Paris, France demanded a guarantee that Frenchmen would thereafter be treated as the "most favored foreigners" on Tahiti. Queen Pomare politely agreed, but as soon as the warship left Papeete, she sent a letter to Queen Victoria, asking for British protection. Britain declined to interfere, which in 1842 opened the door for a Frenchman to trick several Tahitian chiefs into signing a document that in effect made Tahiti a French protectorate.

Queen Pomare retreated to Raiatea, which was not under French control, and continued to resist. On Tahiti, her subjects launched an armed rebellion against the French. This French-Tahitian war continued until 1846, when the last native stronghold was captured and the remnants of their guerrilla bands retreated to Tahiti Iti, the island's eastern peninsula. A monument to the fallen Tahitians now stands beside the round-island road near the airport at Faaa, the village still noted for its strong pro-independence sentiment.

Giving up the struggle, the queen returned to Papeete in 1847 and ruled as a figurehead until her death 30 years later. Her son, Pomare V, remained on the throne for 3 more years until abdicating in return for a sizable French pension for himself, his family, and his mistress. In 1903, all of eastern Polynesia was consolidated into a single colony known as French Oceania. In 1957, its status was changed to the overseas territory of French Polynesia.

A BLISSFUL BACKWATER

French Polynesia remained an idyllic backwater until the early 1960s, except for periodic invasions by artists and writers. French painter Paul Gauguin gave up his family and his career as a Parisian stockbroker and arrived in 1891; he spent his days reproducing Tahiti's colors and people on canvas until he died in 1903 on Hiva Oa, in the Marquesas Islands. W. Somerset Maugham, Jack London, Robert Louis Stevenson, Rupert Brooke, and other writers added to Tahiti's romantic reputation during the early years of the 20th century. In 1932, two young Americans—Charles Nordhoff and James Norman Hall—published *Mutiny on the Bounty*, which quickly became a bestseller. Three years later, MGM released the first movie version, with Clark Gable and Charles Laughton in the roles of Christian and Bligh, respectively.

In 1942, some 6,000 U.S. sailors and marines quickly built the territory's first airstrip on Bora Bora and remained there throughout World War II. A number of mixed-race Tahitians claim descent from those American troops.

MOVIES & BOMBS

The backwater years ended in 1960, when Tahiti's new international airport opened at Faaa. Marlon Brando and a movie crew arrived shortly thereafter to film a remake of *Mutiny on the Bounty*. This new burst of fame, coupled with the ability to reach Tahiti overnight, transformed the island into a jet-set destination, and hotel construction began in earnest.

Even more changes came in 1963, when France established the Centre d'Experimentation du Pacifique and began exploding nuclear bombs on Moruroa and Fangataufa atolls, in the Tuamotus, about 1,127km (700 miles) southeast of Tahiti. A huge support base was constructed on the eastern outskirts of Papeete. Thousands of Polynesians flocked to Tahiti to take the new construction and hotel jobs, which enabled them to earn good money and to experience life in Papeete's fast lane. Between 1966 and 1992, the French exploded 210 nuclear weapons in the Tuamotu Archipelago, about 1,208km (750 miles) southeast of Tahiti, first in the air and then underground. Their health repercussions are still being debated.

Led by New Zealand, where French secret agents sank the Greenpeace protest ship *Rainbow Warrior* in 1985, many South Pacific island nations vociferously complained about the blasts. That same year, the regional heads of government, including the prime ministers of New Zealand and Australia, adopted the Treaty of Rarotonga, calling for the South Pacific to become a nuclear-free zone. After a lull,

Impressions

It would have been far better for these people never to have known us.

—Capt. James Cook, 1769

(Fun Facts) **Picking Up a Few Extra Bucks**

Neither Clark Gable nor Charles Laughton came to Tahiti to film the 1935 version of *Mutiny on the Bounty*. While background scenes were shot on Tahiti, they actually performed on Catalina Island, off Southern California. The Mexican actress Maria "Movita" Castenada, who played the chief's young daughter, was later married to Marlon Brando, star of the 1962 version. A young actor named James Cagney, who was vacationing on Catalina at the time, picked up a few extra bucks by playing a sailor for a day.

French Pres. Jacques Chirac decided in 1995 to resume nuclear testing, a move that set off worldwide protests, a day of rioting in Papeete, and a Japanese tourist boycott of French Polynesia. After six underground explosions, the French halted further tests, closed their testing facility, and signed the Treaty of Rarotonga.

TO BE—OR NOT TO BE— INDEPENDENT

In 1977, the French parliament created the elected Territorial Assembly with powers over the local budget. A high commissioner sent from Paris, however, retained authority over defense, foreign affairs, immigration, the police, civil service, communications, and secondary education.

Local politics have long centered on the question of whether the islands should have even more autonomy while remaining French, or whether they should become an independent nation. Politicians have been equally divided roughly into "pro-autonomy" and "pro-independence" camps. On the other hand, neither side wants to give up all that money from Paris!

An additional grant of local control followed in 1984, and in 2004 the islands shifted from an "overseas territory" of France to an "overseas collective within the French republic." The local Assembly gained increased powers over land ownership, labor relations, civil aviation, immigration, education, and international affairs; that is, within the South Pacific region. (The legal status changed again in 2007, this time to an "overseas community," primarily so that France could enact laws specific to its territories and not have them apply equally in metropolitan France.)

The 2004 law called for fresh Assembly elections. In a surprise upset, a coalition led by Oscar Temaru, the mayor of independence-leaning Faaa, narrowly ousted longtime pro-autonomy President Gaston Flosse, who had ruled with an iron fist for more than 20 years—during which he also made several fortunes.

Temaru, who espouses independence over a 15- to 20-year period, was in office less than 5 months before being toppled by Flosse, who ruled for only 4 months until special elections on Tahiti and Moorea returned Temaru to the presidency. Temaru hung on until ousted at the end of 2006 by Gaston Tong Sang, the mayor of Bora Bora and an ally of Gaston Flosse. The presidency again became a game of musical chairs in 2008, when Flosse and Temaru teamed up to boot Tong Sang, only to see him return less than 2 months later. Not amused by the local shenanigans, French President Nicolas Sarkozy threatened to turn off the money tap if Tong Sang were again removed. As I write, the mayor of Bora Bora is still the president of French Polynesia.

3 THE LAY OF THE LAND & THE SEA

A somewhat less-than-pious wag once remarked that God made the French Polynesian islands on the sixth day of creation so He would have an extraordinarily beautiful place to rest on the seventh day. Modern geologists have a different view, but the fact remains that the islands and the surrounding sea are possessed of heavenly beauty and a plethora of life forms.

All these islands were formed by molten lava escaping upward through cracks in the earth's crust as it has inched northwestward over "hot spots" of molten magma, which escaped through the crust and built great seamounts. Tahiti and the other Society Islands, as well as the Marquesas, are called "high islands" because they have mountains soaring into the clouds. In contrast, the atolls of the Tuamotu Archipelago are pancake-flat because they were formed when the islands sank back into the sea, leaving only a thin necklace of coral islets to circumscribe their lagoons and mark their original boundaries. In some cases, geologic forces have once again lifted the atolls, forming "raised" islands whose sides drop precipitously into the sea. Bora Bora and Maupiti are examples of partially sunken islands, with the remnants of mountains sticking up in their lagoons.

FLORA & FAUNA

Most species of plants and animals native to the islands originated in Southeast Asia and worked their way eastward across the Pacific, by natural distribution or in the company of humans. The number of native species diminishes the farther east one goes, so French Polynesia has fewer species than Fiji and other islands to the west.

Very few local plants or animals came from the Americas, the one notable exception being the sweet potato, which may have been brought back from South America by voyaging Polynesians.

PLANTS

In addition to the west-to-east differences, the flora changes according to each island's topography. The mountainous islands make rain from the moist trade winds and thus possess a greater variety of plants. Their interior highlands are covered with ferns, native bush, or grass. The low atolls, on the other hand, get sparse rainfall and support little other than scrub bush and coconut palms.

Ancient settlers brought coconut palms, breadfruit, taro, paper mulberry, pepper (kava), and bananas to the isolated mid-ocean islands because of their usefulness as food or fiber. Accordingly, they are generally found in the inhabited areas of the islands and not so often in the interior bush.

With a few indigenous exceptions, such as the tiare (Tahiti gardenia), tropical flowers also worked their way east in the company of humans. Bougainvillea, hibiscus, allamanda, poinsettia, poinciana (the flame tree), croton, frangipani (plumeria), ixora, canna, and water lilies all give colorful testament to the islanders' love for flowers of every hue in the rainbow. The aroma of the white, yellow, or pink frangipani is so sweet, it's used as perfume here.

ANIMALS & BIRDS

The fruit bat, or "flying fox," and some species of insect-eating bats are the only mammals native to the islands. The early settlers introduced dogs, chickens, pigs, rats, and mice. There are few land snakes or other reptiles in the islands. The notable exceptions are geckos and skinks, those little lizards that seem to be everywhere. Don't go berserk when a gecko walks upside-down across the ceiling of your bungalow: They are harmless and actually perform a valuable service by eating mosquitoes and other insects.

The number and variety of species of bird life also diminish as you go eastward. Most land birds live in the bush away from settlements and the accompanying cats, dogs, and rats. For this reason, the birds most likely to be seen are terns, boobies, herons, petrels, noddies, and others that earn their livelihoods from the sea. Of the introduced birds, the Indian myna exists in the greatest numbers. Brought to the South Pacific in the early 20th century to control insects, the myna quickly became a noisy nuisance in its own right. Mynas are extremely adept at stealing the toast off your breakfast table.

SEA LIFE

The tropical South Pacific Ocean teems with sea life. More than 600 species of coral—10 times the number found in the Caribbean—form the great reefs that make the islands a mecca to divers. Billions of tiny coral polyps build their own skeletons on top of those left by their ancestors, until they reach the level of low tide. Then they grow outward, extending the edge of the reef. The old skeletons are white, and the living polyps present a rainbow of colors; they grow best and are most colorful in the clear, salty water on the outer edge or in channels, where the tides and waves wash fresh seawater along and across the reef. A reef can grow as much as 2 inches a year in ideal conditions. Although pollution, rising seawater temperature, and a proliferation of crown-of-thorns starfish have greatly hampered reef growth—and beauty—in parts of the South Pacific, there are still many areas where the color and variety of corals are unmatched.

Like gigantic aquariums, a plethora of tropical fish and other marine life fill most of the lagoons. Many hotel boutiques and bookstores in the main towns sell pamphlets containing photographs and descriptions of the creatures that will peer into your face mask. Not all sea creatures are harmless, so be sure to read "Be Careful in the Water," (p. 68).

Humpback whales migrate to the islands from June to October, and sea turtles lay their eggs on some beaches from November through February. Sea turtles and whales are on the list of endangered species, and many countries, including the United States, prohibit the importation of their shells, bones, and teeth.

4 THE ISLANDERS

Polynesians had been living on these tiny outposts for hundreds of years before Europeans had the foggiest notion that the Pacific Ocean existed. Even after Vasco Nuñez de Balboa crossed the Isthmus of Panama and discovered this largest of oceans in 1513, and Ferdinand Magellan sailed across it in 1521, more than 250 years went by before Europeans paid much attention to the islands that lay upon it.

Impressions

Sentimentalists who moan against natives improving their diet with refrigerators and can openers—"Why, they live on Chinese bread, Australian beef and American pork and beans"—could complain with equal logic that dear old ladies in Boston no longer dip tallow candles because they prefer electricity.

—James A. Michener, *Return to Paradise*, 1951

Impressions

You who like handsome men would find no shortage of them here; they are taller than I, and have limbs like Hercules.

—Paul Gauguin, 1891

The early European explorers were astounded to find the far-flung South Pacific islands inhabited by peoples who shared similar physical characteristics, languages, and cultures. How had these people—who lived a late–Stone Age existence and had no written languages—crossed the vast Pacific to these remote islands long before Christopher Columbus had the courage to sail out of sight of land? Where had they come from? Those questions baffled the early European explorers, and they continue to intrigue scientists and scholars today.

THE FIRST SETTLERS

The late Thor Heyerdahl drifted in his raft *Kon Tiki* from South America to French Polynesia in 1947, to prove his theory that the Polynesians came from the Americas. Bolstered by recent DNA studies linking the Polynesians to Taiwan, however, experts now believe that the Pacific Islanders have their roots in eastern Asia. The generally accepted view is that during the Ice Age, a race of early humans known as Australoids migrated from Southeast Asia to Papua New Guinea and Australia, when those two countries were joined as one landmass. Another group, the Papuans, arrived from Southeast Asia between 5,000 and 10,000 years ago. Several thousands of years later, a lighter-skinned race known as Austronesians pushed the Papuans inland and out into the more eastern South Pacific islands.

The most tangible remains of the early Austronesians are remnants of pottery, the first shards of which were found during the 1970s in Lapita, a village in New Caledonia. Probably originating in Papua New Guinea, Lapita pottery spread east as far as Tonga. Lapita pottery was used in the South Pacific islands for a millennium, but by the time European explorers arrived in the 1770s, gourds and coconut shells were the only crockery used by the Polynesians, who cooked their meals underground and ate with their fingers off banana leaves.

THE POLYNESIANS

The Polynesians' ancestors stopped in Fiji on their migration from Southeast Asia, but later pushed on into the eastern South Pacific. Archaeologists now believe that they settled in Tonga and Samoa more than 3,000 years ago and then slowly fanned out to colonize the vast Polynesian triangle, which stretches from New Zealand in the south to Hawaii in the north and to Easter Island to the east. In French Polynesia, they landed first in the Marquesas (where the language and culture still have Samoan traces), and then backtracked to Raiatea and the other islands before eventually arriving in Hawaii and New Zealand.

These extraordinary mariners crossed thousands of miles of ocean in large, double-hulled canoes capable of carrying hundreds of people, animals, and plants. They navigated by the stars, the wind, the clouds, the shape of the waves, and the flight pattern of birds—a remarkable achievement for a people who had no written languages.

Their ancestors fought each other with war clubs for thousands of years, and it stands to reason that the biggest, strongest, and quickest survived (many modern Polynesians have become professional football and rugby players). The notion that all Polynesians are fat is incorrect. In the old days, body size did indeed denote wealth and status, but obesity today is more likely attributable to poor diet. On the other hand, village chiefs are still expected to partake of food and drink with anyone who visits to discuss a problem; hence, great weight remains an unofficial marker of social status.

TAHITIAN SOCIETY

Polynesians developed highly structured societies. On Tahiti, they were highly stratified into three classes: chiefs and priests, landowners, and commoners. Among the commoners was a subclass of slaves, mostly war prisoners. One's position in society was hereditary, with primogeniture the general rule. In general, women were equal to men, although they could not act as priests.

A peculiar separate class of wandering dancers and singers, known as the *Arioi*, traveled about the Society Islands, performing ritual dances and shows—some of them sexually explicit—and living in a state of total sexual freedom. Family values were the least of their concerns; in fact, members immediately killed any children born into their clan.

The Tahitians had no written language, but their life was governed by an elaborate set of rules that would challenge modern legislators' abilities to reduce them to writing. Everyday life was governed by a system based on *tabu*, a rigid list of things a person could or could not do, depending on his or her status in life. *Tabu* and its variants *(tapu, tambu)* are used throughout

the South Pacific to mean "do not enter"; from them derives the English word "taboo."

Western principles of ownership have made inroads, but by and large almost everything in Polynesia—especially land—is owned communally by families. In effect, the system is pure communism at the family level. If your brother has a crop of taro and you're hungry, then some of that taro belongs to you. The same principle applies to a can of corned beef sitting on a shelf in a store, which helps explain why most of the grocery shops in French Polynesia are owned by the Chinese. It also explains why you should keep a wary eye on your valuables.

Although some islanders would be considered poor by Western standards, the extended family system insures that few go hungry or sleep without a roof over their head. Most of the thatched roofs in Polynesia today are actually bungalows at the resort hotels; nearly everyone else sleeps under tin. It's little wonder, therefore, that the islands are inhabited for the most part by friendly, peaceable, and extraordinarily courteous people.

A HIERARCHY OF GODS

The ancient Tahitians worshiped a hierarchy of gods. At its head stood Taaroa, a supreme deity known as Tangaroa in the Cook Islands and Tangaloa in Samoa. *Mana,* or power, came down from the gods to each human, depending on his or her position in society. The highest chiefs had so much *mana* that they were considered

---

Impressions

Now the cunning lay in this, that the Polynesians have rules of hospitality that have all the force of laws; an etiquette of absolute rigidity made it necessary for the people of the village not only to give lodging to the strangers, but to provide them with food and drink for as long as they wished to stay.

—W. Somerset Maugham, 1921

(Fun Facts)   **A Flower Behind the Ear**

Tahitians wear flowers tucked behind their ears, which signals the status of their love lives. Behind the left ear means your heart is taken and you are unavailable, while behind the right ear signals you are unattached and available. Flowers behind both ears announce you are married but available, while a backward flower declares you are available immediately!

godlike, if not actually descended from the gods.

The Tahitians worshipped their gods on *maraes* (ancient temples or meeting places) built of stones. Every family had a small *marae,* which served the same functions as a chapel would today, and villages and entire districts—even islands—built large *maraes* that served not only as places of worship but also as meeting sites. Elaborate religious ceremonies were held on the large central *marae.* Priests prayed that the gods would come down and reside in carved tikis and other objects during the ceremonies (the objects lost all religious meaning afterward). Sacrifices were offered to the gods, sometimes including humans, mostly war prisoners or troublemakers. Despite the practice of human sacrifice, cannibalism apparently was never practiced in the Society Islands, although it was fairly widespread in the Marquesas.

The souls of the deceased were believed to return to Hawaiki, the homeland from which their Polynesian ancestors had come. In all Polynesian islands, the souls departed for it from the northwest corner of each island. That's in the direction of Asia, from whence their ancestors came.

THE CHINESE

The outbreak of the American Civil War in 1861 resulted in a worldwide shortage of cotton. In September 1862, an Irish adventurer named William Stewart founded a cotton plantation at Atimaono, Tahiti's only large tract of flat land. The Tahitians weren't the least bit interested in working for Stewart, so he imported a contingent of Chinese laborers. The first 329 of them arrived from Hong Kong in February 1865. Stewart ran into financial difficulties, which were compounded by the drop in cotton prices after the American South resumed production after 1868; this led to the collapse of his empire.

Nothing remains of Stewart's plantation at Atimaono (a golf course now occupies most of the land), but many of his Chinese laborers decided to stay. They grew vegetables for the Papeete market, saved their money, and invested in other businesses. Their descendants and those of subsequent immigrants from China now influence the economy far in excess of their numbers. They run nearly all of French Polynesia's grocery and general merchandise stores, which in French are called *magasins chinois,* or Chinese stores.

5 THE TAHITIAN LANGUAGE

With the exception of some older Polynesians, everyone speaks **French,** the official language. The material in "Appendix B: Useful French Terms & Phrases" will help you get along and make friends while you're at it.

Tahitian, the indigenous language originally of Tahiti and the other Society Islands, is widely spoken by the local Polynesians. Many residents of the Tuamotu Archipelago also speak **Puamotuan,** a dialect similar to Tahitian, and those in the

Marquesas have their own language, known as **Marquesasan.**

English is taught as a third language in most schools (and all of those operated by the Chinese community), and it's a prerequisite for getting a hotel job involving guest relations. You can converse in English with your hotel's professional and activities staff, but not necessarily with the housemaids.

Many young Tahitians are eager to learn English, if for no other reason than to understand the lyrics of American songs, which dominate the radio airwaves in French Polynesia. Accordingly, you will find English spoken in shops, restaurants, and other businesses, especially those frequented by tourists. Many French residents here also speak English.

Once you get off the beaten path, however, an ability to speak what I call *français touristique*—tourist French, as in asking directions to the loo—will be very helpful if not outright essential. I really need my schoolbook French on Maupiti and in the

Tuamotu and Marquesas islands, where English is not widely spoken.

Not to fear: Tahitians are enormously friendly folk, and most will immediately warm to you when they discover you don't speak French, or that you speak it haltingly or with a pronounced accent.

TAHITIAN PRONUNCIATION

A little knowledge of Tahitian will also help you correctly pronounce the tongue-tying place names here.

All Polynesian languages, including Tahitian, consist primarily of vowel sounds, which are pronounced in the Roman fashion—that is, *ah, ay, ee, oh,* and *ou,* not *ay, ee, eye, oh,* and *you,* as in English. Almost all vowels are sounded separately. For example, Tahiti's airport is at Faaa, which is pronounced Fah-*ah*-ah, not Fah. Papeete is Pah-pay-*ay*-tay, not Pa-*pee*-tee. Paea is Pah-*ay*-ah.

The consonants used in Tahitian are *f, h, m, n, p, r, t,* and *v.* There are some special rules regarding their sounds, but you'll

---

Sex & the Single Polynesian

The puritanical Christian missionaries who arrived in the South Pacific during the early 19th century convinced the islanders that they should clothe their nearly naked bodies. They had less luck, however, when it came to sex. To the islanders, sex was as much a part of life as any other daily activity, and they uninhibitedly engaged in it with a variety of partners from adolescence until marriage.

Even today, they have a somewhat laissez-faire attitude about premarital sex. Every child, whether born in or out of wedlock, is accepted into one of the extended families that are the bedrock of Polynesian society. Mothers, fathers, grandparents, aunts, uncles, and cousins of every degree are all part of the close-knit Polynesian family. Relationships sometimes are so blurred that every adult woman within a mile is known as a child's "auntie"—even the child's mother.

Male transvestitism, homosexuality, and bisexuality are facts of life in Polynesia, where families with a shortage of female offspring will raise young boys as girls. Some of these youths grow up to be heterosexual; others become homosexual or bisexual and, often appearing publicly in women's attire, actively seek out the company of tourists. In Tahitian, these males are known as *mahus.*

(Tips) "Oh-oh"—How to Spell Like a Tahitian

When spelling Tahitian words, many cultural activists advocate the use of apostrophes to indicate glottal stops—those slight pauses between some vowels similar to the tiny break between "Oh-oh!" in English. Moorea, for example, is pronounced Moh-oh-ray-ah, with a glottal stop between *Moh* and *oh,* and thus is often spelled Mo'orea. Likewise, you may see Papeete spelled Pape'ete. Abundant apostrophes already appear in written Tongan and Samoan, but in this book I have used the traditional spellings, with apostrophes appearing for some common nouns and also where they are used in an establishment's name, such as Le Taha'a Private Island & Spa. If you want to spell like a Tahitian, look for a handbook such as D. T. Tyron's *Say It in Tahitian.*

be understood if you say them as you would in English. One exception is *r,* which is pronounced with a slight click of the tongue at the top of the mouth behind the top front teeth, like an abbreviated version of the rolled *r* in Spanish.

USEFUL TAHITIAN WORDS

To help you impress the locals with what a really friendly tourist you are, here are a few Tahitian words you can use on them:

English	Tahitian	Pronunciation
hello	**ia orana**	ee-ah oh-*rah*-na (sounds like "your honor")
welcome	**maeva**	mah-*ay*-vah
goodbye	**parahi**	pah-*rah*-hee
good	**maitai**	*my*-tie
very good	**maitai roa**	*my*-tie-*row*-ah
thank you	**maruru**	mah-*roo*-roo
thank you very much	**maruru roa**	mah-*roo*-roo *row*-ah
good health!	**manuia**	mah-*new*-yah
woman	**vahine**	vah-*hee*-nay
man	**tane**	*tah*-nay
sarong	**pareu**	pah-*ray*-oo
small islet	**motu**	*moh*-too
take it easy	**hare maru**	*ha*-ray *mah*-roo
fed up	**fiu**	few

6 TAHITI IN POPULAR CULTURE: BOOKS, FILM, MUSIC & DANCE

Tahiti and her islands have supplied inspiration for bestselling books since shortly after the first European explorers reported the islands' existence. The number of writers who have penned island stories reads like a who's who of letters: Herman Melville, Robert Louis Stevenson, W. Somerset Maugham, Pierre Loti, Jack

London, Zane Grey, James A. Michener, Charles Nordhoff, and James Norman Hall. Several of their novels were turned into movies. Also, television programs have been produced here, including *Survivor: Marquesas* in 2002.

Artists have been here, too, the most famous being Paul Gauguin, who spent the final years of his life in French Polynesia and whose paintings are almost synonymous with French Polynesia.

Although local youths prefer Polynesian versions of reggae and hip-hop, traditional music is like that played in Hawaii—a blend of the guitar, ukulele, and drums. Most hotels and many restaurants will engage a small band to play traditional music during happy hour and dinner.

Of all the arts, Tahiti is most famous for its hip-swinging traditional dance, the most suggestive performed in all of Polynesia except the nearby Cook Islands (see "A Most Indecent Song & Dance" box, p. 35).

BOOKS

Rather than list the hundreds of books about Tahiti and French Polynesia, I have picked my favorites. A few out-of-print island classics have been reissued in paperback by **Mutual Publishing, LLC,** 125 Center St., Ste. 210, Honolulu, HI 96816 (📞 **808/732-1709;** fax 808/734-4094; www.mutualpublishing.com).

GENERAL

If you have time for only one book, read *The Lure of Tahiti* (1986). Editor A. Grove Day, himself an islands expert, includes 18 short stories, excerpts from other books, and essays. There is a little here from many of the writers mentioned below, plus selections from captains Cook, Bougainville, and Bligh.

The National Geographic Society's book, *The Isles of the South Pacific* (1971), by Maurice Shadbolt and Olaf Ruhen, and Ian Todd's *Island Realm* (1974) are somewhat out-of-date coffee-table books, but they have lovely color photographs. *Living Corals* (1979), by Douglas Faulkner and Richard Chesher, shows what you will see underwater.

HISTORY & POLITICS

Several early English and French explorers published accounts of their exploits, but *The Journals of Captain James Cook* stand out as the most exhaustive and even-handed. Edited by J. C. Beaglehole, they were published in three volumes (one for each voyage) in 1955, 1961, and 1967. A. Grenfell Price edited many of Cook's key passages and provides short transitional explanations in *The Explorations of Captain James Cook in the Pacific* (1971).

The explorers' visits and their consequences in Tahiti, Australia, and Antarctica are the subject of Alan Moorehead's excellent study *The Fatal Impact: The*

> ### (Fun Facts) Jotting It Down
>
> No Polynesian language was written until Peter Heywood jotted down a Tahitian vocabulary while awaiting trial for his part in the mutiny on the *Bounty* (he was convicted, but pardoned). The early missionaries who later translated the Bible into Tahitian decided which letters of the Roman alphabet to use to approximate the sounds of the Polynesian languages. These tended to vary from place to place. For example, they used the consonants *t* and *v* in Tahitian. In Hawaiian, which is similar, they used *k* and *w*. The actual Polynesian sounds are somewhere in between.

Invasion of the South Pacific, 1767–1840 (1966), a colorful tome loaded with sketches and paintings of the time.

Three other very readable books trace Tahiti's post-discovery history. Robert Langdon's *Tahiti: Island of Love* (1979) takes the island's story up to 1977. David Howarth's *Tahiti: A Paradise Lost* (1985) covers more thoroughly the same early ground covered by Langdon, but stops with France's taking possession in 1842. *The Rape of Tahiti* (1983), by Edward Dodd, covers the island from prehistory to 1900.

Mad About Islands (1987), by A. Grove Day, follows the island exploits of literary figures Herman Melville, Robert Louis Stevenson, Jack London, and W. Somerset Maugham. Also included are Charles Nordhoff and James Norman Hall, coauthors of the so-called Bounty Trilogy and other works about the islands (see "Fiction," below). *A Dream of Islands* (1980), by Gavan Dawes, tells of the missionary John Williams as well as Melville, Stevenson, and the painter Paul Gauguin.

PEOPLES & CULTURES

The late Bengt Danielsson, a Swedish anthropologist who arrived in Tahiti on Thor Heyerdahl's *Kon Tiki* raft in 1947 and spent the rest of his life there, painted a broad picture of Polynesian sexuality in *Love in the South Seas* (1986). Heyerdahl tells his tale and explains his theory of Polynesian migration (since debunked) in *Kon Tiki* (1950). In 1936, Heyerdahl and his wife lived for a year in the Marquesas; his book *Fatu-Hiva: Back to Nature* (1975) provides an in-depth look at Marquesan

life at the time. Robert Lee Eskridge spent a year on Mangareva; his charming book is titled, appropriately, *Manga Reva* (1931; reprinted by Mutual in 1986).

FICTION

Starting with Herman Melville's *Typee* (1846) and *Omoo* (1847)—semifictional accounts of his adventures in the Marquesas and Tahiti, respectively—the islands have spawned a wealth of fiction. (Though set in the South Pacific Ocean, Melville's 1851 classic, *Moby-Dick,* does not tell of the islands.)

After Melville came Julien Viaud, a French naval officer who fell in love with a Tahitian woman during a sojourn in Tahiti. Under the pen name Pierre Loti, he wrote *The Marriage of Loti* (1880; reprinted by KPI in 1986), a classic tale of lost love.

W. Somerset Maugham's *The Moon and Sixpence* (1919) is a fictional account of the life of Paul Gauguin. Maugham changed the name to Charles Strickland and made the painter English instead of French. (Gauguin's own novel, *Noa Noa,* was published in English in 1928, long after his death.) Maugham also produced a volume of South Pacific short stories, *The Trembling of a Leaf* (1921; reprinted by Mutual in 1985). My favorite is "The Fall of Edward Bernard," about a Chicagoan who forsakes love and fortune at home for "beauty, truth, and goodness" in Tahiti.

Next on the scene were Charles Nordhoff and James Norman Hall (more about them in chapter 5). Together they wrote the most famous of all South Pacific novels, *Mutiny on the Bounty* (1932). They

---

Impressions

I have often been mildly amused when I think that the great American novel was not written about New England or Chicago. It was written about a white whale in the South Pacific.

—James A. Michener, *Return to Paradise,* 1951

(Fun Facts) A Most Indecent Song & Dance

The young girls whenever they can collect 8 or 10 together dance a very indecent dance which they call Timorodee singing most indecent songs and useing most indecent actions in the practice of which they are brought up from their earlyest Childhood.

—Capt. James Cook, after seeing his first Tahitian dance show in 1769

The Tahitian dances described by the great explorer in 1769 left little doubt as to the temptations that inspired the mutiny on the *Bounty* a few years later. At the time Cook arrived, the Tahitians would stage a *heiva* (festival) for almost any reason, from blessing the harvest to celebrating a birth. After eating meals cooked in earth ovens, they would get out the drums and nose flutes and dance the night away. Some of the dances involved elaborate costumes, and others were quite lasciviously and explicitly danced in the nude or seminude, which added to Tahiti's reputation as an island of love.

The puritanical Protestant missionaries would have none of that and put an end to dancing in the early 1820s. Of course, strict prohibition never works, and Tahitians—including a young Queen Pomare—would sneak into the hills to dance. Only after the French took over in 1842 was dancing permitted again, and then only with severe limitations on what the dancers could do and wear. A result of these varied restrictions was that most of the traditional dances performed by the Tahitians before 1800 were nearly forgotten within 100 years.

You'd never guess that Tahitians ever stopped dancing, for after tourists started coming in 1961, they went back to the old ways. Today, traditional dancing is a huge part of their lives—and of every visitor's itinerary. No one goes away without vivid memories of the elaborate and colorful costumes, the thundering drums, and the swinging hips of a Tahitian *tamure* in which young men and women provocatively dance around one another.

The *tamure* is one of several dances performed during a typical dance show. Others are the *o'tea,* in which men and women in spectacular costumes dance certain themes, such as spear throwing, fighting, or love; the *aparima,* the hand dance, which emphasizes everyday themes, such as bathing and combing one's hair; the *hivinau,* in which men and women dance in circles and exclaim "*hiri haa haa*" when they meet each other; and the *pata'uta'u,* in which the dancers beat the ground or their thighs with their open hands. It's difficult to follow the themes without understanding Tahitian, but the color and rhythms (which have been influenced by faster, double-time beats from the Cook Islands) make the dances thoroughly enjoyable.

followed that enormous success with two other novels: *Men Against the Sea* (1934), based on Captain Bligh's epic longboat voyage after the mutiny, and *Pitcairn's Island* (1935), about Lt. Fletcher Christian's demise on the mutineers' remote hideaway. (For a nonfiction retelling of the great tale, see Caroline Alexander's *The Bounty: The True Story of the Mutiny on the Bounty* [2003].)

Nordhoff and Hall later wrote *The Hurricane* (1936), a novel set in American Samoa that has been made into two movies filmed in French Polynesia. Hall also wrote short stories and essays, collected in *The Forgotten One* (1986).

The second-most famous South Pacific novel appeared just after World War II— *Tales of the South Pacific* (1947), by James A. Michener. A U.S. Navy historian, Michener spent much of the war on Espiritu Santo, in the New Hebrides (now Vanuatu). Richard Rodgers and Oscar Hammerstein turned the novel into the musical *South Pacific*, a huge Broadway hit; it was later made into the blockbuster movie.

Michener toured the islands a few years later and wrote *Return to Paradise* (1951), a collection of essays and short stories. He describes the islands as they were after World War II, but before tourists began to arrive via jet aircraft—in other words, near the end of the region's backwater, beachcomber days.

FILM

The most famous of many movies about Tahiti are the two *Mutiny on the Bounty* films based on the novel by Charles Nordhoff and James Norman Hall. The 1935 version starred Clark Gable as Fletcher Christian and Charles Laughton as a tyrannical Captain Bligh. (It was actually the second film based on the *Bounty* story; the first was an Australian production, starring Errol Flynn in his first movie role.) Although the 1935 version contained background shots of 40 Tahitian villages, most of the movie was filmed on Santa Catalina, off the California coast; neither Gable nor Laughton visited Tahiti. The 1962 remake with Marlon Brando and Trevor Howard in the Gable and Laughton roles, however, was actually filmed on Tahiti. It was the beginning of Brando's tragic real-life relationship with Tahiti (see "Marlon's Mana," p. 120). A 1984 version, *The Bounty*, not based on Nordhoff and Hall, was filmed in Opunohu Bay on Moorea and featured Mel Gibson as Christian and Anthony Hopkins as a more sympathetic (and historically accurate) Bligh.

Another Nordhoff and Hall novel, *The Hurricane* (1936), was turned into two movies set in French Polynesia (the novel was about a hurricane striking American Samoa). The 1937 version starring Dorothy Lamour and Jon Hall (a relative of the coauthor) was a hit, while the 1977 remake, starring Mia Farrow and filmed on Bora Bora, was a classical bomb.

Also bombing was 1994's *Love Affair* starring Warren Beatty, Annette Bening, and Katherine Hepburn. The best things about it are the scenes shot on the *Aranui 2* and in Opunohu Bay on Moorea.

7 EATING & DRINKING IN TAHITI & FRENCH POLYNESIA

French Polynesia has a plethora of excellent restaurants. I'm not fabricating when I say I've seldom had a really bad meal here. You are in for a special treat when ordering tomatoes and other locally grown vegetables, for more than likely they will be as fresh as if they had come from your own garden.

Many visitors are shocked at the high prices on the menus and in the grocery stores. Most foodstuffs are imported, and except for sugar, flour, and a few other necessities, are subject to stiff duties. On the other hand, you won't have sales tax added to your bill, and although the practice is widespread here these days, you will not feel compelled to tip the waitstaff, as in the United States. In other words, Americans will not have to add up to 25%

to the cost of restaurant meals. See below for how I save more money on food here.

Except for breakfast buffets, prices in hotel and resort dining rooms are now comparable to those in the better outside restaurants.

LOCAL FARE: MA'A TAHITI

As would be expected, French is the dominant cuisine in these islands. Local French residents demand their steaks in red-wine sauces, mahimahi under a vanilla sauce, and *canard* (duck) with orange sauce, which seem to appear on every menu, as does carpaccio (thinly sliced raw beef or tuna) and sashimi (especially good when it's fresh yellowfin tuna).

While the Tahitians have adopted many of these dishes as well as Chinese ones, they still consume copious quantities of *ma'a Tahiti* (traditional Tahitian food), especially on Sunday. Like their Polynesian counterparts elsewhere, Tahitians still cook meals underground in an earth oven, known here as an *himaa*. Pork, chicken, fish, shellfish, leafy green vegetables such as taro leaves, and root crops such as taro and yams are wrapped in leaves, placed on a bed of heated stones, covered with more leaves and earth, and left to steam for several hours. The results are quite tasty, since the steam spreads the aroma of one ingredient to the others, and liberal use of coconut cream adds a sweet richness.

Many restaurants serving primarily French, Italian, or Chinese cuisine also offer Tahitian dishes. One you will see virtually everywhere is *poisson cru,* French for "raw fish." It's the Tahitian-style salad of fresh tuna or mahimahi marinated in lime juice, cucumbers, onions, and tomatoes, all served in coconut cream. Chili is added to spice up a variation known as Chinese *poisson cru.*

Most of Tahiti's big resort hotels have at least one *tama'ara'a* (Tahitian feast) a week, followed by a traditional, hip-swinging dance show (see the box "A Most Indecent Song & Dance," p. 35).

SNACK BARS & LES ROULOTTES

Tahiti has two McDonald's, but locals still prefer their plethora of snack bars, which they call "snacks." You can get a hamburger and usually *poisson cru,* but the most popular item is the *casse-croûte,* a sandwich made from a crusty French baguette and ham, tuna, *roti* (roast pork), *hachis* (hamburger), lettuce, tomatoes, and cucumbers—or even spaghetti. A *casse-croûte* usually costs about 300CFP (US$3.75/£1.90) or less.

Also in this category are *les roulottes*—or portable meal wagons. A friend of mine says he hates the idea of dining in a parking lot, but *les roulottes* are one of the best values here, with meals seldom topping 1,500CFP (US$19/£9.50). They roll out after dark on most islands. The carnival-like ambience they create on the Papeete waterfront makes them a highlight of any visit to the city (see "Don't Miss *Les Roulottes,"* p. 140).

MONEY-SAVING TIPS

Despite the high prices, you don't have to go broke dining here. In addition to finding the nearest "snack," here are some ways to eat well for the least money:

- Unless you have no choice, do not have breakfast at the resort hotel dining rooms, which charge 3,000CFP (US$38/£19) or more per person. You can have a perfectly good breakfast for less than half that at a snack bar or patisserie.

- Likewise, do not buy a hotel meal package except on remote islands, where your resort's restaurant is your only choice. Dining out is as much a part of the French Polynesian experience as is snorkeling.

- Order breakfast from room service if you don't want to go out and your hotel restaurant serves only an expensive buffet. Room service menus usually are a la carte, meaning you can order individual items whose total may be much less than the full buffet price.

- Dine at *restaurants conventionné,* which get breaks on the government's high duty on imported alcoholic beverages. Wine and mixed drinks in these establishments cost significantly less than elsewhere. They can charge no more than 700CFP (US$8.75/£4.45) for spirits served on the rocks, but cocktails can be more than twice that amount. I buy rum on the rocks and then add my own Coke to it. You can also order *vin ordinaire* (table wine) served in a carafe to save money. The chef buys good-quality wine in bulk and passes the savings on to you.

- Take advantage of *plats du jour* (daily specials), especially at lunch, and prix fixe (fixed-price) menus, often called "tourist menus." These three- or four-course offerings are usually made with fresh produce direct from the market.

- Consider sharing a starter course. Unlike some American menus, which list the main course as an entree, here an entree is the first course, and it is likely to be a more substantial serving than an American appetizer. If you have a light appetite, an entree could suffice as your only course, or you can share one with your mate or a friend. I discreetly glance at other tables to check portion sizes before ordering.

- Make your own snacks or perhaps a picnic lunch to enjoy at the beach. Every village has at least one grocery store. Fresh loaves of French bread cost about 51CFP (65¢/30p) each, and most stores carry cheeses, deli meats, vegetables, and other sandwich makings, many imported from France. Locally brewed Hinano beers sell for about 250CFP (US$3.15/£1.60) or less in grocery stores, versus 500CFP (US$6.25/£3.15) or more at the hotel bars, and bottles of decent French wine cost a fraction of restaurant prices.

Planning Your Trip to Tahiti & French Polynesia

Thanks to tons of euros pouring in from Paris, French Polynesians enjoy a relatively high standard of living. The flip side of that coin is that everyone pays high prices for almost everything, locals and visitors alike. As one resident of these gorgeous islands once told me, "You must pay for paradise."

Indeed, you can pay a king's ransom to vacation here, but French Polynesia doesn't have to cost you both arms and both legs. In this chapter, I will advise you on how to plan your trip, hopefully so that you won't have to declare bankruptcy after visiting this modern paradise.

In planning your trip, keep in mind why you are coming here and what your priorities are. You can go scuba diving to exhaustion or just sit on the beach with a trashy novel. You can share a 300-room hotel with package-tour tourists or get away from it all in an overwater bungalow. You can hide away with your lover or join your fellow guests at lively dinner parties. You can totally ignore the islanders around you or enrich your own life by learning about theirs. You can listen to the day's events on CNN International or see what the South Seas were like a century ago. Lacking the ability to read minds, I must leave those decisions to you.

1 VISITOR INFORMATION

The best source of up-to-date information in advance is **Tahiti Tourisme**, B.P. 65, 98713 Papeete, French Polynesia (© **50. 57.00;** fax 43.66.19; www.tahiti-tourisme. com).

You can also contact Tahiti Tourisme's overseas offices or representatives:

- **United States:** 300 N. Continental Blvd., Ste. 160, El Segundo, CA 90245 (© **310/414-8484;** fax 310/414-8490; www.tahiti-tourisme.com); and 122 E. 42nd St., Ste. 608, New York, NY 10168 (© **212/599-8484**).
- **Australia:** Paramour Productions, 362 Riley St., Surry Hills, NSW 2010 (© **1300 655 563** toll-free in Australia, or 02/9281-6020; fax 02/9211-6589; www.tahiti-tourisme.com.au)

- **New Zealand:** 200 W. Victoria St., Ste. 2A (P.O. Box 106192), Auckland (© **09/368-5262;** fax 09/368-5263; www.tahiti-tourisme.co.nz)
- **United Kingdom:** BGB & Associates, 7 Westminster Palace Gardens, Artillery Row, London SW1P 1RL (© **20/7233- 2300;** fax 20/7233-2301; www.tahiti-tourisme.co.uk)
- **France:** 28 bd. Saint Germain, 75005 Paris (© **01/55426434;** fax 01/ 55426120; www.tahiti-tourisme.fr)
- **Germany:** Travel Marketing Romberg, Swartzbachstrasse, 32 40822, Mettman bei Dusseldorf (© **2104/286672;** fax 2104/912673; www.tahititourisme.de)
- **Italy:** Aigo, Piazza Castello, 3 20 124 Milano (© **02/66-980317;** fax 02/66- 92648; www.tahiti-tourisme.it)

Impressions

It is no exaggeration to say, that to a European of any sensibility, who, for the first time, wanders back into these valleys—away from the haunts of the natives—the ineffable repose and beauty of the landscape is such, that every object strikes him like something seen in a dream; and for a time he almost refuses to believe that scenes like these should have a commonplace existence.

—Herman Melville, 1847

- **Chile:** Officina de turismo de Tahiti y sus islas, av. 11 de Septiembre 2214, Of. 116, Casila 16057, Santiago 9 (✆ **251-2826;** fax 233-1787; www.tahiti-tourisme.cl)
- **Japan:** Tahiti Tourist Promotion Board, Tokyo City Air Terminal 2F 42-1, Nihonbashi-Hakozakicho, Chuo-ku, Tokyo 103-0015 (✆ **3/3639-0468;** fax 3/3665-0581; www.tahiti-tourisme.jp)

Once you're in Papeete, you can get maps, brochures, and other information at the Tahiti Tourisme's **Fare Manihini** visitor bureau (✆ **50.57.12;** www.tahiti-manava.pf), located in the cruise-ship welcome center on the waterfront, on boulevard Pomare at rue Paul Gauguin. See "Fast Facts: Tahiti," in chapter 5.

Most major islands have tourism committees, but they run information offices only on Moorea, Huahine, Raiatea, Bora Bora, Nuku Hiva, and Hiva Oa (see "Fast Facts" in chapters 6, 7, 8, 9, and 12, respectively).

Be sure to pick up the *Tahiti Beach Press,* a free weekly English-language newspaper that lists special events and current activities. Copies are available in most hotel lobbies.

Tahiti Tourisme distributes free maps of each island. Each weekly edition of the free *Tahiti Beach Press* carries artistic maps of the island and Papeete. Librairie Vaima, a large bookstore in Papeete's Vaima Centre, sells several *cartes touristiques.*

The most detailed map is "Tahiti: Archipel de la Société," published by the Institut Géographique National. Although it doesn't include every new road on Tahiti, it shows all the Society Islands in detail, including topographic features. It's available online from **Maptown Ltd.** (www.maptown.com).

USEFUL WEBSITES

The U.S. Department of State maintains a **Travel Advisory** (✆ **202/647-5225**) to keep you abreast of political or other problems throughout the world. It posts travel warnings and other timely information on its website, www.travel.state.gov.

The Tahiti-based **Agence Tahitienne de Presse** (www.tahitipresse.pf) is the best source for breaking local news as well as events and weather. Click on the "English version" link.

The East-West Center at the University of Hawaii gathers news from French Polynesia and other islands on its **Pacific Islands Report** website, http://pidp.eastwestcenter.org/pireport. It includes links to newspapers, news services, and universities.

Other useful websites include:

- **www.airtahitimagazine.com**, with articles from Air Tahiti's in-flight magazine.
- **www.diving-tahiti.com**, for general information and links to dive operators in all of the islands.
- **www.frommers.com**, especially the message boards, where you can read what other travelers have to say about Tahiti and French Polynesia.
- **www.meteo.pf**, the official site of Météo France, the local weather service.

- **www.polynesianislands.com**, with coverage of all the South Pacific islands.
- **www.tahitiguide.com** is one of the most comprehensive commercial sites and has a booking engine for most hotels and many pensions.
- **www.tahiti-nui.com**, where you can see what the weather is doing in Papeete and on Bora Bora through Tahiti Nui Travel's live webcams.
- **www.tahitisun.com**, with links to several other sites that offer a host of information about each island.

2 ENTRY REQUIREMENTS & CUSTOMS

PASSPORTS

For information on how to get a passport, see "Passports" in the "Fast Facts: Tahiti & French Polynesia" section of appendix A. The websites listed provide downloadable passport applications as well as the current processing fees. For an up-to-date, country-by-country listing of passport requirements around the world, go to the "Foreign Entry Requirement" page of the U.S. State Department's website at **www.travel.state. gov.**

VISAS

All visitors except French nationals are required to have a **passport** that will be valid for 6 months beyond their intended stay, as well as a **return or ongoing ticket.** French citizens must bring their national identity cards.

Citizens and nationals of the United States, Canada, Argentina, Bermuda, Bolivia, Brunei, Chile, Costa Rica, Croatia, the Czech Republic, Ecuador, El Salvador, Estonia, Guatemala, Honduras, Hungary, Japan, Latvia, Lithuania, Malaysia, Mexico, New Zealand, Nicaragua, Panama, Paraguay, Poland, Singapore, Slovakia, Slovenia, South Korea, and Uruguay may visit for up to 30 days without a visa.

Nationals of Andorra, Australia, the European Union countries, Monaco, Switzerland, Iceland, Liechtenstein, Norway, St. Martin, and the Vatican, can stay up to 3 months without a visa.

Citizens from all other countries (including foreign nationals residing in the U.S.) must get a visa before leaving home.

French embassies and consulates overseas can issue "short stay" visas valid for 1 to 3 months, and they will forward applications for longer visits to the local immigration department in Papeete. *Note:* Visas issued by French embassies and consulates do not entitle you to visit Tahiti without being stamped *"valable pour la Polynésie Française"*—valid for French Polynesia.

In the United States, the **Embassy of France** is at 4102 Reservoir Rd. NW, Washington, DC 20007 (© **202/944-6000;** www.info-france-usa.org). There are French consulates in Boston, Chicago, Detroit, Houston, Los Angeles, Miami, New Orleans, New York, and San Francisco.

TRANSITING THE U.S.

Nearly all travelers to Tahiti from the U.K. and Europe will stop in Los Angeles on the way and thus must comply with U.S. immigration procedures. Citizens of 27 countries (including the U.K., most European nations, Australia, and New Zealand) can visit and transit the U.S. without a visa, but as of January 12, 2009, they must register online at **https://esta.cbp.dhs.gov** more than 72 hours before leaving home under the Electronic System for Travel Authorization (ESTA) program administered by the U.S. Department of Homeland Security (www.dhs.gov). Citizens of all other countries without a visitor visa to the U.S. must obtain a C-1 transit visa from the U.S. State Department (www. unitedstatesvisas.gov), even if they don't leave the airport.

MEDICAL REQUIREMENTS

No vaccinations are required unless you are coming from a yellow fever, plague, or cholera area. For information on medical requirements and recommendations, see "Health & Safety," in this chapter on p. 64.

CUSTOMS
WHAT YOU CAN BRING INTO FRENCH POLYNESIA

French Polynesia's Customs allowances are 200 cigarettes or 50 cigars, 2 liters of spirits or 2 liters of wine, 50 grams of perfume, .25 gram of toilet water, 500 grams of coffee, 100 grams of tea, and 30,000CFP (US$375/£189) worth of other goods. Narcotics, dangerous drugs, weapons, ammunition, and copyright infringements (that is, pirated videotapes and audiotapes) are prohibited. Pets and plants are subject to stringent regulations (don't even think of bringing your dog).

WHAT YOU CAN TAKE HOME FROM FRENCH POLYNESIA

United States Citizens: Returning U.S. citizens who have been in French Polynesia for at least 48 hours are allowed to bring back, once every 30 days, 200 cigarettes (age 18 and older), 1 liter of alcoholic beverages (age 21 and older), and US$800 worth of merchandise duty-free. You'll be charged a flat rate of 4% duty on the next US$1,000 worth of purchases. Be sure to have your receipts handy, since you must list every item if you're over the duty-free

limits. On mailed gifts, the duty-free limit is US$100. You cannot bring jewelry or other items made of black coral or whalebone into the United States. Nor can you bring fresh foodstuffs; tinned foods, however, are allowed.

For more information about what you can bring back and the corresponding fees, download the invaluable free pamphlet *Know Before You Go* at www.cbp.gov (click on "Travel" and then "Know Before You Go"). Or request the pamphlet from **U.S. Customs & Border Protection (CBP),** 1300 Pennsylvania Ave. NW, Washington, DC 20229 (© **877/287-8667**).

Canadian Citizens: For a clear summary of Canadian rules, write for the booklet *I Declare,* issued by the Canada Border Services Agency (© **800/461-9999** in Canada, or 204/983-3500; www.cbsa-asfc.gc.ca).

U.K. Citizens: For information, contact **HM Customs & Excise** at © **0845/010-9000** (from outside the U.K., 020/8929-0152), or consult their website at **www. hmce.gov.uk.**

Australian Citizens: A helpful brochure available from Australian consulates or Customs offices is *Know Before You Go.* For more information, call the **Australian Customs Service** at © **1300/363-263,** or log on to **www.customs.gov.au.**

New Zealand Citizens: Most questions are answered in a free pamphlet available at New Zealand consulates and Customs offices: *New Zealand Customs Guide for Travellers, Notice no. 4.* For more information, contact **New Zealand Customs,** The Customhouse, 17–21 Whitmore St., Box 2218, Wellington (© **04/473-6099** or 0800/428-786; **www.customs.govt.nz**).

3 MONEY & COSTS

The cost of living in French Polynesia is high for local residents and visitors alike,

which makes it a relatively expensive place to visit. This is especially true for those of

What Things Cost in Tahiti & French Polynesia	CFP	US$	UK£
Taxi from airport into Papeete	2,480	31.00	16.00
Bus from airport into Papeete	132	1.65	82p
Moderate hotel room for two	20,000	250.00	125.00
Inexpensive hotel room for two	8,800	110.00	105.00
Moderate lunch for two, without alcohol	5,120	64.00	32.00
Moderate three-course meal for two, without alcohol	9,360	117.00	59.00
Bottle of Hinano in a bar	440	5.50	2.75
Cup of regular coffee	300	3.75	1.90

us earning the embattled U.S. dollar, whose recent all-time low has added 25% or more to a visit here. You already know this if you prepaid your hotel room, and you will be reminded on your first morning here when you come to breakfast and find that your hotel may charge more than US$35 (£18) per person for its buffet. This is what I call waking up to "breakfast shock."

The flip side of the coin is that French Polynesia is a modern, First World place. You cannot drink the tap water on most islands, but the electricity is reliable, the airplanes and ferries ordinarily depart and arrive on time, the automated teller machines (ATMs) usually have cash to dispense, you can call anywhere in the world from a public phone, and access to the Internet is readily available. In other words, your visit should go as smoothly here as it would in any other developed country.

CURRENCY

The local currency is the *Comptoirs Français du Pacific,* or **French Pacific franc (CFP),** which comes in coins up to 100CFP and in colorful notes ranging from 500CFP into the millions.

The Pacific franc is abbreviated "XPF" by the banks, but in this book I use CFP, the French abbreviation.

The same franc is used in the French Pacific territories of New Caledonia and Wallis and Futuna islands.

U.S. dollar and European euro notes (but not coins) are widely accepted as cash in the islands, although at less favorable exchange rates than at banks.

You will probably get a more favorable rate if you change your money in French Polynesia rather than before leaving home.

ATMS

The easiest and best way to get local currency is from an ATM, known as a *billetterie* in French and sometimes referred to in English as a "cash machine" or "cashpoint." **Banque de Polynésie, Banque Socredo,** and **Banque de Tahiti** have offices with ATMs on the main islands, and many **post offices** have *billetteries* that dispense cash against MasterCard and Visa cards. See the "Fast Facts" sections in the following island chapters for bank and ATM locations (this is essential since some of the smaller islands do not have ATMs or even banks).

The ATMs operate in both French and English, and they usually are reliable at giving cash or cash advances. Nevertheless, I carry some cash or traveler's checks with me in case the local ATM runs out of cash or is out of service.

Be sure you know your four-digit **personal identification number (PIN)** for each credit and debit card—and find out your daily withdrawal limit before you leave home.

The CFP, the U.S. Dollar & the British Pound

The value of the CFP is pegged directly to the European euro at a rate of **1 = 119.332CFP.** At this writing, **US$1 = approximately 80CFP** (or, the other way around, 100CFP = US$1.25), which is the exchange rate I used to calculate the dollar values given in this book. **For British readers:** At this writing, **£1 = approximately 158CFP** (or, 100CFP = 63p), the rate used to calculate the pound values below. *Note:* International exchange rates fluctuate depending on economic and political factors. Thus, the values given in this table may not be the same when you travel to French Polynesia. Use the following table only as a guide. Find the current rates at **www.xe.com**.

CFP	US$	UK£	CFP	US$	UK£
100	1.25	0.65	1,500	19.00	9.50
150	1.90	0.95	2,000	25.00	13.00
200	2.50	1.25	3,000	38.00	19.00
300	3.75	1.90	4,000	50.00	25.00
400	5.00	2.55	5,000	63.00	32.00
500	6.25	3.15	6,000	75.00	38.00
600	7.50	3.80	7,000	88.00	44.00
700	8.75	4.45	8,000	100.00	51.00
800	10.00	5.05	9,000	113.00	57.00
900	11.00	5.70	10,000	125.00	63.00
1,000	13.00	6.30	20,000	250.00	127.00

I carry two debit (that is, "cash" or "check") cards so there's a backup in case one doesn't work in a bank's ATM. You should use them to get local cash for two reasons: You get a better exchange rate than if you exchange traveler's checks, and you avoid the local banks' fees for changing cash and traveler's checks (see below).

Visa and MasterCard tack a 1% currency conversion fee to every debit card withdrawal, and many banks add up to 5% as their own "foreign transaction fee." In addition, many banks impose a fee every time you use a card at another bank's ATM, and that fee can be higher for international transactions (up to $5 or more) than for domestic ones.

How much you will pay depends entirely on your bank. Call your bank's customer service department for information on any applicable charges.

Also, ask if your bank levies a fee even if you pay in dollars, or when you charge a U.S. dollar amount to an overseas company or website and the vendor sends the transaction through a foreign bank. You may be able to avoid fees by paying for your airfare and hotel in U.S. dollars before leaving home, such as through a travel agent.

You can withdraw cash advances from your credit cards at banks or ATMs, but high withdrawal fees make credit card cash advances a pricey way to get cash. In addition to the fees, you'll pay interest from the moment of your withdrawal, even if you pay your monthly bills on time.

CREDIT CARDS

You can use MasterCard and Visa cards to charge your expenses at most island hotels, car-rental companies, restaurants, and large shops. Many also accept American

Express. Only the major hotels and car-rental firms accept Diners Club, however, and none accept Discover cards. Always ask first, and when you're away from the main towns, don't count on putting anything on plastic.

Note that many banks now assess a 1% to 3% "transaction fee" on **all** charges you incur abroad (whether you're using the local currency or your native currency). Personally, I use my Capital One credit card since it charges no foreign transaction fee, nor does it have an annual fee. Read your own card member agreement—or better yet, call your bank's customer service department—for charges.

TRAVELER'S CHECKS

I seldom use them these days, but I carry a few hundred U.S. dollars in traveler's checks in case the local ATM isn't operating. Only in emergencies do I exchange traveler's checks at banks, since all charge 500CFP (US$6.25/£3.15) or more per transaction, regardless of the amount changed.

You can get traveler's checks in most major currencies at most banks. U.S. dollar checks come in denominations of $20, $50, $100, $500, and sometimes $1,000. Generally, you'll pay a service charge ranging from 1% to 4%.

The most popular traveler's checks are offered by **American Express** (ℂ 800/807-6233 or ℂ 800/221-7282 for card-holders—this number accepts collect calls, offers service in several foreign languages, and exempts Amex gold and platinum cardholders from the 1% fee); **Visa** (ℂ 800/732-1322)—AAA members can obtain Visa checks for a $9.95 fee (for checks up to $1,500) at most AAA offices or by calling ℂ 866/339-3378; and **MasterCard** (ℂ 800/223-9920).

Be sure to keep a record of your traveler's checks' serial numbers separate from the checks in the event that they are stolen or lost. You'll get a refund faster if you know the numbers.

Another option is the new prepaid traveler's check cards, reloadable cards that work much like debit cards but aren't linked to your checking account. The **American Express Travelers Cheque Card,** for example, requires a minimum deposit, sets a maximum balance, and has a one-time issuance fee of $14.95. You can withdraw money from an ATM (for a fee of $2.50 per transaction, not including bank fees), and the funds can be purchased in dollars, euros, or pounds. If you lose the card, your available funds will be refunded within 24 hours.

 Converting in Your Head

No decimals are used with Pacific franc units, so prices at first can seem even more staggering than they really are. Although the value of the CFP varies with the European euro, many local residents think of 100CFP as US$1 (the historical benchmark, which explains the unusual 119.332 CFP value against the European euro), and they often express prices that way to visitors. For example, if the price of something is 1,000CFP, they might say it costs US$10. Using their method, you can make a quick conversion without a calculator by thinking of 100CFP as US$1, 500CFP as US$5, 1,000CFP as US$10, and so on. That is, drop the last two zeros, then add or subtract the percentage difference between the actual rate and 100CFP. In the case of US$1 = 80CFP, for example, you would add 20%.

When you change money (or after you've withdrawn local currency from an ATM), ask for some small bills or loose change. Petty cash will come in handy for public transportation (local taxi drivers never seem to have change for large bills). Consider keeping the small money separate from your larger bills, so that it's readily accessible and you'll be less of a target for theft.

4 WHEN TO GO

There is no bad time to go to French Polynesia, but some periods are better than others. The weather is at its best—comfortable and dry—in July and August, but this is the prime vacation and festival season. July is the busiest month because of the *Heiva Nui* festival (see "French Polynesia Calendar of Events," below). Hotels on the outer islands are at their fullest during August, the traditional French vacation month, when many Papeete residents head for the outer islands to get away from it all. In other words, book your air tickets and hotel rooms for July and August as far in advance as possible.

May, June, September, and October have the best combination of weather and availability of hotel rooms.

THE CLIMATE

Tahiti and the rest of the Society Islands enjoy a balmy tropical climate. Tropical showers can pass overhead at any time of the year. Humidity averages between 77% and 80% throughout the year.

The most pleasant time of year is the May-through-October austral winter, or **dry season,** when midday maximum temperatures average a delightful 82°F (28°C), with early morning lows of 68°F (20°C) often making a blanket necessary. Some winter days, especially on the south side of the islands, can seem quite chilly when a strong wind blows from Antarctica.

November through April is the austral summer, or **wet season,** when rainy periods can be expected between days of intense sunshine. The average maximum daily temperature is 86°F (30°C) during these months, while nighttime lows are about 72°F (22°C). An air-conditioned hotel room or bungalow will feel like heaven during this humid time of year.

The central and northern Tuamotus have somewhat warmer temperatures and less rainfall. Since there are no mountains to create cooling night breezes, these islands can experience desertlike hot periods between November and April.

The Marquesas are closer to the Equator, and temperatures and humidity tend to be slightly higher than in Tahiti. Rainfall in the Marquesas is scattered throughout the year, but is most likely from June through August, exactly opposite that of the rest of French Polynesia. The trade winds reach that far north and temper the climate from April to October, but the Marquesas can see hot and sticky days the rest of the year.

The climate in the Austral and Gambier islands, which are much farther south, is more temperate year-round.

French Polynesia is on the far eastern edge of the South Pacific cyclone (hurricane) belt, and storms can occur between November and March.

Another factor to consider is the part of an island that you'll visit. Because the moist trade winds usually blow from the east, the eastern sides of the high, mountainous islands tend to be wetter all year than the western sides.

Also bear in mind that the higher the altitude, the lower the temperature. If you're going up in the mountains, be prepared for much cooler weather than you'd have on the coast.

The local office of **Météo France,** the national weather service, posts the forecasts and climatic observations in French on **www.meteo.pf**.

Average Daytime Temperatures in Tahiti

	Jan	Feb	Mar	Apr	May	June	July	Aug	Sept	Oct	Nov	Dec
Temp °F	80.6	80.8	81.3	80.8	79.5	77.4	76.5	76.3	77	78.1	79.3	79.9
Temp °C	27	27.1	27.4	27.1	26.4	25.2	24.7	24.6	25	25.6	26.3	26.6

THE BUSY SEASON

July and August are the busiest tourist season in French Polynesia. That's when residents of Tahiti head to their own outer islands, in keeping with the traditional July-to-August holiday break in France. Many Europeans also visit the islands during this time. In addition, July brings the *Heiva Nui,* the territory's biggest annual festival (see "French Polynesia Calendar of Events," below), when locals flock to Tahiti to see or participate in dance contests.

Christmas through the middle of January is a good time to get a hotel reservation in the islands, but airline seats can be hard to come by, since thousands of islanders fly home from overseas.

HOLIDAYS

Like all Pacific Islanders, the Tahitians love public holidays and often extend them

---

(Fun Facts) **"Tahiti Time"**

There's an old story about a 19th-century planter who promised a South Pacific islander a weekly wage and a pension if he would come to work on his copra plantation. Copra is dried coconut meat, from which oil is pressed for use in soaps, cosmetics, and other products. Hours of backbreaking labor are required to chop open the coconuts and extract the meat by hand.

The islander was sitting by the lagoon, eating the fruit he had picked from nearby trees while hauling in one fish after another. "Let me make sure I understand correctly," said the islander. "You want me to break my back working for you for 30 years. Then you'll pay me a pension so I can come back here and spend the rest of my life sitting by the lagoon, eating the fruit from my trees and the fish I catch? I may not be sophisticated, but I am not stupid."

The islander's response reflects an attitude still prevalent in Tahiti and French Polynesia, where many people don't have to work in the Western sense. Here life moves at a slow pace. The locals call it "Tahiti time."

Consequently, do not count on the same level of service in hotels and restaurants as you might expect back home. The slowness is not slothful inattention; it's just the way things are done here. Your drink will come in due course. If you must have it immediately, order it at the bar. Otherwise, relax with your friendly hosts and enjoy their charming company.

Ⓜoments **When the Moon Is Full**

The islands are extraordinarily beautiful anytime, especially so at equinox time in late September and late March, when the sun's rays hit the lagoons at just the right angle to highlight the gorgeous colors out in the lagoons. The play of moonlight on the water and the black silhouettes the mountains cast against the sky, make them even more magical when the moon is full. Keep that in mind when planning your trip—and especially if it's your honeymoon.

past the official day. For example, if Ascension Day falls on a Thursday, don't be surprised if some stores and even banks are closed through the weekend. Plan your shopping forays accordingly.

Public holidays are New Year's Day (government offices are also closed on Jan 2), Good Friday and Easter Monday, Ascension Day (40 days after Easter), Whitmonday (the seventh Mon after Easter), Missionary Day (Mar 5), Labor Day (May 1), Pentecost Monday (the first Mon in June), Bastille Day (July 14), Internal Autonomy Day (Sept 8), All Saints' Day (Nov 1), Armistice Day (Nov 11), and Christmas Day (Dec 25).

Tahiti Tourisme publishes an annual list of the territory's leading special events on its website (see "Visitor Information," earlier in this chapter).

FRENCH POLYNESIA CALENDAR OF EVENTS

JANUARY

Chinese New Year. Parade, musical performances, demonstrations of martial arts, Chinese dances, and handicrafts. Between mid-January and mid-February.

Oceania International Documentary Film Festival (FIFO). Films produced by Pacific islanders are shown and judged in Papeete. Last weekend.

FEBRUARY

Tahiti-Moorea Marathon. Prizes worth up to US$15,000 (£7,500) entice some of the world's best runners to trot 42km (26 miles) around Moorea. Second Saturday.

MARCH

Coming of the Gospel. Gatherings on Tahiti commemorate the anniversary of the arrival of the London Missionary Society. March 5.

MAY

Billabong Pro Surfing. World-class surfers compete on the waves off Teuhupoo on Tahiti Iti. First 2 weeks.

Tahiti Pearl Regatta. Yachts sail among Raiatea, Tahaa, Huahine, and Bora Bora. Mid-May.

JUNE

Miss Tahiti, Miss Heiva, Miss Moorea, and Miss Bora Bora Contests. Candidates from around the islands vie to win the titles. It is among the biggest annual events on outer islands. Early to mid-June.

Tahiti International Golf Open. Local and international golfers vie at Atimaono Golf Course, Tahiti. Mid-June.

JULY

Heiva Nui. This is the festival to end all festivals in French Polynesia. It was originally a celebration of Bastille Day on July 14, but the islanders have extended the shindig into a month-long blast (it is commonly called *Tiurai,* the Tahitian word for July). They pull out all the stops, with parades, outrigger canoe races, javelin-throwing contests, fire walking, games, carnivals, festivals, and reenactments of ancient Polynesian ceremonies at restored *maraes.* Highlight for visitors: an extraordinarily colorful contest to determine the best Tahitian dancing troupe for the year—never do the hips gyrate more vigorously. Airline and hotel reservations are difficult to come by during July, so book early and take your written confirmation with you. Last weekend in June through July.

AUGUST

Mini Fêtes. Winning dancers and singers from the *Heiva Nui* perform at hotels on the outer islands. All month.

SEPTEMBER

World Tourism Day. Islanders pay homage to overseas visitors, who get discounts. Last weekend.

OCTOBER

Rotui's Tour. Runners race 15km (9 miles) around Moorea's Mount Rotui. Late October.

Hawaiki Nui Va'a. Outrigger canoe racing, the national sport, takes center stage as international teams race from Huahine to Raiatea, Tahaa, and Bora Bora over 3 days. www.hawaikinuivaa. pf. Late October to early November.

Tahiti Carnival. Parades, floats, and much partying on the Papeete waterfront. Last week.

NOVEMBER

Tatoonesia. Local and foreign tattoo artists gather in Papeete to share designs and techniques. Early November. Followed by Exhibition "Tattoo" in late November.

All Saints' Day. Flowers are sold everywhere to families who put them on graves after whitewashing the tombstones. November 1.

DECEMBER

Tiare Tahiti Flower Festival (The Tiare Days on Tahiti). Everyone on the streets of Papeete and in the hotels receives a *tiare Tahiti,* the fragrant gardenia that is indigenous to Tahiti. Dinner and dancing later. First week in December.

New Year's Eve. A big festival in downtown Papeete leads territory-wide celebrations. December 31.

5 GETTING TO TAHITI & FRENCH POLYNESIA

BY PLANE

A few cruise ships stop in the islands on their way across the Pacific Ocean (see "By Cruise Ship" later in this chapter), yet today, all but a handful of visitors arrive by air.

All international flights arrive at **Tahiti-Faaa International Airport (PPT),** on Tahiti's northwest corner, about 11km (7 miles) west of downtown Papeete. See "Getting Around Tahiti & French Polynesia" later in this chapter, for details on

getting from the airport to Papeete and other points on Tahiti.

THE AIRLINES

• **Air Tahiti Nui** (© **877/824-4846;** www.airtahitinui-usa.com), French Polynesia's award-winning national airline, has more flights—all on relatively new Airbus planes—to and from Tahiti than any other airline. Some of Air Tahiti Nui's flights depart Los Angeles in the afternoon California time and arrive in Papeete in the evening local

155° E 160° E 165° E 170° E 175° E 180° 175° W

Monday / Sunday

Howland Island (U.S.)

0° EQUATOR Baker Island (U.S.)

★ Tarawa

GILBERT ISLANDS

NAURU

K I R I I

New Ireland

New Britain

PAPUA NEW GUINEA

Bougainville

SOLOMON

PHOENIX

Solomon Sea

Honiara ★

Guadalcanal

10° S

ISLANDS

SANTA CRUZ ISLANDS

TUVALU

★ Funafuti

TOKELAU

Rotuma (Fiji)

WALLIS AND FUTUNA (France)

SAMOA

Savai'i Api ★

Wallis

Coral Sea

Espiritu Santo

Malakula

VANUATU

Port Vila ★ Éfaté

Erromango

Tanna

Futuna

Upolu

Vanua Levu

FIJI

Nadi ○

Viti Levu

Taveuni

Suva ★

TONGA

Vava'u

Nuku'alofa ★ Ha'apai

Tongatapu

20° S

Nouméa ★

NEW CALEDONIA (France)

TROPIC OF CAPRICORN

SOUTH

Brisbane ○

30° S

Norfolk Island (Australia)

KERMADEC ISLANDS (New Zealand)

AUSTRALIA

Lord Howe Island (Australia)

Sydney ○

Monday / Sunday

Tasman Sea

Auckland ○

40° S

NEW ZEALAND

Political boundaries

Atoll

Reef

Wellington ★

INTERNATIONAL DATE LINE

CHATHAM ISLANDS (New Zealand)

Christchurch ○

155° E 160° E 165° E 170° E 175° E 180° 175° W

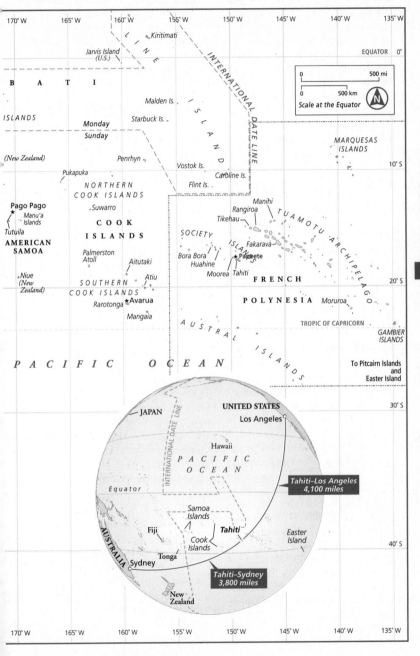

170° W 165° W 160° W 155° W 150° W 145° W 140° W 135° W

Kiritimati

Jarvis Island (U.S.)

EQUATOR 0°

B A T I

ISLANDS

Malden Is.

Starbuck Is.

Monday
Sunday

(New Zealand)

Penrhyn

Vostok Is.

Caroline Is.

Flint Is.

10° S

MARQUESAS ISLANDS

Pukapuka

NORTHERN COOK ISLANDS

Pago Pago
Manu'a Islands
Tutuila
AMERICAN SAMOA

Suwarro

COOK ISLANDS

SOCIETY

Manihi
Rangiroa
Tikehau

TUAMOTU ARCHIPELAGO

Niue
(New Zealand)

Palmerston Atoll

Aitutaki

ISLANDS

Fakarava

Bora Bora
Huahine

Papeete

SOUTHERN
COOK ISLANDS

Atiu

Moorea Tahiti

FRENCH

Rarotonga Avarua

Mangaia

POLYNESIA Moruroa

20° S

AUSTRAL

ISLANDS

TROPIC OF CAPRICORN

GAMBIER ISLANDS

P A C I F I C   O C E A N

To Pitcairn Islands and Easter Island

30° S

0   500 mi
0   500 km
Scale at the Equator

JAPAN

UNITED STATES
Los Angeles

Hawaii

PACIFIC OCEAN

INTERNATIONAL DATE LINE

Equator

Tahiti–Los Angeles
4,100 miles

Samoa Islands

AUSTRALIA

Fiji

Tahiti

Cook Islands

Easter Island

40° S

Tonga

Sydney

Tahiti–Sydney
3,800 miles

New Zealand

170° W 165° W 160° W 155° W 150° W 145° W 140° W 135° W time, thus enabling you to make connections to Moorea or to get a good night's sleep on Tahiti before tackling the islands the next morning. Most of its return flights are overnight, but you arrive in Los Angeles early enough in the morning to make convenient connections to other cities. Air Tahiti Nui also flies between New York's John F. Kennedy International Airport and Papeete from April through October, with a stop in Los Angeles. Those planes keep going to Sydney, which means you can fly between New York and Australia with stops in Los Angeles and Papeete. Air Tahiti Nui also links Paris, Tokyo, Auckland, and Sydney to Papeete. It also code-shares with American Airlines and Northwest Airlines, meaning frequent fliers of those carriers can use their miles to reach Tahiti.

- **Air New Zealand** (© 800/262-1234 or 310/615-1111; www.airnewzealand. com) flies its own planes between Auckland and Papeete, and it code-shares with Air Tahiti Nui between Los Angeles and Papeete. It flies to several Australian cities, so Aussies can reach Tahiti through Auckland. It links Tokyo, Hong Kong, Singapore, Seoul, Taipei, and Beijing to Auckland, with connections on to Papeete. Air New Zealand is a member of the Star Alliance, which includes United Airlines and several other carriers, which means you can get to the islands from many cities in the United States, Canada, and Europe on an Air New Zealand ticket.
- **Air France** (© 800/321-4538; www. airfrance.com) flies to Tahiti from Paris and Los Angeles.
- **Hawaiian Airlines** (© 800/367-5320 in the continental U.S., Alaska, and Canada, or 808/838-1555 in Honolulu; www.hawaiianair.com) has the only direct link between Honolulu and Tahiti, usually once a week. You can fly from Los Angeles, San Francisco,

Portland, or Seattle to Honolulu, and then change plans for Tahiti. *Beware:* The plane change can result in delays and even an unexpected Hawaiian holiday.

- **Lan Airlines** (© 800/735-5526; www. lanchile.com), the Chilean national airline, flies at least weekly between Santiago, Chile, and Tahiti by way of Easter Island.
- **Qantas Airways** (© 800/227-4500; www.qantas.com), the Australian carrier, code-shares flights to and from Papeete with Air Tahiti Nui.

FLYING FOR LESS: TIPS FOR GETTING THE BEST AIRFARE

The Pacific Ocean hasn't shrunk since it took 10 days and more than 83 hours in the air for Australian aviator Charles Kingsford Smith to become the first person to fly across it in 1928. Even though you can now board a jetliner in Los Angeles in the morning and be strolling under the palm trees of Tahiti by dark, the distances still run into the thousands of miles. Consequently, transportation costs may be the largest single expense of your trip to French Polynesia.

Many tour operators specializing in French Polynesia will sell discounted airfare with or without hotel accommodations. I list some of the best under "Packages for the Independent Traveler" later in this chapter. Always check with them.

Here are some other tips:

- You may pay a fraction of the full-fare passengers if you can book your ticket either **long in advance or at the last minute,** or **fly midweek** or **at less-trafficked times**. If your schedule is flexible, say so, and ask if you can secure a cheaper fare by changing your flight plans.
- Search **the Internet** for cheap fares. The most popular online travel agencies are **Travelocity** (www.travelocity.co. uk); **Expedia** (www.expedia.co.uk and

www.expedia.ca); and **Orbitz.** In the U.K., go to **Travelsupermarket** (*©* **0845/345-5708;** www.travelsupermarket.com), a flight search engine that offers flight comparisons for the budget airlines whose seats often end up in bucket-shop sales. Other websites for booking airline tickets online include **Cheapflights.com** and **Priceline.com.**

• Keep an eye on local newspapers for **promotional specials** or **fare wars,** when airlines lower prices on their most popular routes.

• Try to book a ticket **in its country of origin.** If you're planning a one-way flight from London to Tahiti, a U.K.-based travel agent will probably have the lowest fares. For foreign travelers on multi-leg trips, book in the country of the first leg; for example, book New York–Tahiti–Sydney–New York in the U.S.

• **Consolidators,** also known as bucket shops, are wholesale brokers in the airline-ticket game. Consolidators buy deeply discounted tickets ("distressed" inventories of unsold seats) from airlines and sell them to online ticket agencies, travel agents, tour operators, corporations, and, to a lesser degree, the general public. Consolidators advertise in Sunday newspaper travel sections (often in small ads with tiny type), both in the U.S. and the U.K. They can be great sources for cheap international tickets. On the downside, bucket shop tickets are often rigged with restrictions, such as stiff cancellation penalties (as high as 50%–75% of the ticket price). And keep in mind that most of what you see advertised is of limited availability. Several reliable consolidators are worldwide and available online. **STA Travel** (www.statravel.com) has been the world's leading consolidator for students since purchasing Council Travel, but their fares are competitive for travelers of all ages. **Flights.com** (*©* **800/TRAV-800;** www.flights.com) has excellent fares worldwide, particularly to Europe. They also have "local" websites in 12 countries. **FlyCheap** (*©* **800/FLY-CHEAP;** www.1800flycheap.com) has especially good fares to sunny destinations. **Air Tickets Direct** (*©* **800/778-3447;** www.airticketsdirect.com) is based in Montreal and leverages the currently weak Canadian dollar for low fares; they also book trips to places that U.S. travel agents won't touch, such as Cuba.

• **Join frequent-flier clubs.** Frequent-flier membership doesn't cost a cent, but it does entitle you to free tickets or upgrades when you amass the airline's required number of frequent-flier points. You don't even have to fly to earn points; **frequent-flier credit cards** can earn you thousands of miles for doing your everyday shopping. Frankly, credit card miles have very low priority, so good luck trying to cash them in. Also keep in mind that award seats are limited, seats on popular routes are hard to snag, and more and more major airlines are cutting their expiration periods for mileage points—so check your airline's frequent-flier program so you don't lose your miles before you use them. *Inside tip:* Award seats are offered almost a year in advance, but seats also open up at the last minute, so if your travel plans are flexible, you may strike gold. To play the frequent-flier game to your best advantage, consult the community bulletin boards on **FlyerTalk** (www.flyertalk.com) or go to Randy Petersen's **Inside Flyer** (www.insideflyer.com). Petersen and friends review all the programs in detail and post regular updates on changes in policies and trends.

BAGGAGE ALLOWANCES
How many bags you can carry on board and check (and how much they can weigh)

Flying with Film & Video

Never pack **film**—exposed or unexposed—in checked bags, because the new, more powerful airport scanners can fog film. The film you carry with you can be damaged by scanners as well. X-ray damage is cumulative; the faster the film, and the more times you put it through a scanner, the more likely the damage. Film under 800 ASA is usually safe for up to five scans. If you're taking your film through additional scans, U.S. regulations permit you to demand hand inspections. In international airports, you're at the mercy of officials. Store your film in clear baggies so you can remove it easily before you go through scanners. Keep in mind that airports are not the only places where your camera may be scanned: Highly trafficked attractions are X-raying visitors' bags with increasing frequency.

Most photo-supply stores sell pouches designed to block X-rays. The pouches fit both film and loaded cameras. They should protect your film in checked baggage, but they may also raise alarms and result in a hand inspection.

You'll have little to worry about if you are traveling with a **digital camera.** Unlike film, which is sensitive to light, the digital camera and its storage cards are not affected by airport X-rays, according to Nikon.

Carry-on scanners will not damage **videotape** in video cameras, but the magnetic fields emitted by the walk-through security gateways and hand-held inspection wands will. Always place your loaded camcorder on the screening conveyor belt or have it hand-inspected. Be sure your batteries are charged, as you may be required to turn the device on to ensure that it's what it appears to be.

varies somewhat by airline, so always check with your chosen carrier beforehand.

Only one rule is set in stone: Passengers on flights to or from the United States may check two bags each weighing up to 30 kilograms (66 lb.), with total dimensions (height, width, and length) of both not exceeding 158 centimeters (62 in.).

Although domestic U.S. allowances may be lower, you can check this much baggage if you're connecting to an international flight.

In general, first-class passengers on other international flights are entitled to 40 kilograms (88 lb.) of checked luggage, business-class passengers to 30 kilograms (66 lb.), and economy-class passengers to

20 kilograms (44 lb.). Some airlines, including Air New Zealand and Air Pacific, strictly enforce these limits and make you pay extra for each kilogram over the maximum.

In addition to a small handbag or purse, all international passengers are permitted one carry-on bag with total measurements not exceeding 115 centimeters (45 in.). Carry-on hoarders can stuff all sorts of things into a laptop bag; as long as it has a laptop in it, it's still considered a personal item (remember, however, you must remove your laptop and pass it through security separately).

Pack carefully and bring evidence of your international ticket with you, as the baggage limit on both of French Polynesia's domestic airlines is 20 kilograms (44 lb.) per person if you're connecting with an international flight within 7 days, but it's 10 kilograms (22 lb.) per person if you're not. You will face a substantial extra charge for excess weight unless you buy a "Z Class" fare on Air Tahiti, which allows passengers to carry up to 50 kilograms (110 lb.) of luggage, as opposed to 20 kilograms under its economy fare. You can leave your extra belongings in the storage room at your hotel or at Tahiti-Faaa International Airport (see "Baggage Storage" under "Getting Around Tahiti & French Polynesia," later in this chapter).

ARRIVING & DEPARTING

ARRIVING

All international flights arrive at **Tahiti-Faaa International Airport,** 7km (4 miles) west of downtown Papeete.

Once you've cleared Customs, you will see a **visitor information booth** to the right. Group tour operators will be holding signs announcing their presence. Pick up some pocket money at **Banque de Polynésie,** to the left as you exit Customs, or at **Banque Socredo** to the right. Banque de Polynésie opens its exchange window whenever international flights arrive and

depart, while Banque Socredo's office is open only during normal banking hours. Both have ATMs, and Banque Socredo has a machine that will change U.S. dollars and other major notes to CFP (French Pacific francs).

I have spent many hours waiting for flights at the open-air, 24-hour **snack bar** to the right. There's a **McDonald's** next to Air Tahiti's domestic departure lounge, also to the right.

GETTING TO YOUR HOTEL

Unless you're on a package tour or your hotel has arranged a transfer, your only choice of transportation to your hotel between 10pm and 6am will be a **taxi.** Official fares from 8pm to 6am are 1,500CFP (US$19/£9.45) to the hotels on the west coast; 2,500CFP (US$31/£16) to downtown. Add 100CFP (US$1.25/65p) for each bag.

If you arrive when buses are running and you're in good physical condition, haul your baggage across the parking lot in front of the terminal, climb the stairs to the main road, and flag down a local bus. If you're driving a rental car, take Route 1 west to the InterContinental Resort Tahiti, the Sofitel Tahiti Maeva Beach Resort, or

---

Tips Coping with Jet Lag

Except for Air Tahiti Nui's afternoon departures from Los Angeles bound for the islands (see "The Airlines," earlier in this chapter), flights from North America leave after dark, which means you will fly overnight and cross at least two time zones. This invariably translates into jet lag. Here are some tips for combating this malady:

- Reset your watch to your destination time before you board the plane.
- Drink lots of water before, during, and after your flight. Avoid alcohol.
- Exercise and sleep well for a few days before your trip.
- Daylight is the key to resetting your body clock. At the website for **Outside In** (www.bodyclock.com), you can get a customized plan of when to seek and avoid light.
- If you need help getting to sleep earlier than you usually would, some doctors recommend taking either the hormone melatonin or the sleeping pill Ambien—but not together. Take 2 to 5 milligrams of melatonin about 2 hours before your planned bedtime.

Le Meridien Tahiti. Route 1 east passes the Sheraton Hotel Tahiti & Spa on its way to downtown Papeete. If you're going to downtown, watch for the Route 5 signs directing you to the expressway connecting Papeete to the west coast.

See "Getting Around Tahiti & French Polynesia," below, and "Getting Around Tahiti," in chapter 5, for more information.

BAGGAGE STORAGE

Most hotels will keep your baggage for free. The airport's **baggage storage room** (✆ **88.60.08;** hmoea@yahoo.fr) is in the parking lot in front of the international departures gate. It's the small building behind the open-air pavilion where Tahitian women sell leis and flower crowns. Charges range from 640CFP (US$8/£4) per day for regular-size bags to 2,700CFP (US$34/£17) for large items such as surfboards and bicycles. The room opens 2 hours before every international flight departs. Regular hours are Monday 4am to 7pm, Tuesday to Thursday 5am to 11pm, Saturday 5am to 12:30am, Sunday and holidays 1pm to 12:30am. MasterCard and Visa credit cards are accepted for charges in excess of 1,200CFP (US$15/£7.60).

DEPARTING

Check-in time for departing international flights is 3 hours before flight time; for domestic flights, be there 2 hours in advance. All of your bags must be screened for both international and domestic flights leaving Papeete. (There are no security procedures at the outer-island airstrips.)

There is no airport departure tax for either international or domestic flights.

Note: There is no bank or currency exchange bureau in the international departure lounge, so change your money before clearing immigration.

BY CRUISE SHIP

Although the days of great liners plying the Pacific are long gone, occasionally it may be possible to reach the islands on a cruise ship making an around-the-world voyage or being repositioned, say, from Alaska to Australia. In addition to Princess Cruises (see below), other companies likely to have ships in the South Pacific include **Cunard Line** (✆ **800/528-6273;** www.cunardline.com), whose vessels include the *Queen Elizabeth II,* and **Orient Lines** (✆ **800/333-7300;** www.orientlines.com).

Most sell tickets through travel agents, although some offer them directly to the public on their websites.

Lindblad Expeditions (✆ **800/EXPEDITION;** www.expeditions.com) occasionally has exploratory voyages from Easter Island to Tahiti, from there to Fiji, and from Fiji to Papua New Guinea.

You can also go to **www.cruisecritic.com**, where you can check out cruises throughout the world; **www.cruise411.com**, which has itineraries, deck plans, and other information; and **www.cruisepage.com**, with reviews of more than 300 ships.

Your best bet for steaming through the islands, however, is to fly to Tahiti and take one of the ships based here (see "Seeing the Islands by Cruise Ship & Yacht," later in this chapter).

(Tips) **Don't Forget to Reconfirm**

Air Tahiti Nui requires that you reconfirm your return flight within 72 hours of departure. It's mainly so the airline will know how to contact you should the schedule change.

6 GETTING AROUND TAHITI & FRENCH POLYNESIA

BY PLANE

Having Air Tahiti Nui or another carrier book your domestic flights along with your international ticket will greatly simplify matters in case of a local cancellation, and you will avoid an extra fee if you have to change your flights once here.

AIR MOOREA

A subsidiary of Air Tahiti (see below), **Air Moorea** (© **86.41.41;** fax 86.42.99; www.airmoorea.com) provides shuttle service between Tahiti-Faaa International Airport and Temae Airport on Moorea. Its small planes (and I do mean small) leave Faaa on the hour and half-hour daily from 6 to 9am, then on the hour from 10am to 3pm, and on the hour and half-hour again from 4 to 6pm. Each plane turns around on Moorea and flies back to Tahiti. The fare is about 3,700CFP (US$46/£24) each way, half-fare for children. Air Moorea's little terminal is on the east end of Tahiti-Faaa International Airport (that's to the left as you come out of Customs). Air Moorea will take you from the airport to your Moorea hotel for 600CFP (US$7.50/£3.75) each way, but *you must buy your transfer ticket in Papeete.* It is not available after you arrive on Moorea.

AIR TAHITI

The primary domestic carrier is **Air Tahiti** (© **86.44.42;** fax 86.40.99; www.air

---

(Tips) Air Tahiti Fares & Money-Saving Pass

Air Tahiti's approximate one-way adult fares on the usual visitor's circuit are as follows (double the fare for round-trips between any two islands; halve the cost for children):

Tahiti to Moorea	4,200 CFP	(US$53/£27)
Moorea to Huahine	14,800 CFP	(US$185/£94)
Moorea to Bora Bora	21,240 CFP	(US$266/£134)
Huahine to Raiatea	6,300 CFP	(US$79/£40)
Raiatea to Bora Bora	7,200 CFP	(US$90/£46)
Bora Bora to Tahiti	18,100 CFP	(US$226/£115)
Bora Bora to Rangiroa	27,400 CFP	(US$343/£173)
Rangiroa to Tahiti	18,200 CFP	(US$228/£115)

You can save by buying an **Air Tahiti Pass** over the popular routes. For example, the "Bora Bora Pass" permits travel over the popular Papeete–Moorea–Huahine–Bora Bora–Papeete route for about 38,800CFP (US$485/£246), which is about 10,000CFP (US$125/£63) less than the full adult fares. The "Bora Bora–Tuamotu Pass" adds Rangiroa, Tikihau, and Manihi. Whether you save anything will depend on how many islands you plan to visit, so add up the regular fares and compare to the price of the passes (they're explained on Air Tahiti's website). All travel must be completed within 28 days of the first flight, and other restrictions apply. See **www.airtahiti.pf** for details.

It depends on the pilots and how much sightseeing they want to do, but usually you will have the best views of the islands by sitting on the left side of the Air Tahiti aircraft when you're flying from Papeete to the outer islands, on the right side returning. Make sure you have your camera and a lot of film and camera batteries at the ready.

Most hotel dining rooms open for breakfast at 7am and close by 9:30am, so if you're catching an early morning flight to another island, stock up on some munchies and something to drink the night before, and bring them along on the plane.

tahiti.pf), which provides daily flights between Papeete and all the main islands, most in modern ATR turboprop planes seating 44 or 72 passengers. It's wise to reserve your seats as early as possible, especially during school holidays.

Air Tahiti's central downtown Papeete walk-in reservations office is at the corner of rue du 22 Septembre and rue du Maréchal Foche (© **47.44.00**). It also has an office in the Tahiti-Faaa International Airport terminal (© **86.41.84**).

The **baggage limit** on both of these airlines is 20 kilograms (44 lb.) per person if you're connecting with an international flight within 7 days, but 10 kilograms (22 lb.) per person if you're not. You will face a substantial extra charge for excess weight. You can leave your extra belongings in the storage room at your hotel or at Tahiti-Faaa International Airport (see "Arriving & Departing" in chapter 5).

Check-in times vary from 1 to 2 hours in advance, so ask Air Tahiti when you should arrive at the airport.

An alternative to taking Air Tahiti's scheduled flights is chartering a plane and pilot from **Air Moorea, Air Tahiti, Air Archepels** (© **81.30.30;** www.air archipels.com), or **Wan Air** (© **50.44.18;** www.wanair.pf). **Polynesia Hélicoptères** (© **86.60.29;** www.polynesia-helicopter. com) charters helicopters. When the total cost is split among a large enough group of

people, the price per person could be less than airfare on a scheduled airline.

BY FERRY TO MOOREA

Two companies—**Aremiti** (© **50.57.57;** www.aremiti.pf) and **Moorea Ferry** (© **86. 87.47** on Tahiti, or 56.34.34 on Moorea; www.mooreaferry.pf)—run ferries between the Papeete waterfront and Vaiare, a small bay on Moorea's east coast. It can seem like madness when the boats arrive and depart at the wharves, so take your time and be sure to get on one of the fast catamarans, which take 30 minutes to cover the 19km (12 miles) between the islands. The *Aremiti V* is larger, faster, and more comfortable than the *Moorea Express*. Don't get on the *Aremiti Ferry* or the *Moorea Ferry*, which are much slower. The one-way fare on any ferry, whether fast or slow, is about 900CFP (US$11/£5.70).

Since the departure times change from day to day, I usually pick up a schedule at the ferry dock and carry it with me throughout my visit. In general, one or another of them departs Papeete about 6am, 7:30am, 9am, noon, 2:40pm, 4:05pm, and 5:30pm Monday to Friday, with extra voyages on Friday and Monday (Moorea is a popular weekend retreat for Papeete residents). Weekend hours are slightly different on each ferry.

Buses meet all ferries at Vaire, except the midday departures from Papeete, to take you to your hotel or other destination

on Moorea for 500CFP (US$6.25/£3.15) per person. From Vaiare, they take about 1 hour to reach the northwest corner of Moorea.

BY SHIP TO THE OUTER ISLANDS

You can go by ship from Papeete to Huahine, Raiatea, Tahaa, and Bora Bora, but it's neither the quickest nor most comfortable way to travel, nor the most reliable.

Two cargo ferries, the *Vaeanu* (© **41. 25.35;** fax 41.24.34; torehiatetu@mail.pf) and the *Hawaiki Nui* (© **45.23.24;** fax 45.24.44; sarlstim@mail.pf), make three voyages a week. Both have passenger cabins. Usually they depart Papeete about 4pm, arrive at Huahine during the night, and go on to the other Leeward Islands the next day. They return from Bora Bora over the reverse route. Contact the ship owners for fares and schedules, which are at the mercy of the weather and condition of the ships.

Once in the Leeward Islands, you can make the voyage between Bora Bora and Raiatea on the *Maupiti Express* (© **67. 66.69** on Bora Bora, 66.37.81 on Raiatea; maupitiexpress@mail.pf). This small, fast ferry departs Bora Bora for Tahaa and Raiatea at 7am on Monday, Wednesday, and Friday, returning to Bora Bora in the late afternoon. It stops at Tahaa in both directions. On Tuesday, Thursday, and Saturday, it sails from Bora Bora to Maupiti, departing at 8:30am and returning in late afternoon. In other words, it's possible to make day trips from Bora Bora to Raiatea or Maupiti. Fares on either

route are 3,000CFP (US$38/£19) one-way, 4,000CFP (US$50/£25) return.

Except for the excellent *Aranui 3,* which is as much cruise vessel as cargo ship (see "Seeing the Islands by Cruise Ship & Yacht," below), ships to the Tuamotu, Marquesas, Gambier, and Austral island groups keep somewhat irregular schedules in terms of weeks or even months, not days. I once met a young Australian who took a boat to Rapa in the Austral Islands, expecting to return in a few weeks to Papeete. The ship later broke down and went into the repair yard on Tahiti, stranding him for 3 months on Rapa, where he survived on coconuts and the generosity of local residents. Consequently, I cannot recommend them. If you're interested, contact Tahiti Tourisme for a list of inter-island schooners, their fares, and approximate schedules from Tahiti Tourisme. You'd best have a 3-month visa to stay in French Polynesia.

BY RENTAL CAR

Avis and **Europcar** have rental-car agencies (*locations de voiture* in French) on Tahiti, Moorea, Huahine, Raiatea, and Bora Bora. **Hertz** is present on Tahiti, Raiatea, and Bora Bora. See the "Getting Around" sections in the following chapters for details.

A valid **driver's license** from your home country will be honored in French Polynesia.

Service stations are common on Tahiti, but only in the main villages on the other islands. Expect to pay about twice as much per gallon of gasoline (*essence* in French) as in the United States.

Ⓜ**oments**   **Breaking into Tahitian Song**

I was on the last ferry from Moorea to Tahiti when a Tahitian passenger, obviously on his way home from work, started playing a guitar. Within seconds, everyone onboard spontaneously began singing Tahitian songs. If you're lucky, you'll witness something like this and be in for a very special moment.

Drive Defensively!

Except for the four-lane expressways leading into Papeete, the roads here are narrow and winding. Add a penchant for speeding on the part of some locals, and you have the recipe for danger. If you rent a vehicle, keep your eyes on the road and drive defensively at all times.

DRIVING RULES

Driving is on the **right-hand side** of the road, as in North America and continental Europe.

All persons in a vehicle must wear **seat belts.** If you drive or ride on a scooter or motorbike, **helmets** (*casques,* pronounced "casks") are mandatory.

Speed limits are 40kmph (24 mph) in the towns and villages, and 80kmph (48 mph) on the open road. The limit is 60kmph (36 mph) for 8km (5 miles) on either side of Papeete. The general rule on the Route 5 freeway between Papeete and Punaauia, on Tahiti's west coast, is 90kmph (54 mph), although there is one short stretch going down a hill where it's officially 110kmph (66 mph).

Drivers on the main rural roads have the right of way. In Papeete, priority is given to vehicles entering from the right side, unless an intersection is marked with a traffic light or a stop or yield sign. This rule differs from those of most other countries, so be especially careful at all intersections, especially those marked with a *priorité à droite* (priority to the right) sign, and give way accordingly.

Drivers are required to **stop for pedestrians** at marked crosswalks, but on busy streets, don't assume that drivers will politely stop for you when you try to cross.

Traffic lights in Papeete may be difficult to see, since some of them are on the far left-hand side of the street instead of on the driver's side of the intersection.

7 SEEING THE ISLANDS BY CRUISE SHIP & YACHT

Another way to get around the islands is by cruise ship. Indeed, Tahiti and the nearby Society Islands are ideal grounds for cruise ships, since it's barely an hour's steam from Tahiti to Moorea, half a day's voyage on to Huahine, and less than 2 hours each among Huahine, Raiatea, Tahaa, and Bora Bora. That means the ships spend most days and nights at anchor in lovely lagoons, allowing passengers plenty of time to explore the islands and play in the water. Bear in mind, however, that you'll see a lot more of the ship than you will of the islands.

Cruises could also be an affordable way to see the islands in style, since the prices usually include all meals, wine with lunch and dinner, soft drinks, and most onboard activities. You might even find a deal that includes airfare to and from Tahiti.

Likewise, these are wonderful islands for chartering a yacht and setting sail on your own.

TAKING A CRUISE

At press time, **Silversea Cruises** (© 800/ 722-9955; www.silversea.com) had announced plans to station its *Prince Albert II* in French Polynesia from April to

October 2009, with the possibility of repeat visits thereafter. Once known as the *World Discoverer,* the 132-passenger ship has been refitted in order to cruise from Papeete to the seldom-visited Austral Islands and northern Marquesas.

Abercrombie & Kent (© **800/554-7016;** www.abercrombiekent.com) often includes French Polynesia on cruises by the 118-passenger *Clipper Odyssey,* which specializes in out-of-the-way places. For example, its 2-week "Polynesian Paradise" cruise was scheduled to visit Bora Bora, the Tuamotu atolls, and the Marquesas Islands in October 2008, followed by a "South Seas Adventure" cruise west through the Cook Islands and Tonga to Fiji.

ADVENTURES ON THE *ARANUI 3* ★★★

The working cargo ship *Aranui 3* (© **800/972-7268** in the U.S., or 42.36.21 in Papeete; fax 43.48.89; www.aranui.com) is the most interesting way to visit the out-of-the-way Marquesas Islands. See "Exploring the Marquesas on the *Aranui 3,*" p. 256.

Outfitted for up to 200 passengers, this 355-foot freighter makes regular 14-day round-trips from Papeete to 6 of the 10 Marquesas Islands, with stops on the way at Fakarava and Rangiroa in the Tuamotus. While the crew loads and unloads the ship's cargo, passengers spend their days ashore experiencing the islands and islanders. Among the activities: picnicking on beaches, snorkeling, visiting villages, and exploring archaeological sites. Experts on Polynesian history and culture accompany most voyages.

Accommodations are in 10 suites, 12 deluxe cabins, 63 standard cabins, and dormitories. The suites and cabins all have private bathrooms. Suites and deluxe cabins have windows and doors opening to outside decks, and their bathrooms are equipped with bathtubs as well as showers.

Standard cabins lack outside doors and have portholes instead of windows. The ship has a restaurant, bar, boutique, library, video lounge, and pool.

The ship's primary job is to haul cargo, so it does not have stabilizers and other features of a luxury liner. In other words, do not expect the same level of comfort, cuisine, and service as on the other ships cruising these waters. If you only want to sit by the pool, eat prodigious quantities of fine food, and smoke cigars, the *Aranui 3* may not be your cup of tea. But for those who want to go places relatively few people visit, and learn a lot in the process, it is an excellent choice.

Fares for the complete voyage range from about US$2,079 (£1,040) for a dormitory bunk to US$5,445 (£2,723) per person for suites. All meals are included, but you have to pay your own bar bill and your airfare to and from Tahiti.

LUXURY ON THE *PAUL GAUGUIN* ★

The 157m (513-ft.), 318-passenger *Paul Gauguin* (© **877/505-5370** or 904/776-6123 in the U.S., 54.51.00 in Papeete; www.rssc.com) is the most luxurious of Tahiti's cruise ships. It spends most of its year making 7-day cruises through the Society Islands, but occasionally extends to the Tuamotu and Marquesas islands, and it has even ventured as far west as Fiji. It also has environmentalist Jean-Michel Cousteau as guest lecturer on some cruises. All of the ship's seven suites and about half of its 152 staterooms have private verandas or balconies (the least expensive lower-deck units have windows or portholes). All are luxuriously appointed with minibars, TVs and VCRs, direct-dial phones, and marble bathrooms with full-size tubs. Most have queen-size beds, although some have two twins. Fares for the 1-week Society Islands cruises start at US$2,600 (£1,300) per person double occupancy.

A LOT OF COMPANY ON PRINCESS CRUISES

Princess Cruises (✆ **800/774-6237** or 904/527-6660; www.princesscruises.com) will be operating the 700-passenger *Tahitian Princess* on 7- and 10-night cruises in French Polynesia until late 2009, after which it will be renamed the *Ocean Princess* and redeployed to Asia. Its identical sister ship, the *Pacific Princess,* may cruise in French Polynesia thereafter (check the line's website for more information). They are the largest ships operating in French Polynesia, so you won't have the same intimacy as on the other vessels. Princess Cruises are also the least expensive, with prices starting as low as US$1,150 (£575) per person double occupancy for an interior stateroom, depending on time of year and length of voyage. Specials including airfare may be offered during the slow seasons. Passengers can make use of a sun deck, swimming pool, fitness center, casino, cabaret lounge, two bars, and four restaurants. Shore excursions are offered, but unlike the *Paul Gauguin* and the *Star Flyer,* they do not have a stern platform to support onboard watersports activities. Almost 70% of the 280 staterooms and 62 suites open to private terraces.

DINING IN THE LAGOON WITH BORA BORA CRUISES

Bora Bora Cruises, P.O. Box 40186, Papeete (✆ **54.45.05;** fax 45.10.65; www.boraboracruises.com) uses two sleek, luxurious yachts, the *Tu Moana* and the *Tia Moana,* which measure in at 69m (226-ft.) and can carry up to 60 passengers in 30 staterooms spread over three decks. They make 1-week "Nomade" cruises from Bora Bora to Huahine, Raiatea, and Tahaa. The boats are small enough to anchor closer to shore than the other ships here. Consequently, passengers enjoy extras such as breakfast served in the lagoon (that's right, you actually sit at tables in the water) and movies and spa treatments on a beach.

Fares are US$8,990 (£4,495) per person double occupancy.

UNDER SAIL ON THE *STAR FLYER*

As I write, the 170-passenger, 300-foot-long tall ship *Star Flyer* has just begun making 7-, 10-, and 11-day cruises from Papeete through the Society and Tuamotu islands. One of the Monaco-based **Star Clippers** fleet (✆ **800/442-0552;** www.starclippers.com), it resembles an old-time clipper ship, including an Edwardian-style library with a Belle Epoque fireplace, but is loaded with modern amenities and luxuries. Fares start at US$1,845 (£923) per person double occupancy for an interior cabin.

FLY-FISHING FROM THE *HAUMANA*

Avid fishermen can cast lines from the *Haumana* (✆ **50.06.74;** fax 50.06.72; www.tahiti-haumana-cruises.com). This 34m (110-ft.), 42-passenger catamaran specializes in 3-, 4-, and 7-night cruises on the calm, shallow lagoons of Rangiroa and Tikehau in the Tuamotus. Fishing is not the primary focus of the cruises (diving, surfing, and other activities are possible), but this is one of the few vessels to carry rods, reels, and other gear. It's also a much more pleasant way to visit Rangiroa's Pink Sands and Blue Lagoon than riding a speedboat an hour each way (see chapter 11). Although the *Haumana* is smaller than other ships here, its 21 air-conditioned cabins all have large windows or portholes, queen-size beds, sofas or settees, minibars, TVs, VCRs, phones, and shower-only bathrooms with hair dryers. Rates range from US$2,665 to US$5,275 (£1,333–£2,638) per person, double occupancy, including all meals, drinks, fishing, and kayak excursions.

CHARTERING A YACHT

If you are an experienced sailor, you can charter a yacht—with or without skipper and crew—and knock around some of the French Polynesian islands as the wind and your own desires dictate. The best place to start is Raiatea, which shares a lagoon with Tahaa, the only French Polynesian island that can be circumnavigated entirely within a protective reef. Depending on the wind, Bora Bora and Huahine are relatively easy blue-water trips away.

The Moorings, a respected yacht charter company based in Florida (℡ **800/535-7289** or 727/535-1446; www.moorings.com), operates a fleet of monohull and catamaran sailboats based at **Apooti Marina** on Raiatea's northern coast (℡ **66.35.93;** fax 66.20.94; moorings@mail.pf). That's a few minutes' sail to Tahaa. Depending on the size of the boat—they range from 11 to 15m (36–49 ft.) in length—and the season, bareboat rates (that is, without skipper or crew) run about US$450 to US$1,700

(£225–£850) per vessel per day. Provisions are extra. The agency will check to make sure you and your party can handle sailboats of these sizes; otherwise, you pay extra for a skipper.

Also at Apooti Marina, **Sunsail Yacht Charters** (℡ **800/327-2276** in the U.S., 60.04.85 on Raiatea; www.sunsail.com) has a fleet of 11-to-15m (36–49 ft.) yachts. Check its arcane website for bareboat rates.

The French-owned **Tahiti Yacht Charter** (℡ **45.04.00;** fax 45.76.00; www.tahitiyachtcharter.com) has 11-to-14m (36–45 ft.) yachts based at Papeete and Raiatea. It designs cruises throughout the territory, including lengthy voyages to the Tuamotus and Marquesas. Similar services are offered by **Archipel Croisiers** on Moorea (℡ **56.36.39;** fax 56.35.87; www.archipels.com).

8 HEALTH & SAFETY

STAYING HEALTHY

Tahiti and French Polynesia pose no major health problem for most travelers, although it's a good idea to have your tetanus, hepatitis-A, and hepatitis-B vaccinations up-to-date.

If you have a chronic condition, you should consult your doctor before visiting the islands. For conditions like epilepsy, diabetes, or heart problems, wear a **MedicAlert Identification Tag** (℡ **800/825-3785;** www.medicalert.org), which will immediately alert doctors to your condition

and give them access to your records through MedicAlert's 24-hour hot line.

By and large, medical care is very good in Papeete. Every island also has a government clinic, and some have doctors in private practice. I list **hospitals, doctors,** and **emergency numbers** in the "Fast Facts" section of the specific island chapters.

Overseas health-insurance plans are not accepted here, so you will likely have to pay all medical costs upfront and be reimbursed later. See "Insurance," in the "Fast Facts" in appendix A.

(Tips) **Healthy Travels to You**

The following government websites offer up-to-date health-related travel advice:

- **Australia:** www.smartraveller.gov.au
- **Canada:** www.hc-sc.gc.ca/index_e.html
- **U.K.:** www.dh.gov.uk/PolicyAndGuidance/HealthAdviceForTravellers/fs/en
- **U.S.:** www.cdc.gov/travel

The sun in these latitudes can burn your skin in a very short period of time—even on what seems like a cloudy day. Limit your exposure, especially during the first few days of your trip. Be particularly careful from 11am to 2pm. Use sunscreen with a high protection factor (SPF30 or more) and apply it liberally. If you're going snorkeling, wear a T-shirt to avoid overexposure on your back.

Remember to pack **prescription medications** in your carry-on luggage, and carry them in their original containers, with pharmacy labels affixed—otherwise, they won't make it through airport security. Also bring along copies of your prescriptions in case you lose your pills or run out. Carry the generic name of prescription medicines, since local pharmacies primarily carry medications manufactured in France, and the brand names might be different here than in the United States.

And don't forget **sunglasses** and an extra pair of **contact lenses** or **prescription glasses.**

Contact the **International Association for Medical Assistance to Travelers (IAMAT)** (© 716/754-4883 or, in Canada, 416/652-0137; www.iamat.org) for tips on travel and health concerns in the countries you're visiting, and for lists of local, English-speaking doctors. The United States **Centers for Disease Control and Prevention** (© 800/311-3435; www.cdc.gov) provides up-to-date information on health hazards by region or country and offers tips on food safety. **Travel Health Online** (www.tripprep.com), sponsored by a consortium of travel medicine practitioners, may also offer helpful advice on traveling abroad. You can find listings of reliable medical clinics overseas at the **International Society of Travel Medicine** (www.istm.org).

COMMON AILMENTS

Minor illnesses on the islands include the common cold and the occasional outbreaks of influenza and conjunctivitis (pinkeye).

Cuts, scratches, and all open sores should be treated promptly in the Tropics. I always carry a tube of antibacterial ointment and a small package of adhesive bandages.

TROPICAL ILLNESSES

There are plenty of mosquitoes, but they do not carry deadly endemic diseases such as malaria. From time to time, the islands will experience an outbreak of **dengue fever,** a viral disease borne by the *Adès aegypti* mosquito, which lives indoors and bites only during daylight hours. Dengue seldom is fatal in adults, but you should take extra precautions to keep children from being bitten by mosquitoes if the disease is present. (Other precautions should be taken if you are traveling with **children;** see "Specialized Travel Resources," below.)

BUGS, BITES & OTHER WILDLIFE CONCERNS

Living among the friendly Tahitians are some of the world's friendliest ants, roaches, geckos, crabs, and insects.

Indeed, the islands have multitudes of mosquitoes, roaches, ants, houseflies, and other insects. **Ants** are omnipresent here, so don't leave crumbs or dirty dishes lying around your room. A few beaches and swampy areas also have invisible **sand flies**—the dreaded *no-seeums* or *no-nos*—that bite the ankles around daybreak and dusk.

PLANNING YOUR TRIP

3

HEALTH & SAFETY

Avoiding "Economy-Class Syndrome"

Deep vein thrombosis, or "economy-class syndrome," as it's known in the world of flying, is a blood clot that develops in a deep vein. It's a potentially deadly condition that can be caused by sitting in cramped conditions—such as an airplane cabin—for too long. During a flight (especially a long-haul flight), get up, walk around, and stretch your legs every 60 to 90 minutes to keep your blood flowing. Other preventive measures include frequent flexing of the legs while sitting, drinking lots of water, and avoiding alcohol and sleeping pills. If you have a history of deep vein thrombosis, heart disease, or another condition that puts you at high risk, some experts recommend wearing compression stockings or taking anticoagulants when you fly; always ask your physician about the best course for you. Symptoms of deep vein thrombosis include leg pain or swelling, or even shortness of breath.

Insect repellent is widely available in most drug stores and grocery shops. The most effective contain a high percentage of "deet" (N,N-diethyl-m-toluamide).

I light a mosquito coil in my non-air-conditioned rooms at dusk in order to keep the pests from flying in, then start another one at bedtime. Grocery stores throughout the islands carry these inexpensive coils. The Fish brand coils, made by the appropriately named Blood Protection Company, seem to work best.

SUN EXPOSURE

The tropical sun in the islands can be brutal, even on what seems like an overcast day. Accordingly, it's important to use sunscreen whenever you're outdoors, especially at midday. This is particularly true for children.

HIV/AIDS

Sexual relations before marriage—heterosexual, homosexual, and bisexual—are more or less accepted in the islands (abstinence campaigns fall on deaf ears). Both male and female prostitution is common in Papeete. HIV is present in the islands, so if you intend to engage in sex with strangers, you should exercise *at least* the

same caution in choosing them, and in practicing safe sex, as you would at home.

DRINKING WATER

Tap water is safe to drink only in the city of Papeete on Tahiti and on Bora Bora. You can buy bottled spring water in any grocery store. See "Fast Facts" in the chapters that follow for particulars.

WHAT TO DO IF YOU GET SICK AWAY FROM HOME

The main public hospitals and two private clinics in Papeete are up to international standards. Elsewhere you can get a broken bone set and a coral scrape tended, but you may be evacuated to Tahiti for more serious ailments. Tahiti has many well-stocked drug stores (most of their products and medications are from France), and most islands have a pharmacy. Infirmaries and pharmacies are listed under the "Fast Facts" in the specific island chapters.

You may have to pay all medical costs upfront and be reimbursed later. Medicare and Medicaid do not provide coverage for medical costs outside the U.S. Before leaving home, find out what medical services your health insurance covers. To protect yourself, consider buying medical travel insurance (see "Insurance: Tahiti & French Polynesia," in the "Fast Facts" in appendix A).

STAYING SAFE

While international terrorism is a threat throughout the world, the islands are among the planet's safest destinations. Tight security procedures are in effect at Tahiti-Faaa International Airport, but once you're on the outer islands, you are unlikely to see a metal detector, nor is anyone likely to inspect your carry-on.

The islands have seen increasing property theft in recent years, however, including occasional break-ins at hotel rooms and resort bungalows. Although street crimes against tourists are still relatively rare, friends of mine who live here don't stroll off Papeete's busy boulevard Pomare after dark. For that matter, you should stay alert wherever you are after dusk.

Don't leave valuable items in your hotel room, in your rental car, or unattended anywhere. See the "Fast Facts" sections in the following chapters for specific precautions.

Women should not wander alone on deserted beaches at any time, since some Polynesian men may consider such behavior to be an invitation for instant amorous activity.

When heading outdoors, keep in mind that injuries often occur when people fail to follow instructions. Believe the experts who tell you to stay on the established trails. Hike only in designated areas, follow the marine charts if piloting your own boat, carry rain gear, and wear a life jacket when canoeing or rafting. Mountain weather can be fickle at any time. Watch out for sudden storms that can leave you drenched and send bolts of lightning your way.

The French gendarmes will come to rescue you if you get into trouble out in the wild, but believe me, they do not appreciate tourists blundering into trouble.

9 SPECIALIZED TRAVEL RESOURCES

TRAVELERS WITH DISABILITIES

Most disabilities shouldn't stop anyone from traveling, even in the islands, where ramps, handles, accessible toilets, automatic opening doors, telephones at convenient heights, and other helpful aids are just beginning to appear.

Some hotels provide rooms specially equipped for people with disabilities. These improvements are ongoing; inquire when making a reservation whether such rooms are available.

A majority of hotels here consist of bungalows separated from the restaurant, bar, and other facilities, sometimes by long distances. A few upper-end resorts have golf carts or other means of transporting their guests around their properties, but most hotels do not. Anyone who has trouble walking should request accommodations near the central facilities. Make

---

Tips Multitudes of Animals

Don't bother complaining about the multitude of dogs, chickens, pigs, and squawking myna birds running loose out here, even in the finest restaurants. They are as much a part of life as the islanders themselves. And don't be frightened by those little **geckos** (lizards) crawling around the rafters of even the most expensive bungalows. They're harmless to us humans, but lethal to insects.

(Tips) **Be Careful in the Water**

Most of French Polynesia's marine creatures are harmless to humans, but there are some to avoid. Always **seek local advice** before snorkeling or swimming in a lagoon away from the hotel beaches. Many diving operators conduct snorkeling tours. If you don't know what you're doing, go with them.

Wash and apply a good antiseptic or antibacterial ointment to all **coral cuts and scrapes** as soon as possible.

Because coral cannot grow in fresh water, the flow of rivers and streams into the lagoon creates narrow channels known as **passes** through the reef. Currents can be very strong in the passes, so stay in the protected, shallow water of the inner lagoons.

Sharks are curious beasts that are attracted by bright objects such as watches and knives, so be careful what you wear in the water. Don't swim in areas where sewage or edible wastes are dumped, and never swim alone if you have any suspicion that sharks might be present. If you do see a shark, don't splash in the water or urinate. Calmly retreat and get out of the water as quickly as you can, without creating a disturbance.

Those round things on the rocks and reefs that look like pincushions are **sea urchins,** and their calcium spikes can be more painful than needles. A sea-urchin puncture can result in burning, aching, swelling, and discoloration (black or purple) around the area where the spines entered your skin. The best thing to do is to pull any protruding spines out. The body will absorb the spines within 24 hours to 3 weeks, or the remainder of the spines will work themselves out. Contrary to popular advice, do not urinate or pour vinegar on the embedded spines—this will not help.

Jellyfish stings can hurt like the devil but are seldom life-threatening. You need to get any visible tentacles off your body right away, but not with your hands, unless you are wearing gloves. Use a stick or anything else that is handy. Then rinse the sting with saltwater or fresh water, and apply ice to prevent swelling and to help control the pain. If you can find it at an island grocery store, Adolph's Meat Tenderizer is a great antidote.

The **stone fish** is so named because it looks like a piece of stone or coral as it lies buried in the sand on the lagoon bottom with only its back and 13 venomous spikes sticking out. Its venom can cause paralysis and even death. You'll know by the intense pain if you're stuck. Serum is available, so get to a hospital at once. **Sea snakes, cone shells, crown-of-thorns starfish, moray eels, lionfish,** and **demon stingers** also can be painful, if not deadly. The last thing any of these creatures wants to do is to tangle with a human, so keep your hands to yourself.

this absolutely clear when you or your travel agent make your reservations, preferably in writing. Not all hotels remember to honor such requests, so take copies of your request with you, and reiterate it when checking in.

The major international airlines make special arrangements for travelers with disabilities. Be sure to tell them of your needs when you reserve. Repeat it at the check-in counter for Air Tahiti Nui, which does not have a pre-boarding option at all airports, and whose planes often park out on the tarmac at Los Angeles International Airport, where you may ride a bus and then climb up stairs into the aircraft.

Airport security and Customs officials also will make special arrangements for travelers with disabilities, but this is not always obvious and must be requested.

Although Air Tahiti and Air Moorea, the domestic carriers, use small planes that are not equipped for passengers with disabilities, their staff members go out of their way to help everyone get in and out of the craft.

Organizations that offer a vast range of resources and assistance include **Moss Rehab** (ⓒ 800/CALL-MOSS; www.moss resourcenet.org); the **American Foundation for the Blind (AFB)** (ⓒ 800/232-5463; www.afb.org); and **SATH** (Society for Accessible Travel & Hospitality) (ⓒ 212/447-7284; www.sath.org). **Air AmbulanceCard.com** is now partnered with SATH and allows you to preselect top-notch hospitals in case of an emergency.

Access-Able Travel Source (ⓒ 303/232-2979; www.access-able.com) has a comprehensive database on travel agents from around the world with experience in accessible travel; destination-specific access information; and links to such resources as service animals, equipment rentals, and access guides.

Many travel agencies offer customized tours and itineraries for travelers with disabilities. Among them are **Flying Wheels Travel** (ⓒ 507/451-5005; www.flying wheelstravel.com); and **Accessible Journeys** (ⓒ 800/846-4537 or 610/521-0339; www.disabilitytravel.com).

Flying with Disability (www.flying-with-disability.org) is a comprehensive information source on airplane travel. **Avis Rent a Car** (ⓒ 888/879-4273) has an "Avis Access" program that provides services for customers with special travel needs. These include specially outfitted vehicles with swivel seats, spinner knobs, and hand controls; mobility scooter rentals; and accessible bus service. Be sure to reserve well in advance.

Also check out the quarterly magazine *Emerging Horizons* (www.emerginghorizons.com), available by subscription ($16.95 a year U.S.; $21.95 outside U.S.).

The "Accessible Travel" link at **Mobility-Advisor.com** (www.mobility-advisor.com) provides a variety of travel resources.

British travelers should contact **Holiday Care** (ⓒ 0845-124-9971 in U.K. only; www.holidaycare.org.uk) to access a wide range of travel information and resources for travelers with disabilities and seniors.

GAY & LESBIAN TRAVELERS

French Polynesia is a relatively friendly destination for gay men. Just remember that the AIDS virus is present here (see "Health & Safety," earlier in this chapter).

In the islands, many families with a shortage of female offspring rear young boys as girls, or at least relegate them to female chores around the home and village. These males-raised-as-girls are known as *mahus*. Some of them grow up to be heterosexual; others become homosexual or bisexual and, often appearing publicly in women's attire, actively seek the company of tourists. Some dance the female parts in traditional island night shows. You'll see them throughout the islands. Many of them have traveled widely and speak English fluently, making them prime candidates for jobs in hotels and restaurants.

On the other hand, women were not considered equal in this respect in ancient times, so lesbians may not find the islands quite as friendly.

The **International Gay & Lesbian Travel Association (IGLTA)** (ⓒ 800/448-8550 or 954/776-2626; fax 954/776-3303;

www.iglta.org) is the trade association for the gay and lesbian travel industry, and offers an online directory of gay and lesbian-friendly travel businesses; go to their website and click on "Members."

Many agencies offer tours and travel itineraries specifically for gay and lesbian travelers. **MIM Travel** (© **877/844-8055;** www.gay-travel-by-mim.com) recently had a gay cruise aboard the *Tahitian Princess,* while **Now, Voyager** (© **800/255-6951;** www.nowvoyager.com) had one on the *Star Flyer* (see "Seeing the Islands by Cruise Ship & Yacht," earlier in this chapter). Also check out **Above and Beyond Tours** (© **800/397-2681;** www.above beyondtours.com), a gay Australia tour specialist, and **Olivia** (© **800/631-6277;** www.olivia.com), offering lesbian cruises and resort vacations.

Gay.com Travel (© **800/929-2268** or 415/644-8044; www.gay.com/travel or www.outandabout.com), is an excellent online successor to the popular *Out & About* print magazine. It provides regularly updated information about gay-owned, gay-oriented, and gay-friendly lodging, dining, sightseeing, nightlife, and shopping establishments in every important destination worldwide.

The Canadian website **GayTraveler** (**gaytraveler.ca**) offers ideas and advice for gay travel all over the world.

The following travel guides are available at many bookstores, or you can order them from any online bookseller: *Spartacus International Gay Guide, 35th Edition* (Bruno Gmünder Verlag; www.spartacusworld.com/gayguide), *Odysseus: The International Gay Travel Planner, 17th Edition* (www.odyusa.com); and the *Damron* guides (www.damron.com), with separate, annual books for gay men and lesbians.

SENIOR TRAVELERS

Children are cared for communally in the islands' extended family systems, and so are seniors. Many islanders live with their families from birth to death. Consequently, the local governments don't provide as many programs and other benefits for persons of retirement age as in the United States and other Western countries. You won't find many senior discounts.

Nevertheless, mention the fact that you're a senior when you first make your travel reservations. All major airlines and many chain hotels offer discounts for seniors.

Members of **AARP,** 601 E St. NW, Washington, DC 20049 (© **888/687-2277** or 202/434-2277; www.aarp.org), get discounts on hotels, airfares, and car rentals. AARP gives members a wide range of benefits, including *AARP The Magazine* and a monthly newsletter. Anyone age 50 and over can join.

FAMILY TRAVEL

Some of the larger hotels are beginning to cater to families. Best is **Le Meridien Bora Bora** (p. 212).

 Kid-Friendly Hotels

Some French Polynesian hotels are now friendly to children as well as to couples. **Le Taha'a Private Island & Spa** off Tahaa and the **Pearl Resorts** on Moorea, Bora Bora, Manihi, Tikehau, and Nuku Hiva now have a cartoon TV channel and age-appropriate DVDs in each unit. While adults continue to get their welcome baskets full of tropical fruits, youngsters now get their own stash of candies. The **Radisson Plaza Resort Tahiti** (www.radisson.com/aruefrp) allows kids 15 and under to stay free and dine for 50% off. It's a welcome money-saver.

For the most part, however, tourism in French Polynesia is still aimed primarily at honeymooners and other couples. To be blunt, the islands are better known for sand, sea, and sex than for babysitters, nannies, and playgrounds.

That's not to say you and your offspring won't have a marvelous time here. The islanders invariably love children and are very good at babysitting. Just make sure you get one who speaks English. The hotels can take care of this for you.

On the other hand, childhood does not last as long here as it does in Western societies. As soon as they are capable, children are put to work, first caring for their younger siblings and cousins and helping out with household chores, later tending the village gardens. It's only as teenagers, and then only if they leave their villages for Papeete, that they know unemployment in the Western sense. Accordingly, few towns and villages have children's facilities, such as playgrounds, outside school property.

Some resorts do not accept children at all; I point these out in the establishment listings, but you should ask to make sure. Even if they do, check whether the hotel can provide cribs, bottle warmers, and other needs, and if they have children's menus.

Disposable diapers, cotton swabs, and baby food are sold in many main-town stores, but you should take along a supply of such items as children's aspirin, a thermometer, adhesive bandages, and any special medications. Make sure your children's vaccinations are up-to-date before you leave home. If your kids are very small, perhaps you should discuss your travel plans with your family doctor.

Remember to protect youngsters with ample sunscreen. Some other tips: Certain tropical plants and animals may resemble rocks or vegetation, so teach your youngsters to avoid touching or brushing up against rocks, seaweed, and other objects. If your children are prone to swimmer's ear, use vinegar or preventive drops before swimming in freshwater streams or lakes. Have them shower soon after swimming or suffering cuts or abrasions.

WOMEN TRAVELERS

The islands are relatively safe for women traveling alone, but don't let the charm of warm nights and smiling faces lull you into any less caution than you would exercise at home. *Do not* wander alone on deserted beaches. In the old days, this was an invitation for sex. If that's what you want today, that's what you'll likely get. Otherwise, it could result in your being raped. And don't hitchhike alone, either.

Check out the award-winning website **Journeywoman** (www.journeywoman.com), a "real life" women's travel-information network where you can sign up for a free e-mail newsletter and get advice on everything from etiquette and dress to safety. Also see the travel guide *Safety and Security for Women Who Travel*, by Sheila Swan and Peter Laufer (Travelers' Tales, Inc.), for common-sense tips on safe travel.

AFRICAN-AMERICAN TRAVELERS

Among general sources for African-American travelers, **Black Travel Online** (www.blacktravelonline.com) posts news on upcoming events and includes links to articles and travel-booking sites. **Soul of America** (www.soulofamerica.com) is a comprehensive website, with travel tips, event and family-reunion postings, and sections on historically black beach resorts and active vacations.

Agencies and organizations that provide resources for black travelers include **Rodgers Travel** (© 800/825-1775; www.rodgerstravel.com), the **African American Association of Innkeepers International** (© 877/422-5777; www.africanamericaninns.com), and **Henderson Travel & Tours** (© 800/327-2309 or 301/650-5700; www.hendersontravel.com), which has specialized in trips to Africa since 1957.

Go Girl: The Black Woman's Guide to Travel & Adventure (Eighth Mountain Press) is a compilation of travel essays by writers including Jill Nelson and Audre Lorde. *The African-American Travel Guide* by Wayne C. Robinson (Hunter Publishing; www.hunterpublishing.com) was published in 1997, so it may be somewhat dated. *Travel and Enjoy Magazine* (© **866/ 266-6211**; www.travelandenjoy.com) is a travel magazine and guide. The well-done *Pathfinders Magazine* (© **877/977-PATH**; www.pathfinderstravel.com) includes articles on everything from Rio de Janeiro to Ghana to upcoming ski, scuba-diving, golf, and tennis trips.

STUDENT TRAVELERS

Given the high costs of travel to and in French Polynesia, it's not surprising that the islands are not on the usual backpacker trail across the South Pacific. There are many pensions (boardinghouses) here, and a few dormitories and campgrounds, but they are expensive compared to the Cook Islands and Fiji, the two hot college-age destinations out here.

If you're going on to New Zealand and Australia, you'd be wise to get an **international student ID card** from the **International Student Travel Confederation (ISTC)** (www.istc.org), which offers savings on plane tickets. It also provides basic health and life insurance and a 24-hour help line. You can apply for the card online or in person at **STA Travel** (© **800/781- 4040** in North America; www.statravel. com), the biggest student-travel agency in the world; check out the website to locate STA Travel offices worldwide.

If you're no longer a student but are still under 26, you can get an **International Youth Travel Card (IYTC)** for the same price from the same people. The card offers some discounts (but not on museum admissions).

Travel CUTS (© **800/667-2887** or 416/ 614-2887; www.travelcuts.com) offers similar services for both Canadians and U.S. residents. Irish students may prefer to turn to **USIT** (© **01/602-1904**; www.usitnow. ie), an Ireland-based specialist in student, youth, and independent travel.

SINGLE TRAVELERS

Having traveled alone through the islands for more years than I care to admit, I can tell you it's a great place to be unattached. After all, this is the land of smiles and genuine warmth toward strangers. The attitude soon infects visitors: All I've ever had to do to meet my fellow travelers is wander into a hotel bar, order a beer, and ask the persons next to me where they are from and what they have done here.

The top destination for singles is the **Club Med** on Bora Bora (p. 214).

Unfortunately, the solo traveler is often forced to pay a "single supplement" charged by many resorts, cruise lines, and tours for the privilege of sleeping alone.

TravelChums (© **212/799-6464**; www.travelchums.com) is an Internet-only travel-companion matching service hosted by respected New York–based Shaw Guides travel service.

Based in Canada, **Travel Buddies Singles Travel Club** (© **800/998-9099**; www.travelbuddiesworldwide.com) runs small, intimate, single-friendly group trips and will match you with a roommate free of charge and save you the cost of single supplements.

 Leave Fido at Home

Don't even think about bringing your pet to French Polynesia. Fido will be quarantined until you are ready to fly home.

Climate change and rising sea levels resulting from global warming are having a noticeable impact on all the South Pacific islands. Some islanders I have known for more than 30 years tell me the seasons are now unpredictable (it's more likely to rain in the dry season, and vice versa), and the tides are higher than ever (in some places, the lagoons lap directly on dry land at high tide rather than on the beach). Indeed, most islanders don't want to hear any corporate-induced spin about there being no evidence of global warming and its consequences. They know it's true from firsthand experience.

French Polynesia has allowed resort developers to built innumerable bungalows over the lagoons. In fact, manta rays reportedly have disappeared in parts of the Bora Bora lagoon because of the construction. To the islanders beyond Bora Bora, however, their lagoons are not just places where you swim around and look at beautiful corals and sea life; they are major sources of food. Protecting their lagoons and reefs is a matter of survival. Consequently, French Polynesia does have laws protecting its lagoons, reefs, and sea life. You cannot, for example, legally break off a piece of living coral to bring home (a bad idea anyway, since sea life will emit offensive odors as soon as it dies and begins to decay).

For our part, it's up to us visitors to practice **sustainable tourism,** which means being careful with the environments we explore and respecting the communities we visit.

Two overlapping components of sustainable travel are **ecotourism** and **ethical tourism.** The **International Ecotourism Society** (TIES) defines ecotourism as responsible travel to natural areas, which conserves the environment and improves the well-being of local people. TIES suggests that ecotourists follow these principles:

- Minimize environmental impact.
- Build environmental and cultural awareness and respect.
- Provide positive experiences for both visitors and hosts.
- Provide direct financial benefits for conservation and for local people.
- Raise sensitivity to host countries' political, environmental, and social climates.
- Support international human rights and labor agreements.

You can find some eco-friendly travel tips and statistics, as well as touring companies and associations—listed by destination under "Travel Choice"—at the **TIES** website, www.ecotourism.org. Also check out **Ecotravel.com,** which lets you search for sustainable touring companies in several categories (water-based, land-based, spiritually oriented, and so on).

While much of the focus of ecotourism is about reducing impacts on the natural environment, ethical tourism concentrates on ways to preserve and enhance local economies and communities, regardless of location. You can embrace ethical tourism by staying at a locally owned hotel or shopping at a store that employs local workers and sells locally produced goods.

Responsible Travel (www.responsible travel.com) is a great source of sustainable travel ideas; the site is run by a spokesperson for ethical tourism in the travel industry. **Sustainable Travel International** (www.sustainabletravelinternational.org) promotes ethical tourism practices, and manages an extensive directory of sustainable properties and tour operators around the world.

In the U.K., **Tourism Concern** (www. tourismconcern.org.uk) works to reduce

Tips   **It's Easy Being Green**

Here are a few simple ways you can help conserve fuel and energy when you travel:

- Each time you take a flight or drive a car, greenhouse gases release into the atmosphere. You can help neutralize this danger to the planet through "carbon offsetting"—paying someone to invest your money in programs that reduce your greenhouse gas emissions by the same amount you've added. Before buying carbon offset credits, just make sure that you're using a reputable company, one with a proven program that invests in renewable energy. Reliable carbon offset companies include **Carbonfund** (www.carbonfund.org), **TerraPass** (www.terrapass.org), and **Carbon Neutral** (www.carbonneutral.org).

- Whenever possible, choose nonstop flights; they generally require less fuel than indirect flights that stop and take off again. Try to fly during the day—some scientists estimate that nighttime flights are twice as harmful to the environment. And pack light—each 15 pounds of luggage on a 5,000-mile flight adds up to 50 pounds of carbon dioxide emitted.

- Where you stay during your travels can have a major environmental impact. To determine the green credentials of a property, ask about trash disposal and recycling, water conservation, and energy use; also question if sustainable materials were used in the construction of the property. The website **www.greenhotels.com** recommends green-rated member hotels around the world that fulfill the company's stringent environmental requirements. Also consult **www.environmentallyfriendlyhotels.com** for more green accommodations ratings.

- At hotels, request that your sheets and towels not be changed daily. (Many hotels already have programs like this in place.) Turn off the lights and air conditioner (or heater) when you leave your room.

- Use public transport where possible—trains, buses, and even taxis are more energy-efficient forms of transport than driving. Even better is to walk or cycle; you'll produce zero emissions and stay fit and healthy on your travels.

- If renting a car is necessary, ask the rental agent for a hybrid, or rent the most fuel-efficient car available. You'll use less gas and save money at the tank.

social and environmental problems connected to tourism. The **Association of Independent Tour Operators (AITO)** (www.aito.co.uk) is a group of specialist operators leading the field in making holidays sustainable.

Volunteer travel has become increasingly popular among those who want to venture beyond the standard group-tour experience to learn languages, interact with locals, and make a positive difference while on vacation. Volunteer travel usually doesn't require special skills—just a willingness to work hard—and programs vary in length from a few days to a number of weeks. Some programs provide free housing and food, but many require volunteers to pay for travel expenses, which can add up quickly.

For general info on volunteer travel, visit **www.volunteerabroad.org** and **www.idealist.org**.

Before you commit to a volunteer program, it's important to make sure any money you're giving is truly going back to the local community, and that the work you'll be doing will be a good fit for you. **Volunteer International** (www.volunteer international.org) has a helpful list of questions to ask to determine the intentions and the nature of a volunteer program.

Also, see "Ecotravel Tours" in "Special-Interest Trips," p. 78.

11 PACKAGES FOR THE INDEPENDENT TRAVELER

In addition to searching for the lowest airfare, you may want to consider booking your flight as part of a travel package. Buying a package tour is simply a way to get the airfare, accommodations, and other elements of your trip (such as car rentals, airport transfers, and sometimes even meals and activities) at the same time and often at discounted prices—kind of like one-stop shopping. In fact, package tours usually provide the best bargains available.

Package tours are not the same thing as escorted tours, which are structured tours with a group leader (see "Escorted General-Interest Tours," below).

The costs are kept down because wholesale tour operators (known as wholesalers in the travel industry) can make volume bookings on the airlines and at the hotels. Packages traditionally were then sold through retail travel agents, but many wholesalers now deal directly with the public, thus passing savings along to you, rather than part of their commissions to retail agents.

Travel packages are listed in the travel section of many Sunday newspapers. Or

---

Frommers.com: The Complete Travel Resource

For an excellent travel-planning resource, we highly recommend **Frommers.com** (www.frommers.com), voted Best Travel Site by *PC Magazine*. We're a little biased, of course, but we guarantee that you'll find the travel tips, reviews, monthly vacation giveaways, bookstore, and online-booking capabilities thoroughly indispensable. Special features include our popular **Destinations** section, where you can access expert travel tips, hotel and dining recommendations, and advice on the sights to see in more than 3,500 destinations around the globe; the **Frommers.com Newsletter,** with the latest deals, travel trends, and money-saving secrets; and our **Travel Talk** area featuring **Message Boards,** where Frommer's readers post queries and share advice, and where our authors sometimes show up to answer questions. Once you finish your research, the **Book a Trip** area can lead you to Frommer's preferred online partners' websites, where you can book your vacation at affordable prices.

check ads in magazines such as *Arthur Frommer's Budget Travel Magazine, Travel + Leisure, National Geographic Traveler,* and *Condé Nast Traveler.*

Airlines frequently offer air-and-hotel packages, so be sure to check the website of **Air Tahiti Nui** (www.airtahitinui-usa. com).

Tahiti Tourisme has information about agencies selling packages to French Polynesia and provides links to numerous money-saving packages on its North American website (www.tahiti-tourisme. com). See "Visitor Information," earlier in this chapter.

INTERNATIONAL TOUR AGENTS

Following in alphabetical order are some reputable American-based companies selling package tours. Some will discount air tickets and hotel rooms separately; that is, not as part of a package. Be sure to shop for the best deal among them.

- **Blue Pacific Vacations** (© 800/798-0590; www.bluepacificvacations.com), a division of France Vacations, is headed by John Biggerstaff and Ken Jordan, two veterans of Tahiti tourism. They will customize tours to most French Polynesian islands.
- **Brendan Worldwide Vacations** (© 800/421-8446 or 818/785-9696; www. brendanvacations.com) provides packages to French Polynesia.
- **Costco Travel** (© 877/849-2730; www.costco.com) sells island packages to Costco members. The agency was a South Pacific specialist before Costco bought it.
- **GoGo Worldwide Vacations** (© 617/734-2350; www.gogovacationdeals. com), headquartered in Massachusetts, specializes in French Polynesia.
- **Go-Today** (© 800/227-3235; www. go-today.com), based in Washington State, offers discount-priced packages

to French Polynesia and the nearby Cook Islands.

- **Island Escapes** (© 800/983-0210; www.islandescapes.com) has packages to the Society Islands and to Rangiroa and Fakarava in the Tuamotu Archipelago, and it will arrange cruising and yachting vacations.
- **Islands in the Sun** (© 800/828-6877 or 310/536-0051; www.islandsinthesun. com), the largest and oldest South Pacific specialist, sells packages to all the islands.
- **Jetabout Island Vacations** (© 800/348-8145; www.jetabouttahitivacations.com) of El Segundo, California, offers a wide variety of packages to Tahiti. It's the U.S. representative of Qantas Vacations, an arm of the Australian airline.
- **Newmans South Pacific Vacations** (© 800/421-3326; www.newmans vacations.com) offers packages to the islands. It's a long-established New Zealand company.
- **Pacific for Less** (© 800/915-2776; www.pacific-for-less.com), based in Hawaii, has reasonably priced packages to French Polynesia, although its specialty is high-end honeymoons.
- **Pleasant Holidays** (© 800/742-9244; www.pleasantholidays.com), a huge company best known for its Pleasant Hawaiian and Pleasant Mexico operations, offers packages to French Polynesia.
- **South Pacific Direct** (www.south pacificdirect.com) is an Internet-only firm offering deals to all the islands.
- **South Seas Adventures** (© 800/576-7327; www.south-seas-adventures.com) has packages to Samoa and Tonga as well as Fiji, French Polynesia, and the Cook Islands.
- **Swain Tahiti Tours** (© 800/22-SWAIN; www.swaintours.com) obviously knows a lot about Tahiti and French Polynesia.
- **Tahiti Discount Travel** (© 877/426-7262; www.tahiti-discounttravel.com) is owned by former employees of the

defunct Discover Wholesale Travel, once the leader in budget packages. Today they arrange some of the lowest-priced packages to French Polynesia.

- **Tahiti Legends** (🕿 800/200-1213; www.tahiti-legends.com) is run by former officials of Islands in the Sun. It sells tours to French Polynesia, the Cook Islands, and Fiji under the name **Pacific Legends** (www.pacificlegends.com).

- **Tahiti Vacations** (🕿 800/553-3477; www.tahitivacation.com), a subsidiary of Air Tahiti, French Polynesia's domestic airline, specializes in French Polynesia but also has packages to Fiji, the Cook Islands, and Tonga. It frequently offers the least expensive packages available to Tahiti and Moorea.

- **Travelwizard** (🕿 800/330-8820; www.travelwizard.com) specializes in designing luxury travel packages to all the islands but has less expensive offerings as well. It also has adventure, scuba diving, and surfing trips to French Polynesia.

Another tactic is to check with the South Pacific **inbound tour operators**; that is, companies in the islands which put together the local elements of tour packages such as hotel rooms and airport transfers. They have the advantage of being on the scene and thus familiar with the local airlines and hotels. Some sell directly to inbound visitors as well as other tour companies.

In French Polynesia, they range from **Tahiti Nui Travel** (www.tahitinuitravel.com), the largest travel agency, to **True Tahiti Vacations** (🕿 310/464-1490 in the U.S.; www.truetahitivacation.com), operated by American-born Laurel Samuela from her home on Moorea.

Other reputable firms include **Easy Tahiti.com** (www.easytahiti.com); **Islands Adventures/Air Tahiti** (www.islandsadventures.com); **Marama Tours** (www.maramatours.com); **Paradise Tours** (www.paradistourstahiti.com); and **Tekura Tahiti Travel** (www.tahiti-tekuratravelcom).

12 ESCORTED GENERAL-INTEREST TOURS

Escorted tours are structured group tours, with a group leader (I prefer the old-fashioned term "tour guide"). The price usually includes everything from airfare to hotels, meals, tours, admission costs, and local transportation.

Escorted tours are not a big part of the business in these small islands, where it's easy to find your way around and book local tours and activities. Most of the travel agents I mention under "Packages for the Independent Traveler," above, will have someone meet and greet you at the airport upon arrival, take you to your hotel, and make sure you get on any prearranged tours and activities, but you will not have a tour guide.

Some tour companies add a short stopover in Tahiti to their escorted tours of Australia and New Zealand, but these may

not include a guide for the island portion. Leaders in this add-on feature include **Tauck Tours** (🕿; 800/788-7885; www.tauck.com); **Qantas Vacations** (🕿 800/641-8772; www.qantasvacations.com); **Australia Escorted Tours** (🕿 888/333-6607; www.australia-escorted-tours.com), and **Abercrombie & Kent** (🕿 800/652-7986; www.abercrombiekent.com), which adds Fiji and French Polynesia to its high-end escorted tours. Otherwise, I recommend getting a travel agent to track down an escorted tour.

Despite the fact that escorted tours require big deposits and predetermine hotels, restaurants, and itineraries, many people derive security and peace of mind from the structure they offer. Escorted tours let travelers sit back and enjoy the trip without having to drive or worry about details. They're particularly convenient for people with limited mobility and they can be a great way to make new friends.

On the downside, you'll have little opportunity for serendipitous interactions with locals. The tours can be jampacked with activities, leaving little room for individual sightseeing, whim, or adventure—plus they often focus on the heavily touristed sites, so you miss out on many a lesser-known gem.

13 SPECIAL-INTEREST TRIPS

Although outdoor activities take first place in the islands (see "The Active Traveler," below), you can also spend your time learning a new craft, exploring the reefs as part of a conservation project, and whale- and dolphin-watching.

BIRD-WATCHING

Avid bird-watchers are likely to see terns, boobies, herons, petrels, noddies, and many other seabirds throughout the islands. French Polynesia alone has 28 species of breeding seabirds, making memorable a visit to Motu Puarua and Motu Oeone, tiny islets out in Tikihau's lagoon, where noddies and snowy white fairy terns nest (see chapter 11).

The number and variety of land birds diminish as you go eastward. Most live in the bush away from settlements and the accompanying cats, dogs, and rats, so you will need to head into the bush for the best watching.

In French Polynesia, **Société d'Ornithologie de Polynésie (Ornithological Society of Polynesia; ✆ 50.62.09;** www.manu.pf) lists local birds on its website.

A few companies have bird-watching tours to the South Pacific, including the U.K.-based **Bird Quest (✆ 44/1254 826317;** www.birdquest.co.uk) and **Bird-watching Breaks (✆ 44/1381 610495;** www.birdwatchingbreaks.com).

ECOTRAVEL TOURS

The **Oceanic Society (✆ 800/326-7491;** www.oceanicsociety.org), an award-winning organization based in California, has natural history and ecotourism expeditions to the islands. A marine naturalist accompanies its trips, which include village visits and bird-watching excursions.

WHALE- & DOLPHIN-WATCHING

Whale- and dolphin-watching are popular activities in the islands. Dolphins live here year-round, and humpback whales escape the cold of Antarctica and spend from July until October giving birth to their calves in the tropical South Pacific. They can be seen swimming off many islands.

The best dolphin-watching experiences are on Moorea in French Polynesia, where American marine biologist **Dr. Michael Poole** leads daylong excursions to visit some of the 150 spinner dolphins he has identified as regular residents. Honeymooners love to have their pictures taken while swimming with the intelligent mammals in a fenced-in area at **Moorea Dolphin Center,** at the InterContinental Resort & Spa Moorea. See chapter 6 for details.

14 THE ACTIVE TRAVELER

These islands are a dream for active travelers, especially those into diving, snorkeling, swimming, boating, and other watersports. You can also play golf and tennis, or hike into the jungle-clad mountainous interiors of the islands. Kayaking is popular everywhere, and all but a few hotels provide them for free. There's good biking along the many roads skirting colorful lagoons. You can engage in these activities everywhere, although some islands are better than others. I point out the best in the following chapters, but here's a brief rundown of my favorites.

On the Web, **Gordon's Guide** (www. gordonsguide.com) compiles adventure tours from around the world. It's a good place to search for South Pacific adventure trips in a variety of categories. Save time by searching for a specific destination.

BIKING

Relatively flat roads circle most of the islands, making for easy and scenic bike riding. In fact, bicycles are one of my favorite means of getting around. It's simple and inexpensive to rent bikes on all but a few of the islands. In fact, some hotels and resorts provide bikes for their guests to use.

DIVING & SNORKELING

Most of the islands have very good to great diving and snorkeling. Virtually every lagoonside resort has a dive operator on premises or nearby, and many will let snorkelers go along.

French Polynesia is famous for its bountiful sea life, from harmless tropical fish to hammerhead sharks. You'll see plenty of creatures at Moorea, Bora Bora, Huahine, and Raiatea-Tahaa, but the best diving and snorkeling is in the huge lagoons of Rangiroa, Tikehau, Manihi, and Fakarava in the Tuamotu Islands. See chapters 6, 7, 8, 9, and 11.

Most resorts offer dive packages to their guests, and the American-based **PADI Travel Network** (© **800/729-7234;** www. padi.com) puts together packages for divers of all experience levels.

DEEP-SEA FISHING

Charter boats on most islands will take you in search of marlin, swordfish, tuna, mahimahi, and other game fish.

You can also cast your line while living aboard in relative luxury. In the Tuamotu Archipelago, **Haumana Cruises** (www. tahiti-fly-fishing-cruises.com) uses a 17-cabin yacht. See "Seeing the Islands by Cruise Ship & Yacht," earlier in this chapter.

GOLF & TENNIS

French Polynesia now has the **Moorea Green Pearl Golf Course of Polynesia,** an 18-hole set of links on Moorea, to complement the venerable **Olivier Breaud International Golf Course of Atimaono,** on the south coast of Tahiti. See chapters 6 and 5, respectively.

HIKING

These aren't the Rocky Mountains, nor are there blazed trails out here, but hiking in the islands is a lot of fun.

Tahiti and Moorea have several trails into the highlands, some of which run along spectacular ridges. You'll need a guide for the best hikes, but you can easily hire them on both islands. See chapters 5 and 6.

HORSEBACK RIDING

Although I prefer sipping a cold drink, a great way to experience a South Pacific sunset is from the back of a horse while riding along a beach. You can do just that on Moorea and Huahine, where the ranches also have daytime rides into the mountains. See chapters 6 and 7.

KAYAKING

All but a few beachfront resorts have canoes, kayaks, small sailboats, sailboards, and other toys for their guests' amusement. Since most of these properties sit beside lagoons, using these craft is not only fun, it's relatively safe. They are most fun where you can paddle or sail across the lagoon to uninhabited islets out on the reef, such as on Moorea's northwest coast. See chapter 6.

SAILING

The region's reef-strewn waters make charter-boat sailing a precarious undertaking. A major exception is the Leeward Islands in French Polynesia, where you can rent sailboats with or without skippers. Encircled by one lagoon, Raiatea and Tahaa are the centers of sailing here. You can sail completely around Tahaa without leaving the lagoon. Three companies have bases at Raiatea, including **The Moorings** (© 800/535-7289; www.moorings.com), one of the world's leading yacht charter operations. See chapters 4 and 8.

SURFING

The islands have some world-famous surfing spots such as Teahupoo on Tahiti (see chapter 5). All the best are reef breaks; that is, the surf crashes out on coral reefs instead of on sandy beaches. These are no places for beginners, since you could suffer serious injury by landing on a razor-sharp coral reef. (Or as one of my island friends puts it, "You'll become hamburger in a hurry.")

The surf pounds directly on beaches on Tahiti, where you can learn to surf with *Ecole de Surf Tura'i Mataare* (**Tahiti Surf School**) (© 41.91.37; www.tahitisurf school.info). See chapter 5.

15 STAYING CONNECTED

TELEPHONES

All landline communications in and out of French Polynesia are handled by the Office des Postes et Télécommunications (OPT; www.opt.pf). Although relatively expensive, the system is modern and efficient.

HOW TO MAKE CALLS

To call French Polynesia: Dial the international access code (011 from the U.S.; 00 from the U.K., Ireland, or New Zealand; or 0011 from Australia), French Polynesia's country code **689,** and the local number (there are no area codes within French Polynesia).

To make international calls from within French Polynesia: First dial **00**, then the country code (U.S. or Canada 1, U.K. 44, Ireland 353, Australia 61, New Zealand 64), then the area code and phone number. Calls to the U.S., Europe, Australia, and New Zealand are 103CFP (US$1.30/65p) per minute, when dialed directly.

You can make them through your hotel, though with a surcharge, which can more than double the fee.

The least expensive way to make international calls from French Polynesia may be to use a **Top Phone** prepaid card

(© **50.82.08;** www.top-phone.pf), available at many shops and at the Business Center in Tahiti-Faaa International Airport terminal (© **83.63.88;** see "Internet Access" under "Fast Facts: Tahiti," in chapter 5). The cards come in denominations beginning at 1,000CFP (US$13/£6.30), which includes 45 minutes of talk time to the U.S., the U.K., Australia, and New Zealand. That's about 22CFP (US30¢/15p) per minute, assuming you use all 45 minutes. There is no refund for unused time.

For operator assistance: Dial © **3600** if you need assistance making an overseas call. The operators speak English.

To make domestic calls within French Polynesia: No prefix or area code is required for domestic long distance calls, so dial the local number.

For directory assistance: Dial © **3612** for local directory information *(service des renseignements)*. The operators speak English. You can look up local numbers online at **www.annuaireopt.pf** (it's in French).

TOLL-FREE NUMBERS

There are no toll-free numbers in French Polynesia. Calling a 1-800 number in the U.S. or Canada from French Polynesia is

The custom in the Tuamotu and Marquesas islands is to group telephone numbers in two, such as 960 569, but in most of French Polynesia, the local phone numbers are presented as three two-digit numbers—for example, 42.29.17. If you ask someone for a number, he or she will say it like this: *"quarante-deux, vingt-neuf, dix-sept"* in French, or "forty-two, twenty-nine, seventeen" in English.

not toll-free. In fact, it costs the same as an overseas call.

PAY PHONES

Public pay phones are located at all post offices and are fairly numerous elsewhere on Tahiti, less so on the other islands. You must have a *télécarte* to call from public pay phones (coins won't work). The cards are sold at all post offices and by most hotel front desks and many shops in 1,500CFP, 2,000CFP, and 5,000CFP (US$19, US$25, and US$63/£9.50, £13, and £32) sizes. Insert the cards with the electronic chip facing up. Digital readouts on the phones tell you how many *unites* you have left on a card.

CELLPHONES

Known as "mobiles" (moo-*beels*) over here, cellphones are prevalent throughout the islands. No international wireless company operates in French Polynesia, however, and many American phones won't work since French Polynesia uses the Global System for Mobiles (GSM) technology. Although this quasi-universal system is gaining in popularity, only T-Mobile and Cingular/AT&T Wireless use it in the U.S., while some Rogers customers in Canada are GSM. All Europeans and most Australians use GSM. Call your wireless company to see if your phone is GSM.

If you do have a GSM phone, you may be able to use it in the islands if your home provider has a roaming agreement with **Vini** (C **48.13.13;** www.vini.pf), the sole local cellphone company (until 2009, when it will be joined by Mara Telecom).

Call your wireless operator and ask for "international roaming" to be activated for French Polynesia.

There's one big problem if you want to both make and receive calls from within French Polynesia. I can make local calls within French Polynesia on my home cellphone, but calling me requires expensive international calls for French Polynesians. In other words, their calls to my cellphone were routed to the United States and then back to French Polynesia!

You can get around this if (1) your GSM phone transmits and receives on the 900mHz band; (2) it has been "unlocked" from its SIM card, the removable computer chip that stores your and your provider's information; and (3) you buy a local SIM card from Vini.

Prepaid SIM cards are available at stores displaying the vini sign. The least expensive costs about 4,500CFP (US$56/£28) and includes 30 minutes of outgoing calls. Incoming calls are free, but outgoing calls using the least expensive card cost 183CFP (US$2.30/£1.15) a minute, and that's assuming you use all of your 30 minutes.

The **Travel Insider** (www.thetravel insider.info) has an excellent explanation of all this, as well as a phone-unlocking service. Click on "Road Warrior Resources" and "International Cellphone Service."

In a worst-case scenario, you can always rent a phone from Vini.

You can also buy or rent cellphones to take to French Polynesia. The chief advantage to renting a phone or SIM card in advance is that you will have it when you arrive.

I am familiar with **Mobal** (🕾 **888/399-2418;** www.mobal.com), which sells GSM phones that work here and about 150 other countries for as little as US$49 (£25) and SIM cards for less. There are no monthly fees or minimum usage requirements. Calls are billed to your credit card as you make them—US$1.95 (£1) per minute for both incoming and outgoing calls within French Polynesia, US$3.95 (£2) from here to the U.S. and Canada, US$5.95 (£3) to other countries. Mobal gave me a U.K. cellphone number, however, so people in French Polynesia have to make expensive international calls to reach my Mobal phone. For this reason, I buy a local Vini SIM card for my unlocked phone. I still carry my Mobal phone for emergencies, and I can use it when I am traveling in other countries.

CellularAbroad (🕾 **800/287-3020;** www.cellularabroad.com) of Santa Monica, California, rents GSM phones and sells prepaid SIM cards for French Polynesia.

TELEGRAPH, TELEX & FAX

Telegraph, telex, and fax services are provided by the post offices. Most hotels have **fax machines** available for guest use (be sure to ask about the charge to use it).

SKYPE—VOICE-OVER INTERNET PROTOCOL (VOIP)

I save a lot of money by using **Skype** (www.skype.com), a broadband-based telephone service (in technical terms, **Voice-over Internet protocol,** or **VoIP**), to make free international calls from my laptop or in some cybercafes. Talking worldwide on Skype is free if the people you're calling also have it on their computers (that is, computer-to-computer calls). You can also make calls to landline phones for a fee, which is based on the country you are calling, not where you are calling from. Skype calls to landline phones in most Western

countries cost about US2¢ (1p) per minute. Check Skype's website for details.

INTERNET & E-MAIL

E-mail is as much a part of life in French Polynesia as it is anywhere else these days. Although ADSL connections are available here (ADSL is not as fast as DSL or cable access in the U.S. and other countries, but is much speedier than dial-up connections), most Internet connections are still dial-up, which will seem glacially slow if you're used to DSL or cable.

Access is also relatively expensive. **MANA** (🕾 **50.88.88;** www.mana.pf) is the only local Internet service provider (ISP), and it charges by the minute rather than by the month—and many hotels slap a whopping fee on top of that. (My dial-up Internet and phone bills for checking my e-mail and banking sites from Tahiti hotel rooms have topped US$50/£25!) Consequently, don't expect people here to reply to your e-mail immediately. Patience definitely is a virtue when dealing with folks in French Polynesia.

WITHOUT YOUR OWN COMPUTER

All but a few hotels and resorts have computers from which guests can send and receive e-mail and surf the Web. It's less expensive to go a **cybercafe.** I point these out under "Internet Access" in the "Fast Facts" sections in the specific island chapters.

WITH YOUR OWN COMPUTER

Some hotels now have wireless Internet connections, or wired high-speed data-ports in their rooms, which I point out in the hotel listings in this book.

Some cybercafes have wireless connections. MANA, the local provider, has hotspots on Tahiti, Moorea, Huahine, Raiatea, Tahaa, Bora Bora, Nuku Hiva, and Hiva Oa. MANA sells prepaid access cards at its office in Fare Tony, on boulevard

Pomare between the Vaima Centre and the main post office. Hotels within range and some shops also sell them. One hour costs 990CFP (US$12/£6.25).

Since no international service provider has a local access number in the islands, you can't just plug in your laptop, program in the local access number, and go online. On the other hand, you can use your own computer from any hotel room by dialing up MANA's snail-pace "Anonymous" service. To do so, you must configure your laptop, as follows:

When setting up a new Network Connection in Windows, type in **0,368888** as the local access telephone number (0 is the number used to reach an outside line in all hotels here). When you make your first connection, enter *both* your name and your password as **anonymous.** (If your first try fails, retype both in all capital letters.) MANA charges 100CFP (US$1.25/65p) per minute for access time, and the cost of the local call also will be billed to your room. The hotel may well add an additional charge, so it can become very expensive very quickly.

If you bring your laptop, be sure to include a **connection kit** with French power and phone adapters as well as spare phone and Ethernet cables.

16 TIPS ON ACCOMMODATIONS

French Polynesia has a wide range of accommodations, from deluxe resort hotels to mom-and-pop guesthouses and dormitories with bunk beds.

TYPES OF ROOMS

My favorite type of hotel accommodates its guests in individual bungalows set in a coconut grove beside a sandy beach and quiet lagoon; if that's not the quintessential definition of the South Seas, then I don't know what is! Many of these are super-romantic bungalows that actually stand on stilts out over the reef (although some of these overwater units tend to be close together and thus less private than bungalows ashore elsewhere). Others are as basic as tents. In between, they vary in size, furnishings, and comfort. In all, you get to enjoy your own place, one usually built or accented with thatch and other native materials, but containing most of the modern conveniences. An increasing number of these accommodations are air-conditioned, which is a definite plus during the humid summer months from November through March. All but a few bungalows have ceiling fans, which will usually keep you comfortable during the rest of the year. Hotels of this style are widespread in the South Pacific.

SAVING ON YOUR HOTEL ROOM

The rate ranges quoted in this book are known in the hotel industry as **rack rates,** or published rates—that is, the maximum a property charges for a room. These prices are becoming less meaningful as more and more hotels engage in "yield management," under which they change their rates almost daily depending on how many people are booked in for a particular night. In other words, you may not know what the price of a room is until you call the hotel or book online for a particular date. Nevertheless, rack rates remain the best way of comparing prices.

Here are some other money-saving tips:

- **Ask about special rates or other discounts.** At international chain motels, you may qualify for corporate, student, military, senior, frequent flier, trade union, or other discounts.

Guesthouses & Family Accommodations

In general, you'll find a significant difference in quality between French Polynesia's moderate and inexpensive accommodations. Few establishments here are comparable in price or quality to the inexpensive motels found in abundance in the U.S., Canada, Australia, and New Zealand.

The local government is encouraging the development of guesthouses and family pensions, of which there are a growing number. Many owners have used government-backed loans to acquire one-room guest bungalows with attached bathrooms. Although the bungalows are identical, the owners have added decorative touches (in some cases quite tasteful, in others barely so).

Tahiti Tourisme inspects these establishments and distributes lists of those it recommends (see "Visitor Information," earlier in this chapter); some are also recommended in this book. Many promote themselves through an organization known as **Haere-Mai,** whose website (www.haere-mai.pf) is in both French and English, and it gives the current room rates for most properties.

Local families operate most of them, so if you decide to go this route, an ability to speak some French may be essential.

- **Dial direct.** When booking a room in a chain hotel, you'll often get a better deal by calling the individual hotel's reservation desk rather than the chain's main number.
- **Book online.** Many hotels offer Internet-only discounts, or supply rooms to Priceline, Hotwire, or Expedia at rates much lower than the ones you can get through the hotel itself. Be sure to check the individual hotel's site for discounts and specials.
- **Remember the law of supply and demand.** You can save big on hotel rooms by traveling in a destination's off-season or shoulder seasons, when rates typically drop, even at luxury properties.
- **Look into group or long-stay discounts.** If you come as part of a large group, you should be able to negotiate a bargain rate. Likewise, if you're planning a long stay (at least 5 days), you might qualify for a discount. As a general rule, expect 1 night free after a 7-night stay.
- **Sidestep excess surcharges and hidden costs.** Many hotels have adopted the unpleasant practice of nickel-and-diming their guests with opaque surcharges. When you book a room, ask what is included in the room rate, and what is extra. Avoid dialing direct from hotel phones, which can have exorbitant rates. And don't be tempted by the room's minibar offerings: Most hotels charge through the nose for water, soda, and snacks. Finally, ask about local taxes and service charges, which can increase the cost of a room by 15% or more.
- Carefully consider your hotel's meal plan. You will have no choice but to buy a plan at a remote offshore resort, from which it's impossible to stroll over to a nearby restaurant. Unless you're staying out on such a rock, it makes sense to choose a **Continental Plan (CP),** which includes breakfast only, or a **European Plan (EP),** which doesn't include any meals and allows you maximum flexibility. A **Modified American Plan (MAP)** includes breakfast and one

meal. I thoroughly enjoy dining out and sampling local cuisine, so I usually avoid the **American Plan (AP),** which includes three meals.

- **Book an efficiency,** or a "self-contained unit," as rooms with cooking facilities are known in this part of the world. A kitchenette allows you to shop for groceries and cook your own meals. This is a big money saver, especially for families on long stays.
- **Consider enrolling in hotel chains' "frequent-stay" programs,** which are upping the ante lately to win the loyalty of repeat customers. Frequent guests can now accumulate points or credits to earn free hotel nights, airline miles, in-room amenities, merchandise, tickets to concerts and events, and discounts on sporting facilities. Many chain hotels partner with other hotel chains, car-rental firms, airlines, and credit card companies to give consumers additional incentive to do repeat business.

SURFING FOR HOTELS

In addition to the online travel booking sites **Travelocity, Expedia, Orbitz, Priceline,** and **Hotwire,** you can book hotels through **Hotels.com; Quikbook** (www. quikbook.com); and **Travelaxe** (www. travelaxe.net). Frankly, I always go to the hotels' own sites before booking, since many now offer their own Internet specials, which often beat the big-site prices.

One of the best independent websites for South Pacific hotel discount shopping is Fiji-based **Travelmaxia.com,** where scores of properties throughout the region post their specials. You can search by country for resorts, hotels, bed-and-breakfasts, dive operators, and cruises.

The Australian-based **Whotif.com** (© **300/88 7979,** 866/514-3281 in the U.S., 0845 458 4567 in the U.K.; www. whotif.com) discounts rooms in French Polynesia.

Headquartered in London, **www. Pacific-Resorts.com** often has discounted rates for resorts in the islands.

Other websites have reviews and comments about accommodations worldwide. **HotelChatter.com** is a daily webzine offering coverage and critiques. Go to **TripAdvisor.com** or **HotelShark.com** for independent consumer reviews of hotels and resort properties. (Anyone can post reviews on these sites, including hotel owners themselves and "guests" who have never stayed at a property, so I read them with a proverbial grain of salt.)

It's a good idea to **get a confirmation number** and **make a printout** of any online booking transaction.

TOUR OPERATORS

Many of the **international tour operators** listed under "Packages for the Independent Traveler," earlier in this chapter, sell discounted hotel rooms as well as air tickets.

Another tactic is to check with the local **inbound tour operators.** In addition to selling tours and day trips to visitors already in the islands (that is, at hotel activities desks), these companies put together the local elements of tour packages—such as hotel rooms and airport transfers—for overseas wholesalers. They have the advantage of being on the scene and thus familiar with the properties. Some sell direct to inbound visitors as well as other tour companies.

Among more than a dozen Papeete-based companies, **Easy Tahiti.com** (www. easytahiti.com), **Islands Adventures/Air Tahiti** (www.islandsadventures.com), **Marama Tours** (www.maramatours.com), **Paradise Tours** (www.paradistourstahiti. com), **Tahiti Nui Travel** (www.tahiti nuitravel.com), and **Tekura Tahiti Travel** (www.tahiti-tekuratravelcom) have local packages within French Polynesia.

As always, it's a good idea to get a confirmation number and make a printout of any online booking transaction.

LANDING THE BEST ROOM

Somebody has to get the best room in the house. It might as well be you.

You can start by joining the hotel's frequent-guest program, which may make you eligible for upgrades. A hotel-branded credit card usually gives its owner "silver" or "gold" status in frequent-guest programs for free.

Always ask about corner rooms. They're often larger and quieter, with more windows and light, and they often cost the same as standard rooms. When you make your reservation, ask if the hotel is renovating; if it is, request a room away from the construction. Ask about nonsmoking rooms, rooms with views, and rooms with twin, queen-, or king-size beds. If you're a light sleeper, request a room away from vending machines, elevators, bars, and discos. Ask for a room that has been most recently renovated or redecorated.

If you aren't happy with your room when you arrive, ask for a different one. Most lodgings will be willing to accommodate you if another room is available.

Here are some other questions to ask before you book a room:

- What's the view like? If you're a cost-conscious traveler, you might be willing to pay less for a bungalow in the garden, especially if you don't plan to spend much time in the room.
- Does the room have air-conditioning or ceiling fans? This is an important consideration between November and March.
- What's included in the price? Your room may be moderately priced, but if you're charged for beach chairs, towels, sports equipment, and other amenities, you could end up spending more than you bargained for. Also, ask if airport transfers and local hotel taxes are included in the quoted rate.
- How far is the room from the beach and other amenities, especially the bar if the hotel has nighttime entertainment?
- What is the cancellation policy?

Suggested Tahiti & French Polynesia Itineraries

People often ask me where they should go in Tahiti and French Polynesia. Lacking the ability to read minds, I do not have an easy answer. In other words, it all depends on what you want to see and do on your own vacation. What I like is not necessarily what will interest you—but what I can do is give you the benefit of my expertise and advice so that you don't waste your valuable vacation time.

If you live in the United States, Canada, or Europe, the long flights mean you can easily burn a day getting to the islands and a day returning home. A week's worth of vacation suddenly becomes 5 days. If possible, therefore, you should spend more than just a week out here.

However you construct your own itinerary, first find out the airlines' schedules and book both your international and Air Tahiti domestic interisland flights well in advance. This is especially true of the domestic flights; do not wait until you arrive in the islands to take care of this important chore.

And remember the old travel agent's rule: Do not stay at the most luxurious property first. Anything after that will seem inferior, and you may go home disappointed. For example, most resorts on Moorea are neither as luxurious nor as picturesque as those on Bora Bora, so if you can afford to island-hop, start but don't end your visit on Moorea. And even after the luxuries of Bora Bora, you won't regret ending your trip with a bit of pampered chill time at Te Tiare Beach Resort on Huahine (p. 179) or the exquisite Le Taha'a Private Island & Spa (p. 194) on Tahaa.

1 THE ISLANDS IN BRIEF

French Polynesia sprawls over an area of 5.2 million sq. km (2 million sq. miles) in the eastern South Pacific. That's about the size of Europe, excluding the former Soviet Union countries, or about two-thirds the size of the continental United States. The 130 main islands, however, consist of only 3,885 sq. km (1,500 sq. miles), an area smaller than the smallest American state of Rhode Island. Only about 260,000 souls inhabit these small specks.

The territory's five major island groups differ in terrain, climate, and, to a certain extent, people. With the exception of the Tuamotu Archipelago, an enormous chain of low coral atolls northeast of Tahiti, all but a few are "high" islands; that is, they are the mountainous tops of ancient volcanoes eroded into jagged peaks, deep bays, and fertile valleys. All have fringing, or barrier coral reefs, and blue lagoons worthy of postcards.

THE SOCIETY ISLANDS

The most strikingly beautiful and most frequently visited destinations in the South Pacific are the **Society Islands,** so named by Capt. James Cook, the great English explorer, in 1769 because they lie relatively close together (see "Looking at the Past of Tahiti & French Polynesia," p. 16). These include Tahiti and its nearby companion Moorea, which are also known as the Windward Islands because they sit to the east, the direction of the prevailing trade wind.

Tahiti is the most developed island in French Polynesia. Don't be surprised when you take the freeway from the airport into the noisy, bustling capital of Papeete. Chic bistros and high-rise shopping centers long ago replaced the city's stage-set wooden Chinese stores, and the glass and steel of luxury resorts out in the suburbs have supplanted its cheap waterfront hotels. If you're into cities, Papeete will be right up your alley. Even if you're not, Tahiti is well worth seeing, especially its fine museums devoted to the painter Paul Gauguin, the writer James Norman Hall, and the islanders themselves.

Most modern visitors bypass these jewels and quickly head to **Moorea,** just 20km (12 miles) west of Tahiti. The short journey is like being transported to another world. Moorea's mountain peaks and fingerlike bays are world-renowned for their awesome beauty. Even though parts of Moorea are beginning to seem like Papeete suburbs, the island still retains more of old Polynesia than does Tahiti. It also has numerous white-sand beaches, which are in short supply on Tahiti, where most sand is of the black volcanic variety.

To the northwest lie Bora Bora, Huahine, Raiatea, Tahaa, Maupiti, and several smaller islands. Because they are downwind of Tahiti, they are also called the Leeward Islands.

One of the world's top honeymoon destinations, **Bora Bora** is French Polynesia's tourism dynamo, with more resorts than any other island. **Huahine** is almost as beautiful as Moorea and Bora Bora, but with only a handful of hotels, it retains much of its old Polynesian charm. The administrative center of the Leeward Islands, **Raiatea** lacks beaches, but the deep lagoon it shares with Tahaa makes it the sailing capital of French Polynesia. **Tahaa** has only recently opened to tourism, with one of French Polynesia's top resorts now sitting out on a small reef islet. Virtually unscathed by tourism, but a favorite retreat of French residents of Tahiti, **Maupiti** has a few locally owned pensions. It can be visited on a day trip from Bora Bora.

THE TUAMOTU ARCHIPELAGO

Across the approaches to Tahiti from the east, the 69 low-lying atolls of the **Tuamotu Archipelago** run for 1,159km (720 miles) on a line from northwest to southeast. The early European sailors called them the Dangerous Archipelago because of their tricky currents and because they virtually cannot be seen until a ship is almost on top of them. Even today, they are a wrecking ground for yachts and interisland trading boats. Two of them, Moruroa and Fangataufa, were used by France to test its nuclear weapons between 1966 and 1996. Others provide the bulk of Tahiti's well-known black pearls. **Rangiroa,** the world's second-largest atoll and the territory's best scuba-diving destination, is the most frequently visited. Neighboring **Tikehau,** with a much smaller and shallower lagoon, also has a modern resort hotel, as does **Manihi,** the territory's major producer of black pearls. To the south, the reef at **Fakarava** encircles the world's third-largest lagoon.

Out here you'll find marvelous snorkeling and diving in massive lagoons stocked with a vast array of sea life. The atolls may seem anticlimactic after you've seen the high islands, so I suggest visiting them before exploring the Society Islands.

THE MARQUESAS ISLANDS

Made famous in 2002 by the *Survivor* television series, the **Marquesas** are a group of 10 mountainous islands some 1,208km (750 miles) northeast of Tahiti. They are younger than the Society Islands, and because a cool equatorial current washes their shores, protective coral reefs have not enclosed them. As a result, the surf pounds on their shores, there are no encircling coastal plains, and the people live in a series of deep valleys that radiate out from central mountain peaks. The Marquesas have lost their once-large populations to 19th-century diseases and the 20th-century economic lure of Papeete; today, their sparsely populated, cloud-enshrouded valleys have an almost haunting air about them. Archaeological sites with their ancient tikis are prime attractions in the Marquesas.

Of the six inhabited islands, only **Nuku Hiva** and **Hiva Oa** have international standard hotels, and only they and **Ua Huka** and the incredibly beautiful **Ua Pou** have airports.

The Marquesas are best visited via *Aranui 3* cruises, which visit all the inhabited islands including **Fatu Hiva,** another dramatic beauty. (See "Seeing the Islands by Cruise Ship & Yacht," p. 61.)

THE AUSTRAL & GAMBIER ISLANDS

With no hotels or resorts, the **Austral Islands,** south of Tahiti, are seldom visited. They are part of a chain of high islands that continue westward into the Cook Islands. The people of the more temperate Australs, which include **Rurutu, Raivavae,** and **Tubuai,** once produced some of the best art objects in the South Pacific, but these skills have passed into time.

Far on the southern end of the Tuamotu Archipelago, the **Gambier Islands** are the top of a semisubmerged, middle-aged high island similar to Bora Bora. The hilly remnants of the old volcano are scattered in a huge lagoon, which is partially enclosed by a barrier reef marking the original outline of the island before it began to sink. The largest of these remnant islands is **Mangareva.**

2 THE GRAND TOUR IN 2 WEEKS

This itinerary takes you to all the main spots: Tahiti, Moorea, Huahine, and Bora Bora—plus a few days in Rangiroa, the largest atoll in the Tuamotu Archipelago. I suggest going to Rangiroa first because, after seeing the awesome mountainous beauty of the Society Islands, it may seem anticlimactic to end your trip at a flat atoll. Tikehau, Manihi, or Fakarava, Rangiroa's Tuamotuan sisters, are also worthy alternatives to Rangiroa (see chapter 11).

An exceptional alternative—or a terrific add-on if you have a month to spend here—would be a cruise from Papeete to the Marquesas Islands on the *Aranui 3* (p. 256).

For the typical 10-day highlights tour (or honeymoon, as the case may be), leave off Rangiroa and forget Tahiti except while waiting for your flight home. Begin your visit on Moorea, then go to Bora Bora, and finish on Huahine (or Tahaa if you can afford to stay at Le Taha'a Private Island & Spa, p. 195).

1 Tahiti
2–3–4 Rangiroa
5–6–7 Bora Bora
8–9–10 Huahine
11–12–13–14 Moorea

Day 1: Circling Tahiti ★

Unless you arrive in the afternoon or early evening on one of Air Tahiti Nui's flights, you'll probably get here in the wee hours, so spend your first morning on a guided half-day **circle island tour** of Tahiti (p. 111). You won't have to drive or find your way around, so it's a good method of recovering while seeing the island. After a long French lunch, take a **walking tour** of downtown Papeete (p. 107). Even if you aren't staying in a hotel on Tahiti's west coast, head over there to watch the sunset over Moorea, one of the region's most awe-inspiring sights.

Days 2–4: Riding the Rip on Rangiroa ★★

The world's second-largest lagoon demands a full day's excursion by boat to one of its two key sites: **Les Sables Rose (Pink Sands)** or the **Blue Lagoon** (p. 232).

Devote a full day to one of these trips. My choice would be the Blue Lagoon, actually a small lagoon within the large lagoon, though it's hard to pass up the Pink Sands, one of the great beaches here. On another day, don your snorkeling or scuba-diving gear and **ride the riptide** through the main pass into the lagoon. Be sure to watch the dolphins playing in Tiputa Pass at sunset.

Days 5–7: Feeding the Sharks on Bora Bora ★★★

A nonstop flight from Rangiroa will bring you to beautiful **Bora Bora,** which many consider the world's most beautiful island. Spend part of your first day here exploring the interior by four-wheel-drive "safari expedition" (p. 207). Devote a full day to a lagoon tour by boat, the top thing to do on Bora Bora. You'll get a fish-eye view of the island's dramatic peak, snorkel while watching your guide feed a school of reef sharks, and enjoy a fresh-fish lunch on a small islet on the fringing reef (p. 207). Have dinner one night at **Bloody Mary's Restaurant & Bar** (p. 204), another night at **Villa Mahana** (p. 219).

Days ❽–❿: Touring Old Polynesia on Huahine ★★

After the mile-a-minute activities on Bora Bora, **Huahine** will seem like a reserved Polynesian paradise. Spend your first morning on a tour of the historic *maraes* (ancient temples) at Maeva village with Paul Atallah of **Island Eco Tours** (p. 175). The next day, tour the lagoon, swim, snorkel, or go horseback riding. I always have a sunset drink while watching the boats coming and going at **Fare,** the island's charming main town.

Days ⓫–⓮: Sightseeing on Moorea ★★★

While the lagoons are the highlights at Rangiroa and Bora Bora, the ruggedly gorgeous interior draws my eyes on **Moorea.** Whether it's via a regular guided tour, a four-wheel-drive safari excursion, or on your own, go up to the **Belvédère** overlooking **Cook's** and **Opunohu bays.** Moorea's lagoon does have its good features, especially dolphin-watching excursions led by **Dr. Michael Poole** (p. 152). And don't miss a nighttime show at **Tiki Theatre Village,** one of the region's best cultural centers (p. 149). Moorea is only 7 minutes by plane from Tahiti, which makes it a snap to connect to Papeete and your flight home.

---

3 TAHITI & MOOREA IN 1 WEEK

This itinerary outlines how you can spend your time on one of the low-end, 1-week package tours, most of which offer discounted prices for airfare and a week on Tahiti and nearby Moorea. Even if you don't buy a package, this is still the least expensive way to sample the islands, since you won't be forking out a few hundred dollars for interisland airfares and paying the relatively high prices on Bora Bora. You'll get to visit fabled Tahiti and spend a few days frolicking on Moorea. You can pick and choose from this itinerary if you have a 1- or 2-day layover on Tahiti while crossing the Pacific.

Day ❶: Exploring Papeete

Get over your flight by taking it easy on the beach or around the pool this morning. Head into downtown **Papeete** in time for a long French lunch; then take a walking tour of this busy but fascinating city (p. 107). Head back to your hotel for some relaxation before watching the sunset over Moorea.

Day ❷: Circling Tahiti ★★

You can either rent a vehicle or take a guided tour around Tahiti's coastal road (p. 119). Either way, stop at **James Norman's**

Home (p. 105), the **Gauguin Museum** (p. 107), and the **Museum of Tahiti and Her Islands** (p. 106), all of which will inform you about Tahiti's interesting history. If you drive yourself, take along a swimsuit and beach towel for a visit to **Maui Beach,** Tahiti's top sands (p. 115). At night, watch one of the dance shows at the hotels (p. 126).

Day ❸: Taking a Safari Expedition into Tahiti's Interior ★★★

You may think you've seen all of Tahiti after your round-island tour, but not so. A

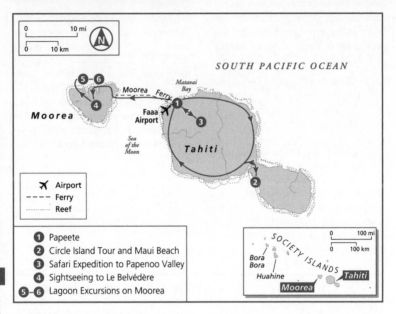

1 Papeete
2 Circle Island Tour and Maui Beach
3 Safari Expedition to Papenoo Valley
4 Sightseeing to Le Belvédère
5–6 Lagoon Excursions on Moorea

safari expedition by four-wheel-drive vehicle (p. 119) will take you into the mountainous interior, which is a very different world from the coastal road. If the weather permits, these trips follow the **Papenoo Valley** into Tahiti's extinct volcanic crater. Have dinner at *les roulottes,* the carnival-like meal wagons on the Papeete waterfront.

Days ❹: Sightseeing on Moorea ★★★

An early morning ferry or plane ride will get to Moorea in time to take a tour of this gorgeous island's north shore, home of the picturesque **Cook's** and **Opunohu bays** and the awesome view over them from **Le Belvédère** lookout. My favorite trip is a four-wheel-drive safari excursion (p. 149), which will take you to the sights, along with a ride into the interior and a dip under a waterfall. After dark, take in the

extraordinary dance show at **Tiki Theatre Village** (p. 149).

Day ❺: Getting Wet in the Moorea Lagoon ★★★

Spending a day out on the water is a must on Moorea, and every hotel offers a half- or full-day **lagoon excursion** (p. 151). The usual route takes you across the water to a *motu* (small islet) out on the reef for some swimming, snorkeling, and a barbecue lunch that may consist of fish your crew caught on the way out.

Day ❻: Dolphin-Watching on Moorea ★★★

You may have spotted dolphins playing on your Moorea lagoon excursion, but you'll learn a lot more about these friendly mammals on a trip with American marine biologist **Dr. Michael Poole** (p. 152), who has identified some 150 of them as Moorea residents.

Day ❼: Finishing Up

You will need to return to Tahiti this afternoon to await your flight home, since most planes leave after dark or in the early morning hours. Enjoy your last supper while taking in the glorious view down over Papeete from **Le Belvédère** (p. 149).

4 THE LEEWARD ISLANDS IN 10 DAYS

The Leeward Islands of Huahine, Raiatea, Tahaa, and Bora Bora are very different from Tahiti, or even Moorea, for that matter. With the exception of Bora Bora, which is French Polynesia's tourism magnet, all are relatively undeveloped. Except when cruise ships are in port, they will let you see what Polynesia is like without hordes of fellow visitors.

Days ❶–❷: Touring Old Polynesia on Huahine ★★

Lovely Huahine will give you a chance to relax and chill after your international flight. On your first morning, take an informative tour of the historic *maraes* (ancient temples) at Maeva village with Paul Atallah of **Island Eco Tours** (p. 175). Have lunch at **Restaurant Mauarii** on gorgeous **Avea Beach** (p. 183), one of French Polynesia's finest strands. On your second day, get out on the water with a lagoon excursion, or perhaps go horseback riding. I always have a sunset drink at **Restaurant Temarara** while watching the boats coming and going at **Fare,** the island's charming main town.

Days ❸–❹: A History Lesson on Raiatea ★★★

If you can spare a day away from the beach, Raiatea will allow a glimpse of Polynesia *sans* tourists—except when cruise ships dock at **Uturoa,** the island's only town and the administrative center of the Leeward Islands. You will get a good lesson in Polynesian history by spending this morning on a tour with Bill Kolans of **Almost Paradise Tours** (✆ 66.23.64) Bill will take you to **Taputapuatea** *Marae,* the largest and most impressive ancient *marae*

in French Polynesia (p. 187). You can spend your second day out on the lagoon, which Raiatea shares with Tahaa.

Days ❺–❽: Enjoying the Lagoon on Bora Bora ★★★

You'll spend 2 days in transit between Bora Bora and other islands, so that leaves just 2 days to experience the beauty of Bora Bora and its lagoon. Though it's barely enough time, you can make the most of the days by spending half of your first one on a four-wheel-drive safari expedition (p. 189). Devote all of the next day to a lagoon excursion, which invariably will include a shark-feeding stop, a picnic on a small islet, and time for snorkeling (p. 207). Be sure to have dinner at **Bloody Mary's Restaurant & Bar** (p. 218) one night, and at **Villa Mahana** (p. 219) the other night.

Days ❾–❿: Chilling in Luxury on Tahaa ★★★

The best way to come down after all the activities of this week is at **Le Taha'a Private Island & Spa,** on a small reef islet off Tahaa (p. 195). While you're here, take a safari excursion into the interior of Tahaa. (If Le Taha'a Private Island & Spa is too rich for your blood, finish your trip on Moorea.)

4

1–2 Huahine
3–4 Raiatea
5–6–7–8 Bora Bora
9–10 Tahaa

5 THE TUAMOTU & MARQUESAS ISLANDS IN 2 WEEKS

Your French Polynesian experience will be much richer if you really do get off the well-worn Tahiti–Moorea–Bora Bora tourist track and visit islands even less developed than Huahine, Raiatea, and Tahaa. (Although four islands in the Tuamotu Archipelago have first-class resorts, the far-flung atolls still meet this criterion.) The Marquesas Islands are even farther off the beaten path. Indeed, they are a world removed from the rest of French Polynesia, since their Polynesian residents have a different culture and even speak a different language than the Tahitians.

Since Air Tahiti has at least one flight a week between Rangiroa in the Tuamotus to Hiva Oa in the Marquesas, it's possible to combine the two groups in this itinerary. Air Tahiti doesn't fly between the Tuamotus every day, either, so your precise itinerary will hinge on its current schedule. Depending on the flights, you can start on Manihi or Tikehau instead of Fakarava (see chapter 11). The easy alternative to all this is taking a 2-week cruise through the Tuamotus and Marquesas on the *Aranui 3* (p. 256).

Days 1–3: Exploring a Large Lagoon & Old Village on Fakarava

An early morning flight from Papeete should put you in Fakarava in time to play in French Polynesia's second-largest lagoon.

Spend your full second day here on a lagoon excursion, especially one that will take you to **Tetamanu** village (p. 246), where you'll see the ruins of an 1834-vintage Catholic church before swimming

①-②-③	Fakarava	
④-⑤-⑥	Rangiroa	
⑦-⑧-⑨-⑩	Hiva Oa	
⑪-⑫-⑬-⑭	Nuku Hiva	

200 mi
200 km
0
0

MARQUESAS ISLANDS

Nuku Hiva
Ua Pou
Hiva Oa
Tahuata
Fatu Hiva

TUAMOTU ARCHIPELAGO

Amanu
Hao

Makemo

Marokau
Ravahere

Takapoto
Takaroa
Kauehi
Raraka

Tahanea
Faaite

Apataki

Manihi
Ahe

Arutua
Rangiroa
Tikehau

Fakarava
Toau
Kaukura
Anaa

FRENCH
POLYNESIA

Papeete
Tahiti
Huahine

INTERNATIONAL
DATE LINE

LINE ISLANDS

Caroline Is.

Vostok Is.
Flint Is.

Tupai
Maupiti
Bora Bora
Tahaa
Raiatea
Maiao
Moorea

SOCIETY ISLANDS

Political
boundaries
Atoll

in the lagoon, riding the riptide in the adjacent pass, and enjoying a beachside picnic.

Days ④–⑥: Swimming with the Sharks at Rangiroa ★★★

As I noted in the Grand Tour earlier, the world's second-largest lagoon demands full-day excursions by boat to its two key sites: **Les Sables Rose (Pink Sands)** and the **Blue Lagoon** (p. 232). On your third day, don your snorkeling or scuba-diving gear and **ride the riptide** through Tiputa Pass into the lagoon. Be sure to watch the dolphins playing in Tiputa Pass at sunset, and don't miss sampling the local vintages at **Cave de Rangiroa** (p. 235). Have dinner one night at **Relais de Josephine,** another night at **Restaurant Le Kai Kai** (p. 238).

Days ⑦–⑩: Following Paul Gauguin to Hiva Oa ★★★

The Air Tahiti flight from Rangiroa to Hiva Oa, administrative center of the Marquesas Islands, will eat up half a day, so spend your first afternoon exploring the village of **Atuona.** The French painter Paul Gauguin died in Atuona in 1903, so visit his grave and the **Tohua Papa Nui/ Paul Gauguin Cultural Center,** where you will see meticulous copies of his great works (p. 276). The center shares space with **Espace Jacques Brel,** dedicated to the French singer Jacques Brel, who also expired here and is buried near Gauguin. Spend the next day on an expedition to lovely **Puamau** village (p. 277), beside a gorgeous settlement next to a half-moon

beach. The snakelike road along on the northeast coast is virtually chiseled into the cliffs above the sea, so the ride out and back will occupy a full day. On another day, you can go fishing, hiking, or exploring the Atuona area on mountain bike or horseback (p. 279).

Days ⑪–⑭: "Surviving" on Nuku Hiva ★★

The *Survivor* TV series brought Nuku Hiva to the world's attention when it was taped here in 2002. However, you'll have a better chance of seeing **Taipivai Valley** if you go to see it on your own. It's where Herman Melville hid after jumping ship in the early 1800s (p. 261). Unless the local helicopter is operating, it's at least a 2-hour ride by four-wheel-drive vehicle across three mountain ranges from the airport to **Taiohae,** Nuku Hiva's only town. Spend half a day exploring the town and the **Herman Melville Memorial** beside its picturesque bay, including a visit to **Taetae Tupuna He'e Tai,** where American Rose Corser shows a fine collection of Marquesan art and sells exquisite handicrafts (p. 265). Later on, you can relax on the town's black-sand beach. Devote the next day to an excursion to the Taipivai Valley and **Hatiheu,** an enormously beautiful bay on the north coast and home to ancient *maraes* with tikis resembling the mysterious statues on Easter Island (p. 261). On your next-to-last day, you can go hiking or horseback riding (p. 262). You will need all of Day 14 for the ride back to the airport and the 3-hour Air Tahiti flight to Papeete.

Tahiti

Large and abundant, Tahiti is the modern traveler's gateway to French Polynesia, just as it was for Capt. James Cook and the other late-18th-century discoverers who used it as a base to explore the South Pacific. In later years, the capital city, **Papeete,** became a major shipping crossroads. Located on Tahiti's northwest corner, the city curves around what is still French Polynesia's busiest harbor.

There wasn't even a village here until the 1820s, when Queen Pomare set up headquarters along the shore, and merchant ships and whalers began using the harbor in preference to the less protected Matavai Bay to the east. A simple town of stores, bars, and billiards parlors sprang up quickly, and between 1825 and 1829 it was a veritable den of iniquity. It grew even more after the French made it their headquarters upon taking over Tahiti in 1842. A fire nearly destroyed the town in 1884, and waves churned up by a cyclone did severe damage in 1906. In 1914, two German warships shelled the harbor and sank the French navy's *Zélée.*

Papeete is a very different place today. Vehicles of every sort now crowd boulevard Pomare, the broad avenue along Papeete's waterfront, and the four-lane expressway linking the city to the trendy suburban districts of Punaauia and Paea on the west coast. Indeed, suburbs are creeping up the mountains overlooking the city and sprawling for miles along the coast in both directions. The island is so developed and so traffic-clogged that many Tahitians commute up to 2 hours in each direction on weekdays. Many are moving to Moorea, a mere 30-minute ferry ride away.

But there is a bright side to Tahiti's development: Using money from a post-nuclear-testing economic restructuring fund, Papeete has done a remarkable job in refurbishing its waterfront, including a cruise-ship terminal and a classy park where families gather and the city celebrates its festivals. It's a real treat now to walk along the promenade fronting this storied South Seas port.

Papeete's chic shops, busy Municipal Market, and lively mix of French, Polynesian, and Chinese cultures are sure to invigorate any urbanite. If you're looking for old-time Polynesia, on the other hand, you will find it on Tahiti's rural east and south coasts and especially on its peninsula, Tahiti Iti. Its three fine museums are reason enough to spend a day or two here.

Even if you plan to leave immediately for Moorea, Bora Bora, and the other less developed islands, you'll likely have to spend at least a few hours here, since all international flights land at Faaa on the northwest coast of this legendary and still very beautiful island.

1 ARRIVING & DEPARTING

ARRIVING

All international flights arrive at **Tahiti-Faaa International Airport,** 7km (4 miles) west of downtown Papeete. With its runway built on a landfill over the reef, it is French Polynesia's only international airport.

Tahitian musicians are usually on hand to welcome international flights, and they'll keep you entertained while waiting in line to have your passport stamped at Immigration. Once you've cleared Customs, you will see a **visitor information booth** straight ahead. Start there for maps and other information. If you're on a tour or have made other prior arrangements, representatives of the local tour operators will be holding signs announcing their presence.

Pick up some pocket money at **Banque de Polynésie,** to the left as you exit Customs, or at **Banque Socredo,** to the right. Both have ATMs, and Banque Socredo has a machine that will change U.S. dollars and other major notes into French Pacific francs.

I have spent many hours waiting for flights at the open-air, 24-hour **snack bar** to the right. There's a **McDonald's** next to Air Tahiti's domestic departure lounge, also to the right.

GETTING TO YOUR HOTEL

Unless you're on a package tour or your hotel has arranged a transfer, your only choice of transportation to your hotel between 10pm and 6am will be a **taxi.** Official fares from 8pm to 6am are 1,500CFP (US$19/£9.50) to the hotels on the west coast, 2,500CFP (US$31/£16) to downtown. Add 100CFP (US$1.25/65p) for each bag.

If you arrive when the local buses are running and you're in reasonably good physical condition, you can haul your baggage across the parking lot in front of the terminal, climb the stairs to the main road, and flag down a bus. See "Getting Around Tahiti," below, for details.

If you're driving a rental car, take **Route 1 W.** to the InterContinental Resort Tahiti, the Sofitel Tahiti Maeva Beach Resort, or Le Meridien Tahiti. **Route 1 E.** passes the Sheraton Hotel Tahiti Resort & Spa on its way to downtown Papeete. If you're going to downtown, watch for the **Route 5** signs directing you to the expressway connecting Papeete to the west coast. See "Getting Around Tahiti," below, for more information.

BAGGAGE STORAGE

Most hotels will store your baggage for free. The airport's **baggage storage room** is in the parking lot in front of the international departures gate. It's the small building behind the pavilion where Tahitian women often sell leis and flower crowns. It isn't cheap: Charges range from 640CFP (US$8/£4) per day for regular-size bags to 1,100CFP (US$14/£7) for surfboards, bicycles, and other large items. The room opens 2 hours before every international flight departs. Regular hours are Monday from 4am to 7pm, Tuesday through Thursday from 5am to 11pm, Saturday from 5am to 12:30am, and Sunday and holidays from 1pm to 12:30am. MasterCard and Visa are accepted.

DEPARTING

Check-in time for departing international flights is 3 hours before flight time; for domestic flights, be there 2 hours in advance. All of your bags must be screened for both international and domestic flights leaving Papeete. (There are few security procedures at the outer-island airstrips.)

There is no airport departure tax for either international or domestic flights.

Note: There is no bank or currency exchange bureau in the international departure lounge, so change your money before clearing Immigration.

Arahoho Blowholes **4**
Arahurahu Marae **13**
Atimaono Golf Course **10**
Bougainville's Anchorage **5**
Captain Cook's Anchorage **7**
Dorence Atwater's Grave **11**
Faarumai Waterfalls **4**
Faatautia Valley **6**
Lagoonarium **15**
La Maison James Norman Hall
(James Norman Hall's
Home) **2**
Maraa Grotto **12**
Musée de Tahiti et Ses Isles
(Museum of Tahiti
and Her Islands) **14**
Musée Gauguin
(Gauguin Museum) **9**
Point Venus **3**
Taravao Plateau **8**
Tomb of Pomare V **1**

Except for the Route 5 expressway between Papeete and Punaauia, and the north-south cross-island road, the island's highway system consists primarily of Route 1, a paved road running for 114km (72 miles) around Tahiti Nui, plus roads halfway down each side of Tahiti Iti. From the isthmus, a road partially lined with trees wanders up to the high, cool Plateau of Taravao, with pastures and pines more like provincial France than the South Pacific.

BY BUS

Although it might appear from the number of vehicles scurrying around Papeete that everyone owns a car or scooter, the average Tahitian gets around by local bus. Modern buses have replaced all but a few of Tahiti's famous *le trucks,* those colorful vehicles called "trucks" because the passenger compartments are gaily painted wooden cabins mounted on the rear of flatbed trucks. The last of them operate between downtown Papeete and Centre Moana Nui, a shopping complex south of the Sofitel Tahiti Maeva Beach Resort. Elsewhere, look for modern buses.

Once upon a time, *le trucks* would stop for you almost anywhere, but today you must catch them and the buses at official stops (called *arrêt le bus* in French).

The villages or districts served by each bus are written on the sides and front of the bus. **Fares** within Papeete are 130CFP (US$1.60/85p) until 6pm and 200CFP (US$2.50/£1.25) thereafter. A trip to the end of the line in either direction costs about 750CFP (US$9.40/£4.75).

BUSES GOING WEST   The few remaining *le trucks* and all short-distance buses going west are painted red and white. They line up on rue du Maréchal-Foch behind the Municipal Market and travel along rue du Général-de-Gaulle, which becomes rue du Commandant-Destremeau and later route de-l'Ouest, the road that circles the island. Buses run along this route as far as the Centre Moana Nui (south of the Sofitel Tahiti Maeva Beach Resort) Monday through Friday at least every 30 minutes from 6am to 6pm, then once an hour between 6pm and midnight. Except for *le trucks* serving tourists at the hotels on the west coast, there is irregular service on Saturday, none on Sunday. Trucks and buses labeled Faaa, Maeva Beach, and Outuamaru will pass the airport and the Sheraton Hotel Tahiti Resort & Spa and InterContinental Resort Tahiti.

BUSES GOING EAST   Short-distance buses going east are painted green and white. They line up in the block west of the Banque de Polynésie on boulevard Pomare, opposite the cruise-ship terminal and near the Municipal Market and rue Paul Gauguin. They proceed out of town via avenue du Prince-Hinoi, passing the cutoff for Hotel Le Royal

---

Tips   Around Tahiti by Bus

Although you had to walk across the Taravao isthmus, it was once possible to circumnavigate Tahiti by *le truck* in a single day. Today, the long-distance buses run only from 6am to noon on weekdays, so it is virtually impossible to go all the way around the island in any reasonable amount of time. I recommend renting a vehicle or taking a guided circle island tour instead.

Impressions

Edward called for him in a rickety trap drawn by an old mare, and they drove along a road that ran by the sea. On each side of it were plantations, coconut and vanilla; now and then they saw a great mango, its fruit yellow and red and purple among the massy green of the leaves, now and then they had a glimpse of the lagoon, smooth and blue, with here and there a tiny islet graceful with tall palms.

—W. Somerset Maugham, "The Fall of Edward Bernard," 1921

Tahitien and the Radisson Plaza Resort Tahiti on their way to Pirae, Arue, and Mahina. They run frequently from 6am to 5pm as far as the Mahina. No buses run at night, so you must rent a car or take a taxi to and from the Radisson and Le Royal Tahitien after dark and on weekends.

LONG-DISTANCE BUSES Buses going in either direction to Tahiti's south coast and Tahiti Iti are painted orange and white. They line up next to the Tahiti Manava visitor bureau on boulevard Pomare at rue Paul Gauguin. They run on the hour from 6am to noon Monday through Friday, but there is only one afternoon trip at 4:30pm back to the villages. They do not run at night or on weekends.

BY TAXI

Papeete has a large number of taxis, although they can be hard to find during the morning and evening rush hours, especially if it's raining. You can flag one down on the street or find them gathered at one of several stations. The largest gathering points are on boulevard Pomare near the market (✆ **42.02.92**) and at the Centre Vaima (✆ **42.60.77**). Most taxi drivers understand some English.

Taxi fares are set by the government and are posted on a board at the Centre Vaima taxi stand on boulevard Pomare. Few cabs have meters, so be sure that you and the driver have agreed on a fare before you get in. Note that *all fares are increased by at least 20% from 8pm to 6am.* A trip anywhere within downtown Papeete during the day starts at 1,000CFP (US$13/£7) and goes up 120CFP (US$1.50/75p) for every kilometer after the first one during the day, 240CFP (US$3/£1.50) at night. As a rule of thumb, the fare from the Papeete hotels to the airport or vice versa is about 1,700CFP (US$21/£11) during the day; from the west coast hotels to the airport, about 1,000CFP (US$13/£7). A trip to the Gauguin Museum on the south coast costs 10,000CFP (US$125/£63) one-way. The fare for a 4-hour journey all the way around Tahiti is about 16,000CFP (US$200/£101). Drivers may charge an extra 50CFP to 100CFP (US65¢–US$1.25/35p–65p) per bag of luggage.

BY RENTAL CAR

Avis (✆ **800/331-1212** or 41.93.93; www.avis.com), **Hertz** (✆ **800/654-3131** or 42.04.72; www.hertz.com), and **Europcar** (✆ **800/227-7368** or 45.24.24; www.europcar-tahiti.com) all have agencies on Tahiti. The best local rental company is **Daniel Location de Voitures,** in the Faaa airport terminal (✆ **81.96.32;** fax 85.62.64; daniel.location@mail.pf). All charge about 9,600CFP (US$120/£61) per day with unlimited kilometers.

DRIVING HINTS In Papeete, priority is given to vehicles entering an intersection from the right side. This rule does not apply on the four-lane boulevard Pomare along the

If you rent a car, consider the unlimited kilometer rate if you intend to drive around Tahiti, since the round-island road is 114km (72 miles) long, not counting Tahiti Iti.

waterfront, but be careful everywhere else, as drivers on your right will expect you to yield the right of way at intersections where there are no stop signs or traffic signals. Be prepared to deal with numerous **traffic circles** in and near town. You must give way to traffic already in the circles.

Outside of Papeete, priority is given to vehicles that are already on the round-island road. The main round-island road is a divided highway east and west of Papeete, which means that to make a left turn, you will have to turn around at the next traffic circle and drive back to your destination.

PARKING   Parking spaces can be as scarce as chicken teeth in downtown Papeete during the day. You must pay to park in most on-street spaces from 8am to 5pm Monday to Saturday, which costs 100CFP (US$1.25/65p) per hour, payable by tickets sold at numerous shops and newsstands displaying signs saying **Parc Chec.** Put the *parc chec* ticket on the dashboard inside the vehicle, not outside under the windshield wiper, where it will be stolen. There are several municipal parking garages, including one under the Hotel de Ville (Town Hall); enter off rue Collette between rue Paul Gauguin and rue d'Ecole des Frères. Some large buildings, such as the Centre Vaima, have garages in their basements. Frankly, if I'm not staying downtown, I usually leave my car at the hotel and take a bus into the city during workdays.

(Fast Facts) **Tahiti**

The following facts apply specifically to Tahiti. For more information, see "Fast Facts: Tahiti & French Polynesia" in appendix A.

American Express   The American Express representative is **Tahiti Tours,** on rue Jeanne-d'Arc (© **54.02.50;** fax 42.25.15), across from the Centre Vaima in downtown Papeete. The mailing address is B.P. 627, 98713 Papeete, Tahiti, French Polynesia.

Bookstores   **Librairie Vaima,** on the second level of the Centre Vaima (© **45.57.57**), has some English-language novels and a wide selection of books on French Polynesia, many of them in English and some of them rare editions. It also has maps of the islands. **Le Kiosk** in front of the Centre Vaima sells the *International Herald Tribune, Time,* and *Newsweek,* as does **La Maison de la Presse,** on boulevard Pomare at Quartier du Commerce (© **50.93.93**).

Business Hours   Although some shops stay open over the long lunch break, most businesses are open Monday to Friday from 8 to 11:30am and 2 to 5pm, give or take 30 minutes, since "flex hours" help alleviate Tahiti's traffic problem. Saturday hours are 8 to 11:30am, although some shops in the Centre Vaima stay open

Saturday afternoon. The Papeete Municipal Market is a roaring beehive from 5 to 7am on Sunday, and many of the nearby general stores are open during those hours. Except for some small groceries, most other stores are closed on Sunday.

Camera & Film Film and 1-hour color print processing are available at several stores in downtown Papeete. One of the best is **Tahiti Photo,** in the Centre Vaima (✆ **42.97.34**), where you can get help in English.

Currency Exchange **Banque de Polynésie, Banque de Tahiti,** and **Banque Socredo** have at least one branch each with ATMs on boulevard Pomare and in many suburban locations where you can cash traveler's checks. See "Money & Costs" in chapter 3 for more information.

Drugstores **Pharmacie du Vaima,** on rue du Général-de-Gaulle at rue Georges La Garde behind the Centre Vaima (✆ **42.97.73**), is owned and operated by English-speaking Nguyen Ngoc-Tran, whose husband runs Pharmacie Tran on Moorea. Pharmacies rotate night duty, so ask your hotel staff to find out which one is open after dark.

Emergencies & Police Consult with your hotel staff. The **emergency police** telephone number is ✆ **17** (but don't expect the person on the other end of the line to speak English). The **central gendarmerie** is at the inland terminus of avenue Bruat (✆ **42.02.02**).

Eyeglasses Papeete has several opticians, including **Optika** (✆ **42.77.54**) in the Centre Vaima.

Healthcare Both **Clinque Cardella** (✆ **42.80.10**), on rue Anne-Marie-Javouhey, and **Clinic Paofai** (✆ **43.77.00**), on boulevard Pomare, have highly trained specialists and some state-of-the-art equipment. They are open 24 hours.

Information **Tahiti Tourisme's Fare Manihini** visitors bureau (✆ **50.57.12;** www. tahiti-manava.pf), on the waterfront on boulevard Pomare at the foot of rue Paul Gauguin, is open 7:30am to 5:30pm Monday to Friday, 8 to 4pm Saturday, 8am to 1pm on Sunday and holidays.

Internet Access Every hotel here has Internet access for its guests to use. **Tahiti Tourisme** has computers in its Fare Manihini visitor center (✆ **50.57.12;** www. tahiti-manava.pf), on the waterfront on boulevard Pomare at the foot of rue Paul Gauguin. It charges 300CFP (US$3.75/£1.90) for 15 minutes of access time, 1,000CFP (US$13/£7) for 1 hour, open 7:30am to 5:30pm Monday to Friday, 8 to 4pm Saturday, 8am to 1pm on Sunday and holidays. **Cybernesia Tahiti,** on the second level of the Vaima Centre (✆ **85.43.67**), has both dial-up and wireless access for 20CFP (US25¢/10p) per minute for the first 10 minutes, 15CFP (US20¢/10p) per minute thereafter. It has English keyboards and the Skype telephone program on some of its computers, and it will burn your digital photos to CD. Open Monday to Friday 8am to 6pm, Saturday 9am to 4pm. **La Maison de la Presse,** on boulevard Pomare at Quartier du Commerce (✆ **50.93.93**) also has English keyboards. It charges 16CFP (US20¢/10p) per minute. The **Tahiti-Faaa Business Center,** next to McDonald's in the airport terminal (✆ **83.63.88**), has access for 300CFP (US$3.75/£1.90) for 15 minutes or 1,000CFP (US$13/£7) for 1 hour. It's open Monday, Tuesday, and Friday 7am to 6pm and 8pm to midnight; Wednesday and Thursday 9am to 6pm and 8pm to midnight; and Saturday 7am to 1pm and 6pm to midnight. The Business Center has fax services and will burn your photos to CDs.

MANA (www.mana.pf), the local Internet service provider, has several wireless hotspots around town, including the main post office, Parc Bougainville, Place Toata, the Fare Tony building on boulevard Pomare, Brasserie des Remparts restaurant, and at Tahiti-Faaa International Airport.

See "Staying Connected," in chapter 3, for more information.

Laundry **Lavomatic du Pont du L'Est,** Gauguin**,** 64 rue Paul Gauguin (© **43.71.59**), at Pont de l'Est, has wash-dry-fold service for 1,400CFP (US$18/£9) a load. Open Monday to Friday 7am to 5:30pm, Saturday 7am to noon.

Libraries The **Office Territorial D'Action Culturelle (Territorial Cultural Center)** on boulevard Pomare, west of downtown Papeete (© **42.88.50**), has a small library of mostly French books on the South Pacific and other topics. Hours are 8am to 5pm Monday to Friday, except on Wednesday when it closes at 4pm.

Mail The main post office is on boulevard Pomare a block west of the Centre Vaima. Open from 7am to 6pm Monday through Friday, 8 to 11am Saturday. The branch post office at the Tahiti-Faaa International Airport terminal is open from 6 to 10:30am and noon to 2pm Monday through Friday, and from 6 to 9am on Saturday, Sunday, and holidays.

Restrooms Both **Tahua Vaite** (the park by the cruise-ship terminal at rue Paul Gauguin) and **Place Toata** on the western end of downtown have free and clean public toilets.

Safety Papeete has seen increasing street crime in recent years. The busy parks on boulevard Pomare along the waterfront generally are safe, but be very careful if you wander onto the side streets after dark.

Telephone & Fax The main post office, the cruise-ship terminal, and Place Toata all have pay phones, where you can use a *télécarte* to make local and international calls. See "Staying Connected" in chapter 3 for more information about pay phones and international calls.

Water You can drink the tap water in Papeete and its nearby suburbs, which includes all the hotels, but not out in the rural parts of Tahiti. Bottled water is available in all grocery stores.

3 TAHITI'S TOP ATTRACTIONS

Tahiti is shaped like a figure eight lying on its side. The "eyes" of the eight are two extinct, eroded volcanoes joined by the flat Isthmus of Taravao. The larger, western part of the island is known as Tahiti Nui ("Big Tahiti" in Tahitian), while the smaller eastern peninsula beyond the isthmus is named Tahiti Iti ("Little Tahiti"). Together they comprise about 670 sq. km (258 sq. miles), about two-thirds the size of the island of Oahu in Hawaii.

Tahiti Nui's volcano has been eroded over the eons so that now long ridges, separating deep valleys, march down from the crater's ancient rim to the coast far below. The rim itself is still intact, except on the north side, where the Papenoo River has cut its way to the sea. The highest peaks, **Mount Orohena,** 2,206m (7,353 ft.), and **Mount Aora,** 2,045m (6,817 ft.), tower above Papeete. Another peak, the toothlike Mount Te Tara O Maiao, or the **Diadème,** at 1,308m (4,360 ft.), can be seen from the eastern suburb of Pirae, but not from downtown.

With the exception of the east coast of Tahiti Iti, where great cliffs fall into the sea, and a few places where the ridges end abruptly at the water's edge, the island is skirted by a flat coastal plain. Tahiti's residents live on this plain, in the valleys, or on the hills adjacent to the plain.

Arahurahu Marae ★★   Arahurahu is the only *marae*—an ancient temple or meeting place—in all of Polynesia that has been fully restored, and it is maintained like a museum. Although not nearly as impressive as the great lagoonside *maraes* on Huahine and Raiatea (see chapters 7 and 8, respectively), this is Tahiti's best example of ancient Polynesian temples and meeting places, and its exhibit boards do a good job of explaining the significance of each part. For example, the stone pens near the entrance were used to keep the pigs before being sacrificed to the gods. Arahurahu is used for the reenactment of old Polynesian ceremonies during the July *Heiva Nui* celebrations.

Paea, 23km (14 miles) west of Papeete. No phone. Free admission. Daily 24 hr.

Lagoonarium de Tahiti   If you won't be diving or snorkeling in the lagoons, then you will enjoy a visit to this underwater viewing room surrounded by pens containing reef sharks, sea turtles, and many colorful species of tropical fish. It's part of the Captain Bligh Restaurant and Bar (p. 135). The view of Moorea from here is terrific.

Punaauia, 12km (7 miles) west of Papeete. ✆ **43.62.90.** Admission 500CFP (US$6.25/£3.15) adults, 300CFP (US$3.75/£1.90) children 11 and under. Daily 9am–5:30pm.

La Maison de James Norman Hall (James Norman Hall's Home) ★★★   This marvelous museum is a required stop for all of us who have ever dreamed of writing successful novels in a lovely lagoonside house. James Norman Hall was a U.S. army pilot in France during World War I, when he was shot down behind German lines and held prisoner. He met Charles Nordhoff in Paris shortly after the war, and together they wrote *The Lafayette Flying Corp,* the story of the American unit that fought for France before the U.S. entered the war. In 1920, they moved to Tahiti, where they sailed around on copra schooners and wrote *Faery Lands of the South Seas.* In 1932, they published *Mutiny on the Bounty,* the first of their three novels about the incident and its aftermath (*Men Against the Sea* and *Pitcairn's Island* are the others). It was turned into the 1935 movie starring Clark Gable and Charles Laughton, and the 1962 remake with Marlon Brando.

TAHITI

5

TAHITI'S TOP ATTRACTIONS

 Tips   **Bone Up on History**

A knowledge of French Polynesia's background will prove very useful as you see the sights, many of which have historical significance. I strongly recommend reading "Looking at the Past of Tahiti & French Polynesia," p. 16, before setting out and referring back to it as you go. Also consider buying a copy of the late Bengt Danielsson's *Tahiti: Circle Island Tour Guide.* French and English editions are available in the local bookstores. Danielsson arrived in French Polynesia on Thor Hyerdahl's *Kon Tiki* raft in the late 1940s. He lived here the rest of his life and understood Polynesian culture as well as any European.

Hall and Nordhoff penned several more books about the islands, including *Hurricane,* which was also turned into two movies.

Hall and his wife, Sarah Teraireia Winchester Hall, lived their entire married lives here in Arue. Their family manages the house, which is an exact reproduction of their home, and has stocked it with Hall's typewriter, original manuscripts, and tons of heirlooms and memorabilia. (One of the three Oscars won by his son, the late Hollywood cinematographer Conrad L. Hall, is here.) The office is adorned with photographs of him with Zane Grey, Robert Dean Frisbee, and other men-of-the-pen when they dropped by for visits. One of Hall's grandsons still lives on the property, so you will need permission to visit his grave on the hill above the house. Staff members lead 30-minute tours and sell coffee and soft drinks. The free parking lot is across the highway beside the lagoon; if coming from Papeete, you'll have to turn around at the next traffic circle and come back to reach it.

Arue, 5.5km (3¼ miles) east of Papeete. ℂ **50.01.60.** www.jamesnormanhallhome.pf. Admission 600CFP (US$7.45/£3.80). Tues–Sat 9am–4pm. Closed public holidays.

Marché Municipale (Municipal Market) ★★★　An amazing array of fruits, vegetables, fish, meat, handicrafts, and other items are sold under the big tin pavilion of Papeete's bustling public market. Unwritten rules dictate that Tahitians sell fruits and traditional vegetables (such as taro and breadfruit), Chinese sell European and Chinese vegetables, and Chinese and Europeans serve as butchers and bakers. If your stomach can handle it, look for hogs' heads hanging in the butcher stalls. The market is busiest early in the mornings, but it's like a carnival here from 5 to 7am every Sunday, when people from the outlying areas of Tahiti, and even from the other islands, arrive to sell their produce. (*Note:* The pickings are slim by 8am.) A Tahitian string band plays during lunch at the upstairs snack bar, which purveys inexpensive island chow.

Papeete, between rue du 22 Septembre and rue François Cardella, 1 block inland from bd. Pomare. No phone. Free admission. Mon–Fri 5am–6pm; Sat 5am–1pm; Sun 4–8am.

Musée de Tahiti et Ses Isles (Museum of Tahiti and Her Islands) ★★★　Set in a lagoonside coconut grove with a gorgeous view of Moorea, this ranks as one of the best museums in the South Pacific. Exhibits show the geological history of the islands, including a terrific topographic map; their sea life, flora, and fauna; and the history and culture of their peoples. Exhibits are devoted to traditional weaving, tapa-cloth making, early tools, body ornaments, tattooing, fishing and horticultural techniques, religion and *maraes,* games and sports, warfare and arms, deaths and funerals, and writers and missionaries (note the 1938 *Tahitian Bible*). Most, but not all, of the display legends are translated into English. Start in the air-conditioned exhibit hall to the left as you enter and proceed outside. Give yourself at least 30 minutes here, preferably an hour.

Punaauia, 15km (9 miles) west of Papeete. ℂ **58.34.76.** Admission 600CFP (US$7.45/£3.80) adults, free for children. Tues–Sun 9:30am–5:30pm. Turn toward the lagoon at the Total station and follow the signs.

Ⓕun Facts　Shipwrecked

While researching the novel *Pitcairn's Island,* which he coauthored with Charles Nordhoff, James Norman Hall disappeared for several months in 1933 after being shipwrecked near Mangareva, between Tahiti and Pitcairn.

Musée Gauguin (Gauguin Museum) ★★★ This museum/memorial to Paul Gauguin, the French artist who lived in the Mataiea district from 1891 until 1893, owns a few of his sculptures, woodcarvings, engravings, and a ceramic vase. It has an active program to borrow his major works, however, and one might be on display during your visit. Otherwise, the exhibits are dedicated to his life in French Polynesia. It's best to see them counterclockwise, starting at the gift shop (which sells excellent prints and reproductions of his works). The originals are in the first gallery. An interesting display in the last gallery shows who owns his works today. The museum has a lagoonside restaurant, although most visitors have lunch at the nearby Restaurant du Musée Gauguin, at PK 50.5 (p. 117).

The museum is adjacent to the lush **Harrison W. Smith Jardin Botanique (Botanical Gardens),** which was started in 1919 by Harrison Smith, an American who left a career teaching physics at the Massachusetts Institute of Technology and moved to Tahiti. He died here in 1947. His gardens, which now belong to the public, are home to a plethora of tropical plants from around the world. This is the wettest part of Tahiti, so bring an umbrella.

Mataiea, 51km (32 miles) west of Papeete. ☎ **57.10.58.** Museum admission 600CFP (US$7.50/£3.80) adults, 300CFP (US$3.75/£1.90) children 12–18. Gardens 600CFP (US$7.50/£3.80), free for children 11 and under. Daily 9am–5pm.

Point Venus ★★★ Capt. James Cook observed the transit of the planet Venus in 1769 at Point Venus, Tahiti's northernmost extremity. The low, sandy peninsula covered with ironwood (casuarina) trees is about 2km (1¼ miles) from the main road. Captains Wallis, Cook, and Bligh landed here after anchoring their ships offshore, behind the reef in Matavai Bay. Cook made his observations of the transit of Venus across the sun in 1769 from a point between the black-sand beach and the meandering river that cuts the peninsula in two. The beach and the parklike setting around the tall white lighthouse, which was completed in 1868 (notwithstanding the 1867 date over the door), are popular for picnics. There are a snack bar, a souvenir and handicrafts shop, and toilets.

Mahina, 10km (6 miles) east of Papeete. No phone. Free admission. Daily 4am–7pm. Snack bar and souvenir shop daily 8am–5pm.

TAHITI

5

WALKING TOUR: PAPEETE

WALKING TOUR PAPEETE

START:	Tahiti Tourisme's visitor center
FINISH:	Papeete Town Hall
TIME:	2 hours
BEST TIME:	Early morning or late afternoon
WORST TIME:	Midday, or Sunday when most establishments are closed

Begin at Tahiti Tourisme's visitor center in Tahua Vaiete, the park by the cruise ship dock, at the foot of rue Paul Gauguin. Stroll westward along Boulevard Pomare. Opposite the tuna boat dock stands Centre Vaima.

❶ Centre Vaima

The chic shops in Papeete's first shopping mall are a mecca for Papeete's French and European residents (the Municipal Market still attracts mostly Tahitians). The infamous Quinn's Bar stood in the block east of the Centre Vaima, where the Noa Noa boutique is now. The Centre Vaima takes its name from the Vaima Restaurant, everyone's favorite eatery in those days, which it replaced.

Across the four-lane boulevard from the Vaima is the wooden boardwalk along the Quay.

❷ The Quay

Cruising yachts from around the world congregate here from April to September,

WALKING TOUR: PAPEETE

TAHITI

5

TAHITI

Papeete

1 Centre Vaima
2 The Quay
3 Parc Bougainville
4 Place Jacques Chirac
5 Eglise Evangélique
6 Place Toata
7 Place Tarahoi
8 Cathédrale de l'Immaculée Conception
9 Marché Municipale
10 Hôtel de Ville (Papeete Town Hall)

⊠ Post office
ⓘ Information

and resident boats are docked here all year. Beyond them, on the other side of the harbor, is **Motu Uta,** once a small natural island belonging to Queen Pomare but now home of the wharves and warehouses of Papeete's shipping port. The reef on the other side has been filled to make a breakwater and to connect Motu Uta by road to **Fare Ute,** the industrial area and French naval base to the right. The interisland boats dock alongside the filled-in reef, and their cargoes of copra (dried coconut meat) are taken to a mill at Fare Ute, where coconut oil is extracted and later shipped overseas to be used in cosmetics.

Walk west along the waterfront, past the main post office, next to which is Parc Bougainville.

❸ Parc Bougainville

This shady park next to the post office is named for the French explorer who found Tahiti a little too late to get credit for its discovery. Two naval cannons flank the statue of Bougainville: The one nearest the post office was on the *Seeadler,* Count von Luckner's infamous World War I German raider, which ran aground in the Cook Islands after terrifying the British and French territories of the South Pacific. The other was on the French navy's *Zélée.* Bougainville's statue stands between the guns. There's a snack bar at the rear of the park.

Walk westward to the traffic circle at the foot of avenue Bruat.

❹ Place Jacques Chirac

Few projects exemplify Papeete's vast road improvements more than the big traffic circle, under which pass the four busy lanes of boulevard Pomare, and the adjacent underground parking garage. On the harbor side, the semicircular-shaped park is known as Place Jacques Chirac, whose name created quite a stir because French tradition says not to name a public place after a living president. Underneath is a public parking garage. The park is the beginning of recent landfills, which have

replaced a black-sand beach that used to **109** run west of here.

Keep going west along the waterfront, to rue l'Arthémise, where you can't miss the big beige church on the mountain side of the boulevard.

❺ Eglise Evangélique

An impressive steeple sits atop Eglise Evangélique, the largest Protestant church in French Polynesia. The local evangelical sect grew out of the early work by the London Missionary Society. Today, the pastors are Tahitian. Outrigger canoe racing is Tahiti's national sport, and the *va'a*—those long, sleek vessels seen cutting the harbor during lunchtime and after work—used to be kept on a black-sand beach across the boulevard from the church. Today, a section of the landfill across the boulevard is reserved for them.

Continue west along boulevard Pomare for 6 more blocks. You'll see a few remaining stately old colonial homes across the boulevard. On the harbor side you will come to Place Toata.

❻ Place Toata

Another project funded by the economic restructuring fund, Place Toata is another park built on the landfill, and it is a favorite gathering place for office workers during the day and families at night. They come to stroll, take in the view, and dine at inexpensive snack bars. Place Toata's outdoor amphitheater hosts concerts all year and the national dance competition during the huge *Heiva Nui* festival in July. Next door, on the banks of Tipaerui River, stands the *Office Territorial d'Action Culturelle,* Tahiti's cultural center and library.

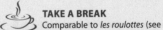

TAKE A BREAK
Comparable to *les roulottes* (see "Where to Dine," later in this chapter) but permanently here, Place Toata's open-air snack bars are great for cold drinks, ice-cream cones, or even a complete lunch. There are clean public restrooms here.

Impressions

To those who insist that all picturesque towns look like Siena or Stratford-on-Avon, Papeete will be disappointing, but to others who love the world in all its variety, the town is fascinating. My own judgment: any town that wakes each morning to see Moorea is rich in beauty.

—James A. Michener, *Return to Paradise*, 1951

Turn around and backtrack east on boulevard Pomare to Parc Bougainville (see number 3, above), cut through the park, and proceed through the park to the spacious grounds of Place Tarahoi.

❼ Place Tarahoi

Place Tarahoi, Papeete's governmental center, was royal property in the old days and site of Queen Pomare's mansion, which the French used as their headquarters after 1842. Her impressive home is long gone, but is replicated by the Papeete Town Hall (see number 10, below). As you face the grounds, the buildings on the right house the French government and include the home of the president of French Polynesia. The modern building on the left is the Territorial Assembly. You can walk around hallways of the Assembly building during business hours. In front stands a monument to Pouvanaa a Oopa (1895–1977), a Tahitian who became a hero fighting for France in World War I and then spent the rest of his life battling for independence for his homeland. During the 1960s and 1970s he spent 15 years in prison in France, but he returned home in time to see more local autonomy granted to the territory. In fact, his fellow Tahitians sent him back to Paris as a member of the French Senate.

Continue 2 more blocks along rue du Général-de-Gaulle, past the rear of Centre Vaima, to Cathédrale de l'Immaculée Conception.

❽ Cathédrale de l'Immaculée Conception

Tahiti's oldest Catholic church, Cathédrale de l'Immaculée Conception houses a series of paintings of the Crucifixion. It's a cool, quiet, and comforting place to worship or just to contemplate.

Rue du Général-de-Gaulle becomes rue du Maréchal-Foch past the church. Follow it for a block. Bear left at rue Colette and continue until you come to Marché Municipale.

❾ Marché Municipale

Take a stroll under the large tin pavilion of Papeete's Municipal Market and examine the multitude of fruits and vegetables for sale (see "Tahiti's Top Attractions," earlier in this chapter).

After sampling the market and the marvelous handicrafts stalls along its sidewalk and upstairs, walk along rue Colette for 2 more blocks, until you come to Papeete Town Hall.

❿ Hotel de Ville (Papeete Town Hall)

This is a magnificent replica of Queen Pomare's mansion, which once stood at Place Tarahoi. This impressive structure, with its wraparound veranda, captures the spirit of the colonial South Pacific. This *Hôtel de Ville* or *Fare Oire* (French and Tahitian, respectively, for "town hall") was dedicated in 1990 by French President François Mitterand during an elaborate celebration. Walk up the grand entrance steps to catch a cool breeze from the broad balconies.

From here you can find your way back to Vaima Centre and some much-needed refreshment at its open-air cafes (see "Where to Dine," later in this chapter).

4 THE CIRCLE ISLAND TOUR ★★

A **Circle Island Tour,** or a drive around Tahiti, is the best way to spend a day seeing the island's outlying sights and a bit of old Polynesia away from Papeete's bustle. It can be done even if you're staying on Moorea (see "Touring Tahiti from Moorea . . . & Vice Versa," p. 121).

The road around Tahiti Nui is 114km (72 miles) long. It's 54km (32 miles) from Papeete to Taravao along the east coast and 60km (40 miles) returning along the west coast. If your car has a trip meter, reset it to zero; if it doesn't, make note of the total kilometers on the odometer at the outset.

On the land side of the road are red-topped concrete **kilometer markers** (*pointes kilomètres* in French, or *PK* for short). They tell the distance every kilometer between Papeete and the Isthmus of Taravao; that is, the distance from Papeete to Taravao in each direction, not the total number of kilometers around the island. The large numbers facing the ocean are the number of kilometers from Papeete; the numbers facing you as you drive along are the number of kilometers you have to go to Papeete or Taravao, depending on your direction. Distances between the PKs are referred to in 10ths of kilometers; for example, PK 35.6 would be 35.6km from Papeete.

THE NORTH & EAST COASTS OF TAHITI NUI

Proceeding clockwise from Papeete, you'll leave town by turning inland off boulevard Pomare and following the broad **avenue du Prince-Hinoi,** the start of the round-island road.

FAUTAUA VALLEY, LOTI'S POOL & THE DIADEME

It's not worth the side trip, but at PK 2.5, a road goes right into the steep-walled Fautaua Valley and the **Bain Loti,** or Loti's Pool. Julien Viaud, the French merchant mariner who wrote under the pen name Pierre Loti, used this pool as a setting for his novel *The Marriage of Loti,* which recounted the love of a Frenchman for a Tahitian woman. Now part of Papeete's water-supply system, the pool is covered in concrete. The road goes into the lower part of the valley and terminates at the beginning of a hiking trail up to the **Fautaua Waterfall,** which plunges over a cliff into a large pool 300m (985 ft.) below. The all-day hike to the head of the valley is best done with a guide (see "Golf, Hiking & Watersports," later in this chapter).

Pull off the main road into the side street opposite the big seaside park at Pirae for a look inland at the **Diadème,** a rocky outcrop protruding like a crown from the interior ridge. (I think it looks like a single worn molar sticking up from a gum.)

 Tips   Avoid Rush Hour & Check on Road Work

If you drive yourself around Tahiti, avoid getting snarled in morning and evening weekday rush hours. Landslides between PK 44 and PK 45 on the east coast can close the round-island road, so ask the car-rental agent or the staff at the Tahiti Manava visitors bureau if it is open all the way around.

Impressions

The air was full of that exquisite fragrance of orange blossom and gardenia which is distilled by night under the thick foliage; there was a great silence, accentuated by the bustle of insects in the grass, and that sonorous quality, peculiar to night in Tahiti, which predisposes the listener to feel the enchanting power of music.

—Pierre Loti (Julien Viaud), *The Marriage of Loti*, 1880

TOMB OF POMARE V ★★

At PK 4.7, turn left at the sign and drive a short distance to a Protestant churchyard commanding an excellent view of Matavai Bay to the right. The **tomb** with a Grecian urn on top was built in 1879 for Queen Pomare. Her remains were removed a few years later by her son, King Pomare V, who abdicated in return for a French pension and later died of too much drink. Now he is buried here, and tour guides like to say the urn is not an urn at all but a liquor bottle, which makes it a monument not to Pomare V, but to the cause of his death.

LA MAISON DE JAMES NORMAN HALL (JAMES NORMAN HALL'S HOME) ★★★

At PK 5.4, on the mountain side of the road just east of the small bridge, stands the home of **James Norman Hall,** coauthor with Charles Nordhoff of *Mutiny on the Bounty.* See "Tahiti's Top Attractions," earlier in this chapter.

ONE TREE HILL ★★

At PK 8, past the new Radisson Plaza resort, you'll come to the top of **One Tree Hill,** so named by Capt. James Cook because a single tree stood on this steep headland in the late 1700s. For many years, it was the site of a luxury hotel, now closed. Pull into the roundabout at the entrance and stop for one of Tahiti's most magnificent vistas. You'll look down on the north coast all the way from Matavai Bay to Papeete, with Moorea looming on the far horizon.

POINT VENUS ★★★

At PK 10, turn left at Super Marché Venus Star and drive to **Point Venus,** Tahiti's northernmost point, where Capt. James Cook observed the transit of the planet Venus in 1769 (see "Tahiti's Top Attractions," earlier in this chapter).

PAPENOO VALLEY

At PK 17.1, Tahiti's longest bridge crosses its longest river at the end of its largest valley at one of its largest rural villages—all named **Papenoo.** The river flows down to the sea through the only wall in Tahiti Nui's old volcanic crater. A cross-island road goes up the valley, literally through the mountains (via a tunnel), and down to Tahiti's south shore. Four-wheel-drive vehicles go into the valley on exciting excursions (see "Safari Expeditions," later in this chapter). You can drive yourself as far as **Relais de la Maroto** (✆ 57. 90.29), a small hotel and restaurant up in the valley.

ARAHOHO BLOWHOLES

At PK 22, the surf pounding against the headland at **Arahoho** has formed overhanging shelves with holes in them. As waves crash under the shelves, water and air are forced through the holes, resulting in a geyserlike phenomenon. One shoots up at the base of a cliff on the mountain side of the road, but be careful because oncoming traffic cannot see you standing there. Pull into the overlook (with free parking and toilets) west of the sharp curve. There's a local snack bar across the road, and a black-sand beach is within sight.

CASCADES DE TEFAARUMAI (FAARUMAI WATERFALLS) ★★

At PK 22.1, a sign on the right just past the blowhole marks a somewhat paved road that leads 1.5km (1 mile) up a small valley to the **Cascades de Faarumai,** Tahiti's most accessible waterfalls. The drive itself gives a glimpse of how ordinary rural Tahitians live in simple wood houses surrounded by bananas and breadfruit. Park near the stand of bamboo trees and take a few minutes to read the signs, which explain a romantic legend. Vaimahuta falls are an easy walk; Haamaremare Iti and Haamaremarerahi falls are a 45-minute climb up a more difficult trail. Vaimahuta falls plunge straight down several hundred feet from a hanging valley into a large pool. Bring insect repellent.

MAHAENA BATTLEFIELD

At PK 32.5, the Tahitian rebellion came to a head on April 17, 1844, when 441 French troops charged several times and many poorly armed Tahitians dug in near the village of **Mahaena.** The Tahitians lost 102 men and the French, 15. It was the last set battle of the rebellion.

BOUGAINVILLE'S ANCHORAGE ★

At PK 37.6, a plaque mounted on a rock on the northern end of the bridge at Hitiaa commemorates the landing of the French explorer **Bougainville,** who anchored just offshore when he arrived in Tahiti in 1768. The two small islands on the reef, Oputotara and Variararu, provided slim protection against the prevailing trade winds, and Bougainville lost six anchors in 10 days trying to keep his ships off the reef. Tahitians recovered one and gave it to the high chief of Bora Bora, who in turn gave it to Captain Cook in 1777.

FAATAUTIA VALLEY

At PK 41.8 begins a view of **Faatautia Valley,** which looks so much like those in the Marquesas that in 1957 director John Huston chose it as a location for a movie version of *Typee,* Herman Melville's novelized account of his ship-jumping adventures among the Marquesans on Nuku Hiva in the 1840s. The project was scrapped after another of Huston's Melville movies, *Moby-Dick,* bombed at the box office. The uninhabited valley surely looks much today as it did 1,000 years ago.

> **Impressions**
>
> *Look to the Northward, stranger / Just over the hillside there / Have you in your travels seen / A land more passing fair?*
>
> —James Norman Hall (on his tombstone)

> **Impressions**
>
> *It came upon me little by little. I came to like the life here, with its ease and its leisure,*
> *and the people, with their good-nature and their happy smiling faces.*
> —W. Somerset Maugham, "The Fall of Edward Bernard," 1921

TARAVAO

At PK 53, after passing the small-boat marina, the road climbs up onto the **Isthmus of Taravao,** separating Tahiti Nui from Tahiti Iti. At the top are the stone walls of **Fort Taravao,** which the French built in 1844 to bottle up what was left of the rebellious islanders on the Tahiti Iti peninsula during the French-Tahitian War of 1844 to 1848. Germans stuck on Tahiti during World War II were interned here. It is now used as a French army training center. The village of **Taravao,** with its shops, suburban streets, and churches, has grown up around the military post. Its snack bars are good places for refueling stops.

THE TAHITI ITI PENINSULA

Tahiti Iti is much less sparsely populated and developed than its bigger twin, Tahiti Nui. Paved roads dead-end about halfway down its north and south sides. A series of cliffs plunge into the sea on Tahiti Iti's rugged east end. While the north shore holds historical interest, the south coast has Tahiti's best beach and its top surfing spot.

TARAVAO PLATEAU

If you have to choose one of three roads on Tahiti Iti, take the one by the school and stadium. It dead-ends high up into the rolling pastures of the **Taravao Plateau.** It begins at the traffic signal on the north-coast road to Tautira and runs up through cool pastures reminiscent of rural France, with huge trees lining the narrow paved road. At more than 360m (1,200 ft.) high, the plateau is blessed with a refreshing, perpetually springlike climate. Near the end of the road, you'll come to the **Taravao Plateau Overlook,** where you'll have a spectacular view of the entire isthmus and down both sides of Tahiti Nui.

THE NORTH COAST TO TAUTIRA

The road on the north coast of Tahiti Iti goes for 18km (11 miles) to the sizable village of **Tautira,** which sits on its own little peninsula. Captain Cook anchored in the bay off Tautira on his second visit to Tahiti in 1773. His ships ran aground on the reef while the crews were partying one night. He managed to get them off, but lost several anchors in the process. One of them was found in 1978 and is now on display at the Museum of Tahiti and Her Islands, which you will come to on the west side of the island.

A year after Cook landed at Tautira, a Spanish ship from Peru named the *Aguila* landed here, and its captain claimed the island for Spain. It was the third time Tahiti had been claimed for a European power. He also put ashore two Franciscan priests. The *Aguila* returned a year later, but the priests had had enough of Tahiti and sailed back to Peru.

When you enter the village, bear left and drive along the scenic coast road as far as the general store, where you can buy a cold soft drink and snack. If you can hold out longer, I usually take my break at La Plage de Maui snack bar on Tahiti Iti's south coast (see below).

THE SOUTH COAST TO TEAHUPOO

The picturesque road along the south coast of Tahiti Iti skirts the lagoon, passing through small settlements. Novelist Zane Grey had a deep-sea-fishing camp at PK 7.3, near the village of **Toahotu,** from 1928 to 1930. He caught a silver marlin that was about 4m (14 ft.) long and weighed more than 454 kilograms (1,000 lb.)—even after the sharks had had a meal on it while Grey was trying to get it aboard his boat. He wrote about his adventures in *Tales of Tahitian Waters.*

According to Tahitian legends, the demigod Maui once made a rope from his sister Hina's hair and used it to slow down the sun long enough for Tahitians to finish cooking their food in their earth ovens (a lengthy process). He accomplished this feat while standing on the reef at a point 8.5km (5 miles) along the south-coast road. Beyond Maui's alleged footprints, now under the road, the **Bay of Tapueraha** provides the widest pass and deepest natural harbor on Tahiti. It was used as a base by a large contingent of the French navy during the aboveground nuclear tests at Moruroa atoll in the 1960s and 1970s. Some of the old mooring pilings still stand just offshore.

Reminiscent of the great Matira Beach on Bora Bora, **La Plage de Maui (Maui Beach)** ★★★ borders the bay and is the best strip of white sand on Tahiti. Get out of the car and take a break at the lagoonside snack bar here. A cave, known as the **Caverne de Maui,** is a short walk inland.

Near Vairao village, you'll pass the modern **IFREMER: Le Centre Océanologique du Pacifique (Pacific Oceanographic Center),** which conducts research into black-pearl oysters, shrimp farming, and other means of extracting money from seawater. The buildings were formerly used for France's nuclear testing program.

The south-coast road ends at **Teahupoo,** the famous *village de surf* (surfing village) whose beachside park overlooks the big waves curling around Havaa Pass. World-class boarders compete in the Billabong Pro tournament here every May. A footbridge crosses the Tirahi River, where a trail begins along Tahiti Iti's rugged eastern shoreline. It's a strenuous and sometimes dangerous hike done only with a guide (see "Golf, Hiking & Watersports," later in this chapter).

THE SOUTH COAST OF TAHITI NUI

As you leave Taravao, heading back to Papeete along Tahiti's south coast, note that the PK markers begin to decrease the nearer you get to Papeete. The road rims casuarina-ringed **Port Phaeton,** which cuts nearly halfway across the isthmus. Port Phaeton and the **Bay of Tapueraha** to the south are Tahiti's finest harbors, yet European settlement and most development have taken place on the opposite side of the island, around Papeete. The shrimps you'll order for dinner come from the aqua farms in the bay's shallow waters.

TAHITI

5

THE CIRCLE ISLAND TOUR

Impressions

Tahiti has unique sex freedom. A bitter critic of the island has sneered that its charm is explainable solely in terms of the" erotic mist" that hangs over the island . . . .
I remember as a boy poring over the accounts of early navigators and coming repeatedly upon that cryptic phrase "so we put into Tahiti to refresh the men."
—James A. Michener, 1951

Fun Facts **R. L. S. Was Here**

Robert Louis Stevenson spent 2 months at Tautira in 1888, working on *The Master of Ballantrae,* a novel set not in Tahiti but in Scotland. Stevenson's mother was with him in Tautira. After she returned to London, she sent the local Protestant church a silver Communion service, which is still being used today.

PAPEARI

At PK 52 stands Tahiti's oldest village. Apparently the island's initial residents recognized the advantages of the south coast and its deep lagoons and harbors, for word-of-mouth history says they came through the Hotumatuu Pass in the reef and settled at **Papeari** sometime between A.D. 400 and 500. Robert Keable, author of *Simon Called Peter,* a bestselling novel about a disillusioned clergyman, lived here from 1924 until he died in 1928 at the age of 40. His home, now a private residence, stands at PK 55. Today, Papeari is a thriving village whose residents often sell fruits and vegetables at stands along the road.

MUSEE GAUGUIN (GAUGUIN MUSEUM) ★★★

At PK 51.2 is the entrance to the museum/memorial to Paul Gauguin, who lived near here from 1891 until 1893 (see "Tahiti's Top Attractions," earlier in this chapter). The museum sits in the lush **Harrison W. Smith Botanical Gardens,** started in 1919 by American Harrison Smith. The museum and gardens are open daily from 9am to 5pm. There's a snack bar here, but your best bet is to continue west.

VAIHIRIA RIVER & VAIPAHI GARDENS

At PK 48, in the village of Mataiea, the main road crosses the Vaihiria River. The new cross-island road from Papenoo on the north coast terminates here. An 11km (7.3-mile) track leads to **Lake Vaihiria,** at 465m (1,550 ft.) above sea level. It is Tahiti's only lake and is noted for its freshwater eels. Cliffs up to 900m (3,000 ft.) tall drop to the lake on its north side. Also in Mataiea is the lush **Jardin Vaipehi (Vaipehi Gardens),** a cool and refreshing spot with a bubbling natural spring and an oft-photographed waterfall (it's closer to the road than any other Tahitian waterfall). The garden is lush with elephant ears, tree ferns, ground orchids, jade vines, and other tropical vegetation. Signs (in French) explain its historical importance, since ancient Tahitian nobles followed the path to the springs in order to be spiritually purified.

ATIMAONO

At PK 41 begins the largest parcel of flat land on Tahiti, site of **Atimaono Golf Course,** French Polynesia's only links. Irishman William Stewart started a cotton plantation here during the American Civil War. Nothing remains of the plantation, but it was Stewart who brought the first Chinese indentured servants to Tahiti. See "Golf, Hiking & Watersports," below.

The knobby *noni* fruit's reputed medicinal properties have created a new industry in the islands, where folks are growing it by the boatload. You can see how it's turned into *noni* juice and other products at **Tahitian Noni International,** at PK 42.2 (© **80.37.50**). Tours are given on Friday by reservation only. Like castor oil, it must be good for you if it tastes this bad!

At PK 36, on the lagoon side of the road in Papara village, stands a Protestant church, under whose paved yard is buried **Dorence Atwater,** American consul to Tahiti after the Civil War. Captured while serving in the Union army, Atwater was assigned to the hospital at the infamous Confederate prisoner-of-war camp at Andersonville, Georgia, where he surreptitiously recorded the names of Union soldiers who died in captivity. He later escaped and brought his lists to the federal government, thus proving that the Confederacy was keeping inaccurate records. His action made him a hero in the eyes of the Union army. He eventually moved to the south coast of Tahiti, married a daughter of a chief of the Papara district, and at one time invested in William Stewart's cotton venture.

MARAA GROTTO

At PK 28.5, on Tahiti's southwest corner, the road turns sharply around the base of a series of headlands, which drop precipitously to the lagoon. Deep into one of these cliffs goes the **Maraa Grotto,** also called the Paroa Cave. It's actually two caves, both with water inside, and they go much deeper into the hill than appears at first glance. Park in the lot, not along the road, and enter at the gazebo to reach the larger of the two caves. A short trail leads from there to the smaller cave and a mini-waterfall.

THE WEST COAST OF TAHITI NUI

North of Maraa, the road runs through the Paea and Punaauia suburbs of Papeete. The west coast is the driest part of Tahiti, and it's very popular with Europeans, Americans, and others who have built homes along the lagoon and in the hills overlooking it and Moorea.

TAHITI

5

THE CIRCLE ISLAND TOUR

(Tips) Take a Circle Island Break

Shoehorned between the road and the sands of Maui Beach, **La Plage de Maui Restaurant** (© **74.71.74**) is my place to stop for refreshment while taking in the gorgeous scenery. Owners Rose Wilkinson and Alain Corre, both veterans of the Sofitel Moorea Beach Resort on Moorea, offer burgers, steaks, *poisson cru* (marinated fish), ice cream, and other temptations. Burgers cost about 800CFP (US$10/£5), while main courses range from 1,900CFP to 2,800CFP (US$24–US$35/£12–18). No credit cards, however. Open daily 10am to 6pm.

The Musée Gauguin has its own restaurant, but most circle island tour buses deposit their passengers for lunch at the lagoonside **Restaurant du Musée Gauguin,** at PK 50.5 (© **57.13.80**), which is worth a stop just for its phenomenal view of Tahiti Iti. The lunch buffet costs about 2,800CFP (US$35/£18) per person Monday through Saturday, 3,700CFP (US$46/£24) on Sunday; sandwiches are also available. Open daily from noon to 3pm.

A less expensive option is **Beach Burger,** at PK 39 (© **57.41.03**), west of the golf course at Atimaono. In addition to burgers, it serves salads, steaks, Chinese fare, and pizzas. Open Sunday through Thursday from 6am to 8pm, Friday and Saturday from 6am to 9:30pm.

The Moon & 21 Million Pounds

In 1891, a marginally successful Parisian painter named Paul Gauguin left behind his wife and six children and sailed to Tahiti. He wanted to devote himself to his art, free of the chains of civilization.

Instead of paradise, Gauguin found a world that suffered from some of the same maladies as the one from which he fled. Poverty, sickness, and frequent disputes with church and colonial officials marked his decade in the islands. He had syphilis, a bad heart, and an addiction to opium.

Gauguin disliked Papeete and spent his first 2 years in the rural Mataiea district, on Tahiti's south coast, where a village woman asked what he was doing there. Looking for a girl, he replied. The woman immediately offered her 13-year-old daughter, Tehaamana, the first of Gauguin's early teenage Tahitian mistresses. One of them bore him a son in 1899.

Tehaamana and the others figured prominently in Gauguin's Impressionist masterpieces, which brought fame to Tahiti but did little for his own pocketbook. After 649 paintings and a colorful career, immortalized by W. Somerset Maugham in *The Moon and Sixpence,* Gauguin died penniless in 1903.

At the time of his death, on Hiva Oa in the Marquesas Islands, a painting by Gauguin sold for 150 French francs. In 2007, his *L'Homme à la Hache* (Man at the Axe) sold for US$40.3 million (£21 million).

ARAHURAHU MARAE ★★

At PK 22.5, a small road on the right of Magasin Laut leads to a narrow valley, on the floor of which sits the restored **Arahurahu Marae** (see "Tahiti's Top Attractions," earlier in this chapter).

MUSEE DE TAHITI ET SES ISLES ★★★

At PK 15.1, turn left at the gas station and follow the signs through a residential area to the lagoon and the **Musée de Tahiti et Ses Isles (Museum of Tahiti and Her Islands),** one of the South Pacific's best museums (see "Tahiti's Top Attractions," earlier in this chapter).

PUNARUU VALLEY

On a cloudless day, you will have a view up the **Punaruu Valley** to the Diadème as you drive from the museum back to the main road. Power lines mar the view, but it's worth stopping to take a look. Tahitian rebels occupied the valley during the 1844 to 1848 war, and the French built a fort to keep them there (the site is now occupied by a television antenna). Later the valley was used to grow oranges, most of which were shipped to California. Villagers sell the now-wild fruit at roadside stands during July and August.

The Route 5 expressway goes as far south as the Punaruu River, just north of the Tahiti Museum. Instead of taking the overpass onto the expressway, stay in the right lane to the traffic circle under the overpass. The first exit off the circle will take you up into the Punaruu Valley. The second exit leads to the Route 5 expressway. The third is Route 1, the old two-lane coast road, which will take you to the Lagoonarium.

I was born to see sights, and no matter how many times I visit French Polynesia, I never tire of its incredible natural beauty. I always spend sunset of my first day on Tahiti's west coast, depleting my camera battery as the sun paints another glorious red-and-orange sky over Moorea's purple ridges. The InterContinental Resort Tahiti and the Restaurant Pink Coconut are my favorite places to watch (see "Where to Stay," and "Where to Dine," respectively, later in this chapter). The sun sets between 5:30 and 6:30pm here, so get there in time.

THE LAGOONARIUM

At PK 11.4, the **Captain Bligh Restaurant and Bar** has a terrific view of Moorea and is home to the **Lagoonarium de Tahiti,** an underwater viewing room (see "Tahiti's Top Attractions," earlier in this chapter).

After the Lagoonarium, Route 1 soon joins the four-lane Route 5 expressway, which passes shopping centers and marinas in Punaauia. It splits just before the Sofitel Tahiti Maeva Beach Resort. The left lanes feed into the Route 5 expressway, which roars back to Papeete. The right lanes take you along Route 1, the old road that goes past the west-coast hotels and the Tahiti-Faaa International Airport before returning to town.

ORGANIZED TOURS AROUND THE COASTAL ROAD

Several companies offer tours along the coastal road around Tahiti Nui. They are a good way to see the island without hassling with traffic. I find them to be an especially fine way to recover from jet lag.

I prefer English-speaking William Leteeg's **Adventure Eagle Tours** (✆ **77.20.03**). William takes you around in an air-conditioned van and lends his experiences growing up on the island to his commentaries. Others include **Tahiti Tours** (✆ **54.02.50;** www.tahiti-tours.com), **Tahiti Nui Travel** (✆ **42.40.10;** www.tahiti-nui.com), and **Marama Tours** (✆ **50.74.74;** www.maramatours.com). They have reservations desks in several hotels. Expect to pay about 4,400CFP (US$55/£28) for a half-day tour, 5,100CFP (US$64/£32) for all day, plus entrance fees to the museums and other attractions and lunch, usually at the Restaurant du Musée Gauguin.

For a spectacular bird's-eye view of Tahiti or Moorea, take a sightseeing ride with **Polynesia Hélicoptères** (✆ **54.87.20;** www.polynesia-helicopter.com). The flights are anything but inexpensive, but if you can afford it, they are well worth the price of about 16,300CFP (US$204/£103) for a flight over Tahiti Nui, 33,700CFP (US$421/£212) for a flight over Tahiti Iti, or 26,300CFP (US$329/£165) for a spectacular view of Moorea. Those fares are per person, with a minimum of four passengers required. The flights last between 20 and 45 minutes, depending on where you go. Reserve as far in advance as possible.

5 SAFARI EXPEDITIONS ★★★

So-called safari expeditions into Tahiti's interior allow for a very different view of the island—and some spectacular views at that. Riding in the back of open, four-wheel-drive vehicles, you follow narrow, often unpaved roads through Tahiti's central crater, usually

Marlon's Mana

The late Marlon Brando did more than star in the remake of *Mutiny on the Bounty* when he came to Tahiti in 1960. He fell in love with his beautiful Tahitian co-star, Tarita Terepaia, the 19-year-old daughter of a Bora Bora fisherman. At first Tarita reportedly wasn't attracted to the then-dashing actor, but his good looks and charm must have won out, for she later became his wife and the mother of two of his children.

Brando also fell for Tetiaroa, an atoll 42km (25 miles) north of Tahiti and Moorea. In the old days, this cluster of 12 flat islets surrounding an aquamarine lagoon was the playground of Tahiti's high chiefs, who frequently were joined by the *Arioi,* traveling bands of sexually explicit entertainers and practitioners of infanticide (see "The Islanders," in chapter 2). High-ranking women would spend months doing a bit of makeover on Tetiaroa, resting in the shade to lighten their skin and gorging on starchy foods to broaden their girth. Men and women of a chiefly rank were said to possess the mystical power called *mana* by the ancient Polynesians, and the bigger the body, the more the *mana.*

For a time, a British dentist who married into the royal family owned Tetiaroa, but it was abandoned when Brando bought it in 1966. He turned one of his islets into a refuge for Tetiaroa's thousands of seabirds. He built a retreat for himself on a second islet and a small, rather rustic resort on a third.

Guests at the resort would seldom see the actor, on whose waistline Tetiaroa apparently worked its expansive magic. During the day, he would stay at home in the shade, playing with his radios and computers. At night, he would go fishing and lobstering.

A series of hurricanes almost blew his resort away in 1983, and Brando's relationship with Tahiti turned to human disaster a decade later when his son Christian—by his first wife, actress Anna Kashfi—shot and killed the boyfriend of his half-sister, Cheyenne, in Brando's Hollywood home. A year later, Cheyenne, then 25, hanged herself at Tarita's home on Tahiti. Brando did not attend her funeral; in fact, he never again returned to Tahiti.

Ex-wife Tarita operated the resort, mostly as a day-trip and weekend destination from Tahiti, until shortly before Brando's death in 2004. Richard Bailey, a long-time family friend and developer of the InterContinental Resort Tahiti and other hotels here, has announced plans to build an upmarket, environmentally friendly resort on Tetiaroa.

via the breathtaking Papenoo Valley. Weather permitting, you'll reach altitudes of 1,440m (4,800 ft.) on the sides of the island's steep interior crater, and in clear conditions you may even cross the island (on the full-day versions of the trip, that is). The cool temperatures at the higher elevations are refreshing, as is a swim in a cold mountain stream.

Tahiti Safari Expedition (© 42.14.15; www.tahiti-safari.com) has been around since owner Patrice Bordes pioneered the concept in 1990. He charges about 5,500CFP

> **ⓘ Tips** **Touring Tahiti from Moorea . . . & Vice Versa**
>
> You can take a circle island tour or safari expedition of Tahiti even if you're stay-ing on Moorea. Catch an early flight or ferry to Papeete, go on the tour or safari expedition, and return to Moorea in the late afternoon. Let the tour companies know you're coming from Moorea when you make your reservation so they can meet you at the airport or ferry dock. If you do it yourself, the rental-car compa-nies can have a vehicle waiting on Tahiti.
>
> By the same token, I would spend a day on Moorea even if I had a short lay-over on Tahiti. You can easily arrange it yourself by ferry or plane, but you will need a rental vehicle on Moorea (Avis or Europcar will have one waiting for you at the Moorea airport or ferry dock). An alternative is to take a Moorea day tour, such as those offered by **Tahiti Nui Travel** (ⓒ **54.02.00;** www.tahitinuitravel. com) and **Marama Tours** (ⓒ **50.74.74;** www.maramatours.com). They charge between 15,000CFP and 28,500CFP (US$188–US$356/£95–£180), depending on whether you fly or take the ferry and whether you simply take a circle island tour or go on a picnic on a small island, an inland safari tour, or a dolphin-watching excursion. Call or book at any hotel activities desk.

(US$69/£35) per person for a half-day trip, 9,500CFP (US$119/£60) for a full day. Another good operator is Arnaud Lucioni of **Natura Exploration** (ⓒ **43.03.83** or 79.31.21). Both Patrice and Arnaud speak French and English. They usually stop for lunch at **Relais de la Maroto** (ⓒ **57.90.29**), or you can bring your own picnic. Don't forget your bathing suit, a towel, hat, sunscreen, insect repellent, and camera. These are popular trips with limited space, so reserve as early as possible at any hotel activities desk.

6 GOLF, HIKING & WATERSPORTS

GOLF

Tahiti's mountainous interior provides a spectacular backdrop to the 27-hole **Olivier Breaud International Golf Course of Atimaono,** PK 40.2 (ⓒ **57.43.41**), which sprawls over the site of William Stewart's 1860s cotton plantation. A clubhouse, pro shop, restau-rant, bar, locker rooms, showers, a swimming pool, a spa pool, and a driving range are on the premises. The club is open daily from 8am until dark. Greens fees are about 5,500CFP (US$69/£35) for 18 holes. The hotel activities desks can book all-day golf outings for about 24,000CFP (US$300/£151) for one golfer, 35,000CFP (US$438/£222) for two, including greens fees, equipment, lunch, and transportation.

HIKING

Tahiti has a number of hiking trails, such as the cross-island Papenoo Valley–Lake Vaihiria route. Another ascends to the top of Mount Aorai, and another skirts the remote and wild eastern coast of Tahiti Iti. This is not the Shenandoah or some other American or New Zealand national park with well-marked trails, and the French gendarmes do not take kindly to rescuing tourists who become lost trying to scale one of Tahiti's peaks.

ⓘ Tips **Pick a Clear Day**

The safari expeditions do not go into the mountains when the weather is bad, and even if it's not raining, clouds atop the mountains can obscure what would otherwise be some fantastic views. It's best, therefore, to pick as clear a day as possible for this thrilling outing. Your best chance for that will be during the drier austral winter, June through early September.

Downpours can occur in the higher altitudes, swelling the streams that most trails follow, and the nights can become bitterly cold and damp. The side of the island that's rainy can shift from one day to the next, depending on which way the wind blows. In addition, the quick-growing tropical foliage can quickly obscure a path that was easily followed a few days before. Permits are required to use some trails that cross government land.

Accordingly, always go with a guide or on organized hikes such as those offered by **Tahiti Evasion** (ⓒ **56.48.77;** www.tahitievasion.com). This Moorea-based company has all-day treks into the Fautaua valley, home of Loti's Pool; the Orofero Valley on Tahiti's south coast; and to the top of Mount Aorai, the island's third-highest peak. The treks start at 5,200CFP (US$65/£33) per person. Hikes along the wild, uninhabited east coast of Tahiti Iti take 3 days and 2 nights of camping (call for prices). All except the Mount Aorai climb are rated as easy walks. Tahiti Evasion will also organize hiking-and-watersports trips of up to 3 weeks throughout the islands.

You can also check with the **Tourisme Tahiti's visitors bureau** in Papeete (ⓒ **50. 57.12**) for the names of guides and hiking clubs.

WATERSPORTS

Based at the InterContinental Resort Tahiti, **Aquatica Dive Centre and Nautical Activities** (ⓒ **53.34.96;** www.aquatica-dive.com) offers the most comprehensive list of watersports activities, and you don't have to be an InterContinental guest to partake. Some sample prices: snorkeling gear rental, 2,000CFP (US$25/£13); snorkeling trips, 4,000CFP (US$50/£25); water-skiing, 6,500CFP (US$81/£42); and kayak rental, 1,800CFP (US$23/£12) per hour. A two-tank dive including equipment and a guide costs 12,000CFP (US$150/£76); and introductory dive, 7,000CFP (US$88/£44). Aquatica also has tours by jet ski and all-terrain vehicles for 19,400CFP (US$243/£123) and 20,600CFP (US$258/£132) per person, respectively. Also contact them about dolphin- and whale-watching tours.

SCUBA DIVING Tahiti is not in the same diving league as the other French Polynesian islands. You can see plenty of smaller fish here, but don't expect daily encounters with sharks, rays, and other large creatures, which are plentiful around the other islands. The popular dive sites are on the west coast of Tahiti Nui, from Papeete down to Punaauia, and off the southern coast of Tahiti Nui. The **Aquarium,** near the end of the Faaa airport runway, and in clear view of Moorea, attracts both divers and snorkelers to see fish swimming around coral heads and several wrecks, including a small aircraft (it didn't crash; it was moved here in the 1990s). Nearby are another aircraft and the hulks of two cargo vessels.

With the exception of **Aquatica Dive Centre and Nautical Activities,** at the InterContinental Resort Tahiti (see above), and **TOPdive Tahiti,** based at the Sheraton Hotel

Tahiti Resort & Spa (© **83.51.26;** www.topdive.com), Tahiti's dive operators cater primarily to local residents, which means you should bring your own equipment. It also helps if you can speak French. Go to Eleuthera Plongee Tahiti's website, **www.dive-tahiti.com,** for more information.

SNORKELING & SWIMMING   Most beaches on Tahiti have black volcanic sand, not the white variety most of us expect in the South Pacific. The most convenient of these is the public beach in front of **Hotel Le Royal Tahitien** (© **50.40.40),** in Pirae 4km (2¹/₂ miles) east of downtown (see "Where to Stay," below). There is some white sand among the pebbles at the **PK 18.5 Plage de Publique (Public Beach),** on the west coast at the Punaauia-Paea border. It has a restaurant and snack bar. The best beach of all is **Plage de Maui** on Tahiti Iti (see "The Tahiti Iti Peninsula: The South Coast to Teahupoo" under "The Circle Island Tour," earlier in this chapter). It's a long haul, but its white sands, clear lagoon, and snack bar make it worth the trip.

SURFING   Tahiti is famous for world-class surfing, especially Teuhupo'o on Tahiti Iti, home of the annual Billabong Pro championships in May. The best big waves crash on jagged reefs offshore, however, so you could be turned into hamburger meat if you've never surfed before. On the other hand, Tahiti is the only major South Pacific island where surf breaks on sandy beaches, upon which **Ecole de Surf Tura'i Mataare (Tahiti Surf School)** (© **41.91.37;** www.tahitisurfschool.info) teaches a half-day of surfing and bodyboarding courses for 4,800CFP (US$60/£30), or you can take private lessons for 12,000CFP (US$150/£76). It's a good way to find out if you have what it takes to "hang ten."

---

7 SHOPPING

There's no shortage of things to buy on Tahiti, especially in Papeete. Black pearls and handicrafts are sure to tempt you. The selection is widest here, but prices on some items may be better on Moorea.

If you just can't live without visiting a modern shopping mall, head for the **Centre Moana Nui,** on the main road in Punaauia about .5km (¹/₄ mile) south of the Sofitel Tahiti Maeva Beach Resort. Here you'll find a huge Carrefour supermarket, several boutiques, a snack bar with excellent hamburgers, a hairdresser, a bar, banks with ATMs, and a post office (open Mon–Fri 8am–5pm, Sat 8am–noon). The local **Centre Artisinant** stands across the parking lot under a tepee-shaped roof (see "Handicrafts," below).

Duty-free shopping is very limited, with French perfumes the best deal. **Duty Free Tahiti** (© **42.61.61),** on the street-level waterside of the Centre Vaima, is the largest duty-free shop. Its specialties are Seiko, Lorus, and Cartier watches and Givenchy, Yves St. Laurent, Chanel, and Guerlain perfumes. The **airport departure lounge** has two duty-free shops.

BLACK PEARLS
Papeete has scores of *bijouteries* (jewelry shops) that carry black pearls in a variety of settings. Some stalls in Papeete's Municipal Market sell pearls, but give them a pass and buy yours from an experienced, reputable dealer. Most of these stores are in or around the Centre Vaima, along boulevard Pomare, and in the Quartier du Commerce, the narrow streets off boulevard Pomare between rue Paul Gauguin and rue d'Ecole des Frères north of the Municipal Market.

Buying Your Black Pearl

French Polynesia is the world's largest producer of black pearls. They are cultured by implanting a small nucleus into the shell of a live *Pinctada margaritifera,* the oyster used here, which then coats it with nacre, the same lustrous substance that lines the mother-of-pearl shell. The nacre produces dark pearls known as "black" but whose actual color ranges from slightly grayer than white to black with shades of rose or green. Most range in size from 10 to 17 millimeters (slightly less than $1/2$ to slightly less than $3/4$ in.).

Size, color, luster, lack of imperfections, and shape determine a pearl's value. No two are exactly alike, but the most valuable are the larger ones that are most symmetrical and have few dark blemishes, and whose color is dark with the shades of a peacock showing through a bright luster. A top-quality pearl 13 millimeters or larger will sell for 960,000CFP (US$12,000/£6,000) or more, but there are thousands to choose from in the 24,000CFP to 80,000CFP (US$300–US$1,000/£150–£500) range. Some small, imperfect-but-still-lovely pearls cost much less.

Of course, the perfect pearl comes down to the eye of the beholder. Just make sure you see your dream pearl in daylight before handing over your credit card.

So many pearls were being produced a few years ago that many small pearl farms closed. Competition is still fierce among the islands' shops (or their agents—commissioned tour guides and bus and taxi drivers), some of which will bombard you with sales pitches almost from the moment you arrive. Pearls are sold at stands in the Tahiti Municipal Market (see "Tahiti's Top Attractions," earlier in this chapter), and even on the street. I would buy only at the stores I recommend in this book, which sell pearls that have been inspected and X-rayed (to determine the thickness of their nacre) by the local marine resources department.

Even at the highest-end shops, discounting is de rigueur. Despite the general rule to avoid haggling in French Polynesia, you shouldn't pay the price marked on a pearl or a piece of jewelry until you have politely asked for a discount.

With most tourists now spending minimum time on Tahiti in favor of the other islands, you might find pearl prices in Papeete to be lower than on Moorea and Bora Bora. That's not always the case, so you should look in shops like **Ron Hall's Island Fashion Black Pearls** (on Moorea) and **Matira Pearls** (on Bora Bora) before making a purchase in Papeete (see "Shopping" in chapters 6 and 9, respectively). Your salespersons in these shops are more likely to speak English fluently.

You can get a **refund** of the 16% **value added tax** (TVA) included in the price of set pearls (but not on loose pearls). The TVA is not added after the purchase like an American sales tax, so you won't see it. Don't believe them if they say you can't get a refund because they've already taken the TVA off a reduced price. Truth is, they'll have to send the government 16% of whatever price you paid. Ask your dealer how to get your money back by sending them an official form after you have left the country (you can mail it after clearing Immigration at Faaa).

Your beginning point should be the **Musée de la Perle Robert Wan** (© **46.15.54**), on boulevard Pomare at rue l'Arthémise, opposite Eglise Evangélique (Protestant Church). Named for Robert Wan, the man who pioneered the local industry back in the 1960s, this museum explains the history of pearls from antiquity, the method by which they are cultured, and the things to look for when making your selection. The museum is open Monday to Saturday from 9am to 5pm. Admission is free.

Adjoining the museum, **Robert Wan Tahiti** (© **46.15.54**) carries only excellent-quality pearls and uses only 18-karat gold for its settings, so the prices tend to be high. Robert Wan has outlets on all the main islands.

On the second level of the Centre Vaima, **Sibani Perles Joallier** (© **41.36.34**) carries the jewelry line of Didier Sibani, another pioneer of the local industry. European-style elegance is the theme here and at the other Sibani outlets throughout the islands.

One of French Polynesia's largest dealers, **Tahia Collins,** has a small outlet on boulevard Pomare at avenue du Prince Hinoi (© **54.06.00**). Another large dealer is **Tahiti Pearl Market,** on rue Collette at rue Paul Gauguin (© **54.30.60**).

HANDICRAFTS

Although most of the inexpensive souvenir items sold here are made in Asia, many local residents, especially on the outer islands, produce a wide range of seashell jewelry, rag dolls, needlework, and straw hats, mats, baskets, and handbags. I love the *tivaivai,* colorful appliqué quilts stitched together by Tahitian women as their great-grandmothers were shown by the early missionaries. You can also buy exquisite shell chandeliers like those adorning many hotel lobbies.

The most popular item by far is the cotton *pareu,* or wraparound sarong, which everyone wears at one time or another. They are screened, blocked, or printed by hand in the colors of the rainbow. The same material is made into other tropical clothing and various items such as bedspreads and pillowcases. *Pareus* are sold virtually everywhere a visitor might wander.

The **Papeete Municipal Market** ★★★ is the place to shop (see "Tahiti's Top Attractions," earlier in this chapter). It has stalls both upstairs and on the surrounding sidewalk, where local women's associations sell a wide selection of handicrafts at reasonable prices. The market is one of the few places where you can regularly find *pareus* for 1,000CFP (US$13/£6.50), bedspreads made of the colorful tie-dyed and silk-screened *pareu* material, and *tivaivai* quilts. By and large, cloth goods are sold at the sidewalk stalls; those upstairs have a broader range of shell jewelry and other items.

Several villages have *centres artisanats,* where local women display their wares. The one in Punaauia, in the Centre Moana Nui parking lot south of the Sofitel Tahiti Maeva Beach Resort, is the best place to look for *tivaivai* quilts, which sell for about 35,000CFP (US$438/£220).

TAHITI

5

SHOPPING

Impressions

It's a comfort to get into a pareu when one gets back from town . . . I should strongly recommend you to adopt it. It's one of the most sensible costumes I have ever come across. It's cool, convenient, and inexpensive.

—W. Somerset Maugham, "The Fall of Edward Bernard," 1921

For finer-quality handicrafts, such as woodcarvings from the Marquesas Islands, shell chandeliers, tapa lampshades, or mother-of-pearl shells, try **Tamara Curios,** on rue du Général-de-Gaulle in Fare Tony (© **42.54.42**).

TROPICAL CLOTHING

You've arrived in Tahiti and you notice that everyone under the sun is wearing print sundresses or flowered aloha shirts. Where do you go to get yours?

Each hotel has at least one boutique carrying tropical clothing, including *pareus*. The prices there reflect the heavy tourist traffic, but they aren't much worse than at the stores in Papeete. Clothing, to put it bluntly, is dear in French Polynesia.

On boulevard Pomare, stop in **Marie Ah You** (© **42.03.31**) and **Aloha Boutique** (© **42. 87.52**), both in the block west of the Vaima Centre. Their selections for women are trendy and a bit expensive.

Maohi Art, in Fare Tony on boulevard Pomare just west of the Vaima Centre (© **42. 97.43**), specializes in block-printed traditional designs (as opposed to the swirls and swooshes with leaves and flowers popular on most *pareus*). Its designs are the most unique in town.

8 WHERE TO STAY

With a few exceptions, Tahiti's accommodations are in four areas: on the west coast, where most properties enjoy at least a partial view of Moorea; in Faaa opposite the airport; in the suburbs east of Papeete, where the beaches are of black volcanic sand; and in the city of Papeete, where you can sample urban life *à la Tahitien*. Consider staying at one of the west-coast, Faaa, or Papeete city hotels if you're stopping here for just a night on your way to or from the other islands or a cruise ship. This is especially true if your connecting flight departs during the horrendous traffic of a weekday morning or evening rush hour.

THE WEST COAST
EXPENSIVE

InterContinental Resort Tahiti ★★★   This is the best all-around resort on Tahiti. Built in the 1960s as the Tahiti Beachcomber Travelodge (most folks here still call it "the Beachcomber"), it sits at Tataa Point on the island's northwest corner, from whence souls supposedly leapt to the ancient Polynesian homeland. Today, planes leap into the air from the nearby airport at Faaa, although the infrequent jet noise seldom penetrates the rooms here. It has a range of accommodations, including smaller rooms dating from its original Travelodge incarnation, newer and more spacious "Panoramic" rooms, and overwater bungalows with unimpeded views of Moorea. Whatever the vintage, all units now are luxuriously appointed with the likes of canopy beds and marble bathrooms, and all have private patios or balconies with views of Moorea. The original overwater units are smaller than newer models on the resort's south end, which have separate sitting areas and steps leading from their decks into the lagoon.

The resort doesn't have a natural beach, but bulkheads separate the sea from white imported sand. Or you can frolic in two pools—one in a large complex sitting lagoonside before the main building, or the other smaller pool with water cascading over its horizon (and apparently into the lagoon). The latter is adjacent to the romantic **Le Lotus,** one of Tahiti's best restaurants (see "Where to Dine," later in this chapter). Features here include

0 — 3 mi
0 — 3 km

Point Venus

Matavai Bay

○ Mahina **1**

○ Orofara

2 2

○ Pirae   ○ Arue

Moorea Ferry
← To Moorea
(12 miles)

3 ★ PAPEETE

Faaa Airport ✈

4

Rte. 5 Freeway

5
6
○ Faaa
6

See Papeete
Accommodations
& Dining map

7
8

Rte. 5 Freeway

9
10
11

S e a   o f   t h e   M o o n

Punaruu River

Mt. Aorai ▲

The Diademe ▲   Mt. Orohena ▲

Papenoo River

○ Punaauia

12

13
13

14

Area of detail

PK 18.5
Plage ↖

○ Paea

★ Papeete

TAHITI NUI

SOUTH PACIFIC OCEAN

0 — 10 mi
0 — 10 km

TAHITI ITI

SOUTH PACIFIC OCEAN

✈ Airport
↖ Beach
- - - Ferry
.... Reef

Point Maraa

15

○ Papara

○ Atimaono

ACCOMMODATIONS ■

Hiti Moana Villa **15**
Hotel Le Royal Tahitien **2**
InterContinental Resort Tahiti **6**
Le Meridien Tahiti **13**
Radisson Plaza Resort Tahiti **1**
Sheraton Hotel Tahiti & Spa **3**
Sofitel Tahiti Maeva Beach Resort **7**
Taaroa Lodge **14**
Tahiti Airport Lodge **5**
Tahiti Airport Motel **5**

DINING ◆

Captain Bligh Restaurant
  and Bar **9**
Casa Bianca **8**
Le Belvédère **4**
Le Carré **13**
Le Cignalon/Pacific
  Burger **12**

Le Lotus **6**
Le Royal Tahitien
  Restaurant **2**
Restaurant Blue
  Banana **9**
Restaurant Pink
  Coconut **8**
Western Grill **11**

an all-night lobby bar, and Tahiti's top watersports center. I love to stay here between jaunts to the outer islands because I can clean my dirty clothes in the free washers and dryers, a real money-saver given the exorbitant cost of laundry services (buy your soap powder before the boutique closes at 7pm). Another plus: The lobby bar serves coffee and snacks all night.

B.P. 6014, 98702 Faaa (8km/5 miles west of Papeete). Ⓒ **800/327-0200** or 86.51.10. Fax 86.51.30. www. tahiti.interconti.com. 214 units. 30,000CFP–44,000CFP (US$375–US$550/£189–£277) double; 79,500CFP– 88,000CFP (US$994–US$1,100/£986–£1,091) suite; 50,000CFP–106,000CFP (US$625–US$1,325/£315– £668) overwater bungalow. AE, DC, MC, V. **Amenities:** 2 restaurants; 2 bars; 2 outdoor pools; tennis courts; health club; Jacuzzi; watersports equipment rentals; concierge; activities desk; car-rental desk; salon; 24-hr. room service; 24-hr. business center w/high-speed Internet access; massage; babysitting; laundry service; coin-op washers and dryers. *In room:* A/C, TV, high-speed dataport, minibar, coffeemaker, hair dryer, iron, safe.

Le Meridien Tahiti ★★ Near the Museum of Tahiti and Her Islands, this luxury resort sits alongside one of Tahiti's few white-sand beaches. It's an excellent choice— provided you don't have to get to Tahiti-Faaa International Airport to catch a flight during the weekday morning traffic jam, when the usual 15-minute ride can take considerably longer. The Melanesian-inspired architecture is stunning, with swayback shingle roofs evoking the "spirit houses" of Papua New Guinea. Imported sand surrounding the wade-in pool augments the pebbly beach and shallow lagoon here. The best accommodations are 12 overwater bungalows, but note that unlike most others, they have neither glass panels in their floors for fish-watching nor steps into the lagoon from their porches, nor are all of them air-conditioned. All of the luxuriously appointed guest quarters have balconies, but try to get a north-facing unit for a Moorea view. Le Meridien provides complimentary *le truck* shuttles into Papeete twice a day and on two evenings a week. **Le Carré** (p. 135) is one of the best resort dining rooms in French Polynesia. A shopping center next door has a grocery store, hairdresser, pharmacy, post office, restaurants, and a patisserie for inexpensive breakfasts.

B.P. 380595, 98718 Punaauia (15km/9 miles south of Papeete, 8km/5 miles south of the airport). Ⓒ **800/ 225-5843** or 47.07.07. Fax 47.07.08. www.starwoodtahiti.com. 150 units. 35,000CFP (US$438/£220) double; 45,000CFP–85,000CFP (US$563–US$1,063/£282–£532) suite; 50,000CFP (US$625/£313) overwater bungalow. AE, DC, MC, V. **Amenities:** 2 restaurants; 2 bars; outdoor pool; tennis court; health club; watersports equipment/rentals; concierge; activities desk; car-rental desk; 24-hr. room service; babysitting; laundry service; Wi-Fi. *In room:* A/C, TV, dataport, minibar, coffeemaker, hair dryer, iron, safe.

Sofitel Tahiti Maeva Beach Resort (Value) Known for several years as the Sofitel Tahiti Resort, this seven-story building resembling a modern version of a terraced Mayan pyramid resides beside the gray sands of Maeva Beach. The murky lagoon off the beach

---

 It Pays to Shop for Room Rates

Like many big hotels these days, those in French Polynesia adjust their room rates according to such factors as the season and how many guests they expect to have on a given day, and many offer Internet specials on their websites. Accordingly, their published "rack rates"—which I am compelled to give in this book—are nearly meaningless. Be sure to check the hotel websites for discounts and other specials. See also "Tips on Accommodations" (p. 83).

isn't as good for swimming and snorkeling as it is for anchoring numerous yachts, whose masts slice the beach's view of Moorea. Equipped with modern European amenities (the bright, lime-green bathrooms nearly blinded me), the smallish rooms open to balconies. Odd-numbered rooms on the upper floors on the north (or "beach") side have views of Moorea, while those on the garden side look south along Tahiti's west coast. The Sofitel is good value by Tahiti standards, but don't expect the same amount of space, luxuries, or amenities as at the InterContinental Resort Tahiti or Le Meridien. I like staying here because I can walk to the big Carrefour supermarket and inexpensive snack bars in Centre Moana Nui in less than 10 minutes.

B.P. 6008, 98702 Faaa (7.5km/4 miles west of Papeete). (C) **800/763-4835** or 86.66.00. Fax 41.05.05. www. accorhotels.pf. 230 units. 21,700CFP–24,300CFP (US$271–US$304/£137–£153) double; 37,100CFP (US$464/£234) suite. AE, DC, MC, V. **Amenities:** 2 restaurants; 2 bars; outdoor pool; tennis courts; watersports equipment rentals; concierge; activities desk; car-rental desk; limited room service; babysitting; laundry service. In room: A/C, TV, minibar, high-speed dataport, coffeemaker, hair dryer, iron, safe.

MODERATE

Slated to open in 2009 is **Manava Suite Resort,** a lagoonside hotel in Punaauia, just south of where the highway splits from the old coastal road. All but 12 of the 121 units will have kitchens, and about a third will have direct views of Moorea. Check it out at http://manavasuiteresorttahiti.blogspot.com or contact South Pacific Management ((C) **800/ 657-3275;** www.pearlresorts.com).

Hiti Moana Villa ★   Beside the lagoon in Papara, on the south coast, this is one of Tahiti's better pensions. The English-speaking Brothersen family keeps everything running smoothly, and son Steve will take you fishing and on guided tours of the island. Half the units here are standard government-issue bungalows with one room for living and sleeping, an attached bathroom to the rear, and a front porch. One of these faces the lagoon, as do two other Mediterranean-style "villa" units with separate bedrooms and their own kitchens. These villas open to a lagoonside swimming pool, which makes up for the lack of a beach. A pier extends over the lagoon, where a wire enclosure traps a school of trevally fish. Guests here get free use of kayaks. Breakfast is available.

B.P. 20055, 98718 Papara (PK 32 in Papara). (C) **57.93.93.** Fax 57.94.44. www.papeete.com/moanavilla. 8 units. 10,000CFP–14,500CFP (US$125–US$181/£63–£92) double. Discounts for 2 nights or more. AE, MC, V. **Amenities:** Outdoor pool; complimentary kayaks; coin-op washer and dryer. In room: TV, kitchen (4 units), no phone.

INEXPENSIVE

Taaroa Lodge   Avid surfer Ralph Sanford bought the two bungalows at his humble lagoonside establishment in ritzy Paea as prefabricated kits in New Zealand; hence, they are larger and have more character than the cookie-cutter *fares* found at most small family-run establishments here. Their porches also present million-dollar views of Moorea, especially the one sitting beside the bulkhead along the lagoon. Each has a kitchen, TV, and ceiling fan. Behind them, an A-frame chalet houses a room with a double bed downstairs and a six-bed dormitory in the loft. The communal kitchen stays busy, as do Ralph's free kayaks (bring your own snorkeling gear). Grocery stores and snack bars are short walks away. In my opinion, this place has the top backpacker accommodations on Tahiti, even if you do have to stay at least 2 nights.

B.P. 498, 98713 Papeete (PK 18.2 in Punaauia). (C)/fax **58.39.21.** www.taaroalodge.com. 1 room, 2 bungalows, 6 dorm beds (shared bathroom). 6,000CFP (US$75/£38) double; 10,000CFP (US$125/£63) bungalow;

2,500CFP (US$31/£16) dorm bed. Rates include breakfast. MC, V. 2-night minimum stay. **Amenities:** Communal kitchen; free kayaks. *In room (bungalows only):* TV, kitchen, coffeemaker, no phone.

IN FAAA

Tahiti Airport Lodge   Perched on the side of a hill in the Cité de l'Air housing development above the airport, Charlie and Margarite Bredin's simple but clean and friendly bed-and-breakfast commands a spectacular view of Moorea from its lovely, open-air guest lounge. Unfortunately, you won't get this view from any of the rather dark rooms, which range from ample motel-size units with king-size beds and private bathrooms down to tiny shared-bathroom units barely big enough to accommodate a double bed. All rooms have fans and electric mosquito deterrents, and all showers dispense hot water. The house is a steep, 5-minute climb from the round-island road, but Charlie will pick you up from the airport or the bus stop. Charlie and Margarite speak English as well as French.

B.P. 2580, 98713 Papeete (PK 5.5, opposite Tahiti-Faaa International Airport). © **82.23.68.** Fax 82.25.00. 10 units (4 w/bathroom). 6,000CFP–8,000CFP (US$75–US$100/£38–£50) double. Rates include breakfast and airport transfers. No credit cards. *In room:* No phone.

Tahiti Airport Motel   Literally carved into a hill directly across Route 1 from the airport terminal, this three-story, walk-up hotel has simply furnished but reasonably comfortable rooms. A communal balcony across the front overlooks the airport and Moorea on the horizon. Although lacking in facilities, this is a convenient and relatively cost-conscious place to sleep off your overnight flight getting here, or to wait for a late-night departure going home. The hotel provides free coffee round-the-clock and sells continental breakfast packs, but it does not provide airport transfers, so you'll have to rent a car, take a taxi, or make the steep climb uphill. The vehicular entry is off route St. Hillare, the road linking the airport to the Route 5 freeway. Restaurants and shops are steps away.

B.P. 2407, 98713 Papeete (PK 5.7, opposite Tahiti-Faaa International Airport). © **50.40.00.** Fax 50.40.01. www.tahitiairportmotel.com. 42 units. 12,800CFP–22,000CFP (US$160–US$275/£81–£140) double. AE, MC, V. **Amenities:** Wi-Fi. *In room:* A/C, TV, fridge, coffeemaker.

EAST OF PAPEETE

Hotel Le Royal Tahitien ★★ (Value)   One of the top values in French Polynesia, this American-owned hotel is the only moderately priced place on the island with its own beach, a stretch of deep black sand from which its suburban neighbors fish and swim. And longtime Australian-born manager Lionel Kennedy (a die-hard baseball fan) and his English-speaking staff are Tahiti's best when it comes to friendly, personalized service. Sitting in an expansive lawn and lush garden traversed by a small stream, the swimming pool sports a Jacuzzi and a waterfall cascading over rocks. The spacious guest rooms are in contemporary two-story wood-and-stone buildings that look like an American condominium complex. Colorful bedspreads and seat cushions add an island ambience to the rooms, however, and the Tropics definitely pervade **Le Royal Tahitien Restaurant** (p. 137), a fine, moderately priced establishment with a 1937-vintage thatched ceiling. Both the beachside restaurant and adjacent bar are popular with local businesspeople. A local band plays on Friday and Saturday evenings. Your fellow guests are likely to be businesspersons living on the other islands and travelers who have made their own arrangements (that is, few groups stay here). It's very popular, so reserve as soon as possible. As with the Radisson Plaza (see

below), you will need to rent a car or take a taxi if going downtown after dark, since the
last local bus passes here about 5pm.

B.P. 5001, 98716 Pirae (4km/2¹/₂ miles east of downtown). 𝒞 **213/878-0283** in the U.S. or 50.40.40. Fax 50.40.41. www.hotelroyaltahitien.com. 40 units. 18,000CFP (US$225/£113) double. AE, DC, MC, V. Take a Mahina bus or follow av. Prince Hinoi to the Total and Mobil stations opposite each other; turn around at next traffic circle and return; turn right to hotel. **Amenities:** Restaurant; bar; outdoor pool; Jacuzzi; laundry service. *In room:* A/C, TV, fridge, coffeemaker.

Radisson Plaza Resort Tahiti ★   This modern resort opened in 2004 beside the deep black sands of Lafayette Beach on Matavai Bay, where the 18th-century explorers dropped anchor. A huge, turtle-shaped thatched roof covers most of the central complex, which holds a restaurant, bar, arts-and-crafts center, full-service spa, and a cozy library devoted to author James Norman Hall. Outside is a horizon-edge pool beside the beach. Currents create an undertow here, so heed the dangerous sea signs when swimming in the lagoon. Seven hotel buildings hold the accommodations, which include standard rooms, two-story town house–style "duplexes" (their upstairs bedrooms have their own balconies), suites, and—my favorites—rooms with hot tubs romantically placed behind louvers on their balconies. Furnishings and decor are tropical with a European flair. The Radisson sends a shuttle to downtown Papeete each morning and afternoon, but public buses do not run out here after 5pm, meaning you will need to rent a car or take a taxi to get to and from downtown after dark. As at Le Meridien Tahiti, rush-hour traffic can make for a long trek to the airport from here.

B.P. 14170, 98701 Arue (on Matavai Bay, 7km/4¹/₄ miles east of downtown). 𝒞 **800/333-3333** or 48.88.88. Fax 43.88.89. www.radisson.com/aruefrp. 165 units. 25,600CFP–31,200CFP (US$320–US$390/£161–£198) double. AE, DC, MC, V. **Amenities:** Restaurant; 2 bars; outdoor pool; exercise room; spa; Jacuzzi; activities desk; car-rental desk; business center; salon; limited room service; massage; babysitting; laundry service; concierge-level rooms. *In room:* A/C, TV, high-speed dataport, minibar, coffeemaker, iron (in suites), safe.

IN PAPEETE
EXPENSIVE
Sheraton Hotel Tahiti & Spa ★★   A 15-minute walk to downtown and a quick drive to the airport, this state-of-the-art hotel was built in 2000–01 on the site of the old Hotel Tahiti, whose massive thatched-roof public areas hosted many a local soiree. With Tahiti's largest meeting space, the Sheraton still serves as one of the city's prime gathering places. Curving steps under a huge shell chandelier lead down to Quinn's Bar, an overwater dining room, and an expansive courtyard with a lagoonside swimming pool and sand piled behind a breakwater, which helps compensate for the lack of a natural beach. A whirlpool perched atop a pile of rocks beside the pool allows for a terrific view of Moorea. Except for 10 suites, which have one or two bedrooms, the spacious units are virtually identical except for the vistas off their private balconies. "Superior" units directly face Moorea, but you actually pay less for them since they are slightly smaller than the "deluxe lagoon" units facing the open ocean or harbor (someone who's never been to Tahiti must have devised that policy). This is a good choice for a short layover when you don't need a beach. TOPdive, one of French Polynesia's best operators, has a base here.

B.P. 416, 98713 Papeete (1km/¹/₂ mile west of downtown, 6km/3¹/₂ miles east of the airport). 𝒞 **800/325-3535** or 86.48.48. Fax 86.48.40. www.starwoodtahiti.com. 200 units. 33,000CFP–41,000CFP (US$413–US$513/£208–£258) double; 75,000CFP–88,000CFP (US$938–US$1,100/£469–£557) suite. AE, DC, MC, V. **Amenities:** 2 restaurants; bar; outdoor pool; health club; exercise room; spa; concierge; activities desk; car-rental desk; Wi-Fi in public areas; salon; limited room service; massage; babysitting; laundry service. *In room:* A/C, TV, high-speed dataport, minibar, coffeemaker, hair dryer, iron, safe.

MODERATE

Hotel Le Mandarin   Attractive primarily to business travelers and cost-conscious tourists heading to the cruise ships, this Chinese-accented hotel is a bit shopworn, but is in a somewhat quieter downtown location—on rue Collette opposite the Town Hall—than is the Hotel Tiare Tahiti Noa Noa (see below). My friend Dick Beaulieu likes to stay at Le Mandarin when he comes over from Fiji because its central-city location puts him close to most offices and many restaurants, thus avoiding a bundle in taxi fares. I don't stay here on Friday, however, since dancers can spill from the noisy nightclub onto the street. Most rooms are rather smallish, but many have narrow balconies with mountain views. There's a coffee shop in the hotel, and **Le Mandarin** dining room next door is one of the city's better Chinese restaurants.

B.P. 302, 98713 Papeete. © **50.33.50.** Fax 42.16.32. 37 units. 15,500CFP–17,500CFP (US$194–US$219/ £98–£110) double. AE, MC, V. **Amenities:** 2 restaurants; 2 bars; laundry service. *In room:* A/C, TV, dataport, fridge.

Hotel Tiare Tahiti Noa Noa   This upstairs, five-story facility, on boulevard Pomare a block west of the Centre Vaima, is simple but clean. Amenities are scarce, but the friendly front-desk staffers speak English and are adept at helping you arrange tours and other activities. Many overseas guests here are on low-budget package tours or are heading to one of the cruise ships. The rooms are minimally furnished and can be noisy, since most face directly onto the busy boulevard. Be sure to request a unit on the upper floors, which are quieter and have better views from their slim, unfurnished balconies. Continental breakfast is available in an open-air room on the second floor.

B.P. 2359, 98713 Papeete. © **50.01.00.** Fax 43.68.47. hoteltiarietahiti@mail.pf. 38 units. 13,500CFP–15,000CFP (US$169–US$188/£85–£95) double. AE, MC, V. **Amenities:** Restaurant (breakfast only); laundry service. *In room:* A/C, TV.

INEXPENSIVE

Ahitea Lodge ⓕⁱⁿᵈˢ   Tucked away on an alley between Prince Hinoi and Chef Vairaatoa avenues, about 5 blocks inland from the Moorea ferry docks, this modern, two-story house provides an oasis in the midst of a closely packed Tahitian neighborhood with the usual collection of roosters and dogs. A high fence surrounds the lush yard with an outdoor pool and a pond stocked with tropical fish. The least expensive units are in an attached building, but these all share toilets and showers, and they have small fresh-air vents instead of windows. Preferable are bedrooms in the main house, especially those upstairs that open to a balcony overlooking the pool and pond. Best of these is a corner unit with TV, fridge, private bathroom, and air-conditioning (it is the only air-conditioned unit here); it is so popular that you should reserve it several months in advance. The hosts provide a tropical breakfast in the communal kitchen each morning. Staying here will expose you to modern urban life as lived by middle- and working-class Tahitians.

Av. Chef Vairaatoa, 98713 Papeete. © **53.13.53.** Fax 42.09.35. www.ahitea-lodge.com. 13 units (9 with bathroom). 8,500CFP–13,500CFP (US$106–US$169/£54–£85). Rates include tropical breakfast. AE, MC, V. **Amenities:** Outdoor pool; communal kitchen. *In room:* A/C (1 unit), TV (2 units), fridge (1 unit), no phone.

Fare Suisse ★ ⓥᵃˡᵘᵉ   Beni Huber moved to Tahiti from Switzerland and opened this spotlessly clean guest house in 2006. It's uphill on rue Venus, a side street in the Paofai

TAHITI

5

WHERE TO STAY

ACCOMMODATIONS ■
Ahitea Lodge 2
Fare Suisse 14
Hotel Le Mandarin 4
Hotel Tiare Tahiti Noa Noa 10
Pension Puea 1
Sheraton Hotel Tahiti & Spa 15
Teamo Hostel 8

DINING ◆
Brasserie des Remparts 6
L'Api'zzeria 13
L'O a la Bouche 11
Le Retrot 9
Les 3 Brasseurs 3
Les Roulottes 5
L'Oasis du Viama 9
Lou Pescadou 12
Polyself 7

⊠ Post office
ⓘ Information

neighborhood and just 3 blocks inland from Place Toata and the waterfront. Sea breezes usually cool the light, airy rooms, two of which are upstairs off a large lounge and communal kitchen. One of these has over-and-under double beds and a convertible sofa; it sees double duty as a dormitory. An apartment downstairs has its own kitchen and two bedrooms, one of which can be rented separately. The dorm and one of the upstairs rooms share a bathroom; the other three units have their own private facilities. Breakfast is available at this home away from home. Beni speaks German and English better than he does French.

B.P. 20355, 98713 Faaa (rue Venus, south of rue des Poilus Tahitiens). ☎/fax **42.00.30.** www.fare-suisse. com. 4 units (3 w/bathroom), 2 dorm beds. 9,000CFP–12,000CFP (US$113–US$150/£57–£76) double; 4,800CFP (US$60/£30) dorm bed. MC, V. **Amenities:** Communal kitchen; Wi-Fi. *In room:* Kitchen (1 unit), no phone.

Pension Puea (Finds)   About a block from Ahitea Lodge (see above), this simple but friendly pension appeals to backpackers and other cost-conscious travelers who want to stay without frills in Papeete. Guests swap yarns in the TV lounge under a lean-to roof, which covers the open-air communal kitchen and lounge with plastic tables and chairs (breakfast is served here daily). The bright, well-ventilated rooms are all upstairs. Largest and best are the three air-conditioned family units with either two double beds or a double and a single. One of these also has a private bathroom (the other units share two toilets and two showers). It lacks the convenience and in-room amenities of Teamo Hostel (see below).

B.P. 5597, 98716 Pirae (87 rue Pasteur Octave Moreau, Papeete). ☎ **85.43.43.** Fax 42.09.35. pension. puea@mail.pf. 6 units (5 with shared bathroom). 6,500CFP–8,500CFP (US$81–US$106/£42–£53). Rates include tropical breakfast. MC, V. **Amenities:** Communal kitchen. *In room:* A/C (3 units), no phone.

Teamo Hostel   Although it has been around for more than 2 decades, this guesthouse-cum-hostel is much improved now that friendly, English-speaking owner Gerald Teriierooiterai has added TVs and fridges to all the rooms and air conditioners to some. In a primarily residential neighborhood 6 blocks from the waterfront, it occupies a wood-frame house built around 1880. Rooms were small in those days, so don't expect them to be spacious today. Some rooms upstairs have balconies. Two downstairs units have six bunk beds each and are used for male and female dorms. There's a comfy lounge at the front of the house and a communal kitchen on a covered patio out back.

B.P. 60113, Faaa (rue du Pont-Neuf off rue du Général Castelnau). ☎ **42.47.26** or 42.00.35. Fax 43.56.95. teamohostel@mail.pf. 11 units (all w/bathrooms), 12 dorm beds. 5,800CFP–7,000CFP (US$73–US$88/£37–£44) double; 2,300CFP (US$29/£15) dorm bed. Rates include continental breakfast. MC, V. **Amenities:** Communal kitchen. *In room:* A/C (4 units), TV, fridge, coffeemaker.

9 WHERE TO DINE

Tahiti has a plethora of excellent French, Italian, and Chinese restaurants. Those I recommend below are but a few of many; don't hesitate to strike out on your own.

Food is relatively expensive in French Polynesia, whether on the shelves of grocery stores or placed before you at a restaurant or snack bar.

Downtown Papeete has a **McDonald's** at the corner of rue du Général-de-Gaulle and rue du Dr. Cassiau behind Centre Vaima, and there's a second on the main road in Punaauia. If you want to make your own meals or a picnic, the downtown **Champion**

supermarket is on rue du Général-d
On the west coast, head for the hug
south of the Sofitel Tahiti Maeva Be

THE WEST COAST
EXPENSIVE

Le Carré ★★ (Value) FRENCH   Alt
Continental Resort Tahiti (see below), l
under a round thatched roof and roman
the resort's wade-in swimming pool—bu
French, the cuisine has numerous island
different methods of preparing the same d
courses.

At Le Meridien Tahiti, PK 15, Punaauia. © **47.07.07.**
3,800CFP (US$39–US$48/£20–£25); fixed-price dinne
DC, MC, V. Daily noon–2pm and 7–10pm.

Le Coco's ★★ FRENCH   Along with Le L ̄ ̄ (see below), this lagoonside restaurant
shares top rank as Tahiti's most romantic place to dine, especially the tables out on the
lawn, where you will have a gorgeous look at Moorea (moonlit nights are awesome).
Other tables shaded by a thatched cabana also share the view. The cuisine is light in the
French nouvelle cuisine tradition, with island influences such as shrimp marinated in
lime juice and coconut milk. If your credit card can withstand 12,400CFP (US$155/£78)
per person, you will be surprised during the five-course, fixed-price "at the humor of the
chef" menu. There's also a scaled-down tourist menu. Arrive early enough for a drink or
glass of fine champagne while the sun sets over Moorea.

PK 13.5, Punaauia. © **58.21.08.** Reservations recommended. Main courses 2,900CFP–3,800CFP (US$36–
US$48/£19–£24); tourist menu 5,850CFP (US$73/£37). AE, MC, V. Daily 11:30am–1:30pm and 7–9:30pm.

Le Lotus ★★★ FRENCH/CONTINENTAL   With two round, thatched-roof dining rooms extending over the lagoon and enjoying an uninterrupted view of Moorea, Le
Lotus has the best setting of any restaurant in the South Pacific. The widely spaced tables are
all at the water's edge (a spotlight between the two dining rooms shines into the lagoon,
attracting fish in search of a handout). The gourmet French fare and attentive but unobtrusive service more than live up to this romantic scene. The resort often invites some of
Europe's top master chefs to take working vacations here. Whomever is in residence, you're
in for a gastronomic delight, be it à la carte or a one- to four-course, fixed-price menu.

In InterContinental Resort Tahiti, Faaa (7km/4 miles west of Papeete). © **86.51.10,** ext. 5512. Reservations highly recommended. Main courses 3,100CFP–4,800CFP (US$39–US$60/£20–£30); fixed-price dinners 3,950CFP–10,300CFP (US$49–US$129/£25–£65). AE, DC, MC, V. Daily noon–2:30pm and 6:30–
9:30pm.

MODERATE

Captain Bligh Restaurant and Bar ★ TRADITIONAL FRENCH   One of
Tahiti's last large, thatched-roof buildings covers this restaurant beside the lagoon (you
can toss bread crumbs to the fish swimming just over the railing). The food is not the
best on the island, but you can't beat the old Tahitian charm. Specialties of the house are
grilled steaks and lobster. Get here early to graze the all-you-can-eat lunchtime salad bar,
which is so popular with locals that it quickly disappears. One of the island's top Tahitian

...d Saturday nights after a seafood buffet—the ...price is an excellent value compared to the resort ... You can sample local food at the *ma'a Tahiti* buffet ...ut to the Lagoonarium here (see "Tahiti's Top Attractions,"

...Lagoonarium (3.9km/21/3 miles south of Sofitel Tahiti Maeva Beach Resort on ...d; Paea buses go by it during the day; take a taxi at night). (C) **43.62.90.** Reservations ...n weekends. Burgers 1,300CFP (US$16/£8); lunch salad bar 1,700CFP (US$21/£11); main ...0CFP–3,400CFP (US$23–US$43/£12–£22). AE, MC, V. Restaurant Tues–Sun 11am–2:30pm ...9pm. Bar Tues–Sun 9am–10pm.

asa Bianca ITALIAN   Formerly known as Casablanca Cocktail Restaurant, this now-Italian establishment is perched beside the yachts moored in Marina Taina, Tahiti's prime yachting facility. The menu consists primarily of pizza and pasta with a few meat and fish courses. Servings are relatively small, but are nevertheless a good value. The food isn't as good as at either L'Api'zzeria or Lou Pescadou in Papeete (see below), but the setting is more pleasant. Try to get a table in one of the romantic gazebos out in the yard. There's live music Friday and Saturday night in the Dinghy Bar, which dispenses home-brews from Papeete's Les 3 Brasseurs (see below).

PK 9, Punaauia, at Marina Taina. (C) **43.91.35.** Reservations recommended. Pizza and pasta 1,100CFP–1,800CFP (US$14–US$23/£7–£12); meat courses 1,950CFP–2,400CFP (US$24–US$30/£12–£15). AE, MC, V. Daily noon–2:30pm and 7–10:30pm. Heading south, turn right into marina after first traffic circle. Restaurant is straight ahead.

Restaurant Blue Banana (Kids) FRENCH/ITALIAN   Opened in 2007 by Steven Baker, son of an American father and Chinese-Tahitian mother, this family-oriented restaurant has an unimpeded view of Moorea from premises formerly occupied by Auberge du Pacifique, for years one of Tahiti's finest restaurants. Steve installed a play area to keep the kids busy while their parents choose from a menu including very big burgers, Italian fare such as spaghetti, lasagna, and pizzas from a wood-fired oven, and traditional French steaks and fish. Be sure to reserve a table with a Moorea view. The food is better at Steve's Restaurant Pink Coconut (see below), but children will have more fun here.

PK 11.2, Punaauia. (C) **42.22.24.** Reservations recommended. Burgers 1,650CFP–1,850CFP (US$21–US$23/ £11–£12); pizza 1,250CFP–1,750CFP (US$16–US$22/£8–£11); main courses 1,550CFP–3,100CFP (US$19–US$39/£10–£20). AE, MC, V. Tues–Sat 11:30am–2:30pm and 6:30–10pm; Sun 11:30am–2:30pm.

Restaurant Pink Coconut ★★ INTERNATIONAL   Another recent Steven Baker creation, this open-air restaurant commands a view of Moorea through the masts of yachts moored stern-to at Marina Taina. Most tables are under a roof, but unless it's raining or too hot, I opt for one outside on the terrace. The bill of fare ranges the globe. My delicious shrimp in curry and coconut cream was much spicier than the usual local versions, and it was accompanied by terrific puréed squash. The seafood pasta with shrimp, salmon, scallops, and tuna was excellent. Whole tropical lobsters, steaks, and braised lamb shanks also appear. Reduced priced drinks from 5 to 6pm makes this a great place to watch the sunset over Moorea. The Pink Coconut and **Restaurant Quai des Isles** ((C) **81. 02.38**), a French seafood restaurant that shares the building, often have live music on weekend nights. There's a children's menu here.

PK 9, Punaauia, at Marina Taina. (C) **42.22.23.** Reservations recommended. Main courses 2,100CFP–4,500CFP (US$26–US$56/£13–£28). AE, MC, V. Restaurant Mon–Sat 11:30am–2pm and 7–10pm. Bar Mon–Sat 5–11pm. Heading south, turn right into marina after first traffic circle and follow the signs.

Western Grill AMERICAN   After a few weeks of French fare, my American stomach
begins to yearn for some good ole Yankee food. Granted, the Western Grill is a theme
restaurant—wagon wheels and swinging saloon doors—but it's also one of the best places
on Tahiti to get a grilled steak *sans* buttery sauce. Rump steak Texas, filet Nebraska,
brochette de coyote, lamb chops Geronimo, plus jambalaya, fajitas, tacos, and chili con
carne. You get the picture. The "menu Pat Garrett" includes a *plat du jour* with an appetizer, dessert, and a glass of draft brewed by Papeete's Les 3 Brasseurs (see below).

PK 12.6, Punaauia. (ℂ **41.30.56.** Reservations recommended on weekends. Burgers 1,500CFP–1,700CFP
(US$19–US$21/£10–£11); main courses 1,600CFP–3,000CFP (US$20–US$38/£10–£19). MC, V. Mon–Fri
11:45am–2pm and 7–9:30pm; Sat 7–9:30pm.

INEXPENSIVE

Le Cignalon/Pacific Burger (Value) PIZZA/SNACK BAR   Cost-conscious guests at
Le Meridien Tahiti resort walk next door to Pacific Burger, the open-air snack bar side
operated by Le Cignalon (an Italian restaurant) for good, reasonably priced salads, *poisson
cru*, sashimi, burgers (beef, chicken, or fish), grilled rib-eye steaks and fish with or without sauce, and very good two-person pizzas from a wood-fired oven. A big tarp covers
plastic patio tables and chairs in front of the fast-food-style counter. The menu is in
French and English. The Tahiti museum is a few blocks away, so this is a good place to
stop for refreshment on your round-island tour.

PK 15, Punaauia. (ℂ **42.40.84.** Burgers 450CFP–850CFP (US$5.60–US$11/£2.80–£6); pizza and pasta
1,000CFP–1,900CFP (US$13–US$24/£7–£12); main courses 1,800CFP–2,500CFP (US$23–US$31/£12–£16).
MC, V. Tues–Thurs 10am–3pm and 5:30–9pm; Fri–Sun 10am–3pm and 5:30–9:30pm.

EAST OF PAPEETE

Le Royal Tahitien Restaurant ★★ (Value) INTERNATIONAL   Occupying a
charming open-air building constructed in 1937 beside the black-sand beach in Pirae,
the Hotel Le Royal Tahitien's dining room provides views of the lagoon and Moorea to
accompany its very good international fare. Like the hotel, it also offers excellent value
for the quality of its food. The cuisine is primarily French, such as fresh mahimahi in
meunière sauce, but you will find island influences here, such as very good *poisson cru*
and shrimp served in half a pineapple. You can also order off a snack menu, including
juicy Aussie-style burgers, the best on Tahiti. Locals flock here for the big lunchtime
salads, as well as for live music in the adjacent bar on Friday and Saturday evenings. Be
sure to talk baseball with Australian-born Lionel Kennedy, the hotel's general manager.

At Hotel Le Royal Tahitien, PK 4, Pirae. Reservations recommended at dinner. Snack menu 850CFP–
1,500CFP (US$11–US$19/£6–£10); main courses 2,000CFP–2,900CFP (US$25–US$36/£13–£18). AE, DC,
MC, V. Daily 6:30–10am, 11:30am–2:30pm, and 7–10pm.

IN PAPEETE
EXPENSIVE

L'O a la Bouche ★★★ INTERNATIONAL   One of the top restaurants in all of
French Polynesia, this charming bistro's sophisticated, muted ambience would make it at
home in the wine countries of Napa or Baroosa—except for the vintage labels pictured
on the walls, which are all French. Although the chef offers several traditional French
dishes, this is anything but a typical French restaurant. His talent soars with creations
such as a moon fish steak under passion-fruit and ginger sauce (the ginger perfectly
tempered the fruit's sweetness). I preceded that with a smoked salmon and shrimp salad
with *pamplemousse* (local grapefruit), which was delightfully refreshing after a day of

(Value) **Dining with a Belle View**

I like to spend my last evening on Tahiti up at **Le Belvédère** (☎ **42.73.44**), for this innlike establishment has a spectacular view of the city and Moorea from its perch 600m (2,000 ft.) up in the Fare Ape Valley above Papeete. The restaurant provides round-trip transportation from your hotel up the narrow, one-lane, winding, switchback road that leads to it (I don't encourage anyone to attempt this drive in a rental car). Take the 5pm pickup so you'll reach the restaurant in time for a sunset cocktail. They'll drop you back at the airport if you're leaving that night. The specialty of the house is fondue Bourguignonne served with six sauces. The 5,600CFP (US$70/£35) fixed price includes three courses, wine, and transportation, so it is a reasonably good value. The quality of the cuisine doesn't match the view, however, so treat the evening as a sightseeing excursion, not as a fine-dining experience. Reservations are required; American Express, MasterCard, and Visa are accepted. Closed Wednesdays.

tramping around Papeete. Next time, I'm going with scallops marinated with red peppers, or perhaps scorched tuna with a light curry sauce. The list of French wines is short but excellent. The menu is in both French and English here.

Passage Cardella (btw. rue du Général-de-Gaulle and rue Anne-Marie Javouhey). ☎ **45.29.76.** Reservations recommended, especially on weekends. Main courses 2,950CFP–3,700CFP (US$37–US$46/£19–£24). AE, MC, V. Mon–Fri 11:30am–2:30pm and 7:15–10pm; Sat 7:15–10pm.

MODERATE

Brasserie des Remparts ★ FRENCH   The blues cascade from speakers at this American-style, brass-and-dark-wood pub, whose food is much better than at the otherwise comparable Les 3 Brasseurs (see below). Despite the 5¢-pay-toilet sign and other American memorabilia hanging on the walls, the chow is definitely French, with the likes of andouille sausage in mustard sauce, mahimahi meunière, an Alsatian-style casserole, Moroccan couscous, and rib-eye steaks with Roquefort, pepper, or béarnaise sauces. The plate-size salads make healthy meals unto themselves. Try for a sidewalk table.

Av. Georges Clemenceau, at Rond Pont de L'Est traffic circle. ☎ **42.80.00.** Reservations accepted. Main courses 1,950CFP–3,000CFP (US$24–US$38/£12–£19). AE, MC, V. Mon–Fri 7am–3pm and 6:30–11pm.

L'Api'zzeria ★★ (Value) ITALIAN   On par with Lou Pescadou (see below) but with a garden setting, this restaurant in a grove of trees across from the waterfront has been serving very good pizza and pasta since 1968. I prefer a table outside under the trees rather than inside, which resembles an Elizabethan waterfront tavern accented with nautical relics. The food, on the other hand, is definitely Italian. Both pizzas and tender steaks are cooked in a wood-fired oven. The menu also features spaghetti, fettuccine, lasagna, steak Milanese, veal in white or Marsala wine sauce, and grilled homemade Italian sausage.

Bd. Pomare, between rue du Chef Teriirooterai and rue l'Arthémise. ☎ **42.98.30.** Reservations not accepted. Pizza and pasta 450CFP–1,750CFP (US$5.60–US$22/£2.80–£11); meat courses 1,700CFP–2,600CFP (US$21–US$33/£11–£17). MC, V. Mon–Sat 11:30am–10pm.

Les 3 Brasseurs FRENCH   The quality of its food tends to be up and down, but this sidewalk microbrewery is the nearest thing Papeete has to an American-style bar-and-grill. The sidewalk tables are fine for a cold one while waiting for the Moorea ferry at the docks across the boulevard. The tabloid menu is all in French, but those on the waitstaff speak enough English to explain the dishes. Choose from sandwiches, salads, roast chicken served hot or cold, and grilled steaks, mahimahi, and tuna plain or with optional sauces. *Jarret de porc,* smoked ham hocks served with sautéed potatoes and sauerkraut, reminds me of the Southern soul food of my youth. The best deal here is the *croque brasseurs,* a ham sandwich served under melted Gruyère cheese and accompanied by a glass of beer and a green salad with excellent vinaigrette dressing, all for 900CFP (US$11/£5.50).

Bd. Pomare, between rue Prince Hinoi and rue Clappier, opposite Moorea ferry docks. ℭ **50.60.25.** Sandwiches and salads 900CFP–1,700CFP (US$11–US$21/£6–£11); main courses 1,500CFP–2,700CFP (US$19–US$34/£10–£17). MC, V. Daily 9am–1am.

Lou Pescadou ★ Ⓥⓐⓛⓤⓔ ITALIAN   A lively young professional clientele usually packs this quintessential Italian trattoria (red-and-white-checked tablecloths, dripping candles on each table, Ruffino bottles hanging from every nook and cranny). They come for good, fresh, and tasty Italian fare at reasonable prices (be prepared to wait for a table). The individual-size pizzas are cooked in a wood-fired oven; the excellent pasta dishes include lasagna, spaghetti, and fettuccine under tomato, carbonara, and Roquefort sauces.

Rue Anne-Marie Javouhey at passage Cardella. ℭ **43.74.26.** Pizza and pasta 1,000CFP–1,750CFP (US$-3–US$22/£6.50–£11); meat courses 1,750CFP–2,650CFP (US$22–US$33/£11–£17). MC, V. Mon–Sat 11:30am–2pm and 6:30–11pm. Take the narrow passage Cardella, a 1-block street that looks like an alley, directly behind Centre Vaima.

INEXPENSIVE

Le Retrot FRENCH/ITALIAN/SNACKS   You'll find better food elsewhere, but this Parisian-style sidewalk cafe is Papeete's best place to rendezvous or to grab a quick bite, a drink, or an ice cream while watching the world pass along the quay. A diverse selection of salads, sandwiches, pizzas, and pastas gets attention from the cafe crowd.

Bd. Pomare, front of Centre Vaima, on waterfront. ℭ **42.86.83.** Salads, sandwiches, and burgers 500CFP–1,450CFP (US$6.25–US$18/£3.15–£9); pizza and pasta 900CFP–1,800CFP (US$11–US$23/£6–£12); main courses 1,750CFP–2,150CFP (US$22–US$27/£11–£14). AE, MC, V. Daily 6am–midnight.

L'Oasis du Vaima SNACK BAR   You'll find me having a breakfast of a small quiche or a tasty pastry with strong French coffee at this kiosklike building on the southwest corner of Centre Vaima. In addition to dishing out ice cream and milkshakes to passersby at a sidewalk counter, it serves up a variety of goodies, from crispy *casse-croûtes* to two substantial *plats du jour* selections each day, on a covered dining terrace and in an air-conditioned dining room upstairs.

Rue du Général-de-Gaulle at rue Jeanne d'Arc (at the corner of Centre Vaima, opposite Cathédrale de l'Immaculée Conception). ℭ **45.45.01.** Sandwiches, quiches, omelets, small pizzas 350CFP–900CFP (US$4.40–US$11/£2.20–£5.50); meals 1,500CFP–2,100CFP (US$19–US$26/£10–£13). No credit cards. Mon–Sat 5am–5pm.

Polyself CAFETERIA   I have stopped by this cafeteria for a quick breakfast or lunch for years. The stainless-steel counter in this air-conditioned, nonsmoking establishment presents a selection of sandwiches, salads, Chinese dishes, and French fare such as chicken in cream sauce. No English is necessary; just point to what you want. Dim-sum dumplings augment such traditional French breakfast fare as croissants and coffee, or you

Don't Miss Les Roulottes

Although prices in some hotel dining rooms and restaurants here can be shocking, you don't need to spend a fortune to eat reasonably well in French Polynesia. In fact, the best food bargains in Papeete literally roll out after dark on the cruise-ship docks: portable meal wagons known as *les roulottes.*

Some owners set up charcoal grills behind their trucks and small electric generators in front to provide plenty of light for the diners, who sit on stools along either side of the vehicles. A few operate during the daytime, but most begin arriving about 6pm. The entire waterfront soon takes on a carnival atmosphere, especially on Friday and Saturday nights. So many cruise-ship passengers and other tourists eat here that most truck owners speak some English.

The traditional menu includes charbroiled steaks or chicken with french fries (known, respectively, as *steak frites* and *poulet frites*), familiar Cantonese dishes, *poisson cru*, and *salade russe* (Russian-style potato salad, tinted red by beet-root juice) for 900CFP to 1,700CFP (US$11–US$21/£5.50–£11) per plate. Glassed-in display cases along the sides of some trucks hold actual examples of what's offered at each (not exactly the most appetizing exhibits, but you can just point to what you want rather than fumbling in French). You'll find just as many trucks specializing in crepes, pizzas, couscous, and waffles *(gaufres)*. Even if you don't order an entire meal at *les roulottes,* stop for a crepe or waffle and enjoy the scene.

Although they now have permanent homes, the open-air restaurants at **Place Toata,** on the western end of the waterfront, were born as roulottes, and they still offer the same fare and prices as their mobile siblings. They're open for lunch Monday through Saturday, for dinner Friday and Saturday.

can order eggs cooked any way you like them. The food isn't the best in town, but you get a lot of it for the money.

Rue Paul Gauguin, between bd. Pomare and rue Colette. ✆ **43.25.32.** Reservations not accepted. Sandwiches and salads 100CFP–250CFP (US$1.25–US$3.10/65p–£1.55); main courses 600CFP–950CFP (US$7.50–US$12/£4–£6). No credit cards. Mon–Fri 5am–12:30pm.

10 ISLAND NIGHTS ON TAHITI

A 19th-century European merchant wrote of the Tahitians, "Their existence was in never-ending merrymaking." In many respects this is still true, for after the sun goes down, Tahitians like to make merry as much today as they did in the 1820s, and Papeete has lots of good choices for visitors who want to join in the fun.

TAHITIAN DANCE SHOWS ★★★

Traditional Tahitian dancing isn't as indecent as it was in Captain Cook's day (see "A Most Indecent Song & Dance," p. 35), but seeing at least one show should be on your agenda. You'll have plenty of chances, since nightlife on the outer islands consists almost exclusively of dance shows at the resorts, usually in conjunction with a feast of Tahitian **141** food.

Each of Tahiti's big resort hotels has shows at least 1 night a week. Not to be missed is the **Grande Danse de Tahiti** ★★★ troupe, which usually performs at the InterContinental Resort Tahiti (✆ **86.51.10**) on Wednesday, Friday, and Saturday evenings (the Sat show is a reenactment of the dance that seduced the crew of HMS *Bounty*). Call the resort to confirm the schedule. Another good place to catch a show is the **Captain Bligh Restaurant and Bar** (✆ **43.62.90**), which usually has them on Friday and Saturday at 8:30pm. Expect to pay from 5,000CFP (US$63/£32) for the show and dinner at the Captain Bligh to 8,500CFP (US$106/£54) at the big resorts.

PUB-CRAWLING

Papeete has a nightclub or watering hole to fit anyone's taste, from upscale private *(privé)* discothèques to down-and-dirty bars and dance halls where Tahitians strum on guitars while sipping on large bottles of Hinano beer (and sometimes engage in fisticuffs after midnight). If you look like a tourist, you'll be allowed into the private clubs. Generally, everything gets to full throttle after 9pm (except on Sun, when most pubs are closed). None of the clubs are inexpensive. Expect to pay a cover of at least 1,000CFP (US$13/£6.50), which will include your first drink. After that, beers cost at least 500CFP (US$6.25/£3.15), with most mixed drinks in the range of 1,000CFP to 1,500CFP (US$13–US$19/£6.50–£9.50).

The narrow rue des Ecoles is the heart of Papeete's *mahu* district, where male transvestites hang out. The **Piano Bar** (✆ **42.88.24**) is the most popular of the "sexy clubs" along this street, especially for its late-night strip shows featuring female impersonators. It's open daily from 3pm to 3am. The multistory **Mana Rock Cafe,** at boulevard Pomare and rue des Ecoles (✆ **48.36.36**), draws a more mixed crowd to its bars and discothèque (you can check your e-mail between sips here).

You're unlikely to be groped or get into a fight at **Hotel Le Royal Tahitien,** in Pirae (✆ **50.40.40**), where a live band plays Tahitian music for dancing on Friday nights. It's a much better behaved version of Quinn's and Tahiti's other infamous old joints. The moderately priced seaside restaurant here (p. 137) has very good food for the money, so you can make Friday a dining-and-dancing evening. General Manager Lionel Kennedy, who came here as a drummer in a rock band in the mid-1960s and never went back to Australia, revives his skills during the hotel's Wednesday night jazz jams.

You don't have to pay to be entertained on Friday, which is "cruise-ship day" on the Papeete waterfront. Arts and crafts are on display, and Tahitians make music from 8am to 5pm at the Tahiti Manava visitors bureau at the foot of rue Paul Gauguin. Tahitian bands perform afterward out on Place Vaiate by the cruise ship docks.

Impressions

They have several negative comments on the beachcombing life in Tahiti: Not much cultural life. No intellectual stimulus. No decent library. Restaurant food is disgraceful . . . But I noticed that Saturday after Saturday they turned up at Quinn's with the most dazzling beauties on the island. When I reminded them of this they said, "Well that does compensate for the poor library."

—James A. Michener, *Return to Paradise,* 1951

Moorea

Like most visitors to French Polynesia, I soon grab the ferry to Moorea, just 20km (12 miles) west of Tahiti. James Michener may have thought Bora Bora was the world's most beautiful island, but Moorea is my choice. In fact, it's so stunningly gorgeous that I have trouble keeping my eyes on the road here. Hollywood often uses stock shots of Moorea's jagged mountains, deep bays, and emerald lagoons to create a South Seas setting for movies that don't even take place in French Polynesia.

Geologists attribute Moorea's rugged, otherworldly beauty to a great volcano, the northern half of which either fell into the sea or was blown away in a cataclysmic explosion, leaving the heart-shaped island we see today. In other words, Moorea is only half of its old self. The remaining rim of the crater has eroded into the jagged peaks and spires that give the island its haunting, dinosaurlike profile. Cathedral-like Mount Mouaroa—Moorea's trademark "Shark's Tooth" or "Bali Hai Mountain"—shows up on innumerable postcards and on the 100CFP coin.

Mount Rotui stands alone in the center of the ancient crater, its black cliffs and stovepipe buttresses dropping dramatically into Cook's Bay and Opunohu Bay, two dark blue fingers that cut deep into Moorea's interior. These mountain-shrouded bays are certainly among the world's most photographed bodies of water.

Perched high up on the crater's wall, the Belvédère overlooks both bays, Mount Rotui, and the jagged old crater rim curving off to left and right. Do not miss the Belvédère, for it is one of the South Pacific's most awesome panoramas.

With traffic choking Tahiti, and Moorea only a 30-minute ferry ride away from Papeete, the island is already a bedroom community for its big sister. Still, it has maintained its Polynesian charm to a large extent. Its hotels and resorts are spread out enough so that you don't feel like you're in a tourist trap, and the locals don't feel inundated by us. They still have time to stop and talk with visitors.

Most of Moorea's 20,000 or so residents live on the coastal plain fringing the island, many of them in small settlements where lush valleys meet a lagoon enclosed by an offshore coral reef. This calm blue lagoon makes Moorea ideal for swimming, boating, snorkeling, and diving. Unlike the black sands of Tahiti, white beaches stretch for miles on Moorea.

1 GETTING AROUND MOOREA

All ferries from Papeete land at Vaiare on Moorea's east coast 5km (3 miles) south of **Temae Airport** (see "Getting Around Tahiti & French Polynesia," in chapter 3).

BY BUS

The only scheduled buses on Moorea are those that carry passengers from and to the morning and afternoon ferries at Vaiare. Tell the drivers where you're going; they will show you which vehicle is going to your hotel. The trip from Vaiare to the end of the line at the old Club Med site takes about 1 hour. The buses also return from the Petite Village

From Tahiti, Moorea seems to have about 40 separate summits: fat thumbs of basalt, spires tipped at impossible angles, brooding domes compelling to the eye. But the peaks which can never be forgotten are the jagged saw-edges that look like the spines of some forgotten dinosaur.

　　　　　　　　　　　　　　　　—James A. Michener, *Return to Paradise*, 1951

shopping center in Haapiti to Vaiare, leaving the shopping center about 1 hour prior to each ferry departure. They go by the hotels, so ask the front-desk staff when you can expect the next bus to pass. Or you can flag them down along the road elsewhere. The one-way fare is 500CFP (US$6.25/£3.15), regardless of direction or length of ride.

BY TAXI

Unless you catch a ferry bus or rent a vehicle, you're at the expensive mercy of Moorea's taxi owners, who don't run around looking for customers. The only **taxi stand** is at the airport (© **56.10.18**). It's staffed daily from 6am to 6pm. Your hotel desk can call one for you, or else phone **Pero Taxis** (© **56.14.93**), **Albert Tours** (© **56.13.53**), or **Justine Taxi** (© **77.48.26**). Make advance reservations for service between 6pm and 6am.

Fares are 800CFP (US$10/£5) during the day, 1,700CFP (US$21/£11) at night, plus 110CFP (US$1.35/70p) per kilometer. They double from 8pm to 6am. Expect to pay about 2,000CFP (US$25/£13) one-way from the ferry or airport to the Cook's Bay area, about 4,000CFP (US$50/£25) one-way from the airport or Cook's Bay to the Haapiti area, less for stops along the way. Be sure that you understand what the fare will be before you get in.

BY RENTAL CAR & SCOOTER

Avis (© **800/331-1212** or 56.32.68; www.avis.com) and **Europcar** (© **800/227-7368** or 56.34.00; www.europcar-tahiti.com) both have booths at the Vaiare ferry wharf and at several hotels. Although I usually rent from Avis, Europcar is the more widespread and slightly less expensive of the two, with unlimited-kilometer rates starting at 9,300CFP (US$116/£59) a day. The local firm **Albert Rent-a-Car** (© **56.19.28**) is the least expensive, with unlimited-kilometer rates starting at 8,000CFP (US$100/£50) for a day.

In addition to automobiles, Europcar also rents little "Bugsters" (noisy contraptions with two seats and no top) for about 8,800CFP (US$110/£55) a day. They are fun to drive on sunny days. So are scooters, which Albert rents starting at 5,000CFP (US$63/£32) for 4 hours and 6,000CFP (US$75/£38) for 24 hours, including full insurance, and unlimited kilometers.

Making reservations for cars and scooters is a very good idea, especially on weekends, when many Tahiti residents come to Moorea.

BY BICYCLE

The 60km (36-mile) road around Moorea is relatively flat. The two major hills are on the west side of Cook's Bay and just behind the Sofitel Moorea Ia Ora Beach Resort (the latter is worth the climb, as it has a stupendous view of Tahiti). Some resorts have bikes for their guests to use, and **Europcar** (see above) rents mountain bikes for about 1,600CFP (US$20/£10) for 8 hours, 2,000CFP (US$25/£13) all day.

(Fast Facts   **Moorea**

The following facts apply specifically to Moorea. For more information, see "Fast Facts: Tahiti & French Polynesia," in appendix A.

Bookstores **Kina Maharepa,** in the Maharepa shopping center (© 56.22.44), has English-language novels and magazines. **Supersonics,** in Le Petit Village shopping center opposite Club Med (© 56.14.96), carries some English-language magazines and newspapers.

Camera & Film The hotel boutiques, along with the aforementioned **Kina Maharepa** and **Supersonics** (see above), all sell film.

Currency Exchange **Banque Socredo, Banque de Tahiti,** and **Banque de Polynésie** have offices and ATMs in or near the Maharepa shopping center. Banque de Polynésie has an ATM and a currency-exchange machine (but not an office) in Le Petit Village shopping center in Haapiti. Bring cash or traveler's checks if you're staying on the northwest corner, or be prepared to put most of your expenditures on a credit card. Banks are open Monday through Friday from 8am to noon and 1:30 to 4:30pm.

Drugstores **Pharmacie Moorea** (© 56.10.51) is in Maharepa. The owner, Tran Thai Thanh, is a Vietnamese refugee who speaks English. It's open Monday to Friday from 7:30am to noon and 2:30 to 4:30pm, Saturday from 8am to noon and 3:30 to 6pm, and Sunday and holidays from 8 to 10am. The owner speaks English.

Emergencies & Police The **emergency police** phone number is © **17.** The phone number for the **gendarmerie** in Cook's Bay is © **56.13.44.** Local police have offices at Pao Pao (© **56.13.63**) and at Haapiti (© **56.10.84**), near Club Med.

Eyeglasses Try **Optique Moorea** in the Maharepa shopping center (© **56.55.44**).

Healthcare The island's **infirmary,** which has an ambulance, is at Afareaitu on the southwest coast (© **56.24.24**). Several doctors are in private practice; ask your hotel staff for a recommendation.

Internet Access Every hotel has Internet access for its guests. In Cook's Bay, **Top Phone** (© **56.57.57**) has fast Internet access for 200CFP (US$2.50/£1.25) for 15 minutes. It also sells VINI cellphone SIM cards. Open Monday to Friday 8am to 5pm, Saturday 8am to noon. In Haapiti, **Polynesian Arts** (© **70.66.38**), in Le Petit Village, also has fast access at 20CFP (US25¢/15p) a minute. Open Monday to Saturday 8:30am to 6pm. You can burn your digital photos onto CDs at either.

Mail Moorea's main post office is in the Maharepa shopping center. It's open Monday through Thursday from 7:30am to noon and 1:30 to 4pm, Friday from 7:30am to noon and 1:30 to 3pm, and Saturday from 7:30 to 9:30am. A post office in Papetoai village is open Monday through Thursday from 7:30am to noon and 1:30 to 4pm, Friday from 7:30am to noon and 1:30 to 3pm, and Saturday from 8 to 10am.

Taxes Moorea's municipal government adds 100CFP to 150CFP (US$1.25–US$1.85/65p–95p) per night to your hotel bill. Don't complain: The money helps keep the island litter-free.

Visitor Information The **Moorea Visitors Bureau,** B.P. 1121, 98279 Papetoai (C **56.29.09;** www.gomoorea.com), has an office at Le Petit Village shopping center in Haapiti. Open Monday to Thursday 8am to 4pm, Friday 8am to 3pm, holidays 8am to noon (more or less; they sometimes change).

Water Tap water on Moorea is not safe to drink, so buy bottled water at any grocery store. Some hotels filter their water; ask if it's safe before drinking from the tap.

2 EXPLORING MOOREA: THE CIRCLE ISLAND TOUR ★★★

Most of the island's accommodations, along with activities and attractions, are found along Moorea's north coast, between the ferry wharf at **Vaiare** and the area known as **Haapiti** on the island's northwestern corner. A large Club Med dominated Haapiti until it closed in 2002, and locals still say "Club Med" when referring to this area.

The sights of Moorea may lack great historical significance, but the physical beauty of the island makes a tour—at least of Cook's and Opunohu bays and up to the Belvédère lookout—a highlight of any visit here. There are few places on earth this gorgeous.

As on Tahiti, Moorea's round-island road—about 60km (36 miles) long—is marked every kilometer with a PK post. Distances are measured between the intersection of the airport road with the main round-island coastal road and the village of Haapiti on Moorea's opposite side. In other words, the distances indicated on the PKs increase from the airport in each direction, reaching 30km near Haapiti. They then decrease as you head back to the airport.

The hotel activities desks offer tours around Moorea and up to the Belvédère lookout in the interior. **Albert Tours** (C **56.13.53**) and **Moorea Explorer** (C **56.12.86**) have half-day circle island tours, including the Belvédère, for about 3,500CFP (US$44/£22) per person. The tour buses all stop at one black-pearl shop or another (guess who gets a commission when you buy the orb of your dreams?). See "Buying Your Black Pearl" (p. 124) and "Shopping," later in this chapter, before making a purchase.

TEMAE & MAHAREPA

Begin at the airstrip on Moorea's northeast corner. The airstrip is on the island's only sizable area of flat land. At one time it was a *motu,* or small island, sitting on the reef by itself. Humans and nature have since filled the lagoon except for Lake Temae, which you can see from the air if you fly to Moorea.

> ### Impressions
>
> *Nothing on Tahiti is so majestic as what faces it across the bay, for there lies the island of Moorea. To describe it is impossible. It is a monument to the prodigal beauty of nature.*
>
> —James A. Michener, *Return to Paradise,* 1951

MOOREA

6

EXPLORING MOOREA: THE CIRCLE ISLAND TOUR

Head west from the junction of the round-island road and airport road. **Temae,** 1km (¹/₂ mile) from the junction, supplied the dancers for the Pomare dynasty's court in the 19th century and is still known for the quality of its performers. Herman Melville spent some time here in 1842 and saw the famous, erotic *upaupa,* which he called the "lory-lory," performed clandestinely, out of sight of the missionaries. Today, Moorea's golf course is here (see "Fishing, Golf, Watersports & Other Outdoor Activities," later in this chapter).

The relatively dry north shore between the airport and the entrance to Cook's Bay is **Maharepa,** the island's commercial center. The road skirts the lagoon and passes the Moorea Pearl Resort & Spa and soon reaches the island's main shopping center.

COOK'S BAY ★★★

As the road curves to the left, you enter **Cook's Bay,** the fingerlike body of water virtually surrounded on three sides by the jagged peaks lining the semicircular "wall" of Moorea. The tall thumb with a small hole in its top is **Mount Tohiea.** Coming into view as you drive farther along the bay is **Mount Mauaroa,** Moorea's trademark cathedral-like "Shark's Tooth" mountain buttressed on its right by a serrated ridge.

Huddled along the curving beach at the head of the bay, the village of **Pao Pao** is the site of Moorea's public schools. The *Cooperatif de Pêche Moorea* (**Moorea Fish Market**) is open Monday through Saturday from 5am to 5pm and Sunday from 5 to 8am. The paved road that seems to run through the school next to the bridge cuts through the valley between Cook's Bay and Opunohu Bay. It intersects with the main road between Opunohu Bay and the Belvédère lookout.

The small **St. Joseph's Catholic Church** sits on the shore on the west side of Cook's Bay, at PK 10 from the airport. Inside is a large mural that artist Peter Heyman painted in 1946 and an altar decorated with mother-of-pearl. From the church, the road climbs up the side of the hill, allowing for some fine views, and then descends back to the lagoon's edge.

Watch on the left for the road leading inland to **Jus de Fruits de Moorea** (**Moorea Fruit Juices;** ⓒ 56.22.33), a factory and distillery that turns the island's produce into the Rotui juices and the potently alcoholic Tahiti Drink you will see in every grocery store. I like to refresh here by tasting the yummy fruit liqueurs. Every souvenir imaginable is for sale, too. Hours are Monday through Thursday from 8:30am to 4:30pm, Friday and Saturday from 8:30am to 3:30pm.

OPUNOHU BAY ★★★

Towering over you is jagged **Mount Rotui,** the huge green-and-black rock separating Moorea's two great bays. Unlike Cook's Bay, Opunohu is virtually devoid of development,

> **Fun Facts**　**Pai's Spear**
>
> Tahitian lore says the legendary hero Pai made the hole in the top of Mount Tohiea when the god of thieves attempted to steal Mount Rotui in the middle of the night. Pai threw his spear from Tahiti and pierced Mount Tohiea. The noise woke up Moorea's roosters, whose commotion alerted the citizenry to put a stop to the dastardly plan.

Belvédère Lookout 6
Jardin Kellum 4
Jus de Fruits de Moorea
  (Moorea Fruit Juices) 7
Lycée Agricole d'Opunohu
  (Opunohu Agricultural
  School) 5
Papetoai Temple
  Protestant 2
Robinson's Cove 3
Ron Hall's Island Fashion
  Black Pearls 8
Tiki Theatre Village 1
Toatea Overlook 9

✈ Airport
← Beach
--- Ferry
····· Hiking trail
      Reef
      Unpaved road

SOCIETY ISLANDS
Moorea
Bora Bora
Huahine
Tahiti

Moorea Ferry (to Tahiti)
To Tahiti → (12 miles)

Sea of the Moon

Temae
Temae Airport
Temae Plage Publique
Lake Temae
Temae
Maharepa
Vaiare
Motu Ahi
Afareaitu
Maatea
Atiraa Waterfall
Mt. Tohiea
Pao Pao
Cook's Bay
Mt. Rotui
Three Coconuts Pass
Mareto Plage Publique
Opunohu Bay
Mt. Mouaroa
Haapiti
Papetoai
Mt. Mouapu
Old Club Med Site

SOUTH PACIFIC OCEAN

2 mi
2 km

Impressions

Seen for the first time by European Eyes, this coast is like nothing else on our workaday planet; a landscape, rather, of some fantastic dream.
—Charles Nordhoff and James Norman Hall, *Mutiny on the Bounty*, 1933

a testament to efforts by local residents to maintain the natural beauty of their island (they have ardently resisted efforts to build a luxury resort and golf course here).

As soon as the road levels out, you can look through the trees to yachts anchored in **Robinson's Cove,** one of the world's most photographed yacht anchorages. Stop here and put your camera to work.

Near the cove, at PK 17.5, stands **Jardin Kellum,** the bayside home and botanical garden of the late Medford and Gladys Kellum, an American couple who once owned all of Opunohu Valley. The Kellums arrived here in 1925, aboard Medford's parents' converted lumber schooner, and they lived for 65 years in a clapboard colonial-style house. Their daughter, Marimari Kellum, resides here today and gives tours of the home and garden to groups that book in advance (© 56.18.52).

From the garden, the road soon curves right along a black-sand beach backed by shade trees and the Opunohu Valley at the head of the bay. The beach was turned into Matavai Bay on Tahiti for the 1983 production of *The Bounty,* starring Mel Gibson and Anthony Hopkins.

The major cruise ships now anchor in Opunohu Bay rather than in Cook's Bay, and you soon will pass the dock where they land their passengers. Although the location is gorgeous, it is also remote from shops, restaurants, and other facilities. Locals say the relocation was engineered by Moorea's most aggressive black-pearl merchant so that the ships' passengers would go ashore closer to his shop in Haapiti rather than competing dealers in Cook's Bay (see "Shopping," later in this chapter).

BELVEDERE LOOKOUT ★★★

After the bridge by the beach, a paved road runs up Moorea's central valley through pastureland, across which Warren Beatty and Annette Bening strolled in their flop movie *Love Affair* (the scenes with Katharine Hepburn were filmed in the white house on the hill to your right). You can stop at **Lycée Agricole d'Opunohu (Opunohu Agricultural School),** on the main road (© 56.11.34), to see plantations for vanilla and other crops. It's open Monday through Friday from 8am to 4:30pm, Saturday from 9am to 12:30pm.

At the head of the valley, the road climbs steeply up the old crater wall to the restored **Titiroa Marae,** which was part of a concentration of *maraes* and other structures. Higher up, you'll pass an archery platform used for competition (archery was a sport reserved for high-ranking chiefs and was never used in warfare in Polynesia). A display in the main *marae* parking lot explains the history of this area. You can walk among the remains of the temples, now shaded by towering Tahitian chestnut trees that have grown up through the cobblestone-like courtyards.

The narrow road then ascends to **Belvédère Lookout,** whose awesome panorama of the valley and the bays on either side of Mount Rotui is unmatched in the South Pacific. You won't want to be without film or camera batteries here. There's a snack bar in the parking lot, so grab a cold drink or ice cream while you take in this remarkable vista.

PAPETOAI

Back on the coastal road, the sizable village of **Papetoai** was the retreat of the Pomare dynasty in the 1800s and the base from which Pomare I launched his successful drive to take over all of Tahiti and Moorea. It was also headquarters for the London Missionary Society's work throughout the South Pacific. The road to the right, past the new post office, leads to the octagonal **Papetoai Temple Protestant,** built on the site of a *marae* dedicated to Oro, son of the supreme Taaroa and the god of war. The original church was constructed in the 1820s, and although advertised as the oldest European building still in use in the South Pacific, the present structure dates from the late 1880s.

HAAPITI

From Papetoai, the road runs through the Haapiti hotel district at Pointe Hauru, Moorea's northwestern corner. A long stretch of white-sand beach wraps around the point and conspires with two islets out on the reef's edge and great sunset views to make the Haapiti area popular with tourists. Beginning in the 1970s, a 300-bungalow Club Med generated much business here, including Le Petit Village shopping center across the road. Although it closed in 2002, many locals still refer to the Club Med when giving directions. The area has been a bit depressed since the club closed. Still, this is your last chance to stop for refreshment before the sparsely populated southern half of Moorea. There are several choices here (see "Where to Dine," later in this chapter).

About 4km (2½ miles) beyond Le Petit Village, look for the **Tiki Theatre Village** ★★★, a cultural center consisting of thatched huts on the coastal side of the road. It's the only place to see what a Tahitian village looked like when Captain Cook arrived, so pull in. See "Tiki Theatre Village," below, for details.

When the first Europeans arrived, the lovely, mountain-backed village of **Haapiti** was home to the powerful Marama family, which was allied with the Pomares. It became a center of Catholic missionary work after the French took over the territory, and it is one of the few villages with a Catholic church as large as its Protestant counterpart. Stop here and look up behind the village for a view of Mount Mouaroa from a unique perspective.

THE SOUTHEAST COAST

South of Haapiti, just as the road curves sharply around a headland, is a nice view of a small bay with the mountains towering overhead (there's no place to park on the headland, so stop and walk up for the view). In contrast to the more touristy north shore, the southeast and southwest coasts have retained an atmosphere of old Polynesia.

The village of **Afareaitu,** on the southeast coast, is the administrative center of Moorea, and the building that looks like a charming hotel across from the village church actually is the island's *mairie,* or town hall.

(Moments) The View from Belvédère Lookout

If the view from Le Belvédère restaurant on Tahiti doesn't thrill me enough, the scene from the Moorea lookout of the same name certainly does. I never tire of standing at the base of that cliff and watching dramatic Mount Rotui separate the deep-blue fingers of Cook's and Opunohu bays.

MOOREA

6

EXPLORING MOOREA: THE CIRCLE ISLAND TOUR

(**Moments**) **Tahiti in All Its Glory**

My neck strains every time I cross the hill behind Moorea's Sofitel Moorea Ia Ora Beach Resort, for there, across the Sea of the Moon, sits Tahiti in all its green glory. What amazement the early explorers must have felt when those mountains appeared over the horizon!

About half a kilometer (¹/₄ mile) beyond the town hall, opposite an A-frame house on the shore, an unpaved road runs straight between several houses and then continues uphill to the **Atiraa Waterfall ★★**. Often called Afareaitu Waterfall, it plunges more than 32m (100 ft.) down a cliff, into a small pool. You can drive partway to the falls and then walk 20 minutes up a steep, slippery, and muddy trail. Wear shoes or sandals that have good traction if you make this trek, for in places the slippery trail is hacked into a steep hill; if you slip, it's a long way down to the rocks below. Villagers will be waiting at the beginning of the footpath to extract a small fee.

Beyond Afareaitu, the small bay of **Vaiare** is a beehive of activity when the ferries pull in from Papeete. On workdays, commuters park their vehicles at least 1km (¹/₂ mile) in either direction from the wharf.

TOATEA OVERLOOK & TEMAE PLAGE PUBLIQUE ★★★

Atop the hill north of the Sofitel Moorea Ia Ora Beach Resort is the **Toatea Overlook ★★★**. Here you'll have a magnificent view of the hotel, the green lagoon flecked with brown coral heads, the white line of the surf breaking on the reef, the deep blue of the Sea of the Moon, and all of Tahiti rising magnificently from the horizon. There's a parking area at the overlook.

The unpaved road to the right at the bottom of the hill leads to the **Temae Plage Publique (Temae Public Beach),** Moorea's finest stretch of public beach. Follow the left fork through the coconut grove to the lagoon. This is a continuation of the Sofitel Moorea Ia Ora Beach Resort's beach, except that here you don't have a staff to rake the leaves and coral gravel from the sand. Locals often sell snacks and souvenirs, especially on weekends. Bring insect repellent if you go on the beach here.

3 SAFARI EXPEDITIONS, LAGOON EXCURSIONS & DOLPHIN-WATCHING

SAFARI EXPEDITIONS ★★

You can see the sights and learn a lot about the island on a four-wheel-drive excursion through Moorea's mountainous interior. Every hotel activities desk will book you on one of these adventures. **Albert Tours** (② **56.13.53**) and **Moorea Explorer** (② **56.12.86**) both have them. I've been with Alex and Gheslaine Haamatearii's **Inner Island Safari Tours** (② **56.20.09;** intersaf@mail.pf), which will take you through the valleys, up to Belvédère Lookout, and then down to a vanilla plantation in Opunohu Valley. They

Tiki Theatre Village

The best cultural experience in French Polynesia is at **Tiki Theatre Village,** at PK 31, or 2km (1¼ miles) south of old Club Med (℃ **55.02.50;** www.tikivillage.pf). Founded by Olivier Briac, a Frenchman whom the local Tahitians call *Le Sauvage Blanc* (White Savage), it's built in the fashion of ancient Tahitian villages. This cultural center has old-style *fares* (houses) in which the staff demonstrates traditional tattooing, tapa-cloth making and painting, wood and stone carving, weaving, cooking, and making costumes, musical instruments, and flower crowns. There's even a "royal" house floating out on the lagoon, where you can learn about the modern art of growing black pearls.

Tiki Theatre Village will even arrange a traditional beachside wedding. The bride is prepared with flowery *monoi* oil like a Tahitian princess, and the groom is tattooed (with a wash-off pen). Both wear traditional costumes.

The village is open Tuesday to Saturday from 11am to 3pm. Admission and a guided tour cost 1,500CFP (US$19/£9.50).

Not to be missed is the authentic Tahitian feast and dance show here on Tuesday, Wednesday, Friday, and Saturday nights. They pick you up from your hotel and deposit you on the beach for a rum punch and sunset. After the staff uncovers the earth oven, they take you on a tour of the village. A buffet of both Tahitian and Western foods is followed by an energetic 1½-hour dance show with some of the most elaborate yet traditional costumes to be seen in French Polynesia. The dinner and show cost 8,700CFP (US$109/£55) per person, or you can come for the 9pm show for 4,300CFP (US$54/£57). Kids 3 to 12 pay half-price. Add 1,150CFP (US$14/£7.25) for round-trip transportation.

explain the island's flora and fauna along the way. The best trips end with a drive around Moorea's south coast and a hike up to Atiraa Waterfall for a refreshing swim (see "The Southeast Coast" under "Exploring Moorea: The Circle Island Tour," earlier in this chapter). Expect to visit a black pearl shop and Jus de Fruits de Moorea (see "Shopping" below). These half-day trips cost about 5,000CFP (US$63/£32) per person.

In a variation on this theme, **Mahana ATV Tours** (℃ **56.20.44**) takes you on all-terrain vehicles into the Opunohu Valley.

LAGOON EXCURSIONS ★★★

The lagoon around Moorea is not as beautiful or diverse as Bora Bora's, but it's worth a day's outing. Most hotel activities desks will book you on a lagoon excursion, the best way to experience the magnificent setting. The full-day version of these excursions invariably includes a "*motu* picnic"—a lunch of grilled fresh fish, *poisson cru,* and salads served on a *motu* (little islet) out on the reef. Quite often, the fresh fish is caught on the way. You'll have an opportunity to snorkel in the lagoon and learn how to husk a coconut. Some tours also include shark- and ray-feeding, one of the most interesting and exciting things to do in the water here. Wear shoes that you don't mind getting wet. The cost is about 7,000CFP (US$88/£44) per person.

(Tips) Lunch & Swim on a Motu

You can pop over for a swim, snorkeling, and a French or Tahitian lunch at **Motu Moea** (© **74.96.96**), one of the small islets off Moorea's northwestern corner. Book at your hotel activities desk, since reservations are essential for a boat shuttle leaving the InterContinental Resort & Spa Moorea at 10am, noon, or 2pm daily. Round-trip boat transfers cost about 1,600CFP (US$20/£10), while main courses average about 2,000CFP (US$25/£13). You'll be on your own out here, so follow the advice of the activities staff and don't swim in the pass between the islets.

DOLPHIN- & WHALE-WATCHING ★★★

Watching and swimming with dolphins is as much a part of the Moorea experience as is swimming with the sharks on Bora Bora (see chapter 9). You also stand a good chance of seeing humpback whales offshore from July until October, when they migrate from Antarctica to calve.

The best way to observe the animals in their natural habitat is on a dolphin- and whale-watching excursion led by American marine biologist **Dr. Michael Poole** (© **56. 23.22** or 77.50.07; www.drmichaelpoole.com). An expert on sea mammals and a leader in the effort to have French Polynesian waters declared a whale sanctuary, Dr. Poole will take you out beyond the reef to meet some of the 150 acrobatic spinner dolphins he has identified as regular Moorea residents. In calm conditions, and if the animals are agreeable, you can don snorkeling gear and swim with them. You'll also be on the lookout for pilot whales that swim past year-round and giant humpback whales that frequent these waters from July to October. The half-day excursions cost about 7,500CFP (US$94/£47) for adults, half-price for kids, including pickup at most hotel docks. Make reservations in advance, and be prepared not to go if the sea isn't calm.

Among the many activities at the InterContinental Resort and Spa Moorea (see "Watersports," below) and by far the most popular is the **Moorea Dolphin Center** ★★ (© **55.19.48**; www.mooreadolphincenter.com). The intelligent sea mammals are sure to excite young and old alike—and many honeymooners love to have their photos taken face-to-face with "smiling" dolphins. The animals live in a fenced area, although the center professes to be dedicated to their care and conservation. Kids 16 and older can join adults in snorkeling with the mammals in deeper water (all must be good swimmers) for 24,300CFP (US$304/£153) per person. A 1-hour "dolphin discovery" excursion in shallow water costs 19,800CFP (US$248/£125) per person. There's a 1-hour children's program (ages 5–11) that costs 12,000CFP (US$150/£76) per kid, and there are family programs, too. They'll even take honeymooners on their own private encounter.

4 FISHING, GOLF, WATERSPORTS & OTHER OUTDOOR ACTIVITIES

Most hotels have active watersports programs for their guests, such as glass-bottom-boat cruises and snorkeling in, or sailing on, Moorea's beautiful lagoon. Moorea has no public tennis courts, so pick a hotel that has them if tennis is important to you.

FISHING

Chris Lilley, an American who has won several sport-fishing contests, takes guests onto the ocean in search of big-game catch on his *Tea Nui* (© **55.19.19**, ext. 1903, or 56.15.08 at home; teanuiservices@mail.pf). In keeping with South Pacific custom, you can keep the little fish you catch; Chris sells the big ones. Contact Chris for rates and reservations.

GOLF

Encompassing Lake Temae west of the airport, the **Moorea Green Pearl Golf Course of Polynesia** (© **56.27.32;** www.mooreagolf-resort.com) opened in 2007 with 18 holes designed by Jack Nicklaus. The par-70 course measures 6,002m (6,596 yards). Greens fees are 12,000CFP (US$150/£76) for 9 holes, 18,000CFP (US$225/£113) for 18 holes, including a cart. Rental equipment is available. The course and clubhouse are open daily from 7:30am to 5:30pm. You can practice by driving balls into the lake. Plans call for the 154-room **Warwick Moorea Golf Spa Resort** to open here in 2010 (www.warwickhotels.com).

HIKING

You won't need a guide to hike from the coast road up the Opunohu Valley to Belvédère Lookout. Up and down will take most of a day. It's a level, but hot walk along the valley floor and gets steep approaching the lookout. Bring lots of water.

Several unmarked hiking trails lead into the mountains, including one beginning in Cook's Bay and ending on the east coast near the Vaiare ferry dock, another from the southwest coast near Haapiti village across Three Coconuts Pass and into Opunohu Valley. Go with a guide on longer hikes up in the mountains. Moorea-based **Tahiti Evasion** (© **56.48.77;** www.tahitievasion.com) has half-day treks to the archaeological sites in the Opunohu Valley, across Three Coconuts Pass between the Belvédère and the south coast, and to the Afareaitu waterfall and the pierced Mount Tohiea. Prices range from 4,500CFP to 8,000CFP (US$56–US$100/£29–£51) per person.

HORSEBACK RIDING

Landlubbers can go horseback riding along the beach and into the interior with **Ranch Opunohu Valley** (© **56.28.55**). Rates are about 6,000CFP (US$75/£38) for a 1¹/₂-hour ride. Advance reservations are essential.

WATERSPORTS

The most extensive array of sporting activities is at the **InterContinental Resort and Spa Moorea** (© **55.19.19**), and its facilities can be used by both guests and visitors who are willing to pay. Options include scuba diving, parasailing (magnificent views of the bays, mountains, and reefs), water-skiing, wake-boarding, scooting about the lagoon and Opunohu Bay on jet skis, viewing coral and fish from Aquascope boats, walking on the lagoon bottom while wearing diving helmets, line fishing, and speedboat rentals. Nonguests can also pay to use the pool, snorkeling gear, and tennis courts, and to be taken over to a small islet. Call the hotel for prices, schedules, and reservations, which are required.

SCUBA DIVING

Although Moorea's lagoon is not in the same league with those at Rangiroa, Fakarava, or even Bora Bora, its outer reef has some decent sites for viewing sea life, and especially the whitetip and blacktip reef sharks. Since the northern side of Moorea fell away from the rest of the island eons ago, the reef slopes away gently here, as opposed to the precipitous drop-offs found on Tahiti and most other South Pacific islands. The shallow lagoon has mostly dead coral, so you must dive to deeper depths in order to see the colors of the living reef.

Most sites are within short boat rides of the northwest-coast resorts and require dives of 10 to 20m (33–70 ft.). The **Tiki,** off the island's northwestern point, is popular thanks to the shark-feeding (as on Bora Bora, many dives feature shark-feeding, although not all of Moorea's operators engage in this practice). Even novice divers can pet the friendly rays at **Stingray World,** just off the InterContinental Resort and Spa Moorea. **Opunohu Canyons,** off the mouth of the bay, is another favorite shark-feeding site. You can drift dive through **Taotoi Pass,** to the west of Opunohu Bay. Experienced divers can see a huge expanse of flat montipora coral at the **Roses,** at a depth of 30 to 40m (100–130 ft.) halfway between Opunohu and Cook's bays. Inside the lagoon, the **Wreck** is an old ship that was sunk to provide an artificial reef home to a multitude of fish.

The island's best diving operator is **TOPdive** (☎ 56.17.32; www.topdive.com), at the Sheraton Moorea Lagoon Resort & Spa. Also excellent is Gilles Pétré's **Moorea Diving Center** (☎ 55.17.50; www.bluenui.com) at the Moorea Pearl Resort & Spa. On the northwest coast, the InterContinental Resort and Spa Moorea is home to **Bathy's Diving** (☎ 55.19.19, ext. 1139; www.bathys.net), and **Scubapiti Moorea** (☎ 56.20.38; www. scubapiti.com) resides at Hotel Les Tipaniers. All charge about 6,500CFP (US$81/£41) for a one-tank dive, including equipment (gauges are metric).

SNORKELING & SWIMMING

Sharing the lagoon with the Sofitel Moorea Ia Ora Beach Resort, the gorgeous **Temae Plage Publique (Tamae Public Beach)** has some of the island's best snorkeling, and it's relatively safe (p. 150). Also good is the lagoon around the islets off Haapiti, but watch out for strong currents coming in and out of the nearby reef passes.

Another favorite with locals for sunning and swimming is **Mareto Plage Publique (Mareto Public Beach),** in a coconut grove west of the Sheraton Moorea between the two bays. Go around the barbed-wire fence on the eastern end.

There's good snorkeling over coral gardens off **Pianapo (Pineapple) Beach** (☎ 74. 96.96; www.painapo.com), on the Haapiti coast. This picturesque little playground charges a one-time 2,000CFP (US$25/£13) for a day pass, including use of snorkeling gear. I love to fill up on Sunday at the restaurant here (see "A Sunday Tahitian Feast" under "Where to Dine," later in this chapter).

The lagoon off Moorea's northwest corner is blessed with offshore *motus,* small islets where you can sunbathe, swim, and snorkel (but beware of strong currents), plus have lunch on **Motu Moea** (p. 152). You can rent a boat to get over there from **Moorea Locaboat** (☎ 78.13.39), based next to Hotel Les Tipaniers, or take a transfer from **Tip Nautic** next door (☎ 73.76.73) for 700CFP (US$8.75/£4.45) round-trip. Tip Nautic also rents snorkel gear for 500CFP (US$6.25/£3.15) for a half-day and kayaks starting at 500CFP (US$6.25/£3.15) per hour, and it has water-skiing and dolphin-watching trips as well.

5 SHOPPING

THE SHOPPING SCENE

The island's primary commercial center is at **Maharepa,** where you'll find black-pearl shops, banks, grocery stores, hairdressers, the main post office, and other services. The neocolonial buildings of **Le Petit Village** shopping center anchor the northwestern corner, where numerous stores sell *pareus,* T-shirts, and souvenirs. **Supersonics** (© **56. 29.73**) carries film, camera batteries, stamps, magazines, and other items. There's also a grocery store.

Boutiques and art galleries are numerous on Moorea, but they come and go as frequently as their owners arrive from France and then decide to go home. The shops below should still be here when you arrive. One of the most reliable places to look for *pareus,* tropical dresses, aloha shirts, bathing suits, T-shirts, shell jewelry, and handicrafts is **La Maison Blanche (White House)**, in Maharepa near the Moorea Pearl Resort & Spa (© **56. 13.26**). It's housed in a whitewashed vanilla planter's house with a railing enclosing a magnificent veranda, which alone makes it worth a stop. Open daily from 8:30am to 5pm.

ART

Boutique d'Art Marquisien (Marquesan Art Boutique)   A family from the Marquesas Islands runs this attractive shop, where they sell exquisite art and handicrafts from their native archipelago. Woodcarvings top their list, including intricately carved tables that will cost a fortune to ship home. More manageable are war clubs, paintings, stone work, masks, tikis, and carved coconut shells. Open Monday through Saturday from 8am to 5:30pm. Cook's Bay, in Cooks Bay Center shops. © **56.23.37.**

Galerie van der Heyde ★★   Dutch artist Aad van der Heyde has lived and worked on Moorea since 1964. One of his bold Impressionist paintings of a Tahitian woman was selected for French Polynesia's 100CFP postage stamp in 1975, and his landscape of Bora Bora appeared on a 2004 stamp. Aad will sell you an autographed lithograph of the paintings. Some of his works are displayed on the gallery's garden wall. He has also produced excellent videos of the islands and will gladly sell you a copy on DVD. In addition, you'll see a small collection of pearls, woodcarvings, tapa cloth, shell and coral jewelry, and primitive art from Papua New Guinea. Open Monday through Saturday from 8am to 5pm. East side of Cook's Bay. © **56.14.22.**

Sculpture Par Woody ★   Woody Howard was studying horticulture at the University of Hawaii when he came to Moorea in 1982 to work on Hotel Bali Hai's plantation. Like so many others, he stayed. He's more likely to be off running his pearl farm in the Tuamotus these days, but if you're lucky, he'll be here carving award-winning images of dolphins, fish, Polynesian wildlife, and women. He also has a reasonably priced selection of black pearls. Open Monday through Saturday from 8am to 5pm. Papetoai, btw. village and InterContinental Resort and Spa Moorea. © **56.37.00** or 56.17.73.

BLACK PEARLS

Moorea has more pearl shops than you can visit on a normal vacation. In fact, many of the stores will come looking for you, with offers of free transportation to and from your hotel or the cruise-ship landing in Opunohu Bay, and tour operators are likely to deposit you at the shop offering the highest commission at the end of your excursion. But Moorea also has small, family-owned shops that carry quality pearls that cost less, since the shops don't have high overheads and promotion expenses. Always shop around—and read "Buying Your Black Pearl" (p. 124) before making your purchase.

Among several stores near the old Club Med site in Haapiti is **Tahia Collins** (© **55. 05.00;** www.tahiacollins.com). Owner and chief designer Tahia Collins was a Miss Moorea and is a scion of the Albert Haring family (you will see the Albert name all over the island). Her husband, Marc Collins, was born in Hawaii of an American father and

Tahitian mother. Theirs is the most aggressive pearl dealership on Moorea, and since they have the concession on some of the cruise ships, Tahia Collins will be the first dealer many of you will encounter here. Others worth visiting in this area are **Herman Perles** (© **56.42.79**) and **Pai Moana Pearls** (© **56.25.25**).

My favorites are the lower-key shops on the other side of the island, to wit:

Ann Simon Boutique   The French owner of this shop, Ann Simon, specializes in darker pearls—those with rich blue and green hues—set in 18-karat gold. That combination makes them anything but inexpensive, but this is a good place to see what high-quality black pearls look like. Some of Ann's designs are unique. Open Monday through Saturday from 9am to 6pm. Maharepa, west of the post office. © **56.44.55.**

Eva Perles   Eva Frachon, the French gemologist who owns this little shop, graduated from the University of Wisconsin at Oshkosh with a bachelor's degree in photography and art metals; thus, she does her own creative settings, and speaks American-style English. She carries high-quality orbs in all price ranges. Eva and Ron Hall's Island Fashion Black Pearls (see below) are the only Cook's Bay dealers who can legally send a courtesy shuttle to pick you up. Open Monday through Saturday from 9:30am to 5:30pm. Maharepa, opposite the post office. © **56.10.10.**

Ron Hall's Island Fashion Black Pearls ★★★ (Value)   Ron Hall sailed from Hawaii to Tahiti with the actor Peter Fonda in 1974. Peter went home; Ron didn't. Now Ron and his son, Heimata, run this air-conditioned Moorea retail outlet. It's worth a stop to see the antiques and old photos, including one of the infamous Quinn's Bar and a William Leeteg painting of a Tahitian *vahine* (Ron's wife and Heimata's mother, Josée, was herself a championship Tahitian dancer). In 15 minutes of "pearl school," you will learn the basics of picking a pearl. They will have your selection set in a mounting of your choice, their prices are fair, and they donate 10% of every pearl purchase to Dr. Michael Poole's dolphin and whale research (see "Dolphin- & Whale-Watching," above). They also carry one of Moorea's best selections of bathing suits, aloha shirts, and T-shirts. Open Monday through Saturday from 9am to 6pm. East side of Cook's Bay. © **56.11.06.**

MOOREA

6

WHERE TO STAY

6 WHERE TO STAY

Most of Moorea's hotels and restaurants are grouped in or near Cook's Bay, between Cook's and Opunohu bays, or in the Haapiti district on the northwest corner of the island around the old Club Med site. With the exception of the Sofitel Moorea Ia Ora Beach Resort, those in or near Cook's Bay do not have the best beaches on the island, but the snorkeling is excellent and most have unsurpassed views of the mountains. The establishments between the two bays have beaches, but they are a bit inconvenient to the facilities at both Cook's Bay and Haapiti. Those on the northwest corner have generally fine beaches, lagoons like giant swimming pools, and unobstructed views of the sunset, but not of Moorea's famous mountains. The areas are relatively far apart, so you might spend most of your time near your hotel unless you rent a vehicle or otherwise make a point to see the sights. An alternative is to split your stay between the areas.

THE COOK'S BAY AREA

Plans have been announced to build the 154-room **Warwick Moorea Golf Spa Resort** (www.warwickhotels.com) in Temae next to the Moorea Green Pearl Golf Course of Polynesia. Opening is scheduled for 2010.

Moorea Ferry
(to Tahiti)

To Tahiti →
(12 miles)

Sea of
the Moon

Temae Airport
Temae Plage Publique

Lake Temae

Temae

Vaiare

Motu Ahi

Maharepa

Afareaitu

Atiraa Waterfall

Belvédère Lookout

Mt. Tohiea

Maatea

Pao Pao

Cook's Bay

Mt. Rotui

Three Coconuts Pass

Mareto Plage Publique

Opunohu Bay

Mt. Mouaroa

Haapiti

Papetoai

Mt. Mouapu

SOUTH PACIFIC OCEAN

SOCIETY ISLANDS

Moorea

Tahiti

Huahine

Bora Bora

Camping Chez Nelson **1**
Club Bali Hai **10**
Fare Manuia **16**
Fare Vaihere **6**
Fare Vai Moana **1**
Hotel Hibiscus **2**
Hotel Kaveka **9**
Hotel Les Tipaniers **3**
InterContinental Resort and Spa Moorea **5**
La Baie de Naurei **12**
Legends Resort **4**
Mark's Place Paradise **14**
Moorea Pearl Resort & Spa **11**
Pension Motu Iti **8**
Residence Linareva **15**
Sheraton Moorea Lagoon Resort & Spa **7**
Sofitel Moorea Ia Ora Beach Resort **13**

✈ Airport
⤹ Beach
--- Ferry
······ Hiking trail
~~~ Reef
▭▭▭ Unpaved road

MOOREA

6

WHERE TO STAY

Moorea Pearl Resort & Spa ★★★   You can easily walk from this multifaceted resort to Maharepa's shops and restaurants. Forget a great view, since the resort faces the open ocean, and its 28 overwater bungalows block most of the sea view. On the other hand, snorkeling is excellent here, especially from the decks of the 20 deluxe, overwater bungalows perched out on the edge of the clifflike reef. They and 18 beach bungalows with private pools in their courtyards are the pick of a mixed litter of accommodations. Some of the garden bungalows are stand-alone, while others are in less private duplex units. Sporting private backyards with plunge pools, the bungalows are identical inside, with tasteful native wood accents, ceiling fans, king-size beds, and ample shower-only bathrooms. The least expensive units are 30 spacious hotel rooms in two-story blocks away from the lagoon. They all have king-size beds and balconies or patios, and eight family rooms add two single beds. Big thatched roofs cover a large dining room and pool-level bar, which hosts Tahitian dance shows twice a week. The smallish beach and big infinity swimming pool serve as centers for numerous outdoor activities.

B.P. 3410, 98728 Maharepa, Moorea. ☏ **800/657-3275** or 55.17.50. Fax 55.17.51. www.pearlresorts.com. 95 units. 30,200CFP–35,800CFP (US$378–US$448/£190–£226) double; 40,300CFP–76,100CFP (US$504–US$951/£254–£480) bungalow. AE, DC, MC, V. **Amenities:** 2 restaurants; bar; outdoor pool; spa; Jacuzzi; watersports equipment rentals; bike rentals; activities desk; car-rental desk; limited room service; massage; babysitting; laundry service. *In room:* A/C, TV, dataport, kitchen, minibar (bungalows only), fridge, coffeemaker, hair dryer, irons, safe.

Sofitel Moorea Ia Ora Beach Resort ★★★   Known as the Sofitel Moorea Beach Resort until 2005, when it was shuttered for a complete overhaul, this sprawling resort sits beside Moorea's best lagoon and beach (it's known as Temae Public Beach north of the resort). The Sofitel is the only resort with a view of Tahiti, whose green, cloud-topped mountains seem to climb out of the horizon beyond the reef. Given its already superb location, the renovations have made it the best all-around resort on Moorea. All its original, 1960s-vintage bungalows were replaced with modern, luxurious units, and 19 overwater units were added to the 20 already here. Most overwater units face the lagoon rather than Tahiti, however, so try to get bungalow no. 117, 119, 120, 122, or 215 through 218. Ashore, the best views are from three deluxe bungalows on the south end of the property; these are the most private units here, although the beach is much better on the north side. Least expensive are the garden bungalows whose views are squeezed through the beachfront units. The thatched-roof, sand-floor gourmet restaurant here is both extremely romantic and reasonably priced (reservations are required).

B.P. 28, Maharepa, Moorea (Temae, on the northeast coast facing Tahiti). ☏ **800/763-4835,** 55.03.55, or 41.04.04 in Papeete. Fax 41.05.05. www.accorhotels.com. 119 units. 36,700CFP–85,000CFP (US$459–US$1,063/£231–£536) double. AE, DC, MC, V. **Amenities:** 2 restaurants; bar; outdoor pool; 2 tennis courts; watersports equipment rentals; bike rentals; activities desk; car-rental desk; bicycle rentals; spa; massage; babysitting; laundry service. *In room:* A/C, TV, minibar, coffeemaker, iron, safe.

MODERATE

Club Bali Hai ⟮Value⟯   The last property operated by Moorea's two surviving Bali Hai Boys (see the "The Bali Hai Boys" box, below), this basic hotel has an incredible view of Moorea's ragged mountains across Cook's Bay, a scene epitomizing the South Pacific. Under a bayside thatched roof, **Snack l'Ananas Bleu (Blue Pineapple;** p. 168) serves breakfast and lunch (see "Where to Dine," later in this chapter). It also is the scene for Muk McCallum's bring-your-own happy hours from 5:30 to 7pm Thursday to Tuesday, when he "talks story" about the good old days on Moorea. It's worth stopping by the

The Bali Hai Boys

Californians Jay Carlisle, Don "Muk" McCallum, and the late Hugh Kelley gave up their budding business careers as stockbroker, lawyer, and sporting-goods salesman, respectively, and in 1960 bought an old vanilla plantation on Moorea. Instead of planting, they refurbished a beachfront hotel that stood on their property (now occupied by the Moorea Pearl Resort & Spa). Taking a page from James A. Michener's *Tales of the South Pacific,* they renamed it the Bali Hai and opened for business in 1961. With construction of Tahiti-Faaa International Airport across the Sea of the Moon, their timing couldn't have been better. With Jay managing the money, Hugh building the resort, and Muk entertaining their guests, they quickly had a success on their hands. Travel writers soon dubbed them the "Bali Hai Boys."

Supplies and fresh produce weren't easy to come by in those days, so they put the old vanilla plantation to work producing chickens, eggs, and milk. It was the first successful poultry and dairy operation on the island.

Thank Jay, Muk, and Hugh for overwater bungalows—those cabins sitting on pilings over the lagoon, with glass panels in their floors so that we can watch the fish swim below. They built the world's first in 1968 on Raiatea. A novelty at the time, their romantic invention is now a staple at resorts well beyond French Polynesia.

club's Wednesday-night Tahitian dance shows, too. A swimming pool with a rock water-fall augments the man-made beach here. Half of the guest units are part of a timeshare operation, but that means they come equipped with cooking facilities, which is a plus for budget-minded travelers. The overwater bungalows are the least expensive in French Polynesia, while the beachfront bungalows have huge bathrooms with gardens growing in them, another trademark of the Bali Hai Boys. Most other units are in one- or two-story, motel-style buildings. All are simply but comfortably furnished. *Note:* Some units have air conditioners in their bedrooms but not in their living areas. This is good value if you don't need a phone in your room or other such luxuries. On the other hand, the view is worth a million bucks.

B.P. 8, 98728 Maharepa, Moorea. ✆ **56.13.68.** Fax 56.13.27. www.clubbalihai.com. 39 units. 14,000CFP (US$175/£89) double; 14,800CFP–19,600CFP (US$185–US$245/£94–£124) bungalow. AE, DC, MC, V. **Amenities:** Restaurant (breakfast and lunch); bar; outdoor pool; activities desk; car-rental desk; bicycle rentals; complimentary kayaks; coin-op washers and dryers. *In room:* A/C, kitchen, fridge, coffeemaker, no phone.

Hotel Kaveka (Value) Another modest property with a marvelous view, Greg Hardee's compact, all-bungalow hotel sits behind a rock wall along the road, but its other side opens to Cook's Bay. Noted for its fish burgers, the hotel's overwater **Kaveka Restaurant** (p. 171) enjoys a view rivaled only by Snack l'Ananas Bleu (Blue Pineapple) at the Club Bali Hai (see later in this chapter). The white-sand beach here is small (a breakwater fronts most of the property), but snorkeling is very good, especially off the hotel's pier. Recently refurbished, the bungalows are made of timber with shingle roofs covering pandanus ceilings. Most have attractive mat walls, single and king-size platform beds, and shower-only bathrooms. Two units have two double beds and larger bathrooms. The least expensive lanai units lack porches and air conditioners. All units have ceiling fans, but none of their windows is screened. The few-frills Kaveka often is the least expensive hotel offered in package trips to French Polynesia.

B.P. 373, 98728 Maharepa, Moorea. 🕐 **877/354-5902** or 56.50.50. Fax 56.52.63. www.hotelkaveka.com. 25 units. 11,500CFP–23,500CFP (US$144–US$294/£73–£148) double. AE, MC, V. **Amenities:** Restaurant; bar; bicycle rentals; watersports equipment rentals; laundry service. *In room:* A/C (in bungalows), TV, fridge, no phone.

La Baie de Nuarei   You can see Tahiti from this small pension, on the north side of Temae Public Beach and near the Sofitel Moorea Ia Ora Beach Resort. Owner Tamara Kindynis, who also operates a thalassotherapy spa here, has three bungalows in her beachside compound, which is enclosed by a privacy fence. With tin-topped thatched roofs, two of her bungalows can each sleep up to three persons, while a larger family unit can accommodate four. All have kitchen facilities.

B.P. 605, 98728 Maharepa, Moorea (in Temae). 🕐/fax **56.15.63.** www.labaiedenuarei.pf. 3 units. 12,000CFP–14,000CFP (US$150–US$175/£76–£88). No credit cards. **Amenities:** Spa; free use of bicycles, canoes, and snorkeling gear. *In room:* TV, kitchen, no phone.

BETWEEN COOK'S & OPUNOHU BAYS
EXPENSIVE

Sheraton Moorea Lagoon Resort & Spa ★★   This luxury hotel is not particularly convenient to restaurants and activities, but it does provide shuttles to the Tiki Village Theatre and the Vaiare ferry dock. Two stunning, conical thatched roofs cover the reception area and a French restaurant overlooking a decent beach. Steps lead down to a beachside pool with its own sunken bar. You'll get some serious pampering in the resort's full-service Mandara spa. All the guest bungalows are identical except for their location. A Y-shaped pier—with its own sundowner bar—leads to half of them out over the lagoon. These all have glass floor panels for fish-viewing and decks with steps down into the clear, 4-foot-deep water. The others are situated in a coconut grove by the beach. Every unit is equipped with niceties such as CD players, complimentary snorkeling gear, plush robes, and claw-foot bathtubs, in addition to walk-in showers.

B.P. 1005, 98279 Papetoai, Moorea (btw. Cook's and Opunohu bays). 🕐 **800/325-3535** or 55.11.11 in Moorea. Fax 86.48.40. www.sheraton.com. 106 units. 45,500CFP–86,000CFP (US$569–US$1,075/£288–£544) bungalow. AE, DC, MC, V. **Amenities:** 2 restaurants; 3 bars; outdoor pool; 2 tennis courts; health club; spa; watersports equipment rentals; bike rentals; concierge; activities desk; car-rental desk; business center; 24-hr. room service; massage; babysitting; laundry service. *In room:* A/C, TV, CD player, dataport, minibar, coffeemaker, iron, safe.

MODERATE

Fare Vaihere   On the eastern shore of Opunohu Bay, this pension has four small bungalows in its tropical gardens and a family-size unit beside the beach and lagoon. Although the buildings all have tin roofs, they sport Polynesian decor inside. Each has a front porch. Guests in the family unit have their own kitchen, while everyone else gets a complimentary tropical breakfast and can share cooking facilities in a separate lounge building. You can explore the lagoon with kayaks and snorkeling gear, either from the beach or from a long pier reaching deep water beyond the fringing reef.

B.P. 1806, 98729 Papetoai, Moorea (PK 15.5, btw. Cook's and Opunohu bays). 🕐/fax **56.19.19** or 79.00.97. www.farevaihere.com. 5 units. 17,800CFP (US$223/£113). Rates include continental breakfast. MC, V.

Pension Motu Iti   Auguste and Dora Ienfa's little pension sits beside the lagoon about 800m (2,625 ft.) west of the Sheraton Moorea Lagoon Resort & Spa. They have no beach, only a bulkhead along the shore, but a pier goes to an overwater cabana for relaxing. Their five bungalows are clean, comfortable, and reasonably spacious, and there's also a small dormitory over the main building. The dining room serves breakfast, lunch, and dinner daily, although the food at **Restaurant Aito** (p. 171) next-door is much more interesting.

B.P. 189, 98728 Maharepa, Moorea (btw. Cook's and Opunohu bays). © 55.05.20. Fax 55.05.21. www. pensionmotuiti.com. 5 units. 10,500CFP–12,000CFP (US$131–US$150/£66–£76) bungalow; 1,650CFP (US$21/£10) dorm bed. AE, MC, V. **Amenities:** Restaurant; bar; free kayaks, canoes, snorkeling gear. *In room:* TV, no phone.

THE NORTHWEST COAST
EXPENSIVE
InterContinental Resort and Spa Moorea ★★★   Although relatively isolated about 2.5km (1¹/₂ miles) east of the Club Med area, Moorea's busiest resort is famous as home to the Moorea Dolphin Center (see "Safari Expeditions, Lagoon Excursions & Dolphin-Watching," earlier in this chapter). The beach and sometimes murky lagoon here aren't the island's best, but the resort has the widest range of watersports activities on the island—all of them available both to guests and to nonguests who are willing to pay (see "Fishing, Golf, Watersports & Other Outdoor Activities," earlier in this chapter). The airy central building with a shingle roof opens to a large pool area surrounded by an ample sunning deck. Most of the guest bungalows extend partially over the water from man-made islands. Although the construction style is European, mat walls and rattan furnishings lend tropical ambience. A curving two-story building holds 52 spacious hotel rooms; they all have patios or balconies facing the beach, and their combination tub-showers are a rarity on Moorea. The Tahitian dance show on the beach is one of Moorea's most colorful. *Note:* The resort has done away with its children's program, which had made it attractive to families.

B.P. 1019, 98729 Papetoai, Moorea (btw. Papetoai and Haapiti). © **800/327-0200** or 55.19.19. Fax 55.19.55. www.interconti.com. 52 units, 102 bungalows. 32,900CFP–36,500CFP (US$411–US$456/£208–£231) double; 53,000CFP–87,400CFP (US$662–US$1,093/£335–£553) bungalow. AE, DC, MC, V. **Amenities:** Restaurant; bar; outdoor pool; tennis courts; spa; free snorkeling gear, kayaks, canoes; watersports equipment rentals; bike rentals; activities desk; car-rental desk; limited room service; babysitting; laundry service. *In room:* A/C, TV, minibar, coffeemaker, hair dryer.

Legends Resort   Opened in 2008, this property consists of 46 luxury-laden villas on a hillside opposite the InterContinental Resort and Spa Moorea. Ranging from one to three bedrooms, the thatched-roof houses have full kitchens, two bathrooms, washers and dryers, and Jacuzzi-equipped sun decks with either sea or mountain views. The Balinese-style tropical decor is identical throughout. Serving as a clubhouse for guests, a central building houses a deli-style restaurant and opens to a small, infinity-edge swimming pool overlooking the sea. Complimentary shuttles take guests around the property, to a beach across the road, and to a small private island, which has a daytime snack restaurant and bar. Legends is a good bet for families and get-away-from-it-all couples, but it is more like a suburban housing development and is definitely not a beachside resort.

B.P. 4546, 98713, Papeete (btw. Papetoai and Haapiti). (℃ **55.15.15.** Fax 55.15.01. www.legendsresort.fr. 46 units. 40,810CFP–83,530CFP (US$530–US$1,085/£265–£543) double. AE, MC, V. **Amenities:** 2 restaurants; 2 bars; outdoor pool; tennis court; exercise room; complimentary watersports equipment; massage; Wi-Fi. *In room:* A/C, TV, kitchen, coffeemaker.

MODERATE

Fare Manuia★ Beside a beach of spectacularly white sand on Moorea's southwestern coast, Jeanne Salmon's pension consists of seven thatched-roof bungalows flanking a large, palm-accented lawn. Choice among them is unit no. 1, whose large porch overlooks the beach. It has a bedroom with a queen-size bed, and there are two single beds in the living room. Other units are larger and can accommodate up to six persons. The bungalows are Tahitian-style, with unscreened, push-out windows, but they all have kitchens, electric fans, and hot-water showers. This is a good choice for families, although I recommend ample use of insect repellent. The location is a bit remote, so unless you want to be away from it all, consider renting a car.

PK 30, 98729 Papetoai, Moorea. (℃ **56.26.17.** Fax 56.10.30. www.tahitiguide.com. kinarei@hotmail.com. 7 units. 15,000CFP–18,000CFP (US$188–US$225/£95–£114). No credit cards. **Amenities:** Complimentary washers. *In room:* TV, kitchen, no phone.

Fare Vai Moana The best thing about this little hotel is its charming French restaurant and bar, housed in a beachside building with a natural thatched roof. Otherwise, it's in the center of a busy, crowded neighborhood, which can give it a Grand Central Terminal ambience, especially during mealtimes. On the other hand, more restaurants and a multitude of shops are short walks away. The guest bungalows also have thatched roofs, but most are close together, and some are duplex units, meaning you could have neighbors sharing a common wall. Your best choice is one of three units beside the beach, with unobstructed lagoon views from their porches. These are not screened, but they do have mosquito nets over their beds plus ceiling fans, and a mezzanine holds extra beds, meaning each unit can sleep up to five persons.

B.P. 1181, 98729 Papetoai, Moorea (west of old Club Med site). (℃ **56.17.14.** Fax 56.28.78. www.pacific-resorts.com. 13 units. 15,000CFP–22,000CFP (US$188–US$275/£95–£139). MC, V. **Amenities:** Restaurant; bar; watersports equipment/rentals; activities desk; limited room service. *In room:* Fridge, safe, no phone.

Hotel Hibiscus Occupying a lagoonside coconut grove in the Haapiti restaurant-and-shopping district, this hotel has been around for years. Although its 29 bungalows are showing their age a tad, they still have traditional island charms, such as natural thatched roofs extending over front porches. They also have ceiling fans and kitchenettes, making the Hibiscus attractive for longer-term stays. Next to the pool, a newer building holds 12 less charming, but air-conditioned hotel-style rooms. All units have kitchens, a relative rarity here. The beach is minimal, but a section of the lagoon has been walled off to make a safe swimming hole for children. The beachside **Sunset Restaurant and Pizzeria** serves decent pizzas and pastas, and it's a fine place to sip a cocktail at sunset.

B.P. 1009, 98279 Papetoai, Moorea (in Haapiti, east of old Club Med site). (℃ **56.12.12.** Fax 56.20.69. www.hotel-hibiscus.pf. 41 units. 14,000CFP (US$175/£89) double; 16,400CFP–27,000CFP (US$205–US$338/£104–£171) bungalow. AE, MC, V. **Amenities:** Restaurant; bar; outdoor pool; watersports equipment/rentals. *In room:* A/C (hotel rooms only), kitchen.

Hotel Les Tipaniers ★★ Value One of Moorea's best values, this friendly, French-owned establishment sits in a coconut grove beside the sandy beach wrapping around the island's northwestern corner. The widely spaced bungalows stand back in the trees, which gives the small complex an open, airy atmosphere. They also are far enough from the road to be quiet. The "standard superior" bungalows have L-shaped settees facing sliding glass doors to covered porches. Behind the settee, a raised sleeping area supports a queen-size bed, and behind that, a fully tiled bathroom has a sizable shower and vanity space. To the rear of the property, other bungalows are equipped with kitchens and can sleep up to five persons. Also out back, a building houses four small, hotel-style rooms equipped with twin beds (you can push them together), reading lights, and ample tiled bathrooms with showers. Okay for couples, these rooms are the least expensive yet comfortable place to stay on Moorea. Unlike the others, however, they do not have phones, fridges, or safes. All units here have ceiling fans but not air conditioners.

Les Tipaniers Restaurant de la Plage (Restaurant by the Beach; p. 163), with a deck over the white sands, is open during the day, while the hotel's very good **Restaurant Les Tipaniers** (p. 169) serves Italian and Frenchy cuisine at dinner. Guests can make free use of canoes and bicycles, or pay Tip Nautic for kayaking, water-skiing, *motu* trips, and diving with Scubapiti, which is based here.

If you'd like to have a bungalow without the hotel accouterments, consider **Les Tapaniers Iti,** a five-unit annex near Papetoai village. A shuttle will bring you to the main hotel, where you can make use of its facilities. Rates at the annex are lower than at the main property, and discounts are given for longer stays.

B.P. 1002, 98729 Papetoai, Moorea (in Haapiti, east of old Club Med). ✆ **56.12.67.** Fax 56.29.25. www. lestipaniers.com. 22 units. 6,900CFP (US$86/£44) double; 13,950CFP (US$174/£88) bungalow without kitchenette; 13,950CFP–15,950CFP (US$174–US$199/£88–£101) double w/kitchenette. AE, DC, MC, V. **Amenities:** 2 restaurants; 2 bars; watersports equipment rentals; canoes and bicycles; babysitting; laundry service. *In room:* Kitchen (13 units), fridge (9 units), safe (17 units).

Residence Linareva Owner Eric Lussiez has accommodations of varying size beside a very fine beach on Moorea's southwest coast. All are tropically attired with thatched ceilings, split bamboo walls, and bright fabrics, and all have porches and cooking facilities. They range from the least expensive duplex garden studios, which can sleep two persons, to an air-conditioned beachside bungalow, which can sleep up to six. The restaurant will send breakfast to your unit for an extra fee. This is a gay-friendly establishment.

B.P. 1H, 98729 Papetoai, Moorea (PK 34.5, on the southwest coast). ✆ **55.05.65.** Fax 55.05.67. www. linareva.com. 8 units. 13,500CFP–21,500CFP (US$169–US$269/£85–£136). AE, MC, V. **Amenities:** Restaurant; bar; free use of kayaks, canoes, and snorkeling gear; bike rentals; Wi-Fi. *In room:* A/C (some units), TV, kitchen, coffeemaker, no phone.

INEXPENSIVE

Camping Chez Nelson All guests share toilets, cold-water showers, and communal kitchen facilities at this campground and hostel in a beachside coconut grove about 183m (600 ft.) west of the former Club Med. In addition to camping space on a shade-less lawn, basic accommodations here include tiny bungalows for couples (just enough room for a double bed), four blocks of small rooms (two beds each), and four other thatched-roof hostel bungalows down the road (and still on the beach).

B.P. 1309, 98279 Papetoai, Moorea (in Haapiti, west of old Club Med). ✆/fax **56.15.18.** www.camping-nelson.pf. 4 bungalows, 15 rooms, 20 dorm beds. 1,200CFP–1,300CFP (US$15–US$16/£7.60–£8.20) per camper; 1,600CFP–2,000CFP (US$20–US$25/£10–£13) dorm bed; 4,300CFP–6,300CFP (US$54–US$79/£27–£40) double; 4,500CFP–5,000CFP (US$56–US$63/£29–£32) bungalow. Lower rates for stays of more than 1 night. AE, DC, MC, V. *In room:* No phone.

> ## (Tips) Bring Traveler's Checks, or Card It
>
> The only banking facility on Moorea's northwest corner is Banque de Polynésie's ATM in Le Petit Village shopping center, opposite the old Club Med site. Since you cannot be assured of withdrawing cash from this machine, and it's a long and expensive trip to the banks at Maharepa, bring traveler's checks if you're staying in this area, or be prepared to put most of your expenditures on a credit card.

Mark's Place Paradise A cabinetmaker from Idaho, Mark Walker moved to French Polynesia in 1980 and has put his skills to work on the creatively rustic units at this retreat in the Haapiti Valley. No two alike, his units range in size from a honeymoon unit that has a TV with DVD player to one large enough for groups or use as a dormitory. Bungalows have TVs, kitchens, and private bathrooms. Dorm residents share toilets, showers, and the communal kitchen, but everyone else has a private bathroom. Although it isn't on the beach, this is a good place for backpackers and other adventurous souls.

B.P. 41, 98279 Papetoai, Moorea (at PK 23.5 in Haapiti valley). (C) **56.43.02** or 78.93.65. www.marks-place-paradise.com. 5 bungalows (all w/bathroom), 26 dorm beds. 8,000CFP (US$100/£51) bungalow; 2,500CFP (US$31/£16) dorm bed. MC, V. Minimum 2-night stay required. **Amenities:** Bike and kayak rentals; Wi-Fi. *In room:* TV, kitchen, coffeemaker, no phone.

7 WHERE TO DINE

The restaurant scene changes quickly on Moorea, so I can only hope the ones I recommend below are still in business when you get here. As on Tahiti, you can save by eating at snack bars for breakfast, lunch, or an early dinner.

THE COOK'S BAY AREA

Nicely spiced pies come from the wood-fired oven at **Allo Pizza,** in Cook's Bay near the gendarmerie ((C) **56.18.22**). There are only two tables, so most folks carry out or call for delivery if they're staying between the Sofitel Moorea Ia Ora Beach Resort and the Sheraton Moorea Lagoon Resort & Spa. Prices range from 1,000CFP to 2,000CFP (US$13–US$25/£6.30–£13). Open Tuesday to Saturday from 11am to 2pm and 5 to 9pm, Sunday from 5 to 9pm.

EXPENSIVE

Restaurant Honu Iti (Chez Roger) CLASSIC FRENCH This bayside restaurant is the domain of owner-chef Roger Iqual, who once won the *Concours National de la Poêle d'Or* (Golden Pot Contest) in Cannes for a sea-bass concoction. The scenic setting beside Cook's Bay is terrific. Roger devotes much of his time now to painting (his works hang on the walls here), but oversees his and wife Sui-Lane's two sons back in the kitchen. They specialize in fresh seafood prepared in the classic French fashion. Be sure to try the lightly smoked slices of mahimahi or haddock served over a piquant potato salad, or the delicate mahimahi mousse. One note of caution: Although I've had very good meals here, some of my friends on Moorea have not.

Alfredo's **11**
Allo Pizza **13**
Chez Jean-Pierre **10**
Kaveka Restaurant **14**
Le Cocotier **17**
Le Mahogany **18**
Le Mayflower **2**
Le Motu Pizza Grill **3**
La Petite Maison
(Chez Lydie) **9**
La Plantation **3**
Le Sud **16**
Les Tipaniers Restaurant de la
Plage (Restaurant by
the Beach) **5**
Maria Tapas **15**
Motu Moea **4**
Patisserie Caraméline **16**
Patisserie La Polynésienne **1**
Painapo (Pineapple) Beach **6**
Restaurant Aito **7**
Restaurant Honu Iti
(Chez Roger) **10**
Restaurant Les Tipaniers **5**
Roulotte Jules & Claudine **10**
Rudy's **16**
Snack l'Ananas Bleu
(The Blue Pineapple) **12**
Snack Rotui **8**

Pao Pao, north of Municipal Market. ℭ **56.19.84.** Reservations recommended. Main courses 2,900CFP–3,800CFP (US$36–US$48/£18–£24); tourist menu 5,000CFP (US$63/£32). AE, MC, V. Daily 11:30am–2pm and 6:30–9pm.

MODERATE

Alfredo's ITALIAN/FRENCH   Gregarious French restaurateur Christian Boucheron, who worked at hotels in the Washington, D.C., suburbs for 19 years, will make you feel right at home in this old building, a short walk from the Club Bali Hai. In fact, many guests are Americans and other English-speaking visitors who come here more for the fun than the food. The menu features pizzas, pastas, and a variety of both Italian and French main courses.

Pao Pao, near Club Bali Hai. ℭ **56.17.71.** Reservations recommended. Pizza 1,650CFP (US$21/£11); main courses 2,450CFP–3,850CFP (US$31–US$48/£16–£24). MC, V. Daily 11am–2:30pm and 5:30–9:30pm.

Kaveka Restaurant (Value) FRENCH/CHINESE/ITALIAN   Even if I'm not staying at Hotel Kaveka, I come in for Moorea's best mahimahi burger and the terrific view of Cook's Bay from its overwater restaurant. Pizzas, pastas, Chinese stir-fries, and French steaks and chicken are inferior to the fish burgers, but they are good value nonetheless, especially considering the view. A portable bar rolls out on the hotel's pier, making it a great place to watch the sunset (from this vantage, it disappears into the sea, but also paints the mountains surrounding Cook's Bay with a phenomenal array of colors). A Tahitian string band usually performs here during dinner on Friday and Saturday.

Cook's Bay, in Hotel Kaveka. ℭ **56.50.50.** Reservations recommended for dinner. Burgers and sandwiches 850CFP–1,950CFP (US$11–US$24/£5.40–£12); pizza and pasta 1,650CFP–1,800CFP (US$21–US$23/£11–£12); main courses 1,100CFP–2,850CFP (US$14–US$36/£7–£28). AE, MC, V. Daily 6:30–9:30am, 11:30am–2pm, and 6:30–9pm.

La Petite Maison (Chez Lydie) (Finds) FRENCH/MEDITERRANEAN/CHINESE   Lydie Pache worked at Le Mahogany for many years before opening her little restaurant near the bridge in Pao Pao village. Ask for one of the bayside tables on the covered veranda; they look north toward the yachts anchored in Cook's Bay. As at Le Mahogany, she serves Cantonese Chinese dishes (less expensive here), but her best offerings are fresh seafood treated in the Mediterranean fashion. I was impressed with her *poêlée,* a mixed seafood casserole with butter, cream, and garlic. Paella and couscous appear here, too. Lydie brings a bowl of peanuts for munching before your first course arrives.

Paopao, east side of bridge. ℭ **56.34.80.** Reservations recommended. Main courses 1,000CFP–2,800CFP (US$13–US$35/£7–£18). MC, V. Daily 11am–3pm and 6–10pm.

Le Cocotier ★ TRADITIONAL FRENCH   One of Moorea's more consistent restaurants, Le Cocotier has widely spaced tables under a natural thatched roof, which helps make it one of the island's more romantic places to dine. The chef specializes in

---

(Value) **Call for Transportation**

Most Moorea restaurants will either come get you or pay half, if not all, of your taxi fare if you make reservations for dinner. Although they restrict this service to nearby guests, depending on the size of your group, it pays to call ahead and ask.

mahimahi steamed in paper with basil sauce, tuna steak in a green-pepper sauce, and other seafood prepared the traditional French way. For a change of pace, I enjoyed his homemade ham (like the sugar-cured version we get in Virginia) in a port-wine sauce. For dessert, don't miss the bananas roasted in coconut cream and served with vanilla ice cream.

Maharepa. ✆ **56.12.10.** Reservations recommended. Main courses 2,050CFP–2,950CFP (US$26–US$37/ £13–£19). MC, V. Mon–Fri 9:30am–2pm and 6–10pm; Sat 6–10pm.

Le Mahogany ★★ ⓥ Value FRENCH/CHINESE   French chef François Courtien spent 30 years cooking at the former Hotel Bali Hai before joining Tahitian Blondine Agnia at her pleasant little dining spot next to the local gym. It's a favorite with local expatriates who appreciate value and friendly service. Polished mahogany tables, art-adorned walls, and a window opening to a garden provide tropical ambience. A rich avocado-and-shrimp cocktail is a good way to start. Consistently good are Moorea-grown shrimp with curry or Provençal sauce, and shrimp and scallops in a puff pastry with a light cream sauce. The Cantonese main courses are better than those at any Chinese restaurant here. Or you can opt for the special tourist menu of a salad, mahimahi grilled or with meunière sauce, and ice cream for dessert. Otherwise, end with a *tarte tatin,* a caramelized apple pie served with vanilla ice cream.

Maharepa. ✆ **56.39.73.** Reservations recommended. Main courses 1,450CFP–2,950CFP (US$18–US$37/ £9–£19); tourist menu 3,250CFP (US$41/£21). MC, V. Thurs–Tues 11am–2:30pm and 6–9:30pm.

Le Sud ★ SOUTHERN FRENCH   For a pleasant change of French pace, head to this little white house in the Maharepa shopping district for paella, Provençal-style fish dishes, and seafood pastas from *le sud* (the south) of France. The spices definitely reflect Spanish and Italian influences. The *plats du jour* are very good value, especially at lunch. Torches contribute to romantic nighttime dining on the patio.

Maharepa. ✆ **56.42.95.** Reservations recommended. Main courses 1,900CFP–2,900CFP (US$24–US$36/£12–£18). MC, V. Tues–Sat 11am–2pm and 6–9pm; Sun 6–9pm.

Rudy's ⓕ Finds FRENCH/STEAKS   This hacienda-style steakhouse is the latest creation of Tahiti-born Syd Pollack, who has started several restaurants and other projects both here and in Hawaii. This one is named for his son Rudy, who oversees the kitchen here. In addition to tender New Zealand steaks, there is fresh local seafood. I always check the specials board for the likes of parrotfish grilled and stuffed with crab, or beef in a red-wine sauce, but with island influences.

Maharepa, west of post office. ✆ **56.58.00.** Reservations recommended. Main courses 2,200CFP–3,200CFP (US$28–US$40/£14–£20). MC, V. Daily 11am–2:30pm and 5:30–10pm.

INEXPENSIVE

Chez Jean-Pierre CANTONESE   When my body tells me to eat my vegetables, I get off the tourist track and join the locals at this plain but clean Chinese family restaurant beside Cook's Bay. You can try very good Chinese-style *poisson cru* (it's spicy) or chicken with sweet Moorea pineapple. Everything's fresh and tasty here.

Pao Pao, near Municipal Market. ✆ **56.18.51.** Main courses 1,350CFP–2,150CFP (US$17–US$27/£8.55–£14). MC, V. Mon–Tues and Thurs–Sat 11:15am–2:30pm; Thurs–Tues 6:15–9:30pm.

MariaTapas FRENCH/TEX-MEX   You'll hear conversations being held in French, English, and Tahitian—sometimes all three simultaneously—at this lively pub, where the offspring of Moorea's many expatriate residents like to hang out. Happy hours from 6 to

7pm on Thursday and Friday and entertainment on Friday and Saturday evenings really pack them in, especially when live music is on. Although Tex-Mex is the official specialty, I stick to burgers, salads, steaks, and French fare. Friendly owner Julie Berten stocks a wide selection of European beers.

Cook's Bay, PK 6 in Kilupa Centre. © **55.01.70.** Reservations accepted. Most items 950CFP–2,400CFP (US$12–US$30/£6–£15). MC, V. Restaurant Mon and Wed–Thurs 11:30am–2:30pm and 6:30–9:30pm; Fri 11:30am–2:30pm and 6:30pm–1am; Sat 6pm–1am. Bar Mon–Thurs 9am–11pm; Fri 9am–1am; Sat 6pm–1am.

Patisserie Caraméline (Value) PATISSERIE/SNACKS   A good choice for a cooked breakfast, this patisserie also offers a selection of pastries, crepes, pizzas, salads, omelets, quiches, burgers, sandwiches, *poisson cru,* shrimp in coconut curry sauce, grilled tuna and mahimahi, fruit plates, ice cream, sundaes, and other goodies. The patio tables here are a relaxing spot to write a postcard.

Maharepa, next to the post office. © **56.15.88.** Breakfasts 700CFP–1,550CFP (US$8.75–US$19/£4.45–£9.80); snacks and light meals 500CFP–1,800CFP (US$6.25–US$23/£3.15–£11). MC, V. Daily 7am–5pm.

Snack l'Ananas Bleu (Blue Pineapple) (Value) BREAKFAST/SNACKS   Matahi Hunter's "snack" occupies what was once the sunken bayside bar at the Club Bali Hai, where a stupendous view of Cook's Bay accompanies the cooked or continental breakfasts and the lunches of big juicy beef, fish, or teriyaki burgers and french fries. Ice cream and fruit drinks provide relief from the midday heat. There's a seafood barbecue on Wednesday night following the hotel's Tahitian dance show.

Pao Pao, in Club Bali Hai. © **56.12.06.** Breakfast 600CFP–1,650CFP (US$7.50–US$21/£3.80–£10); burgers and sandwiches 800CFP–1,650CFP (US$10–US$21/£5–£11); main courses 1,450CFP–2,350CFP (US$18–US$30/£9–£15). MC, V. Daily 7am–3pm.

Snack Rotui SNACK BAR   On the shore of Cook's Bay, this walk-up "snack" is run by a Chinese family, and for about 550CFP (US$6.85/£3.50) you can get a sandwich, a soft drink, and a slice of delicious homemade cake. The owners prepare Chinese plate lunches across the road and bike them over here. A few tables under a roof beside the beach catch the breezes off the bay; for more than 20 years, I've taken in this splendid view while munching a *casse-croûte* sandwich.

Pao Pao, west of the bridge at the head of Cook's Bay. © **56.18.16.** Sandwiches 200CFP–350CFP (US$2.50–US$4.40/£1.25–£2.20). No credit cards. Tues–Sun 7am–6pm.

(Tips)   Check Out Moorea's Roulottes

As on Tahiti, your best bet for inexpensive nighttime meals is the local *roulottes* (see "Don't Miss *Les Roulottes*," p. 140). The best of these meal wagons, **Roulotte Jules & Claudine,** at the fish market in Pao Pao (© **56.25.31**), serves a mixed menu of *poisson cru,* chow mein, and char-grilled steaks, chicken, and fish, but the best item is local shrimp in a tasty coconut-curry sauce. Prices range from 1,000CFP to 1,800CFP (US$13–US$23/£6.30–£11). No credit cards. Open Monday through Saturday from 6:30 to 8:30pm. You'll find another *roulotte* near Le Petite Village shopping center in Haapiti.

BETWEEN COOK'S & OPUNOHU BAYS

Restaurant Aito FRENCH/CORSICAN   Extending out over the lagoon, this open-air cafe preserves the old South Seas ambience better than any other restaurant on Moorea. Adding to the charm are big *aito* (ironwood) trees growing through the deck and thatched roof (hence the restaurant's name). Owner Jean-Baptiste Cipriani grew up in Marseilles on the cooking of his Corsican ancestors, and he repeats some of those dishes here, including a luscious tomato sauce that requires 10 hours to prepare. You can dip your bread into some *very* spicy Corsican peppers while waiting. This isn't the cleanest place on Moorea, but it's a terrific spot for a lagoonside meal, as many celebrity visits attest.

PK 13.1, west of Sheraton Moorea btw. Cook's and Opunohu bays. ✆ **56.45.52.** Reservations recommended. Main courses 1,850CFP–2,800CFP (US$23–US$35/£12–£18). MC, V. Wed–Mon 11am–2:30pm and 6–9pm.

THE NORTHWEST COAST

EXPENSIVE

La Plantation ★★ FRENCH/CAJUN   It's not exactly New Orleans quality, but Nathalie Richard and Bertrand Jardon do a fine imitation of Louisiana fare at this large restaurant with tables inside or on a plantation-like veranda. Spicy gazpacho, jambalaya, and whole crab Cajun-style offer relief from the French sauces that rule elsewhere. Two fixed-price menus offer three courses each of either French or Cajun fare. Nathalie and Bertrand turn down the lights at night, creating romantic ambience.

Haapiti (opposite old Club Med). ✆ **54.45.10.** Reservations recommended. Main courses 2,400CFP–4,500CFP (US$30–US$56/£15–£28); fixed-price dinners 4,500CFP–5,100CFP (US$56–US$64/£28–£32). MC, V. Wed 6:30–9:30pm; Thurs–Mon 11:30am–9:30pm.

MODERATE

Le Mayflower ★★★ Value CASUAL FRENCH   This roadside restaurant draws mostly local residents, who rightly proclaim it to be Moorea's best for both food and value. The sauces are lighter than you will experience elsewhere, and there is always a vegetarian selection. I like to start with a salad of warm local shrimp over cool, fresh greens. The house special—lobster ravioli in a cream sauce—is a worthy main choice, as are seafood pasta under pesto or the reliable shrimp in coconut curry. Mahimahi in a lobster sauce highlights a special tourist menu here.

Haapiti, west of old Club Med site. ✆ **56.53.59.** Reservations recommended. Main courses 1,650CFP–2,650CFP (US$21–US$33/£10–£17). AE, MC, V. Tues–Sun 11:30am–2pm and 6:30–10:30pm.

Restaurant Les Tipaniers ★ Value ITALIAN/FRENCH   This romantic, thatched-roof restaurant is popular with visitors and Moorea's permanent residents, who come here for delicious pizzas with a variety of toppings and homemade spaghetti, lasagna, tagliatelle, and gnocchi served with Bolognese, carbonara, or seafood sauce. French dishes include pepper steak and filets of mahimahi in butter or vanilla sauce. Discounted transportation is available for Haapiti-area hotel guests.

Haapiti, at Hotel Les Tipaniers, east of old Club Med. ✆ **56.12.67.** Reservations recommended. Pasta and pizza 1,000CFP–1,550CFP (US$13–US$20/£6.30–£10); main courses 1,850CFP–2,550CFP (US$23–US$32/£12–£16). AE, DC, MC, V. Daily 6:30–9:15pm.

INEXPENSIVE

Le Motu Pizza Grill SNACK BAR   You can get grilled steak or fish with french fries at this open-air restaurant, but it's best for pizzas, crepes, and large hamburgers. Light

Moments **A Sunday Tahitian Feast**

Locals love to partake of huge *ma'a Tahiti* feasts on Sunday afternoon, and I join them at Ron Sage's **Painapo (Pineapple) Beach** (☎ **74.96.96;** www.painapo. com), on the southwestern coast. It's a lovely setting with tables under a natural thatched-roof restaurant (with sand floor) as well as outside under the shade of a sprawling beachside tree. Ron's all-you-can-eat Sunday buffet of traditional Tahitian foods costs 3,500CFP (US$44/£22), a steal in these expensive islands. He also serves an à la carte menu of fresh grilled fish for 1,900CFP to 2,500CFP (US$24–US$31/£12–£16) Monday to Thursday, when Pineapple Beach is open from 9am to 3pm. Bring cash, for Ron does not accept credit cards. See "Eating & Drinking in Tahiti & French Polynesia" (p. 36) for more information about Tahitian chow.

fare includes salads, crepes, and soft ice cream, and a selection of soft drinks, beer, and wine.

Haapiti, opposite old Club Med. ☎ **56.16.70.** Burgers, sandwiches, and salads 500CFP–1,400CFP (US$6.25–US$18/£3.15–£8.85); pizza 1,050CFP–1,300CFP (US$13–US$16/£7–£8). MC, V (2,000CFP minimum). Mon–Sat 9:30am–9pm; Sun 9:30am–3pm.

Les Tipaniers Restaurant de la Plage (Restaurant by the Beach) ★ ITALIAN/ SNACK BAR   Under a soaring thatched roof and opening to the lagoon, this is the best place in Haapiti for a lagoonside lunch or sunset cocktail. It offers a good selection of salads (some with fruit) and a big juicy burger. Or you can select one of the pastas that make the hotel's nighttime restaurant popular (see above). Breakfast is also served here.

Haapiti, at Hotel Les Tipaniers, east of old Club Med. ☎ **56.19.19.** Salads, sandwiches, burgers 550CFP–1,300CFP (US$6.90–US$16/£3.80–£8.20); pastas 1,000CFP–1,700CFP (US$13–US$21/£6.30–£11). AE, DC, MC, V. Daily 6:30–9:30am and noon–2:15pm. Bar daily 6:30am–7pm.

Patisserie La Polynésienne BREAKFAST/SNACKS   Next door to Le Mayflower, this is a good place to start your day with croissants and coffee or a full American-style breakfast (served all day). Later, you can stop for crepes, burgers, sandwiches, small pizzas, quiches, and pastries. The low-slung building has six tables on a sand floor under cover.

Haapiti, west of the Club Med site. ☎ **56.20.45.** Reservations not necessary. Breakfast 600CFP–1,800CFP (US$7.50–US$23/£3.80–£11); crepes and salads 400CFP–900CFP (US$5–US$11/£2.55–£5.70). No credit cards. Mon–Fri 7:30am–1pm and 3–6pm; Sat–Sun 7am–6pm.

8 ISLAND NIGHTS ON MOOREA

The one required nighttime activity here is an authentic feast and dance show at **Tiki Theatre Village** in Haapiti (☎ **55.02.50**). For details, see p. 149.

Moorea's major resorts also have Tahitian feasts and dance shows at least once a week. The most elaborate is the Saturday-evening lagoonside show at the InterContinental

(Moments) Sunsets with Muk at Club Bali Hai

If I'm on Moorea, you'll find me beside Cook's Bay at the **Club Bali Hai** (© **56.13.68**) swapping yarns with Muk McCallum, one of the original Bali Hai Boys. His bring-your-own happy hours run Thursday through Tuesday between 5:30 and 7pm. This is one of the great vistas in the South Pacific; you'll want to become a modern Paul Gauguin in order to capture the changing colors of the bay, sky, and jagged mountains.

Resort and Spa Moorea. Most charge 8,000CFP to 9,500CFP (US$100–US$119/£51–£60) per person for the dinner and dance show.

One notable exception is a free show at the **Club Bali Hai** (© **56.13.68**) every Wednesday at 6pm. It's followed by an à la carte seafood barbecue at Snack l'Ananas Bleu (Blue Pineapple). Meals range from 1,800CFP to 3,900CFP (US$23–US$49/£11–£25). Reservations are required for the barbecue.

Among the restaurants, **Maria@Tapas** (© **55.01.70**) has entertainment on Friday and Saturday evenings (expect a cover charge when bands perform unless you dine there). Scottish-born guitarist Ron Falconer appears at **Restaurant Aito** (© **56.45.52**) on Friday night. And a string band plays traditional Tahitian tunes on Friday and Saturday nights at **Kaveka Restaurant** (© **56.50.50**). See "Where to Dine," earlier in this chapter. In the Haapiti hotel district, **PK0** (© **56.55.46**) has live music on Friday and Saturday. It's Haapiti's version of Maria@Tapas.

Huahine

Pronounced Wa-ee-nee by the French (who never sound an "h") and *Who*-a-hee-nay by the Tahitians (who always do), Huahine ranks with Easter Island and Raiatea (see chapter 8) as the three most important Polynesian archaeological sites. Here, the ancient chiefs built a series of *maraes* on the shores of **Lake Fauna Nui,** which separates the north shore from a long, *motu*-like peninsula, and on Matairea Hill above the lakeside village of **Maeva.** These have been restored, and informational markers explain their history and purposes.

Many honeymooners and other visitors are making Huahine their last vacation stop, drawn by its relaxed ambience, Moorea-esque bays, lovely beaches, and friendly people. **Baie Avea (Avea Bay),** on the far southwestern coast of Huahine Iti, is fringed by one of French Polynesia's most glorious beaches. Another beach is right in the small hamlet of **Fare,** one of the region's best examples of what the South Seas were like in the days of trading schooners and copra planters.

Personally, I think Huahine is the third most beautiful of the Society Islands (behind Moorea and Bora Bora). Geographically, it is actually two islands—**Huahine Nui** and **Huahine Iti** (Big Huahine and Little Huahine, respectively)—enclosed by the same reef and joined by a short bridge, which, in turn, separates two picturesque bays, Maroe and Bourayne. With basaltic thumbs reaching from jagged mountains on either side of the bays, this vista reminds me of Moorea.

France did not annex Huahine until 1897, more than 50 years after it took over Tahiti, and its 5,500 residents are still independent in spirit. When the first Europeans arrived, Huahine was governed as a single chiefdom and not divided into warring tribes as were the other islands, and this spirit of unity is still strong. Pouvanaa a Oopa, the founder of French Polynesia's independence movement, hailed from here. Unrushed by hordes of tourists, the friendly people of Huahine still say *"Ia orana"* to us visitors.

1 GETTING AROUND HUAHINE

Huahine's airport is on the flat peninsula paralleling the north side of the island, 3km (2 miles) from Fare. Unless you have previously reserved a rental car or are willing to walk into Fare, take your hotel minibus; at other times, **Moe's Taxi** (© **72.80.60**) or **Enite's Taxi** (© **68.82.37**). Fares are 600CFP (US$7.50/£3.80) from the airport into Fare, and 2,500CFP (US$31/£16) to the southern end of Huahine Iti.

Avis (© **800/230-4898** or 68.73.34; www.avis.com), **Europcar** (© **800/227-7368** or 68.82.59; www.europcar-tahiti.com), and **Hertz** (© **800/654-3131** or 68.76.85; www.hertz.com) have agents in Fare. Europcar's starts at 9,400CFP (US$118/£60) a day. Avis charges 12,000CFP (US$150/£76) a day for air-conditioned cars. Europcar's scooters are 6,200CFP (US$78/£39) a day; bicycles are 2,000CFP (US$25/£13) a day. **Huahine Lagoon,** (© **68.70.00**) has bicycles for 1,500CFP (US$19/£9.50) for 8 hours. On Huahine Iti, **Moana Turquoise** (© **68.85.57**), rents scooters for 6,500CFP (US$81/£41) a day and bicycles for 2,500CFP (US$31/£16) a day.

Aérodrome de Huahine-Fare

SOUTH PACIFIC OCEAN

Lac Fauna Nui

1 ○ Manunu *Marae* ■
Maeva

12
11
Passe Avamoa

○ Fare

10

Passe Avapeihi

▲ Turi

Baie de Cook

HUAHINE NUI

○ Fitii

2 ○ Faie

Baie Faie

Passe Tiare

9

3

Passe Farerea

8

Baie Maroe

Maroe ○

HUAHINE ITI

Tefarerii ○

Baie Bourayne

Haapu ○

Mahuti River

📷

Parea ○

0 ___ 1 mi
0 ___ 1 km
Ⓝ

Baie Avea
4
5
6
Avea Beach 🏖 **7**

SOUTH PACIFIC OCEAN

✈ Airport
🏄 Beach
···· Reef
📷 Scenic view
⌁ Unpaved road

ACCOMMODATIONS ■
Chez Guynette **10**
Fare Ie **7, 11**
Huahine Camping **5**
Huahine Vacances **3**
Pension Fare Maeva **12**
Pension Mauarii **4**
Pension Vaihonu Océan **12**
Rande's Shack **11**
Relais Mahana **5**
Te Tiare Beach Resort **9**
Villas Bougainville **3**

ATTRACTIONS ●
Anini Marae **6**
Eden Parc **8**
Huahine Nui Pearls & Pottery **2**
Maeva maraes **1**

SOCIETY ISLANDS
Bora Bora
Huahine
Moorea
Tahiti

0 ___ 100 mi
0 ___ 100 km

Each district has local **buses,** which run into Fare at least once a day, but the schedules are highly irregular. If you take one from Fare to Parea, for example, you might not be able to get back on the same day.

(Fast Facts) Huahine

The following facts apply specifically to Huahine. For more information, see "Fast Facts: Tahiti & French Polynesia," in appendix A.

Camera & Film **AO Api New World,** upstairs over the Manava Huahine Visitors Bureau (☎ **68.70.99**), burns digital photos to CDs. See "Internet Access," below.

Currency Exchange **Banque Socredo** is in Fare, on the road that parallels the main street and bypasses the waterfront. **Banque de Tahiti** is on Fare's waterfront. Both have ATMs.

Drugstore The pharmacist at the drugstore, on the main road between Fare and the airport, speaks English (☎ **68.80.90**). Open Monday to Friday 7:30am to noon and 2:30 to 5pm, Saturday 8am to noon, Sunday and holidays 8 to 9am.

Emergencies & Police The emergency **police** telephone number is ☎ **17.** The phone number of the **gendarmerie** in Fare is ☎ **68.82.61.**

Healthcare The **government infirmary** is in Fare (☎ **68.82.48**). Ask your hotel for the names of doctors and dentists in private practice.

Internet Access You can pick up e-mail at **AO Api New World** (☎ **68.70.99**), upstairs over the Manava Huahine Visitors Bureau. Open Monday to Friday 8:30am to noon and 4 to 7:30pm, Saturday 4:30 to 9:30pm. Access costs 15CFP (US20¢/10p) a minute. Restaurant New Temarara, on the Fare waterfront (☎ **68.89.31**), has wireless access for 700CFP (US$8.75/£4.45) an hour.

Mail The colonial-style post office is in Fare, on the bypass road north of the waterfront area. Hours are Monday to Thursday 7:30am to 3pm, Friday 7am to 2pm.

Restrooms There are public toilets on the Fare wharf opposite the visitors bureau, but don't expect them to be clean. I use them for emergencies only.

Visitor Information On Fare's main street opposite the wharf, **Manava Huahine Visitors Bureau** (☎/fax **68.78.81**) is open Monday to Saturday 8am to noon (more or less). Some local pensions and tour operators have banded together to host **www.iaorana-huahine.com**.

Water Don't drink the tap water on Huahine. Bottled water is available at all grocery stores.

---

2 EXPLORING HUAHINE

VISITING THE MARAES & FARE POTEE ★★★

The village of **Maeva,** beside the pass where Lake Fauna Nui flows toward the sea, was a major cultural and religious center before Europeans arrived in the islands. All of Huahine's chiefly families lived here. More than 200 stone structures have been discovered between the lakeshore and **Matairea Hill,** which looms over Maeva, including some 40 *maraes* (the others were houses, paddocks, and agricultural terraces).

To see the *maraes* on your own, start west of Maeva village at the big reed-sided building known as **Fare Potee,** which houses an excellent museum (✆ **24.16.63**). Flanked by *maraes* and extending out over Lake Fauna Nui, Fare Potee is modeled after a large meetinghouse that stood here in 1925, but was later destroyed by a hurricane. Take time to read the historical markers outside, which expertly explain the history and use of the *maraes*. Inside, you'll observe *adzes* (stone axes), fishhooks, and other artifacts uncovered during restoration work by Dr. Yoshiko H. Sinoto, the chairman of the anthropology department of the Bernice P. Bishop Museum in Honolulu. He restored this and many other *maraes* throughout Polynesia. Fare Potee is open Monday through Friday 9am to noon and 2 to 4pm, Saturday 9am to noon. Admission is 200CFP (US$2.50/£1.25) per person.

Ask at Fare Potee for directions to six *maraes* and other structures (some were built as fortifications during the 1844 to 1848 French-Tahitian war) on Matairea Hill. The track up the hill can be muddy and slippery during wet weather, and the steep climb is best done in early morning or late afternoon. Better yet, take a tour (see below).

Easier to reach, the large **Manunu Marae** stands on the beach about 1km (¹⁄₂ mile) across the bridge on the east end of Maeva. Follow the left fork in the road after crossing the bridge. The setting is impressive.

From the bridge, you will see several stone **fish traps.** Restored by Dr. Sinoto, they work as well today as they did in the 16th century, trapping fish as the tide ebbs and flows in and out of the narrow passage separating the lake from the sea.

HISTORICAL TOURS

The most informative way to see the historical sites—and much of Huahine, for that matter—is with Paul Atallah of **Island Eco Tours** ★★★ (✆ **68.79.67;** www.island-eco-tours.com). Paul is an American who graduated from the University of Hawaii with a major in anthropology and a minor in Polynesian Island archaeology. He has lived in French Polynesia for more than a decade. His is more than a typical safari expedition, for he gives in-depth commentary about the Maeva *maraes* and other historical sites. He charges 5,000CFP (US$63/£32) for either morning or afternoon trips from Monday through Friday. The 3¹⁄₂- to 4-hour trips depart daily at 8am and 1pm. He will pick you up at your hotel. Paul can also guide you to the *maraes* on Matairea Hill by special arrangement.

TOURING THE ISLAND

You can rent a vehicle and tour both parts of Huahine in half a day. The main roads around both islands are about 32km (20 miles) long and are paved. Be careful on the

HUAHINE

7

EXPLORING HUAHINE

Ⓕun Facts   Say Hello to Dorothy

Be sure to say hello to Dorothy Levy, who oversees the Fare Potee museum at the Maeva *maraes*. Dorothy's Tahitian father came to Hollywood in the 1930s to work with Clark Gable on the original *Mutiny on the Bounty* movie. He later participated in the first film version of *Hurricane* with Dorothy Lamour, for whom he named this Dorothy.

(Fun Facts Adzes, Fishhooks & Ornaments

When construction began on the now-defunct Hotel Bali Hai Huahine on the north side of Fare in 1973, workers discovered some artifacts while excavating the lily ponds—the only remnants of the hotel left today. Dr. Yoshiko of the Bernice P. Bishop Museum in Honolulu just happened to be on the island and took charge of further excavations. During the next 2 years, the diggers uncovered *adzes*, fishhooks, and ornaments that had been undisturbed for more than 1,000 years, according to radiocarbon dating of a whale bone found with the items.

steep *traversière* (cross-island road) that traverses the mountains from Maroe Bay to Faie Bay on the east coast. (I would not ride a scooter or bicycle over this road.) Heading clockwise from **Fare,** you skirt the shores of Lake Fauna Nui and come to the *maraes* outside Maeva village (see "Visiting the *Maraes* & Fare Potee," above).

From Maeva, the road heads south until it turns into picturesque Faie Bay. Here you'll pass the landing for **Huahine Nui Pearls & Pottery ★** (© **78.30.20;** www.huahine pearlfarm.com), a pearl farm and pottery studio (p. 179). Once you're past Faie village at the head of the bay, the road starts uphill across the *traversière* (see above). At the top, you'll be rewarded with a view down across Moorea-esque **Maroe Bay,** which splits Huahine into two islands.

Turn right at the dead-end by the bay and drive west to the main west-coast road. Turn left and follow it across the bridge over the narrow pass separating Huahine Nui from Huahine Iti. A right turn past the bridge will take you along the winding west-coast road to **Avea Bay,** where Relais Mahana (p. 180) and Pension Mauarii (p. 181) sit beside one of the South Pacific's greatest beaches. Either is an excellent place to stop for refreshment.

Sitting at the end of the peninsula at the south end of Huahine Iti, **Anini Marae** presents a glorious view of the island's southern coast. Nearby on the grounds of Fare Ie (see "Where to Stay," below), another small *marae* bears the **Taiharuru Petroglyphs. Parea** is one of Huahine's largest villages. From there, you'll skirt the shoreline until you come to the village of **Tefarerii** on the east coast. In between is a pull-off with a marvelous view over the reefs and sea. From here, it's an easy drive to Maroe Bay. The large cruise ships land their passengers at Maroe village on the south side of the bay.

REVISITING THE OLD SOUTH SEAS IN FARE

The main village of **Fare ★★★** (*Fah*-ray) is hardly more than a row of Chinese stores and a wharf opposite the main pass in the reef on the northwest shore, but it takes us back to the days when trading schooners were the only way to get around the islands. Even today, trucks and buses arrive from all over Huahine with passengers and cargo when the interisland boats put in from Papeete. The rest of the time, Fare lives a lazy, slow pace, as people amble down its tree-lined main street and browse through the stores facing the town wharf. A monument on the waterfront designates it as **Place Hawaiki,** the starting point for October's big outrigger canoe race to Raiatea and Bora Bora.

Beginning at the Restaurant New Temarara (p. 183), a pebbly promenade leads north along the waterfront to a sandy swimming beach, which has a daytime snack bar.

> **(Tips)** **Fruit Juice & an Exotic Lunch**
>
> On your way back to Fare from Huahine Iti, turn off the main road toward Bourayne Bay and drive 2km (1¼ miles) to **Eden Parc** (✆ **68.86.58;** www.edenparc.org), a lush tropical garden where you can get freshly squeezed fruit juice or enjoy an "exotic" lunch made from produce organically grown on the premises. It's a hot and steamy site, so get out your insect repellent. Open Monday through Saturday from 8am to 2pm.

3 LAGOON EXCURSIONS & SAFARI EXPEDITIONS

LAGOON EXCURSIONS

As on Moorea and Bora Bora, one of the most enjoyable ways to see the island is on a lagoon excursion that includes snorkeling and a picnic on an islet out on the reef. The biggest difference here is that with relatively few tourists around, you and your companions are likely to have the islet all to yourselves.

The all-day excursion with **Huahine Nautique** (✆ 68.83.15; www.huahine-nautique. com) takes you by outrigger canoe through Maroe Bay and around Huahine Iti. You'll stop for snorkeling and a picnic featuring freshly made *poisson cru,* and you will observe shark-feeding before returning to Fare. Huahine Nautique's canoes have shade canopies, and the guides speak English as well as French. **Poetaina Cruises** (✆ 60.60.06) also does all-day trips, but I can't guarantee that you'll have shade on your outrigger. Don't be surprised if you visit Huahine Nui Pearls & Pottery (p. 176). The excursions cost about 8,500CFP (US$106/£54) per person.

SAFARI EXPEDITIONS

As on most of the Society Islands, you can make four-wheel-drive expeditions into the mountains here. You will see a bit of the interior of Huahine Nui with Paul Atallah on his **Island Eco Tours** (see "Historical Tours," above), which I would take first. You will repeat seeing the Maeva *maraes,* but either **Huahine Land** (✆ 68.89.21), which is owned by American expatriate Joel House, or **Huahine Explorer** (✆ 68.87.33) will also take you to Huahine Iti on its half-day expeditions. Both charge about 5,100CFP (US$64/£32) per person.

4 WATERSPORTS & OTHER OUTDOOR ACTIVITIES

FISHING

For lagoon or deep-sea fishing, contact **Huahine Marine Transports** (✆ 68.84.02; hua. mar.trans@mail.pf), owned by American expatriate Rich Shamel, who has lived on Huahine for many years and who runs the transfer boats for Te Tiare Beach Resort (p. 179). Rich charges 64,000CFP (US$800/£400) for a half-day and (US$1,200/£600) for a full

(Moments) **Sailboats & Sunsets at Fare**

I thoroughly enjoy strolling along the wharf, poking my head into the shops across the main street, observing the cruising yachts anchored in the harbor, and watching the boats come and go. With Raiatea, Tahaa, and Bora Bora resting on the western horizon, Fare is one of my favorite places to watch the sunset.

day of fishing on his 11m (36-ft.) Hatteras sport-fishing boat. He lives and works at the resort's transfer base, just across the bridge on the south side of Fare.

HORSEBACK RIDING

One of the best horseback-riding operations in French Polynesia is **La Petite Ferme** (**Little Farm;** ℂ **68.82.98;** www.huahine-lapetiteferme.com), on the main road north of Fare, just before the airport turnoff. It has Marquesas-bred horses that can be ridden with English or Western saddles along the beach and around Lake Fauna Nui. Prices range from 5,500CFP (US$69/£35) for 2 hours to 11,000CFP (US$138/£70) for an all-day trail ride. The farm also has accommodations, from a dormitory to bungalows.

SAILING

You can go for a half- or full-day cruise with Claude and Martine Bordier of **Sailing Huahine Voile** (ℂ/fax **68.72.49;** www.sailing-huahine.com) on their *Eden Martin,* a 15m (50-ft.) yacht, which they sailed from France in 1999. A half-day of sailing costs about 7,200CFP (US$90/£45) per person; a whole day, 12,500CFP (US$156/£79). They also have sunset cruises for 6,600CFP (US$83/£42) per person. That's assuming Claude and Martine are on Huahine and not on a 1- or 2-week charter cruise in the Leeward or Tuamotu islands.

SCUBA DIVING

Huahine's lagoon and fringing reef have several dive sites with a multitude of sea life, and you don't have to be an experienced diver to see much of it. You'll need a boat to get to it, but even snorkelers will enjoy the **Seafari Aquarium,** inside the barrier reef off Avea Beach on Huahine Iti. Tropical fish congregate around the colorful coral heads that dot the lagoon here, and rays troll the sandy bottom. The aquarium is only 2 to 3m (7–10 ft.) deep. Novice divers can also explore the canyons beyond **Tiare Pass,** off Faie Bay on the eastern side of Huahine-Nui. You will need intermediate skills to explore Huahine's most famous site, **Avapeihi Pass,** the entry through the reef off Cook's Bay and a short boat ride from Fare. Conditions in the pass draw feeding schools of barracuda and other fish, which in turn get the attention of gray reef sharks.

Pacific Blue Adventure (ℂ **68.87.21;** fax 68.80.71; www.divehuahine.com) and **Mahana Dive** (ℂ **73.07.**17; www.mahanadive.com) have offices on the Fare wharf. Both charge about 6,000CFP (US$75/£38) for a one-tank dive.

SNORKELING & SWIMMING

You don't have to leave Fare to find a fine little swimming and snorkeling beach; just follow the seaside promenade north past Restaurant New Temarara. Huahine's best, however, is the magnificent crescent of sand at **Avea Beach,** skirting Baie Avea on Huahine Iti. A hilly peninsula blocks the brunt of the southeast trade winds, so the speckled

5 SHOPPING

You are not as likely to be pestered to buy black pearls on Huahine as on Tahiti, Moorea,
and Bora Bora—another of Huahine's appealing attributes, in my opinion. One stop you
should make is **Huahine Nui Pearls & Pottery** ★ (© **78.30.20;** www.huahinepearl
farm.com), a pearl farm and pottery studio operated by American expatriate Peter Owen
on a *motu* off Baie Faie (see "Touring the Island," above). Peter offers free tours daily from
10am to 4pm, with the boat leaving Faie Bay every 15 minutes. If you aren't going to the
Tuamotus, this is a good place to see how black pearls are grown.

Local women sell shell jewelry, bedspreads, and other handicrafts at **Huahine Mata
Aiai** (no phone) in a thatch building at the south end of the Fare waterfront. Be sure to
look in the small art galleries and other shops along the waterfront, especially **Pacific Art**
(© **68.70.09**).

6 WHERE TO STAY

7

EXPENSIVE

Te Tiare Beach Resort ★★★   Rudy Markmiller made a fortune in the overnight
courier business in California and then spent more than a decade—and a sizable chunk
of his loot—building this luxury resort, one of French Polynesia's finest. Although it's on
the main island, guests are ferried here from Fare, which makes this seem like a remote
offshore resort (never fear: a shuttle boat makes the 10-min. run to and from Fare every
hour from 5:30am–11pm). You will land at a thatched-roof, overwater structure housing
a reception area, lounge, bar, and dining room serving excellent international cuisine. A
long pier connects this central complex to a westward-facing, white-sand beach with
gorgeous sunsets over Raiatea and Tahaa out on the horizon. The lagoon is not deep here,
but it's still good for swimming and snorkeling over coral heads close to shore. You can
use canoes, paddleboats, and kayaks, or cool off in a beachside swimming pool equipped
with its own terrific bar serving libations and snacks all afternoon. Diving, sailing, fishing, picnicking on a *motu*, horseback riding, and touring the *maraes* cost extra. Jet skis
and water-skiing are available, though not in front of the resort.

The 41 spacious bungalows are as luxuriously appointed as any in French Polynesia.
You won't have a fish-viewing glass panel in the floor, but you can step out to a huge
L-shaped deck, half of it under the shade of a thatched roof. The decks also have privacy

---

Fun Facts   **The Swimsuit Models Were Here**

Those extraordinarily beautiful women seen briefly—in both time and clothing—
at Te Tiare Beach Resort were here to model for the 2006 swimsuit issue of *Sports
Illustrated* magazine.

screens so your neighbors can't see you dining in the nude, or whatever. Steps lead into the lagoon from the decks of the 11 "deep overwater" bungalows that have spa tubs as well as showers in their bathrooms (all other units, including five "shallow overwater" models, have large showers). Six bungalows sit beside the beach, but the garden units (the least expensive here) don't have unimpeded views of the lagoon.

B.P. 36, 98731 Fare, Huahine (in Fitii District, 10 min. by boat from Fare). © **888/600-8455** or 60.60.50. Fax 60.60.51. www.tetiarebeach.com. 41 units. 39,000CFP–78,000CFP (US$488–US$975/£247–£494) double. AE, DC, MC, V. **Amenities:** Restaurant; 2 bars; outdoor pool; watersports equipment rentals; activities desk; car-rental desk; limited room service; massage; babysitting; laundry service. *In room:* A/C, TV, minibar, coffeemaker, hair dryer, iron (overwater units only), safe.

MODERATE

Fare Ie   Instead of a bungalow, you'll have your own genuine South African safari tent at this establishment's two locations. One is north of Fare and within walking distance of town. The other is on the outskirts of Paea village, near Huahine Iti's southernmost point. The Paea location is remote, but the beach is very good, and it's actually on the grounds of an ancient *marae* bearing the Taiharuru Petroglyphs. The tents are all screened and have electric fans, two beds, and their own bathrooms. Two larger tents at Paea also have kitchens just outside under thatched roofs. Guests share communal kitchens at both locations.

B.P. 746, 98331 Fare, Huahine (north of Fare and in Paea village, Huahine Iti). ©/fax **60.63.77.** www.tahitisafari.com. 6 units. 16,500CFP–27,000CFP (US$206–US$338/£104–£171) per tent. No credit cards. **Amenities:** Communal kitchen; complimentary bicycles, kayaks, snorkeling gear. *In room:* No phone.

Relais Mahana (Value)   This hotel has one of the South Pacific's best beach-lagoon combinations, for half of it sits beside Avea Beach, the white sand stretching along the peninsula on Huahine's south end. A pier from the main building runs out over a giant coral head, around which fish and guests swim. Just climb down off the pier and swim with the fishes. Choice guest quarters are the deluxe models beside the beach. These were remodeled recently and, although a bit smaller than at other resorts, they have king-size beds and their showers open to private rear gardens. Other units here are somewhat larger, but they're north of the central building where the beach has been eroded. All in all, Relais Mahana is good value.

B.P. 30, 98731 Fare, Huahine (Avea Bay, Huahine Iti). © **60.60.40.** Fax 68.85.08. www.relaismahana.com. 32 units. 23,900CFP–31,600CFP (US$299–US$395/£151–£200). AE, MC, V. **Amenities:** 2 restaurants; bar; watersports equipment rentals; bicycle rental; activities desk; car-rental desk; babysitting; laundry service. *In room:* TV, dataport, minibar, coffeemaker, iron.

INEXPENSIVE

Chez Guynette (Value)   Marty and Moe (*Mo*-ay) Temahahe (wife Marty is American; husband Moe is Tahitian) operate this friendly hostel across the main street from the Fare waterfront. A corridor runs down the center of the building to the kitchen and lounge at the rear. The simple but clean rooms and dorms flank the hallway on either side. The rooms have screens, ceiling fans, and their own bathrooms with hot-water showers. The dorms also have ceiling fans; they share two toilets and showers. Marty and Moe serve breakfast and lunch (sandwiches, burgers, salads, and *poisson cru,* plus wine and beer) on their street-side patio. It's the best place in Fare to slake a thirst and get into a good conversation—in English.

B.P. 87, 98731 Fare, Huahine (opposite the town wharf). © **68.83.75.** chezguynette@mail.pf. 7 units (all with bathroom), 8 bunks. 1,750CFP–2,000CFP (US$22–US$25/£11–£13) dorm bed; 5,900CFP–6,200CFP

(US$74–US$78/£37–£39) double (higher rates apply to 1-night stays). MC, V. **Amenities:** Restaurant; bar.
In room: No phone.

Pension Fare Maeva   Located between Fare and the airport, this pension has some features that make it seem more like a cost-conscious resort. It sits beside a white-sand beach, although the lagoon here is so rocky and shallow that you cannot wade in for a swim. You can take a dip in the pool, though, which resides in a beachside lawn in front of the restaurant. The latter is open daily for breakfast and lunch, and occasionally for island feasts and Tahitian music after dark. You can order a cold one at the bar and escape the midday sun under the tin roof of a *fare potee,* or outdoor lounge, beside the pool. The 20 units here are evenly divided between bungalows and hotel-style rooms, all in tropical gardens rather than on the beach. The bungalows are more expensive, but come with kitchens and separate bedrooms. Accommodations are rather spartan, but tin roofs, tile floors, porches, and simple bathrooms with hot-water showers are common to all units. You'll get a fan, but not window screens. Pension Vaihonu Océan (see below) is a short walk away.

B.P. 675, 98731 Fare, Huahine (2.5km/1½ miles north of Fare). © **68.75.53.** Fax 68.70.68. www.fare-maeva. com. 20 units. 7,000CFP (US$88/£44) double; 12,100CFP (US$151/£76) bungalow. MC, V. **Amenities:** Restaurant (breakfast and lunch); bar; outdoor pool; bike rentals. *In room:* Kitchen (bungalows only), no phone.

Pension Mauarii ★   Beside Avea Beach, this little pension may not have all the comforts of home, but it oozes charm. Its buildings are constructed of thatch, bamboo, tree trunks, and other natural materials. Although cleverly designed, they seem to be slapped together, which adds to the ambience. Most units are in the tropical gardens, but the rooms open to a long porch right on the beach, as does the one beachside bunga-low—my favorite here. All units have ceiling fans, but not all have bathrooms, and their windows aren't screened. The pension provides a host of waterborne activities. Unless the owners haven't moved it to the inland side of the road to make room for more bungalows, the restaurant here is the most charming on the island (see "Where to Dine," below).

B.P. 473, 98731 Fare, Huahine (Baie Avera, Huahine-Iti). © **68.86.49.** Fax 60.60.96. www.mauarii.com. 5 bungalows (3 with bathroom), 4 rooms (2 with bathroom). 9,500CFP (US$119/£60) double; 11,500CFP–20,000CFP (US$144–US$250/£73–£126) bungalow. AE, MC, V. **Amenities:** Restaurant; bar; watersports equipment rentals; bike rentals; activities desk; massage; laundry service. *In room:* No phone.

Pension Vaihonu Océan   On the shore a few meters south of Pension Fare Maeva (see above), with which it shares a beach beside the shallow, rocky lagoon, this pension offers a wider range of accommodations than any other inexpensive establishment here. Top of the line are two duplex apartments with a kitchen and bathroom; the mezzanine level has two double beds. In the middle are three "beach huts"—actually small, simple bungalows with plywood walls, tin roofs, unscreened windows, and shaded verandas—facing the lagoon across a lawn. Guests in the huts and in the dormitory share toilets, showers, and a sand-floor communal kitchen with campers who pitch their own tents on the lawn. Huahine Camping (see below) has a better beach and a more picturesque set-ting, but the location here is much more convenient to Fare, just 2.5km (1½ miles) away.

B.P. 302, 98731 Fare, Huahine (2.5km/1½ miles north of Fare). © **68.87.33.** Fax 68.77.57. www.iaorana-huahine.com/en/vaihonu.html. 2 apts, 5 beach huts, 7 dorm beds (shared bathrooms), 8 campsites. 8,000CFP (US$100/£51) apt; 5,000CFP (US$63/£32) double beach hut; 1,800CFP (US$23/£11) per person in dormitory or camping. MC, V. **Amenities:** Communal kitchen; free use of bikes; laundry service. *In room:* Kitchen (apts only), no phone.

American Rande Vetterli has two clean, well-equipped houses for rent at **Rande's Shack,** on the shore north of Fare (© **68.86.27;** www.haere-mai.pf; randeshack@mail.pf). Both have TVs, fans, and kitchens. One house has two bedrooms and can sleep five people; a one-bedroom model can sleep three people. Rates are 10,000CFP and 15,000CFP (US$125 and US$188/£63 and £95), respectively.

The two lodgings below, both on the north shore of Maroe Bay, represent good value since they throw in the use of a car and motorboat in their rates. Neither is a hotel or pension; you get a modern house to yourself.

Huahine Vacances (Value)   Bordeaux native Michel Sorin learned to speak English while living in Canada before relocating to the islands in the early 1980s. Although his modern villas could be at home in most suburbs, the tin roofs and fretwork around the eaves add an old-plantation touch. Two have three bedrooms and two bathrooms, while the third has two bedrooms and a single bathroom. Both are good choices for groups or families. You'll have a fully equipped kitchen (including a microwave), a large front porch from which to observe the bay, window screens, and your own bathroom with hot-water shower. Michel's Tahitian wife, Jacqueline, will babysit the kids while you drive your car into Fare for dinner. The Sorins provide linens, but you do the housework.

B.P. 10, 98731 Fare, Huahine (north shore of Maroe Bay). ©/fax **68.73.63.** www.huahinevacance.pf. 3 units. 20,500CFP–27,500CFP (US$256–US$344/£130–£174) depending on number of guests. Reduced rates for long stays. MC, V. **Amenities:** Free use of car, motorboat, canoes, fishing rods; babysitting. *In room:* TV, kitchen, coffeemaker, hair dryer, washing machine, no phone.

Villas Bougainville (Value)   Near Huahine Vacances (see above), the three houses here are a bit larger, as are the surrounding tropical gardens. The two- and three-bedroom villas have wraparound verandas, modern kitchens, and bathrooms with hot-water showers. The bedrooms are somewhat spartan, but all have ceiling fans and some have air conditioners (for which you must pay extra). Cribs and babysitting are available, but not housekeeping.

B.P. 258, 98731 Fare, Huahine (north shore of Maroe Bay). © **60.60.30** or 79.70.59. Fax 60.60.31. www. villas-bougainville.com. 3 units. 20,500CFP–32,500CFP (US$256–US$406/£130–£206) depending on number of guests and air-conditioning. Reduced rates for long stays. AE, MC, V. **Amenities:** Free use of car, motorboat, canoes, fishing rods; babysitting. *In room:* A/C, TV, kitchen, coffeemaker, hair dryer, washing machine, no phone.

CAMPING

You can pitch a tent or rent a rudimentary thatched-roof *fare* (cabin) at Cecèle and Hubert Bremond's **Huahine Camping** (© **68.85.20** or 68.83.78), on the southern end of Avea Beach. The shoreline here has as many coral ledges as it has sand, but the shady grounds are appealing. Guests share a communal kitchen, tables under a thatched roof, toilets, and cold-water showers (don't expect a shower head). The cabins have either a double bed or two single beds and cost 6,000CFP (US$75/£38), while tent sites are 1,800CFP (US$23/£11) per person.

7 WHERE TO DINE

You'll meet the locals having breakfast or lunch while watching the passing scene from the patio at **Chez Guynette** in Fare (p. 180). You can also enjoy the fine dining room at

Te Tiare Beach Resort (p. 183), though you will need to make reservations and pay 500CFP (US$6.25/£3.15) for the boat ride there and back.

You'll find Huahine's *roulottes* on the Fare wharf. They're open for both lunch and dinner. See "Don't Miss *Les Roulottes*" (p. 140) for details.

Restaurant Mauarii FRENCH/TAHITIAN   Assuming the owners haven't taken leave of their senses and moved this restaurant across the road, it will still be sitting almost over the sand, with a great view southward along Avea Beach. It's a charmer, with a thatch-lined ceiling and tables hewn from tree trunks. Lunchtime sandwiches include a "Killer" baguette loaded with grilled fish and french fries (yes, in the sandwich) under your choice of vanilla or other sauces. For my money, this is a good place to sample Tahitian treats such as *fafa ru* (chicken with taro leaves in coconut cream), or sample different dishes on a Polynesian platter. Ask for a menu in English if the friendly staff doesn't figure you out first.

Avea Beach, Huahine Iti (at Pension Mauarii). (ℂ) **68.86.49.** Reservations recommended for dinner. Sandwiches and burgers 600CFP–1,200CFP (US$7.50–US$15/£3.80–£7.60); main courses 1,600CFP–3,500CFP (US$20–US$44/£10–£22). AE, MC, V. Daily noon–2pm and 6–8pm.

Restaurant New Temarara ★ FRENCH   Facing due west beside the lagoon at the north end of Fare's wharf, this is my favorite place for a sundown cocktail or cold Hinano beer during half-price happy hour from 5:30 to 6:30pm. The *poisson cru* is outstanding, as is the coconut-crumbed mahimahi, a spicy version of breaded fish. If offered, you might also try the parrotfish with lemon butter. You can get a good beef or fish burger here, as well as steaks and fish with French sauces.

Fare, north end of wharf. (ℂ) **68.89.31.** Reservations accepted. Burgers 800CFP–900CFP (US$10–US$11/£5.05–£5.70); main courses 1,600CFP–2,100CFP (US$20–US$26/£10–£13). MC, V. Mon–Sat 11:30am–9pm. Bar open all day, to 11pm Fri–Sat.

Raiatea & Tahaa

The mountainous clump of land you can see on the horizon from Huahine or Bora Bora may appear to be one island, but it actually is two, Raiatea and Tahaa, which are enclosed by a single barrier reef. Cruising yachts can circumnavigate Tahaa without leaving the lagoon, and Huahine and Bora Bora are relatively easy hauls from here. Accordingly, this is French Polynesia's yacht-chartering center. There are no beaches on either Raiatea or Tahaa other than a few on islets out on the reef, and except for sailing and cruise-ship visits, tourism is not an important part of their economies, which are based on agricultural produce and, in the case of Raiatea, government salaries.

Raiatea, the largest of the Leeward Islands, is by far more important than Tahaa, both in terms of the past and the present. In the old days, it was the religious center of all the Society Islands, including Tahiti. Polynesian mythology has it that Oro, the god of war and fertility, was born in **Mount Temehani**, the extinct flat-top volcano that towers over the northern part of Raiatea. **Taputapuatea,** on its southeast coast, was at one time the most important *marae* in the

islands. Legend also has it that the great Polynesian voyagers who discovered and colonized Hawaii and New Zealand left from there. Archaeological discoveries have substantiated the link with Hawaii.

Today, Raiatea (pop. 10,000) is still important as the economic and administrative center of the Leeward Islands. Next to Papeete, the town of **Uturoa** (pop. 4,000) is the largest settlement and is one of the most important transportation hubs in French Polynesia. A modern cruise-ship terminal and welcome center dominate Uturoa's waterfront. Although most prefer anchoring offshore in order to use their watersports platforms, Uturoa is the only island port other than Papeete where the larger cruise ships spend their nights tied up to a wharf.

Tahaa (pronounced *Tah*-ah-ah) is much smaller than Raiatea in terms of land area, population (about 1,500), and the height of its terrain. It's a lovely island, with a few very small villages sitting deep in bays that cut into its hills. Tahaa has a few family-operated pensions, but other than sailors and guests at resorts out on its reef islets, few visitors see it, and most of those who do, see it on day tours from Raiatea.

1 GETTING AROUND RAIATEA & TAHAA

The Raiatea airstrip, 3km (2 miles) north of Uturoa, serves both islands. You have to rent a vehicle or take a taxi, for there is no regular public transportation system on either Raiatea or Tahaa.

Europcar (© 800/227-7368 or 66.34.06; www.europcar-tahiti.com) and **Hertz** (© 800/654-3131 or 66.44.88; www.hertz.com) have rental-car offices here. Europcar's prices start at 9,700CFP (US$121/£61) a day, including insurance and unlimited kilometers. It also rents scooters, bicycles, and open-air "Bugster" vehicles. Europcar also has an office at Tupuamu Wharf on Tahaa's west coast (© 65.67.00), so you can take the ferry there, rent a car, and drive around the island. You must take a water taxi back to Uturoa.

RAIATEA & TAHAA

8

GETTING AROUND RAIATEA & TAHAA

0 ─── 2 mi
0 ─── 2 km

✈ Airport
↖ Beach
····· Reef

Motu
Tehotu

1

Motu
2 Tu Vahine

Patio

Hipu

3

Motu
Tautau

Tapuamu Bay

T A H A A

Faaaha

4 Faaaha Bay

Tapuamu

Haamene
Village

Tiva

Haamene Bay

5

Hurepiti Bay

Poutoru _Apu_

Bay Vaitoare

ATTRACTIONS ●

Apooiti Marina **6**

Faaroa Bay **14**

La Maison de Vanille
(The House of Vanilla) **5**

Taninuu Marae **13**

Taputapuatea Marae **15**

Temehani Plateau **11**

Airport

6

✈

Uturoa

See Uturoa map

7

8

ACCOMMODATIONS ■

Hawaiki Nui Hotel **8**

Hotel Atiapiti **16**

Hotel La Pirogue **1**

Hotel Mirimiri **10**

Le Taha'a Private Island
& Spa **3**

L'Hibiscus **4**

Pension Manava **12**

Pension Tepua **9**

Sunset Beach Motel **7**

Vahine Island
Private Resort **2**

Vai Poe (Chez Patricia
et Daniel) **4**

10

9

Temehani
Plateau

11

12

Motu
Nao Nao

Avera

Tevaitoa

13

14

Faaroa Bay

▲
Mt. Tefatua

Opoa Bay

15

Tehurui

R A I A T E A

Opoa

16 _Hotopuu Bay_

Vaiaau

Vaiaau Bay

Faaroa Bay

Puohine

Fetuna

Motu
Nao Nao

Maupiti

SOCIETY ISLANDS

0 ─── 100 mi
0 ─── 100 km

Bora
Bora

Huahine

Raiatea
& Tahaa

Moorea

Tahiti

Trudy Tours (✆ 78.23.36) provides transfers from the airport to the hotels and to Apooti Marina for 500CFP to 700CFP (US$6.25–US$8.75/£3.15–£4.45) per person. There is a taxi stand near the cruise-ship terminal in Uturoa, or you can contact **René Guilloux** (✆ 66.31.40), **Marona Teanini** (✆ 66.34.62), or **Apia Tehope** (✆ 66. 36.41). Fares are about 600CFP (US$7.50/£3.80) from the airport to town and 1,200CFP (US$15/£7.60) to the Raiatea Hawaiki Nui Hotel.

The passenger ferry *Tamarii Tahaa* (✆ 65.67.10) docks in front of the Champion store on Uturoa's waterfront and runs from there to Patio on Tahaa's northern coast. It departs from Uturoa Monday to Friday, usually at 10am and 4pm, Saturday at 10am. You should make sure it will return to Uturoa on the same day it leaves. Fares range from 500CFP to 750CFP (US$6.25–US$9.40/£3.15–£4.75) one-way. **Dave's Tours** (✆ 65. 62.42) also runs a shuttle from Uturoa to Tahaa, departing Monday to Saturday at 9am, returning at 4:30pm. Fares are 1,500CFP (US$19/£9.50) one-way, 2,500CFP (US$31/ £16) round-trip. **Water-taxi** service is available at the waterfront (✆ 65.66.64); rides cost about 2,000CFP (US$25/£13).

ⓕ *Fast Facts*   **Raiatea & Tahaa**

The following facts apply specifically to Raiatea and Tahaa. For more information, see "Fast Facts: Tahiti & French Polynesia," in appendix A.

Currency Exchange French Polynesia's three banks have offices with ATMs on Uturoa's main street. There is no bank on Tahaa.

Drugstores **Pharmacie de Raiatea** (✆ 66.34.44) in Uturoa carries French products. Open Monday to Friday 7:30am to noon and 1:30 to 5:30pm; Saturday 7:30am to noon; Sunday 9:30 to 10:30am.

Emergencies & Police The emergency police telephone number is ✆ 17. The telephone number of the **Uturoa gendarmerie** is ✆ 66.31.07. The **Tahaa gendarmerie** is at Patio, the administrative center, on the north coast (✆ 65. 64.07).

Eyeglasses **Optique Te Mata Ore** is on Uturoa's main street (✆ 66.16.19).

Healthcare Opposite the post office, the **hospital** at Uturoa (✆ 66.32.92) serves all the Leeward Islands. Tahaa has an **infirmary** at Patio (✆ 65.63.31). **Dr. Sonia Andreu** and **Dr. Pascal Diochin** (✆ 66.23.01) practice together on Uturoa's main street.

Internet Access **ETS,** in the Gare Maritime on the Uturoa waterfront (✆ 60.25.25), has computers with Internet access for 500CFP (US$6.25/£3.15) for 35 minutes. Open Monday to Friday 7:30am to noon and 1 to 5pm, Saturday 7:30am to noon. It will burn your digital photos to CDs.

Post Office The post and telecommunications office is in a modern building north of Uturoa on the main road (as opposed to a new road that runs along the shore of reclaimed land on the north side of town). It is open Monday to Thursday 7:30am to 3pm, Friday 7am to 2pm, and Saturday 8 to 10am. There's a small branch upstairs in the Gare Maritime on the waterfront.

Restrooms The Gare Maritime on the waterfront has clean restrooms.

Telephone There are *télécarte* phones on the waterfront and at the post and telecommunications office.

Visitor Information **Tourisme Tahiti** (✆ **60.07.77;** fax 60.07.76; www.tahiti-tourisme.pf) has a visitor information office in the Gare Maritime on the waterfront. Open daily 8am to 4pm.

Water Don't drink the tap water on either Raiatea or Tahaa.

2 EXPLORING RAIATEA & TAHAA

Highlights of your time here will include visits to the ancient *maraes,* day trips to and around Tahaa, picnics on small islands on the outer reef, and four-wheel-drive excursions into the mountains.

A paved road runs for 150km (92 miles) around the shoreline of rugged **Raiatea,** the second-largest island in French Polynesia, behind only Tahiti. Its tallest peak, **Mount Tefatoaiti,** at 1,017m (3,337 ft.), occupies the triangular-shaped island's southern end. To the north, the flat top of sacred **Mount Temehani** soars to 792m (2,598 ft.). Much of Mount Temehani is a high plateau, where the five-petal *tiare apetahi* flower grows (see "Delicate Petals," p. 188). Polynesians in ancient times believed that when they died, their souls ascended to the plateau, where they faced a fork in the road. If they were told to go right, they went to Paradise. If they went left, it was into the crater and their version of Purgatory.

Several rivers carve steep valleys on their way from the Raiatea highlands to six bays indenting the coast. One of them, the **Faaroa River,** is the only navigable waterway in French Polynesia. It empties into mountain-sided **Faaroa Bay,** which provides a protected anchorage for yachts and other small craft. Most charter-boat operators, however, are based at **Apooti Marina** on the north shore beside the strait separating Raiatea and Tahaa.

With 88 sq. km (34 sq. miles), **Tahaa** is about one-third the size of Raiatea, but it is still French Polynesia's fourth-largest island. Its main villages are **Tapuamu** on the west coast, **Patio** on the north side, and **Haamene** in the center. Tahaa is a rugged island, with its tallest peak, **Mount Ohiri,** reaching to 598m (1,975 ft.). The island's inhabitants live along a narrow coastal plain and at the head of four narrow bays, two of which—**Haamene** and **Harepiti**—almost cut Tahaa into two. Completely surrounded by a deepwater lagoon, and with the sheltered bays providing fine anchorages, Tahaa is a sailor's heaven.

VISITING THE MARAE

Raiatea is known as the "Sacred Island" because of its religious importance in pre-European times. On the outskirts of **Opoa** village, 29km (18 miles) south of Uturoa, the **Taputapuatea Marae** ★★★ is the second-most-significant archaeological site in all of Polynesia, behind only Easter Island. Legend says that Te Ava Moa Pass offshore was the departure point for the discovery and settlement of both Hawaii and New Zealand. The large *marae* on the site was actually built centuries later by the Tamatoa family of chiefs. Vying for supremacy, the Tamatoas mingled religion with politics by creating Oro, the

(Fun Facts) **Delicate Petals**

Found nowhere else except in Raiatea's mountains, the *tiare apetahi* is a one-sided white flower of the gardenia family. Legend says that its five delicate petals are the fingers of a beautiful Polynesian girl who fell in love with a prince but couldn't marry him because of her low birth. Just before she died, heartbroken, in her lover's arms, she promised to give him her hand to caress each day throughout eternity. At daybreak each morning, accordingly, the *tiare apetahi* opens its five petals.

ferocious god of war and fertility supposedly born on Mount Temehani, and by spreading his cult. It took almost 200 years, but Oro eventually became the most important god in the region. Likewise, the Tamatoas became the most powerful chiefs. They were on the verge of conquering all of the Society Islands when the missionaries arrived in 1797. With the Christians' help, Pomare I became king of Tahiti, and the great *marae* the Tamatoas built for Oro was soon left to ruin, replaced by the lovely Protestant church in nearby Opoa village.

The *marae* was restored in the 1960s and, more recently, Tahiti Museum archaeologists discovered human bones under some of the structures, apparently the remains of sacrifices to Oro. The *marae's* huge *ahu,* or raised altar of stones for the gods, is more than 45m (150 ft.) long, 9m (30 ft.) wide, and 3.3m (11 ft.) tall. Flat rocks, used as backrests for the chiefs and priests, still stand in the courtyard in front of the ahu. The entire complex is in a coconut grove on the shore of the lagoon, opposite Te Ava Moa Pass, and legend says that bonfires on the *marae* guided canoes through the pass at night.

Taputapuatea is worth a visit not only for the *marae* itself, but also for the scenery here and along the way. The road skirts the southeast coast and follows Faaroa Bay to the mouth of the river, and then back out to the lagoon.

On the west coast, 15km (9 miles) from Uturoa, **Taninuu Marae** was also dedicated to Oro. Stones bordering the foundation of the ancient chief's home bear petroglyphs of turtles. This is a place of Christian history, too, since the lovely white Eglise Siloama is one of the oldest churches in French Polynesia.

WALKING AROUND UTUROA

There was not even a village at Uturoa before the Rev. John Williams, who proselytized throughout the South Pacific, set up a London Missionary Society headquarters here in the 1820s. The settlement later became the Leeward Islands' administrative center and major trading post. A number of Chinese-owned stores still line Rue Centrale, Uturoa's main street, but the center of activity is the glistening **Gare Maritime,** a cruise-ship terminal built with money from France's economic restructuring fund. You can't miss this big Mediterranean-style building that houses restaurants, shops, the island's visitor information office, and public restrooms. Needless to say, the waterfront is busiest when a cruise ship arrives, and local women sell handicrafts and souvenirs in small thatch buildings next door known as *fares des mamas* (mamas' houses). Across the street is the *Marché Municipale,* the local produce market.

DINING ◆
Brasserie Maraamu 4
Le Napoli 1
Sea Horse Restaurant 3
Snack Moemoea 2

approximate scale

↖ Beach
ⓘ Information
✉ Post office

You can make a walking tour of Uturoa by following the four-lane road northward from the town docks along the shore, past a park built on landfill to the public yacht marina on the northern edge of town. From the traffic circle, follow Rue Centrale back through the business district. Although Rue Centrale was once along the shoreline, landfill has left the street a block inland from the waterfront. Behind it on the mountain side, an expressway speeds vehicles past downtown (there's a traffic circle on each end).

3 SAFARI EXPEDITIONS & LAGOON EXCURSIONS

SAFARI EXPEDITIONS

Either **Raiatea 4×4** (ⓒ **66.24.16**) or **Jeep Safari Raiatea** (ⓒ **66.15.73**) will take you via four-wheel-drive jeep into Raiatea's interior, including a ride up to the plateau and into the ancient crater of Mount Temehani; both stop at Taputapuatea Marae before heading back to Uturoa. These expeditions are less thrill ride and more oriented to history and culture than those on Bora Bora. I would opt for Raiatea 4×4, especially if the highly informative Ronnie Moufat is to be your guide. Each outfitter has two trips a day, requires reservations a day in advance, and charges about 4,500CFP (US$56/£28) per person.

The mountains of Tahaa have much less dramatic scenery than on Raiatea, and the island lacks the historical importance of its big sister. Consequently, safari expeditions here include visits to **La Maison de Vanille (House of Vanilla; ☎ 57.61.92**), where visitors are informed about the cultivation and uses of vanilla (Tahaa's major product), and to a black-pearl farm. Most tours follow a four-wheel-drive trail through the mountains from Patio, on the north coast, to Haamene, in the center of the island. These invariably include a refreshment stop high on a ridge with a view over Haamene Bay. I thoroughly enjoyed my expedition guided by the energetic and engaging Roselyne Atiniu of **Dave's Tours (☎ 65.62.42**). You can also go with **Vai Poe Tours (☎ 65.60.83**). Either will pick you up at Uturoa.

LAGOON EXCURSIONS

If you can put together your own group (because a minimum of four persons is required), you can take a variety of lagoon excursions and see firsthand the Raiatea-Tahaa lagoon, one of the most beautiful in French Polynesia. All trips include snorkeling, and most include picnics on the *motus* (tiny islets) sitting on the outer reef; unlike the mainland of Raiatea and Tahaa, they have beautiful white-sand beaches. **Motu Toahotu** and **Motu Mahena** are equipped with restrooms and other facilities, for which the locals extract a 500CFP (US$6.25/£3.15) per-person entrance fee. **Dave's Tours (☎ 65.62.42**) will take you out from Uturoa.

Marie and Tony Tucker (she's French; he's South African) of **West Coast Charters (☎ 66.45.39**) offer a complete tour around Tahaa with swimming, guided snorkeling over the magnificent coral gardens next to Le Taha'a Private Island & Spa, a shark-feeding stint, a pearl-farm visit, and lunch for 8,500CFP (US$106/£54) a person. Both Marie and Tony speak fluent English as well as French.

Andrew Brotherson of **Manava Excursions (☎/fax 66.28.26;** maraud@mail.pf) also charges 7,500CFP (US$94/£47) per person for his all-day trips to Tahaa. They include visits to a vanilla plantation and pearl farm, a picnic on a *motu*, and snorkeling over the coral gardens. He also takes a boat trip up the Faaroa River and on to the Taputapuatea Marae, priced at 4,500CFP (US$56/£28) per person.

> (Fun Facts) **Omai Scores a Hit in London**
>
> Capt. James Cook discovered Raiatea during his first expedition to the islands in 1769. On his second voyage, in 1773, he took home with him a young Raiatean named Mai, or Omai to the English, who was living on Huahine at the time. Like Ahutoru, a Tahitian brought to Paris by the French explorer Antoine de Bougainville 2 years earlier, Omai was seen as living proof of philosopher Jean-Jacques Rousseau's theory of humans as "noble savages." The first Polynesian to visit England, Omai became an instant hit with London society and even met King George III and Queen Charlotte, who apparently were impressed with his grace and good manners. Great artists painted him, and writers spun many words about him (including some pornography). High society soon lost interest, however, and Cook brought Omai home in 1777 on his third and last great voyage of discovery.

> **(Tips) Avoid Cruise-Ship Days**
>
> Unless you're on one of them, try to avoid visiting Raiatea when cruise ships are in port, since their passengers can monopolize all organized activities here.

Another option is Bruno Fabre's **L'Excursion Bleue** (✆ **66.10.90;** www.tahaa.net), whose full-day trip around Tahaa costs 9,500CFP (US$119/£60).

4 HIKING, SAILING & WATERSPORTS

HIKING
Just north of downtown Uturoa, the street to the left as you face the gendarmerie leads to a four-wheel-drive track ascending to the television towers atop 291m (970-ft.) **Papioi Hill.** (Be sure to close the gates, which keep the cows out of the station.) From the top, you can see Uturoa, the reef, and the islands Tahaa, Bora Bora, and Huahine.

Serious hikers can take another trail leading to the plateau atop Mount Temehani. The route begins with a four-wheel-drive track about 183m (600 ft.) south of the bridge at the head of Pufau Bay on the northwest coast. It is not marked, so a guide is advisable. Contact the local visitor information office about hiring one (see "Fast Facts: Raiatea & Tahaa," earlier in this chapter).

SAILING ★★★
As noted in "Seeing the Islands by Cruise Ship & Yacht" (p. 61), **The Moorings** (✆ **800/ 535-7289** or 727/535-1446; www.moorings.com) and **Sunsail Yacht Charters** (✆ **800/ 327-2276** or 207/253-5400 in the U.S., or 60.04.85 on Raiatea; fax 66.23.19; www. sunsail.com) are based on Raiatea. Both charter sailboats with or without crew. If a boat is available, it can be chartered on a daily basis. Arrangements for longer charters ordinarily should be made before leaving home.

The Moorings keeps its boats at Apooti Marina on the north shore, which is more convenient to the popular cruising grounds around Tahaa. Sunsail is based on the north shore of Faaroa Bay.

SCUBA DIVING & SNORKELING
Raiatea may not have beaches, but the reef and large, clear lagoon are excellent for scuba diving and snorkeling.

SCUBA DIVING The best wreck dive site in all of French Polynesia is a descent of 15 to 27m (50–90 ft.) above the **S.S. _Norby,_** a three-masted Danish schooner that sunk off Uturoa in 1900. Its main deck has collapsed, so even novice divers can explore its topside. Intermediate divers can swim through the 150-foot-long hull and see a multitude of sea life, including black coral. Although the lagoon can be murky here, the _Norby_ makes for good night diving. Nearby, novices can drift dive at Teavapiti Pass, where a coral wall just outside the reef attracts fish, rays, and gray, whitetip, and blacktip sharks. Other sites here, such as the **Little Caves** and the **Mounts of Céran,** both off Tahaa's eastern coast, are known for spectacular underwater scenery.

With bases at the Raiatea Hawaiki Nui Hotel and at Apooti Marina, Hubert Clot's **Hémisphère Sub Raiatea** (② **66.12.49;** fax 66.28.63; www.multimania.com/diveraiatea) takes divers on one-tank excursions for 6,500CFP (US$81/£41).

SNORKELING   You'll have to take a lagoon excursion (see above) to experience the best snorkeling near the offshore islands, especially over the coral gardens off Le Taha'a Private Island & Spa on Tahaa's northwestern coast. Or you can don mask, snorkel, and fins at the Raiatea Hawaiki Nui Hotel (p. 192), where the overwater bungalows are perched atop a clifflike reef face.

5 SHOPPING

The Gare Maritime on the waterfront has several black-pearl and other shops. The best is **My Flower** (② **66.19.19**), where owner Flora Hart carries not just floral arrangements, but also excellent tapa drawings and woodcarvings—some from the Marquesas Islands, others done in *hue papaa* wood, a specialty of Raiatea's own carvers.

Other shops line Rue Centrale, the main street. These days, most are built of concrete and steel, but one wooden building hearkens back to the bygone days of clapboard Chinese stores. In it, you'll find the unique **Magasin Vanira** (② **66.30.06**), where owner Jeanne Chane—the *préparatrice de vanille*—prepares many products from vanilla beans: extract, powder, even vanilla soup. The wonderful aroma alone makes it worth a visit.

6 WHERE TO STAY

ON RAIATEA
EXPENSIVE
Raiatea Hawaiki Nui Hotel ★   This hotel is of historical importance in its own right, for it was here in 1968 that Moorea's "Bali Hai Boys" built the world's first overwater bungalows (see "The Bali Hai Boys," p. 159). It was their way of compensating for the lack of a beach here. The hotel has gone through several name changes since its days as the Hotel Bali Hai Raiatea, but those bungalows still stand out on the edge of the reef; from them, you can climb right into the water and get the sensation of flying as you snorkel along the clifflike face.

Also, this is still Raiatea's best hotel. The friendly and helpful staffers speak English, but the ambience is definitely French these days. The land-based bungalows, some of which have two units under their thatched roofs, are either along the seawall or in the gardens beyond. The least expensive units are hotel rooms, which have the same amenities as the bungalows and are air-conditioned. Opening to the pool and lagoon, and serving French fare and libations all day, the hotel's restaurant and bar are favorite local haunts.

B.P. 43, 98735 Uturoa, Raiatea (2km/1¼ miles south of town). ② **800/657-3275** or 66.20.23. Fax 66.20.20. www.pearlresorts.com. 32 units. 26,000CFP (US$325/£165) double; 26,000CFP–36,000CFP (US$25US–$450/£165–£228) bungalow. AE, MC, V. **Amenities:** Restaurant; bar; outdoor pool; tennis court; bike

rentals; activities desk; car-rental desk; babysitting; laundry service. *In room:* A/C (some units), TV, fridge, **193**
coffeemaker, safe.

MODERATE

Hotel Atiapiti   Virtually next-door to Taputapuatea Marae, this remote but pleasant little hotel sits beside the lagoon facing Te Ava Moa Pass and Huahine. There is no natural beach here, but a row of coconut palms and sand behind a bulkhead makes it seem like a beach resort. Five of the six bungalows directly face this vista. All have stucco sides and wood-shingled roofs that extend over front porches, some strung with hammocks. Each beachfront unit has a separate bedroom with a king-size bed, while each garden unit has a double bed and two singles in its main room, plus a small second room with a single bed. Owner Marie-Claude Rajaud, who speaks several languages including English, applies her cooking skills to fresh seafood in the French country–style restaurant. It's an excellent stop for lunch while you're visiting the *marae,* but call ahead for reservations if you're not a guest here. This is a relaxing place to stay if you don't mind being a long way from everything except the *marae.*

B.P. 884, 98735 Uturoa, Raiatea (east coast, 30km/18 miles south of Uturoa). ✆/fax **66.16.65.** atiapiti@ mail.pf. 7 units. 13,900CFP (US$174/£88) double. MC, V. **Amenities:** Restaurant; bar; free use of snorkeling gear; watersports equipment/rentals; bike rentals; laundry service. *In room:* TV, kitchen, no phone.

Raiatea Lodge Hotel   Formerly the Hotel Mirimiri, and the Hotel Tenape before that, this plantation-style hotel sits in a large lawn across the main road from the lagoon on the west coast. The restaurant and bar in the middle of the two-story clapboard building open onto the swimming pool out in the front yard. The rooms and one suite extend to each side. The medium-size units are identical, with pine floors, tables, desks, balconies with a view of the lagoon, and bathrooms with open, French-style showers. The suite adds two bedrooms. A pier gives access to the lagoon for boating and swimming. The location is a bit remote, but the setting is so peaceful that you can hear the birds singing outside your room.

B.P. 1147, 98735 Uturoa, Raiatea (west coast, 8km/5 miles from town). ✆ **60.20.00.** Fax 66.20.02. www. raiateahotel.com. 16 units. 12,000CFP (US$150/£76) double; 24,000CFP (US$300/£152) suite. AE, DC, MC, V. **Amenities:** Restaurant; bar; outdoor pool; bike rentals; Wi-Fi; laundry service. *In room:* A/C, TV, dataport, safe.

INEXPENSIVE

Pension Manava   Roselyne and Andrew Brotherson rent two rooms in their house and have four bungalows in their gardens, across the road from the lagoon. The two rooms share a bathroom and the Brothersons' kitchen. The bungalows have corrugated tin roofs, screened louvered windows, double and single beds, and large bathrooms with hot-water showers. Two of them also have kitchens. Roselyne will cook breakfast and provide free dinner transportation to town on request.

B.P. 559, 98735 Uturoa, Raiatea (6km/3¹/₂ miles south of town). ✆ **66.28.26.** www.manavapension.com. 6 units. 4,700CFP (US$59/£30) rooms; 8,000CFP (US$100/£51) bungalow. No credit cards. *In room:* Kitchen (2 units), no phone.

Pension Tepua   There's a lot packed into this small parcel of land next to the lagoon south of Uturoa, including a swimming pool and Raiatea's only dormitory, making this pension a good choice for backpackers. Despite being shoehorned into the property, the buildings are tropically attractive, with split bamboo siding and shingle roofs. The choice bungalow sits right beside the lagoon, with a view of Hotel Hawaiki Nui across a small bay. It's the only unit here with a television. Three other bungalows stand away from the lagoon near the pool. Another building houses four hotel-style rooms and the dormitory. The restaurant provides breakfast and lunch to guests and is open to the public at dinner. Dorm residents share toilets and showers, but all other units have private bathrooms with hot-water showers.

B.P. 1298, 98735 Uturoa, Raiatea (2.7km/1¹/₂ miles south of Uturoa). ✆ **66.33.00.** Fax 66.32.00. www. raiatea.com/tepua. 8 units, 12 dormitory beds (shared bathrooms). 5,000CFP–7,500CFP (US$63–US$94/£32–£47) double; 10,000CFP–13,000CFP (US$125–US$163/£63–£82) bungalow; 2,500CFP (US$31/£16) dormitory bed. MC, V. **Amenities:** Restaurant; bar; outdoor pool; communal kitchen. *In room:* TV (1 unit), no phone.

Sunset Beach Motel ★ (Value)   One of the best values in French Polynesia, this is not a motel, but rather a collection of cottages set in a coconut plantation on a peninsula sticking out west of the airport. The cottages sit in a row just off a palm-draped beach, the only one on Raiatea. The lagoon here is very shallow, but the beach enjoys a gorgeous westward view toward Bora Bora, and a long pier stretches to deep water (guests can paddle free kayaks from it). Of European construction rather than Polynesian, the bungalows are spacious, comfortably furnished, and have fully equipped kitchens and large covered verandas facing the sea. Part of the grove is set aside for campers, who have their own building with toilets, showers, and kitchen (bring your own tent). Manager Steve "Moana" Boubée speaks English. There is no restaurant here, but you can order breakfast in your bungalow.

B.P. 397, 98735 Uturoa, Raiatea (in Apooiti, 5km/3 miles northwest of Uturoa). ✆ **66.33.47.** Fax 66.33.08. www.sunset.raiatea.com. 22 units. 10,000CFP (US$125/£63) double bungalow; 1,100CFP (US$14/£6.95) per person camping. MC, V. **Amenities:** Free kayaks; rental bikes; laundry service. *In room:* TV, kitchen, no phone.

ON TAHAA

Except for Hotel Le Pirogue, Vahine Island Private Resort, and the superluxurious Le Taha'a Private Island & Spa, all out on islets by themselves, Tahaa's accommodations fall into the anything-but-luxurious pension category. This may change soon, however, since new high-end properties are planned for the *motus* out on the reef.

EXPENSIVE

Hotel La Pirogue   Beside a white-sand beach and shallow lagoon on Motu Porou, a small reef islet off Hipu village on Tahaa's northeastern coast, this is the least expensive

---

 Stuck After Dark

If you've been to Bora Bora, you'll know that hotel launches regularly ply between the *motu* resorts there, which means guests can easily get over to the main island for activities and dining. Such is not the case at Tahaa. Here, you cannot run over to the mainland from Hotel La Pirogue, La Taha'a Private Island & Spa, or Vahine Island Private Resort and save a few bucks on dinner. They are wonderful places to relax, but once you're out on one of Tahaa's *motus,* you are pretty much stuck out here after dark.

of the offshore resorts here. All of the buildings have natural thatched roofs. Four of the guest bungalows, including a suite, sit beside the beach and have platforms extending out over the sand, where you can sit and take in the sunsets behind Tahaa and Bora Bora off in the distance. Needless to say, these are the most expensive models. Each unit also has a front porch, a mosquito net over the king-size bed, a television, and a phone. Separate buildings hold the seafood restaurant and bar. The staff will take you over to Hipu, where you can use bicycles to explore Tahaa.

B.P. 668, 98735 Uturoa, Raiatea (on Motu Porou). © **60.81.45.** Fax 60.81.46. www.hotel-la-pirogue.com. 8 units. 26,000CFP–42,000CFP (US$325–US$525/£165–£266) bungalow. AE, MC, V. **Amenities:** Restaurant; bar; free use of bicycles, canoes, and snorkeling gear; limited room service. *In room:* TV, dataport.

Le Taha'a Private Island & Spa ★★★

When I was traveling by yacht back in 1977, we anchored near Motu Tautau, an islet on the reef off Tahaa's west coast, and went ashore to get an unsurpassed view of Bora Bora from its outer edge. There was nothing on Tautau then except palm trees, a brackish lake, and several million mosquitoes. Since 2002 the "mossies" have mostly resided on the sea side of the *motu,* while one of French Polynesia's most luxurious and architecturally creative resorts has occupied the lagoon shoreline. A 40-minute boat ride from the Raiatea airport, or 15 minutes by helicopter from Bora Bora, this Relais & Châteaux–affiliated hotel sports the territory's most tastefully decorated bungalows. Most stand out over the hip-deep lagoon, where their large decks have privacy fences screening covered sitting areas under thatched roofs. Most face hilly Tahaa, but a few have views of Bora Bora through a shallow reef pass between Tautau and its neighboring *motu.* Ashore beside the brilliant white-sand beach, 10 villa suites are even larger and more private. The villas all have living rooms, bedrooms, and courtyards with plunge pools hidden behind high rock walls. Two Royal Villas enlarge on them by adding a separate bungalow within their compounds, 24-hour butler service, and private shows and barbecues on the beach.

At the center of it all is a stunning, two-story central building, where stairs built in a tree lead up to the main bar and casual gourmet restaurant with both indoor and outdoor tables, all with a view. The most romantic tables sit by themselves on extensions from the terrace. Or you can retire to the air-conditioned, fine-dining restaurant. The resort's infinity pool, a lunchtime restaurant and bar, full-service spa and air-conditioned gym are on one end of the property, thus removing most daytime activities from the vicinity of the bungalows. There's much to do here, from snorkeling to safari expeditions on Tahaa. This is a marvelous place to chill after the rigors of Bora Bora.

B.P. 67, 98733 Patio, Tahaa (on Motu Tautau). © **800/657-3275** or 60.84.00. Fax 60.84.01. www.letahaa. com. 60 units. 92,000CFP–230,000CFP (US$1,150–US$2,875/£582–£1,456) bungalow. AE, DC, MC, V. **Amenities:** 2 restaurants; 2 bars; outdoor pool; tennis court; spa; Jacuzzi; watersports equipment rentals; concierge; activities desk; business center; fitness center; limited room service; massage; babysitting; laundry service. *In room:* A/C, TV, CD player, dataport, minibar, coffeemaker, safe.

Vahine Island Private Resort ★★

In a coconut grove on flat Motu Tuuvahine, off Tahaa's northeastern coast, this intimate little hotel offers bungalows both beside a brilliant white-sand beach and built out over a shallow lagoon beautifully speckled with coral heads. The three thatched-roof overwater units are the pick, since they are larger and more private than the beachside units—and they have a stunning view of Bora Bora on the far horizon. The bungalows ashore have shingle roofs, but all are decorated in traditional Polynesian style, with native lumber and bamboo trim. Each sports a porch in front and a shower-only bathroom to the rear. Ceiling fans and mosquito nets make up for the lack of air-conditioning and window screens. The dining room serves good French fare with island touches. There's a guest lounge with a collection of books and videos in both English and French. Most of the guests are from Europe, but the staff makes everyone feel welcomed at this little gem.

B.P. 510, 98735 Uturoa, Raiatea (on Motu Tuuvahine). ℂ **65.67.38.** Fax 65.67.70. www.vahine-island.com. 9 units. 37,000CFP–58,000CFP (US$463–US$725/£234–£367) double. AE, DC, MC, V. **Amenities:** Restaurant; bar; free use of kayaks, canoes, and snorkeling gear; laundry service. *In room:* TV, fridge, coffeemaker, hair dryer.

MODERATE

Pension Vai Poe (Chez Patricia et Daniel)   Owners Patricia and Daniel Amaru have five tin-roof bungalows across the road from their Haamene Bay pearl farm, where you can learn how the orbs are grown and produced. They also operate Vai Poe safari expeditions (see "Safari Expeditions & Lagoon Excursions," earlier in this chapter). Two of their bungalows are suitable for couples, while the other three can accommodate small families. Each has a private bathroom with hot-water shower and a fridge. L'Hibiscus is a short walk away (see below).

B.P. 104, 98734 Haamene, Tahaa (north shore of Haamene Bay). ℂ/fax **65.60.83.** v.p@mail.pf. 5 units. 12,000CFP (US$150/£76) double. Rates include breakfast. AE, MC, V. *In room:* TV, kitchen, no phone.

INEXPENSIVE

L'Hibiscus   This lively little pension beside Haamene Bay is the domain of Leo Morou, a bearded Frenchman who "went troppo" years ago, and his charming Tahitian wife, Lolita. I stayed here in the early 1990s when they had three simple bungalows sharing communal showers and toilets. The Morous have added four government-issued bungalows, each with its own bathroom as well as front porch. The bungalows climb a hill across the road from a 200-seat waterside restaurant and bar, a long pier, and moorings out in the bay, which attract dozens of yachties for a bit of libation and a meal. Parties, music, and Tahitian dance shows have been known to extend well into the night. The lagoon is a protected area for sea turtles, thanks to Leo's Foundation Hibiscus.

B.P. 184, 98734 Haamene, Tahaa (north shore of Haamene Bay). ℂ **65.61.06.** Fax 65.65.65. www.tahaa-tahiti.com. 7 units (3 with shared bathroom). 9,500CFP (US$119/£60) double. MC, V. **Amenities:** Restaurant; bar; free use of snorkeling gear. *In room:* Fridge, no phone.

---

7 WHERE TO DINE

ON RAIATEA

Les roulottes, Raiatea's inexpensive meal wagons, congregate after dark near the Gare Maritime in the middle of Uturoa's business district, and in the seaside park north of the business district. They stay open past midnight on Friday and Saturday. See "Don't Miss *Les Roulottes*" (p. 140) for details.

An inexpensive daytime option is **Snack Hai Ling** (ℂ **66.10.11**), a walk-up snack bar in the public square opposite the Gare Maritime. It has the usual *roulotte* menu of burgers, steaks, and Chinese dishes.

Brasserie Maraamu ⟨**Value**⟩ CHINESE/TAHITIAN   Before it moved into the Gare Maritime, this restaurant occupied a waterfront shack and was widely known for its simple but good Chinese dishes, *poisson cru,* and fried chicken and steaks served with french fries. The chow is still good, as witnessed by the number of local office workers who head here for lunch. Local business types like to hang out here over strong cups of morning coffee served French-style in soup bowls (the better to dunk your baguette).

In Gare Maritime, Uturoa waterfront. ☎ **66.46.64.** Breakfast 700CFP–1,200CFP (US$8.75–US$15/£4.45–£7.60); main courses 1,000CFP–1,800CFP (US$13–US$23/£6.30–£11). MC, V. Mon–Fri 7am–2pm and 6:30–9pm; Sat 10am–2pm.

Le Napoli ★ ITALIAN   A stack of firewood beside a pond (note the Tahitian eels swimming about) hints that the very good pizzas and steaks are cooked in a wood-fired oven in this restaurant, which is dolled up with bamboo trim. The 15 varieties of pizza are all two-person size, so unless you are famished, forget the special tourist menu that adds *poisson cru* and a dessert. I like the smoked salmon and cream sauce pasta here.

Main road north of Uturoa, near airport. ☎ **66.10.77.** Reservations recommended. Pizza and pasta 1,350CFP–1,500CFP (US$17–US$19/£8.55–£9.50); main courses 1,450CFP–2,100CFP (US$18–US$26/£9.15–£13). MC, V. Tues–Fri 11am–2pm and 6:30–9pm; Sat–Sun 6:30–9pm.

Sea Horse Restaurant CHINESE   Proprietor Alphonse Léogite, scion of a major Raiatea family, lived in the United States for 15 years before returning home and opening this excellent establishment in the Gare Maritime. You can dine outside on the plaza or inside, where tropical furniture, potted plants, and linen tablecloths set a refined but relaxed ambience for very good Chinese cuisine. Most items on the menu will be familiar, such as sautéed beef with peanut sauce. Check the specials board for the day's fish selections.

In Gare Maritime, Uturoa waterfront. ☎ **66.16.34.** Reservations recommended on weekend evenings. Main courses 1,150CFP–2,100CFP (US$14–US$26/£7.30–£13). MC, V. Mon–Sat 10am–1:30pm and 6–9:30pm.

Snack Moemoea SNACKS/FRENCH/CHINESE   Predating the Gare Maritime by many years, this old corner storefront has tables both outside on the sidewalk and inside on the ground floor or on a mezzanine platform. It's another good place for breakfast, from croissants to omelets. The lunch menu includes *casse-croûte* sandwiches, fine hamburgers, grilled fish and steaks, and Raiatea's best *poisson cru.* I love to slake my thirst here with an ice-cold coconut.

Waterfront, Uturoa (in Toporo Building). ☎ **66.39.84.** Breakfast 600CFP–1,500CFP (US$7.50–US$19/£3.80–£9.50); burgers and sandwiches 400CFP–800CFP (US$5–US$10/£2.55–£5.05); main courses 1,500CFP–1,900CFP (US$19–US$24/£9.50–£12). No credit cards. Mon–Fri 6am–5pm; Sat 6am–2pm.

ON TAHAA

If you're chartering a yacht, you can have dinner at one of the offshore resorts listed under "Where to Stay: On Tahaa," above. Clients of the Moorings can even dine at the ritzy La Taha'a Private Island & Spa, provided they make reservations in advance.

Chez Louise ★ TAHITIAN   This local restaurant beside the lagoon in Tiva village, on Tahaa's west coast, is a popular stop for cruise-ship passengers, and it's close enough to Le Taha'a Private Island & Spa that its guests come here for lunch or dinner, too (call for dinner pickup at Tapuamu wharf). The *ma'a Tahiti* fare is first-rate, as are lobster and other fresh seafood items. There's a gorgeous view of Bora Bora from here, so come in time for a sunset drink.

Tiva village, lagoonside. © **65.68.88** or 72.59.18. Reservations highly recommended. Full meals 3,500CFP–5,600CFP (US$44–US$70/£22–£35). MC, V. Daily 11am–2pm and 6–9pm.

Restaurant Tahaa Maitai FRENCH   Chef Bruno François cooks excellent French fare at his restaurant on the waterfront in Haamene village, at the head of the bay. He also serves salads and burgers, making this the best stop for lunch on a tour of Tahaa. The crab salad is excellent, as is Bruno's mahimahi in beer sauce. His fixed-priced tourist menu includes a cocktail and three courses. The nighttime clientele is mostly local, but yachties often tie up at the dock out front.

Haamene village, on the waterfront. © **65.70.85.** Reservations recommended. Burgers 1,350CFP (US$17/£8.55); main courses 1,300CFP–2,400CFP (US$16–US$30/£8.20–£15); tourist menu 3,950CFP (US$49/£25). MC, V. Tues–Fri 10am–2:30pm and 6:40–8pm; Sat 6:40–8pm; Sun 10am–2:30pm.

Bora Bora

Because of its fame and extraor-dinary beauty, little Bora Bora is a playground for the well-to-do, occasionally the famous, and honeymooners blowing a wad of cash. As French Polynesia's tourist magnet, it now has more hotel rooms per capita than any other island, their piers reaching out like tentacles to multitudinous bungalows standing over its gorgeous lagoon. Some of the piers are so long that the Moorings has added them to its sailing charts as hazards to navigation!

Some of us who remember the island in its more pristine state often bemoan that development has ruined it. But I frequently meet people making their first visit, and usually they are as blown away by Bora Bora as I was when I spent a week camping here in 1977. If you can ignore the jet skis occasionally whizzing past your bungalow, and look beyond the tourists hanging under parasails over the lagoon, you will appreciate why James A. Michener wrote that this is the world's most beautiful island.

Of course, there are more tourists here than on any other French Polynesian island. Thus, some lovers now like to polish off

their honeymoons on the more peaceful Tahaa or Huahine after the mile-a-minute pace here.

Lying 230km (143 miles) northwest of Tahiti, Bora Bora is a middle-aged island consisting of a high center completely surrounded by a lagoon that's enclosed by coral reef. It has a gorgeous combination of sand-fringed *motus* (small islets) sitting on the outer reef enclosing the multihued lagoon, which cuts deep bays into the high central island. Towering over it all is Bora Bora's trademark, the basaltic tombstone known as **Mount Otemanu** (725m/2,379 ft.). Standing next to it is the more normally rounded **Mount Pahia** (660m/2,165 ft.).

One of the best beaches in French Polynesia stretches for more than 3km (2 miles) around the flat, coconut-studded peninsula known as **Point Matira,** which juts out from the island's southern end.

Bora Bora is so small that the road around it covers only 32km (19 miles) from start to finish. All the 7,000 or so Bora Borans live on a flat coastal strip that quickly gives way to the mountainous interior.

1 ARRIVING & GETTING TO YOUR HOTEL

Bora Bora's airport is on **Motu Mute,** a flat island on the northwestern edge of the barrier reef. U.S. marines built the airstrip during World War II when Bora Bora was a major refueling stop on the America-to-Australia supply line.

You will see the lagoon close up soon after landing because all passengers are ferried across it from the airport. Some resorts send boats to pick up their guests (be sure to tell them your flight number when making your reservations). The major resorts have welcome desks in the terminal to greet you and steer you to the correct boat. It can be a tad confusing out on the dock, where baggage is unloaded. You do not want to end up on the wrong *motu,* so pay attention, and ask someone if you are not sure which boat is yours.

Impressions

I saw it first from an airplane. On the horizon there was a speck that became a tall, blunt mountain with cliffs dropping sheer into the sea. And about the base of the mountain, narrow fingers of land shot out, forming magnificent bays, while about the whole was thrown a coral ring of absolute perfection.... That was Bora Bora from aloft. When you stepped upon it the dream expanded.

—James A. Michener, *Return to Paradise,* 1951

If your hotel does not send a boat, you will take Air Tahiti's launch to **Vaitape,** the only village and the center of most commerce. Buses will take you from Vaitape to your hotel. Get in the bus displaying the name of your hotel, or ask the driver if you are not sure. Bus fare from Vaitape to the Matira Point hotel district is 500CFP (US$6.25/£3.15).

See "Getting to Tahiti & French Polynesia" and "Getting Around Tahiti & French Polynesia," in chapter 3, for more information.

2 GETTING AROUND BORA BORA

There is no regularly scheduled public transportation system on Bora Bora. Buses do ferry passengers from Vaitape to the Matira hotel district on cruise-ship days, though, and anyone can catch a ride for 300CFP (US$3.75/£1.90).

Some hotels on the main island shuttle their guests to Vaitape and back once or twice a day, but the frequency can vary depending on how many guests they have. Except for the Bora Bora Pearl Beach Resort, whose shuttles go to Chancelade on the northwestern corner, resorts out on the western islets run shuttle boats to Vaitape. Resorts on the eastern *motus* send their *navettes* (shuttle boats) to remote Anau village on the east coast. Take this into account if you plan to spend time on the main island.

BY RENTAL CAR, SCOOTER & BICYCLE

Europcar (© 800/227-7368 or 67.70.15; www.europcar-tahiti.com) is the biggest and best firm here. Both it and a local firm, **Fare-Piti Rent a Car** (© 67.65.28), have offices at Vaitape wharf. Europcar's rates start at 10,100CFP (US$126/£64) a day for their smallest cars, including unlimited kilometers and insurance. Both rent open-air Bugsters for about 9,300CFP (US$116/£59) a day. Both have bicycles for about 1,800CFP (US$23/£11) all day.

The 32km (19 miles) of road around Bora Bora are paved, but always drive or ride slowly and carefully, and be on the lookout for pigs, chickens, pedestrians, and especially dogs.

BY TAXI

No taxis patrol Bora Bora looking for passengers, but several firms have transport licenses, which means they can come get you if someone calls. The hotel desks and restaurants will do that for you, or you can phone **Taxi Simplet** (© 79.19.31), **Léon** (© 70.69.16), **Otemanu Tours** (© 67.70.49), **Jacques Isnard** (© 67.72.25), or **Dino's Land & Water Taxi** (© 79.29.65). Fares between Vaitape and the Matira Point

ACCOMMODATIONS ■

Chez Nono **8**
Bora Bora Lagoon Resort
& Spa **4**
Bora Bora Nui Resort & Spa **5**
Bora Bora Pearl Beach Resort **2**
Club Med Bora Bora **13**
Hotel Bora Bora **6**
Hotel Maitai Polynesia **10**
Hotel Matira **7**
InterContinental Le
Moana Resort **8**

InterContinental Resort and
Thalasso Spa Bora Bora **15**
Le Meridien Bora Bora **16**
Mai Moana Island **1**
Novotel Bora Bora Beach
Resort **11**
Pension Robert et Tina **8**
Rohutu Fare Lodge **14**
Sofitel Bora Bora Marara
Beach Resort **12**
Sofitel Bora Bora Motu
Private Island **9**

St. Regis Resort
Bora Bora **17**
Village Temanuata **10**

ATTRACTIONS ●

Aehautai Marae **18**
Marotetini Marae **20**
Old Hyatt Site **22**
TOPdive Bora Bora **3**
U.S. guns **19**
U.S. wharf **21**

hotel district are at least 1,500CFP (US$19/£9.50) from 6am to 6pm and 2,000CFP (US$25/£13) from 6pm to 6am. A ride between Vaitape and Anau village costs 5,000CFP (US$63/£32) anytime. (Add up your expected fares; it may be more economical to rent a vehicle.) The taxis aren't metered, so make sure you and the driver agree on a fare before setting out.

If you're staying at a resort on an islet and don't want to wait for the next boat shuttle, you can call **Dino's Land & Water Taxi** (☏ **79.29.65**) or **Taxi Motu** (☏ **67.60.61**). The ride to the main island costs about 2,500CFP (US$31/£16).

⟮*Fast Facts*   **Bora Bora**

The following facts apply specifically to Bora Bora. For more information, see "Fast Facts: Tahiti & French Polynesia," in appendix A.

Babysitters The hotels can arrange for English-speaking babysitters, or you can contact **Robin Teraitepo** at Chez Ben's (☏ **67.74.54**).

Bookstores & Newsstands **La Maison de la Press,** across the main road from the Vaitape small boat harbor (☏ **60.57.75**), carries the *International Herald Tribune* and *USA Today,* though not today's edition. It also sells film, camera batteries, and prepaid SIM cards for your cellphone.

Camera & Film **Jeanluc Photo Shop,** at the Vaitape harbor (☏ **72.01.23**), offers professional photo services and overnight processing of color print film.

Currency Exchange **Banque de Tahiti, Banque Socredo,** and **Banque de Polynésie** have branches with ATMs in Vaitape.

Drugstores **Pharmacie de Bora Bora,** north of the small boat harbor in Vaitape (☏ **67.70.30**), is open Monday through Friday from 8am to noon and 2:30 to 6pm, Saturday from 8am to noon and 5 to 6pm, and Sunday and holidays from 9 to 11am.

Emergencies & Police The **emergency police** phone number is ☏ **17.** The **gendarmerie** (☏ **67.70.58**) is opposite the Vaitape harbor.

Healthcare The island's **infirmary** is in Vaitape (☏ **67.70.77**), as is **Dr. Azad Roussanaly** (☏ **67.77.95**).

Internet Access **Aloe Cafe,** in the Centre Commercial Le Pahia just north of the Vaitape wharf (☏ **67.78.88**), has a computer terminal with Skype, which costs about 40CFP (US50¢/25p) per minute of online time. See "Where to Dine," later in this chapter, for more about this pastry shop.

Mail The Vaitape post office is open Monday from 8am to 3pm, Tuesday through Friday from 7:30am to 3pm, and Saturday from 8 to 10am.

Restrooms The wharf at Vaitape has public restrooms, in the small octagonal building on the wharf itself and in a small white building to the north of the visitor and handicrafts centers. It can be a long wait for a shuttle boat back to your resort, so take preventive action as necessary.

Taxes Bora Bora's municipal government adds 100CFP to 150CFP (US$1.25–US$1.90/ 65p–95p) per night to your hotel bill.

Visitor Information The **Bora Bora Comité du Tourisme,** B.P. 144, Vaitape, Bora Bora (*©* **67.76.36;** info-bora-bora@mail.pf), has a visitor center in the large building on the north side of the Vaitape wharf. Open Monday to Friday, and on cruise-ship days, from 9am to 4pm.

Water Bora Bora has a huge desalinization plant, so the tap water is safe to drink. Most local residents still drink bottled water, available at all groceries.

3 EXPLORING BORA BORA: THE CIRCLE ISLAND TOUR

Most of Bora Bora's residents live on the flat coastal strip that rings the island. The paved round-island road skirts the shoreline and runs in and out of the bays. Because the road is only 32km (19 miles) long, many visitors see it by bicycle (give yourself a full day), scooter, or car.

Some of the sights mentioned below may not be easy to find, however, so consider taking a guided tour around the island. **Otemanu Tours** (*©* **67.70.49;** otemanu.tours@ mail.pf) still uses one of the traditional, open-air *le truck* vehicles, which adds an extra dimension to its trips, but be sure your tour is in *le truck* and not an air-conditioned bus. The cost is about 4,000CFP (US$50/£25) per person; you can book at any hotel activities desk.

You can get a spectacular bird's-eye view of the island with **Polynesia Hélicoptères** (*©* **54.87.20;** www.polynesia-helicopter.com). It charges about 16,300CFP (US$204/ £103) per person for a 15-minute sightseeing flight over Bora Bora and its lagoon. If you've never seen an atoll and aren't going to the Tuamotu Islands, consider a 30-minute flight over Bora Bora and out to Tupai, a ring of flat islets enclosing a lagoon north of Bora Bora; the cost is about 27,000CFP (US$338/£171) per person. A minimum of four passengers is required on all flights. Polynesia Hélicoptères also provides transfers between Bora Bora and Le Taha'a Private Island & Spa, off Tahaa (p. 195).

VAITAPE

Either driving or biking, you should begin at the small boat harbor in **Vaitape,** Bora Bora's only town and its administrative center. The harbor is the center of attention in Vaitape, as Air Tahiti, the cruise ships, and the shuttle boats from the resorts on Motu Toopua (the large islet offshore) land their passengers here. The island's visitor information center and women's handicrafts center are in the large building beside the harbor. Vaitape's only street is lined with boutiques, black-pearl shops, and other establishments designed to wrench money from your pockets. The post office is to the right as you face the mountains, but most business activity takes place north of the harbor, especially at the modern Centre Commercial La Pahia.

In the parking lot, opposite the gendarmerie, is a monument to famed French socialite, author, and yachtsman **Alain Gerbault,** who single-handedly skippered his boat *Firecrest* around the world between 1923 and 1929, stopping for an extended period in French Polynesia. Gerbault returned to French Polynesia in 1933 and championed the cause of the islanders against the colonial bureaucracy. He also introduced soccer to the locals. Gerbault was interned on Moorea at the outbreak of World War II in Europe

> **(Tips) A Killer View**
>
> The round-island road curves along the shore of **Povai Bay,** where Mount Otemanu
> and Mount Pahia tower over you. Take your time along this bay; the views here
> are the best on Bora Bora. When you reach **Bloody Mary's Restaurant & Bar,** go
> out on the pier for a killer view back across the water at Mount Otemanu.

because he favored the pro-Nazi Vichy government in Paris, while French Polynesians sided with Gen. Charles de Gaulle and the Free French. He was released on the condition he leave the territory. He sailed to Indonesia, where he died on Timor in 1941. Six years later, the French navy returned his ashes to Bora Bora, his favorite island.

From the harbor, walk northward through Vaitape, taking in its large Christian church, which stands at the base of soaring Mount Pahia. When you've seen enough of this Polynesian village, turn south and head counterclockwise around the island.

MATIRA BEACH ★★★

After following the shore of semicircular Povai Bay, the road climbs the small headland, where a huge banyan tree marks the entrance to the Hotel Bora Bora on **Raititi Point,** and then follows curving **Matira Beach,** one of French Polynesia's finest. Some of the island's best snorkeling is in the shallow, sand-bottom lagoon off these powdery white sands. People have homes on the other side of the road, but the beach itself is still remarkably undeveloped.

The road follows the beach and then curves sharply to the left at the south end of the island. Watch here for a narrow paved road to the right. This leads to **Matira Point,** the low, sandy, coconut-studded peninsula that extends out from Bora Bora's south end. Down this track about 46m (150 ft.) is a **public beach** on the west side of the peninsula, opposite the InterContinental Le Moana Resort. The lagoon is shallow all the way out to the reef at this point, but the bottom is smooth and sandy. When I first came to Bora Bora in 1977, I camped for a week on Matira Point; the InterContinental Le Moana Resort is now just one of many structures in what was then a virtually deserted coconut grove completely surrounded by unspoiled beach.

THE EAST COAST

After rounding the point, you'll pass through the island's busy hotel-and-restaurant district before climbing a hill above the Club Med, which sits beside Faaopore Bay. A steep trail begins at a set of steps on the mountain side of the road and goes up to a lookout over the bay. Another trail cuts off to the right on the north side of the hill and goes to the **Aehautai Marae,** one of several old temples on Bora Bora. This particular one has a great view of Mount Otemanu and the blue outlines of Raiatea and Tahaa islands beyond the *motu* on the reef.

You will go through a long stretch of coconut plantations before entering **Anau,** a typical Polynesian village with a large church, a general store, and tin-roof houses crouched along the road. Anau is the landing point for boats going to and from Le Meridien Bora Bora and the InterContinental Resort and Thalasso Spa Bora Bora, whose overwater bungalows you will see out on Motu Pitiaau. The St. Regis Resort Bora Bora and the Four Seasons Bora Bora are slated to join them out there (see "Where to Stay," p. 209).

ACCOMMODATIONS ■

Chez Nono **9**

Club Med Bora Bora **20**

Hotel Bora Bora **3**

Hotel Maitai Polynesia **16**

Hotel Matira **8**

InterContinental Le
  Moana Resort **12**

Novotel Bora Bora
  Beach Resort **18**

Pension Robert et Tina **11**

Sofitel Bora Bora Marara Beach
  Resort **19**

Sofitel Bora Bora Motu
  Private Island **15**

Village Temanuata **13**

DINING ◆

Bloody Mary's Restaurant
  & Bar **2**

Chez Ben's **4**

La Bounty **17**

La Matira Beach Restaurant **6**

La Villa Mahana **1**

Restaurant Fare
  Manuia **14**

Restaurant-Snack Moi
  Here **10**

Roulotte Matira **7**

Snack Matira **5**

✈ Airport
🏄 Beach
--- Reef

The road goes over two hills at Point Haamaire, the main island's easternmost extremity, about 4km (2½ miles) north of Anau village. Between the two hills on the lagoon side of the road stands **Aehautai Marae,** a restored temple. Out on the point is **Taharuu Marae,** which has a great view of the lagoon. The Americans installed naval guns in the hills above the point during World War II.

THE NORTH & WEST COASTS

On the deserted northeast coast, you will ride through several miles of coconut plantations pockmarked by thousands of holes made by *tupas* (land crabs). After turning at the northernmost point, you pass a group of overwater bungalows and another group of houses that climb the hill. Some of these are expensive condominiums; the others are part of a defunct project that was to have been a Hyatt resort. The ruins of what was to have been the resort's funicular railway scar the hillside. Across the lagoon are Motu Mute and the airport.

Faanui Bay was used during World War II as an Allied naval base. It's not marked, but the U.S. Navy's Seabees built the concrete wharf on the north shore as a seaplane ramp. Just beyond Farepiti Wharf, the main cargo shipping dock at the point on the southern entrance to Faanui Bay, is the restored **Marotetini Marae,** which in pre-European days was dedicated to navigators. In his novel *Hawaii,* James Michener had his fictional Polynesians leave this point to discover and settle the Hawaiian Islands. Nearby are tombs in which members of Bora Bora's former royal family are buried. If you look offshore at this point, you'll see the only pass into the lagoon. The remains of two **U.S. guns** that guarded it stand on the hill above, but are best visited on a safari tour (see "Safari Expeditions," below).

Entering Vaitape, **Magasin Chin Lee** is a major gathering place for local residents. It's a good place to soak up some island culture while trimming your thirst with a cold bottle of Eau Royale.

4 SAFARI EXPEDITIONS & LAGOON EXCURSIONS

SAFARI EXPEDITIONS ★

The regular tours stick to the shoreline, but safari expeditions venture into the hills in open-air, four-wheel-drive vehicles for panoramic views and visits to the old U.S. Navy gun sites. Compared to safari expeditions on Moorea, Huahine, and Tahaa, which emphasize local culture as well as scenery, here they are more like scenic thrill rides. The journey can be rough, so I do not recommend it for children, the elderly, or anyone prone to carsickness. The mountain roads are mere ruts in places, so you could become stuck if it has been raining.

Your best bet for insight into the island's history and lore is Patrick Tairua of **Patrick's Activities** (© **79.19.11** or 67.69.94; www.maohinui.net). Son of the last Polynesian chief of Bora Bora, Patrick (pronounced Pa-*treek* in French) lived in the U.S. and speaks English fluently. He passes along stories gleaned from spending time with one of the elders responsible for protecting the island's oral history. You'll get out of the jeep and walk through the forest to an ancient *marae* where petroglyphs are carved into the basaltic rock. Patrick's tours are essentially private; that is, he takes a maximum of four persons at a time for 32,000CFP (US$400/£200) per tour. Patrick also leads private lagoon excursions (see below).

A more comfortable choice is **Vavau Adventures** (© **72.01.21;** temana689@mail.pf), which has morning and afternoon expeditions around the island and up into the mountains in an air-conditioned Land Rover. These tours also emphasize Bora Bora's history, culture, flora, and fauna, and they stop at the World War II guns and at a fish farm, where you will see tropical species being raised to restock the magnificent lagoon. They cost 7,400CFP (US$93/£47) per person.

The largest operator is the Levard family's **Tupuna Four-Wheel-Drive Expeditions** (© **67.75.06**), which uses open-air vehicles. On this tour, your last stop will be at the Farm, the Levards' black-pearl operation (see "Shopping," p. 208).

LAGOON EXCURSIONS & SHARK-FEEDING ★★★

Bora Bora has one of the world's most beautiful lagoons, and getting out on it, snorkeling and swimming in it, and visiting the islands on its outer edge are absolute musts. Although it's a widespread activity now, this is where **shark-feeding** began. That is, your guide feeds reef sharks while you watch from a reasonably safe distance. Some conservationists have criticized shark-feeding, but it is guaranteed to leave an indelible imprint on your memory.

Any hotel activities desk can book you on an all-day excursion with one of several operators. My longtime favorite is Nono Levard's **Teremoana Tours** (✆ **67.71.38**), which everyone here calls Nono's Tours. You spend the day going around the lagoon in a speedy outrigger canoe. Depending on the weather, you'll go snorkeling and watch a shark-feeding demonstration in the morning. You'll stop on a *motu* for swimming and a picnic lunch, and then pet stingrays on your way home in the afternoon. Expect to pay about 8,500CFP (US$106/£54) for a full-day outing.

Even if your all-day excursion doesn't feature it, you can still visit the **Bora Bora Lagoonarium** (✆ **67.71.34**), a fenced-in underwater area near Le Meridien Bora Bora. Here you can swim with (and maybe even ride) manta rays and observe sharks (which are on the other side of the fence here). The Lagoonarium has its own morning tour with shark-feeding and lunch on the *motu,* plus an afternoon excursion with fish-watching. The morning excursion costs about 7,800CFP (US$98/£49), the afternoon tour is 6,600CFP (US$83/£42), or you can do both for 10,000CFP (US$125/£63).

You can rent a boat and explore the lagoon yourself, but I strongly suggest this only for those who know what they're doing, and who understand how the color of the water tells its depth. You do not want to ruin your vacation by running onto a shallow reef. If you're still interested in renting a small craft, contact **Taxi Motu,** at the Novotel Bora Bora Beach Resort (✆ **67.60.61**), or **Moana Adventure Tours,** near the Hotel Bora Bora (✆ **67.61.41**).

5 SCUBA DIVING, SNORKELING & OTHER WATERSPORTS

SCUBA DIVING & SNORKELING ★★

While snorkeling off the reef face at the Hotel Bora Bora late one afternoon, I was startled to see a large manta ray gliding by virtually overhead, seemingly just a few feet away. It's one of my most indelible Bora Bora moments. You may have one, too, for both divers and snorkelers can swim among the manta rays, eagle rays, sharks, and some 1,000 species of colorful tropical fish in the lagoon here.

One of the most popular snorkeling sites is over the coral gardens in and near the **Bora Bora Lagoonarium** (see "Lagoon Excursions & Shark-Feeding," above). Even novice divers can explore the site known as Anau, in the lagoon between there and Point Haamaire, where manta rays frequently hang out. Divers and snorkelers also share the lagoon off the eastern side of Motu Toopua and the islet next to it, Motu Toopua Iti.

The most easily accessible dive site outside the reef is off Motu Tapu, the islet just south of Teavanui Pass. Two others—the White Valley, off the airport, and Tupitipiti, on the reef's southeastern corner—both require lengthy boat rides and can experience strong currents.

(Moments)   **Like Flying Underwater**

Shining with every hue on the blue end of the color spectrum, Bora Bora's watery playground is one of my favorite snorkeling spots. Hotel Bora Bora has bungalows sitting right on the edge of a reef that drops precipitously to dark depths. I experience the exhilaration of flying when I drift out over that underwater cliff. If you're lucky, a manta ray will gracefully glide by.

Among the best snorkeling spots are the aptly named "Aquarium," off the southern end of Motu Pitiaau, and around Motu Piti Uuuta, home of the Sofitel Motu. These require boat transportation, but you can walk to the outer reef from the southern tip of Point Matira, thus increasing your chances of seeing more fish than if you snorkel off Matira Beach south of the Hotel Bora Bora. Best of all, in my opinion, are the reef faces, above which sit the Hotel Bora Bora's overwater bungalows.

Every resort has snorkeling gear for its guests as well as a scuba-diving program. They all charge about 6,500CFP (US$81/£41) for 30-minute introductory courses or a one-tank lagoon dive. Open-water and night dives cost about 9,000CFP (US$113/£57).

The island's major dive operator is **TOPdive Bora Bora** (© **60.50.50;** fax 60.50.51; www.topdive.com), which has some of the best equipment and dive boats in French Polynesia. Its base is on the northern outskirts of Vaitape. **Nemo World** (© **67.71.84;** www.boradiving.com) has two bases: Nemo World Bora Bora near the Sofitel Bora Bora Marara Resort, and Nemo Bora Diving Cener near the Hotel Bora Bora. Two-tank dives cost about 14,500CFP (US$181/£92).

Nondivers can walk on the bottom while wearing a diving helmet with Aqua Safari (© **67.71.84**).

OTHER WATERSPORTS

Every hotel has some water toys for its guests to use, and hotel activities desks can arrange fishing, diving, and other watersports. You don't have to stay at the **Novotel Bora Bora Beach Club** (© **60.59.50**) to use its equipment and facilities, but you do have to pay a fee. You can go water-skiing, sail on Hobie Cats, paddle canoes, and get a bird's-eye view of the lagoon while hanging below a parasail.

Matira Jet Tours (© **77.63.63**) offers lagoon excursions by jet ski as well as inland tours via all-terrain vehicles. Many of the people you'll see riding above the lagoon are with **Bora Bora Parasail** (© **78.27.10**).

Most resorts have kayaks for their guests to paddle in the lagoon. Based at Rohutu Fare Lodge (see "Where to Stay," below), **Bora Bora Kayaks** (© **70.77.99;** www.rohotufare lodge.com) rents one- and two-person sea kayaks ranging from 1,500CFP (US$19/£9.50) for 1 hour to 6,500CFP (US$81/£41) for a whole day. These quality boats were made in the United States and come equipped with snorkeling and fishing gear.

6 SHOPPING

Most shopping here is in Vaitape, where you'll find several souvenir shops and upscale black-pearl dealers. Other boutiques and shops are scattered along the main road, especially in the Matira hotel district.

Bora Bora I Te Fanau Tahi   Local artisans display their wares in the large hall at the wharf. It's the least expensive place to shop for straw hats, *pareus,* and other handicrafts items. Open Monday to Friday 8:30am to 4pm, and on the weekend when cruise ships are in port. Vaitape, at the small boat landing. No phone.

Boutique Bora Bora   Catering to the cruise ship crowd, this store has more T-shirts and *pareus* than most others, plus it sells woodcarvings, books, curios, calendars, and a few black pearls. It's a good place to stock up on Hinano beer glasses. A similar sister store, **Boutique Pakalola,** is upstairs next to the post office. Open daily from 9am to 5:30pm. Vaitape, opposite the ferry wharf. ℭ **67.79.72.**

Boutique Gauguin   In a white house 1.5km (1 mile) north of Hotel Bora Bora, Boutique Gauguin is one of the larger stores here, offering a selection of handicrafts, clothing, black pearls, and curios. This is the best place on Bora Bora to shop for prints of Paul Gauguin's paintings. Some of the *pareus* here are particularly artistic. Open daily from 8am to 5:30pm. Povai Bay. ℭ **67.76.67.**

The Farm   You need to know about the Farm, since it's owned by the Levard family and thus you are likely to be deposited here after going on one of their safari excursions. They will show you how pearls are grown, harvested, graded, and turned into jewelry. The final products are for sale in the **Bora Pearl Company,** the showroom here. It's worth a visit here to see how it's all done. Open daily from 9am to 6pm. Raititi Point, near Hotel Bora Bora. ℭ **70.06.65.**

La Galerie Bora Bora   In Vaitape, this air-conditioned gallery carries excellent quality woodcarvings and stone carvings from the Marquesas, *tivaivai* quilts, pillow cases, pottery, tapa cloth, and paintings by local artists. Black pearls, too, of course. Open daily from 9am to 6pm. Vaitape, opposite the post office. ℭ **60.53.25.**

Matira Pearls ★★★ (Value)   You will have ample opportunities to shop for black pearls here (Vaitape village alone has a dozen outlets), but this is my favorite. It's owned by Steve Fearon, whose family once had a piece of the Hotel Bora Bora. Steve's chief assistants are his son, Heirama, who graduated from Pepperdine University in California, and daughter-in-law Tehani, herself educated in Los Angeles (Heirama and Tehani met there, not here). Unlike some other stores, their customized settings emphasize the pearl, not the gold. Set and loose pearls start at 10,000CFP (US$125/£63). Open Monday through Saturday from 9am to 5:30pm, and Sunday, 10am to 5pm. East side of Matira Point. ℭ **67.79.14.**

Mom's Boutique   Erina Gould, wife of Bloody Mary's Restaurant & Bar maitre d' Gregg Gould (see "Where to Dine," later in this chapter), sells only traditional aloha shirts, dresses, *pareus,* straw hats, and handicrafts at her little shop. In other words, the designs are like those prevalent when I first came here in the 1970s. Open Monday through Saturday from 9am to 5:30pm. Vaitape, behind Fashion Bora Bora. ℭ **67.69.29.**

7 WHERE TO STAY

Bora Bora has some of French Polynesia's finest and most expensive resorts, and yet another—the superluxe **Four Seasons Bora Bora** (www.fourseasons.com)—was scheduled to open in September 2008 on Motu Tehotu, on the eastern side of the lagoon.

A mainstay on the island since 1961, the luxurious **Hotel Bora Bora** (✆ **800/421-1490** or 60.44.11; www.amanresorts.com) was slated to close in October 2008 for a complete rebuilding. It is expected to reopen in time for its 50th anniversary in 2011.

EXPENSIVE

Bora Bora Lagoon Resort & Spa ★★

Speedboats shuttle 23 times a day from the Vaitape wharf to this posh resort on the northern end of Motu Toopua, a hilly island facing the rounded peak of Mount Pahia (not Mount Otemanu's tombstone). The main building, under three interlocking thatched roofs, holds a reception area, a bar, and a gourmet restaurant. To the rear, an expansive stone deck surrounds one of French Polynesia's largest swimming pools, where you'll find another bar and daytime restaurant. Long piers with hand-carved railings lead to the 44 overwater bungalows, while the rest of the units sit ashore in tropical gardens. One is a two-bedroom villa well suited to well-heeled families. Three beachside bungalows interconnect to form suites, while three "Motu Suites" have their own swimming pools. Although very good, the accommodations do not quite live up to the resort's exceptional amenities, including an unusual spa with treatment rooms high up in a banyan tree.

B.P. 175, 98730 Vaitape, Bora Bora (on Motu Toopua, 1km/¹/₂ mile off Vaitape). ✆ **800/860-4905** or 60.40.00. Fax 60.40.01. www.boraboralagoon.com. 77 units. 50,000CFP–130,000CFP (US$25–US$1,625/£316–£823) bungalow. AE, DC, MC, V. **Amenities:** 2 restaurants; 2 bars; large outdoor pool; 2 tennis courts; exercise room; spa; game room; watersports equipment rentals; concierge; activities desk; limited room service; laundry service. *In room:* A/C, TV, high-speed dataport, minibar, coffeemaker, safe.

Bora Bora Nui Resort & Spa ★★★

A member of Starwood Hotels' Luxury Collection, this sprawling resort occupies the southern end of hilly Motu Toopua, a 15-minute boat ride off Vaitape. It faces west toward the sea, thus depriving its public areas and all but a handful of its bungalows of the typical Bora Bora view. Only the full-service spa, perched atop the islet's central ridge, has an unimpeded view of Mount Otemanu. A beachside, two-level infinity swimming pool serves as the focal point of activities. It's backed by two public buildings, one with a large boutique and a casual, sand-floor restaurant serving reasonably priced lunches and dinners. The other houses a fine-dining outlet, an air-conditioned library, and a fascinating photo collection of U.S. marines building the airstrip on Motu Mute during World War II. Spread out over 6.4 hectares (16 acres) and nearly a kilometer (¹/₂ mile) of lagoon (you'll soon learn to call for a golf cart to take you to dinner), the 120 luxurious, suite-size units—84 of them overwater—are some of the largest in French Polynesia. The overwater bungalows have separate bedrooms, huge bathrooms with both tubs and walk-in showers, and big decks with privacy screens. Two three-bedroom overwater bungalows with swimming pools in their decks were being planned. Housed in a hillside hotel-style building, the "lagoon-view suites" are the least expensive units, and they interconnect to accommodate families. Top-of-the-line are the huge royal suites.

B.P. 502, 98730 Vaitape, Bora Bora (on Motu Toopua, 1.5km/1 mile off Vaitape). ✆ **800/782-9488** or 60.32.00. Fax 60.32.01. www.boraboranui.com. 120 units. 61,000CFP (US$763/£386) double; 82,000CFP–290,000CFP (US$1,025–US$3,625/£519–£1,835) bungalow; 62,000CFP–68,500CFP (US$775–US$856/£392–£434) suite. AE, DC, MC, V. **Amenities:** 3 restaurants; 2 bars; large outdoor pool; tennis courts; exercise room; spa; Jacuzzi; sauna; watersports equipment rentals; bike rentals; children's programs; game room; concierge; activities desk; 24-hr. room service; massage; babysitting; laundry service. *In room:* A/C, TV, high-speed dataport, minibar, coffeemaker, iron, safe.

Bora Bora Pearl Beach Resort ★★   The most traditionally Polynesian resort on
Bora Bora, the Pearl Beach resides on Motu Tevairoa, the largest of the flat islets dotting
the outer reef, and it has better views of Mount Otemanu across the lagoon than does
the Bora Bora Lagoon Resort to its south (see above). Covered by interconnected conical
thatched roofs, the open-air restaurant, main bar, and library stand on a raised earthen
platform, which enhances their views over a large swimming pool to the lagoon and
mountains. Guests can also enjoy splashing or snorkeling in the natural sand-bottom
lagoon. Gilles Pétré, one of French Polynesia's top dive operators, is in charge of the shop
here (and all other Pearl resorts). Long, curving piers extend out to 50 overwater bungalows, which ooze Polynesian charm. The 15 premium units are worth paying extra for,
because they are more private than the others and enjoy unimpeded views of Bora Bora.
If privacy is more important than the sound of water lapping under your bungalow,
consider one of the garden bungalows, which have private courtyards with sun decks and
splash pools. If you bring the kids, opt for a beachside bungalow with a separate bedroom. Although it lacks a sea view, the gorgeous spa is on an islet surrounded by lily
ponds (among other treatments, you can get a tattoo). An annoying drawback here is that
the resort's shuttle boats land at Chancelade on Bora Bora's northwestern corner, an
expensive taxi ride if you don't catch an infrequent shuttle bus to Vaitape.

B.P. 169, 98730 Vaitape, Bora Bora (on Motu Tevairoa, 1km/¹/₂ mile off Farepiti). ℂ **800/657-3275** or
60.52.00. Fax 60.52.22. www.pearlhotels.com. 80 units. 54,000CFP–86,000CFP (US$675–US$1,075/
£342–£544) bungalow. AE, DC, MC, V. **Amenities:** 3 restaurants; 2 bars; outdoor pool; tennis court; exercise room; spa; watersports equipment rentals; game room; concierge; activities desk; limited room service; massage; babysitting; laundry service. *In room:* A/C, TV, dataport, minibar, coffeemaker, iron, safe.

InterContinental Le Moana Resort Bora Bora ★★★   On the eastern side of the
Matira peninsula, this exclusive resort was until recently known as the InterContinental
Bora Bora Beachcomber Resort. It's one of the older resorts here, although much
improved over the years, especially after a recent renovation. Its bungalows, most of them
overwater, are some of the most charmingly designed here. They were the first in which
you could remove the tops of the glass coffee tables and actually feed the fish swimming
in the turquoise lagoon below. Ashore, 11 beachside bungalows are less enchanting, but
like the overwater units, they have Raiatea and Tahaa in their lagoon views. Two suites—
one overwater, one ashore—have kitchenettes, making them suitable for families. Also
beside the beach, a circular thatched-roof building houses the reception area, a lounge,
and the restaurant and bar, both with outdoor seating. The airy, beachside dining room
offers very fine French selections, with an emphasis on seafood.

B.P. 156, 98730 Vaitape, Bora Bora (east side of Matira Point). ℂ **800/327-0200** or 60.49.00. Fax 60.49.99.
www.interconti.com. 64 units. 83,000CFP–119,000CFP (US$1,038–US$1,488/£525–£753) bungalow;
115,000CFP–271,000CFP (US$1,438–US$3,388/£728–£1,715) suite. AE, DC, MC, V. **Amenities:** Restaurant;
bar; outdoor saltwater pool; spa; watersports equipment rentals; bike rentals; concierge; activities desk;
car-rental desk; 24-hr. room service; massage; babysitting; laundry service. *In room:* A/C, TV, dataport,
kitchens (suites only), minibar, coffeemaker, iron, safe.

> Ⓣⁱᵖˢ   **Be Prepared for Mosquitoes & No-Nos**
>
> Keep in mind that mosquitoes and *no-nos* (sand flies) love to feast on guests on
> Bora Bora's *motus,* so you'll want a good supply of insect repellent if you opt to
> stay at one of the offshore resorts.

InterContinental Resort and Thalasso Spa Bora Bora ★★★ This luxury resort shares the blazing white sands of Motu Piti Aau—an atoll-like island stretching 10km (6 miles) along the southeastern side of the outer reef—with Le Meridien Bora Bora (see below). It has won environmental awards as the world's first resort to be air-conditioned using seawater pumped from 2,500 feet down in the ocean. The 13°C (55°F) seawater also is used by the Thalasso Spa—officially the Deep Ocean Spa by Algotherm, the French company that uses seawater in its beauty products and treatments. The spa is the real star here, especially its three treatment rooms extending over the shallow, sand-bottom lagoon (yes, you can watch fish swimming below while getting a massage). You'll also feel like you're floating on air as you go down the glass-floor aisle of the overwater wedding chapel. All of the 80 suite-size guest bungalows also are built over the lagoon. Extending from two pincer-shaped piers, they are identical except for three two-bedroom, two-bathroom "villa suites" that have kitchens and are thus good choices for well-heeled families. In addition to king-size beds, the regular bungalows also have convertible sofas in their living rooms, so families can stay in them, too. The thatched-roof bungalows and central building are furnished in chic, Balinese tropical style, so the resort lacks Polynesian flair. The restaurants, bars, and infinity-edge swimming pool have fine views of Mount Otemanu, whose tombstone is seen from its narrow end out here. The same cannot be said of most bungalows, which face north-south along the lagoon. Guests here can use the facilities at the InterContinental Le Moana Resort (see above). The hotel's launch shuttles to Anau village.

B.P. 156, 98730 Vaitape, Bora Bora (on Motu Piti Aau, 1km/¹⁄₂ mile off Anau village). 📞 **800/327-0200** or 60.49.00. Fax 60.76.99. www.boraboraspa.intercontinental.com. 80 units. 89,000CFP–123,000CFP (US$1,112–US$1,538/£563–£778). AE, DC, MC, V. **Amenities:** 2 restaurants; 2 bars; outdoor pool; spa; massage; watersports equipment rentals; fitness center; concierge; activities desk; business center; 24-hr. room service; babysitting; laundry service. In room: A/C, TV, high-speed dataport, kitchens (villa suites only), minibar, coffeemaker, iron, safe.

Le Meridien Bora Bora ★★ Located on the northern tip of Motu Piti Aau, this is the best family resort in French Polynesia. Its Melanesian architecture is reminiscent of its sister property on Tahiti (see Le Meridien Tahiti, p. 128). The architects also created a seawater-fed, lakelike lagoon, in which you can swim with endangered sea turtles, bred there as part of the resort's award-winning preservation program. Children love it. Of the 100 identical guest units, 85 are built overwater. Only a few of these have views of Mount Otemanu's skinny side. Standing over waist-deep water, they are notable for their huge glass floors, which make it seem as if you're walking on air (maids cover the glass with carpets at evening turndown). All units here are smaller than those at Bora Bora's other resorts, however, and you could stumble over too much furniture for the space available. Ten otherwise identical "beach" bungalows actually sit beside the man-made lagoon, but most of them have fine views of Bora Bora. Since the shallow man-made lagoon is safe for swimming, they are excellent for families with small children. The broad, brilliantly white main beach here has its own bar. The hotel's launch shuttles to Anau village. Plans were in store to built a full-service spa on its one islet.

B.P. 190, 98730 Vaitape, Bora Bora (on Motu Pitiaau, 1km/¹⁄₂ mile off Anau village). 📞 **800/225-5843** or 60.51.51. Fax 60.51.10. www.lemeridien.com. 100 units. 60,000CFP–106,000CFP (US$750–US$1,325/£380–£671). AE, DC, MC, V. **Amenities:** 3 restaurants; 2 bars; outdoor pool; spa; watersports equipment rentals; children's playground; game room; concierge; activities desk; 24-hr. room service; babysitting; laundry service. In room: A/C, TV, dataport, minibar, coffeemaker, iron, safe.

St. Regis Resort Bora Bora ★★★   Nicole Kidman and Keith Urban were among
the first to honeymoon at this superluxurious resort that opened in 2007 on Motu Omee,
on the northeastern side of the lagoon. They took the 1,208-sq.-m (13,000-sq.-ft.) Royal
Estate, a walled-off compound with its own pool. Apparently the chef even came over
and prepared their meals, for no guest ever caught a glimpse of the celebrity duo. The
Royal Estate sits on land beside its own beach. If I were a quazillionaire, however, I would
have opted for one of the Royal Over Water Villas, which have their own swimming
pools with terrific views of Bora Bora. I am not pulling your leg: They have swimming
pools built into their overwater decks. That's really all I need to say about the St. Regis,
which is over-the-top in all respects, even its Hono Iti kids' club, where your little scions
can surf the Net at high speed. The guest quarters come in eight categories, from land-
based villas with pools to stripped-down overwater bungalows. Stripped down, that is, in
that they do not have pools or even Jacuzzis. Shame on you if you have to settle for one
of those luxurious hovels! Butlers are on call for all units. The overwater units extend
from man-made islets reaching far out into the lagoon, so be prepared for some serious
walking to reach the central complex. Or call for a golf cart.

B.P. 506, 98730 Vaitape, Bora Bora (on Motu Omee, 1km/¹/₂ mile off Anau village). ✆ **800/787-3447** or
60.78.88. Fax 60.78.56. www.stregis.com/borabora. 100 units. 98,000CFP–1,500,000CFP (US$1,225–US$18,750/
£620–£9,494). AE, DC, MC, V. **Amenities:** 3 restaurants; 3 bars; 2 outdoor pools; spa; massage; watersports
equipment rentals; fitness center; children's program; concierge; activities desk; business center; 24-hr.
room service; babysitting; laundry service. *In room:* A/C, TV, high-speed dataport, kitchens (villas only),
minibar, coffeemaker, iron, safe.

Sofitel Bora Bora Marara Resort   Italian movie producer Dino De Laurentis built
this resort, formerly known as the Sofitel Bora Bora Beach Resort, in 1977 to house star
Mia Farrow and the crew working on his box-office bomb *Hurricane.* It was closed for a
year in 2005–06 for an extensive rejuvenation, including the addition of a full-service spa
and 13 overwater bungalows. A beehive-shaped central building houses the restaurant
and bar, both of which open to a walk-in swimming pool sunken into a deck built out
over Matira Beach and the lagoon. The resort has the island's largest array of watersports
activities, which it shares with the Novotel Bora Bora Beach Resort, its Accor Hotels
sibling next-door (the toys are available to both guests and nonguests). The overwater
bungalows here have some of Bora Bora's largest decks, but be sure to ask for a unit away
from the nearby round-island road or you will wonder if you're sleeping over the lagoon.
Overwater units nos. 49, 50, 51, 62, and 64 are the most private and have the best views.
Facing a curving beach of white sand, the land-based bungalows have views of Raiatea
and Tahaa on the horizon. Guests here can dine at the Sofitel Bora Bora Motu Private
Island (see below), but not partake of the activities there.

B.P. 6, 98730 Vaitape, Bora Bora (northeast of Matira Point). ✆ **800/763-4835** or 41.04.04 in Papeete, or
60.55.00 on Bora Bora. Fax 41.05.05 or 67.74.03. www.accorhotels.pf. 64 units. 38,000CFP–85,000CFP
(US$475–US$1,063/£241–£538). AE, DC, MC, V. **Amenities:** 2 restaurants; bar; outdoor pool; tennis court;
watersports equipment rentals; bike rentals; concierge; activities desk; car-rental desk; limited room
service; babysitting; laundry service. *In room:* A/C, TV, dataport, minibar, coffeemaker, iron, safe.

Sofitel Bora Bora Motu Private Island ★★   More exclusive and private than its sister
property, this intimate, adult-oriented resort sits on a rocky, one-hill *motu* and is a 3-min-
ute shuttle-boat ride from the Sofitel Bora Bora Marara Resort. Unlike any other Bora
Bora resort, this one has a gorgeous, picture-postcard view of Mount Otemanu's tombstone face (most but not all overwater bungalows enjoy the view, so ask for unit no. 138,
129, or 130). Often-steep stone pathways lead up and downhill to the guest bungalows;

9

WHERE TO STAY

for this reason, I don't recommend the Motu to travelers with disabilities or anyone who has trouble walking. Most of the luxurious if not overly spacious units are overwater. Those that are ashore extend on stilts from the side of the hill, rendering great lagoon views. The most expensive unit here is a large villa. Several small beaches offer hammocks and easy chairs, and one has a shower mounted on a tree. Guests here can take the free on-demand shuttle boat and use all of the facilities over there. Sofitel Bora Bora Marara Resort guests, on the other hand, are allowed out here only for lunch and dinner. *Note:* The Sofitel Motu was slated for an overhaul in 2008–09, during which a spa and swimming pool were to be added.

B.P. 516, 98730 Vaitape, Bora Bora (on Piti Uuuta, .5km/¹/₄ mile off Matira Beach). © 800/763-4835 or 41.04.04 in Papeete, or 60.56.00 on Bora Bora. Fax 41.05.05 or 60.56.66. www.accorhotels.pf. 31 units. 47,000CFP–89,500CFP (US$588–US$1,119/£297–£566). AE, DC, MC, V. **Amenities:** Restaurant; bar; watersports equipment rentals; activities desk; limited room service; massage; laundry service. *In room:* A/C, TV, dataport, minibar, coffeemaker, iron, safe.

MODERATE

Club Med Bora Bora (Value)

Lush tropical gardens provide the setting for this Club Med beside a good beach in a little half-moon-shaped bay north of Matira Point. The focus of attention is a large thatched-roof beachside pavilion, which houses a reception area, bar, buffet-oriented dining room, and nightclub. Guests pay extra for scuba diving and excursions, but all meals (with wine) and a wide range of activities are included in the rates. Considering the prices elsewhere on Bora Bora, this makes Club Med a good value. The accommodations are in a mix of stand-alone and duplex bungalows and two-story, motel-style buildings. The beachfront bungalows are the preferred choice here, especially for honeymooners and others seeking privacy. The rooms are comfortably if not extravagantly furnished.

B.P. 34, 98730 Vaitape, Bora Bora (northeast of Matira Point). © 800/258-2633, 60.46.04, or 42.96.99 in Papeete. Fax 42.16.83. www.clubmed.com. 150 units. 16,000CFP–30,000CFP (US$200–US$375/£101–£190) per person. Rates include all meals with wine, drinks, and most activities. AE, DC, MC, V. **Amenities:** Restaurant; bar; tennis courts; bike rentals; activities desk; car-rental desk; salon; massage; coin-op washers and dryers. *In room:* A/C, TV, fridge, coffeemaker, safe.

Hotel Maitai Polynesia (Value)

Like the nearby Novotel, this resort has hotel rooms, but here they climb a hill, giving upper floor units spectacular lagoon views. Unlike the Novotel, it also has beachside and overwater bungalows, which are among the more reasonably priced in French Polynesia. The bungalows are smaller than those at the more expensive resorts, but they are packed with Polynesian decor, and those over water have glass floor panels for fish-viewing. The round-island road runs through the property, separating the beach and bungalows from the thatched-roof main building and hotel rooms. Of its two restaurants, one sits beachside.

B.P. 505, 98730 Vaitape, Bora Bora (northeast of Matira Point). © 60.30.00. Fax 67.66.03. www.hotelmaitai. com. 74 units. 24,200CFP–35,500CFP (US$303–US$444/£152–£225) double; 39,000CFP–53,300CFP (US$488–US$666/£247–£337) bungalow. AE, DC, MC, V. **Amenities:** 2 restaurants; 2 bars; watersports equipment rentals; bike rentals; activities desk; car-rental desk; babysitting; laundry service. *In room:* A/C (hotel rooms only), TV, dataport, minibar, coffeemaker, safe.

Hotel Matira

This is not so much a hotel as a collection of bungalows on and near the beach at the northern end of the Matira peninsula. Imported from Indonesia, the teak units have thatched roofs, porches on one corner, shower-only bathrooms, and pairs of double beds. You'll get a ceiling fan, fridge, and coffeemaker, but forget amenities like

TVs, phones, and hair dryers. What you get here is an essentially unscreened cottage, so keep your insect repellent handy. The choicest and most expensive models rest beside Matira Beach, while the others are back in the garden. Ask for a discount if you book directly.

B.P. 31, 98730 Vaitape, Bora Bora (on Matira Beach, south of Hotel Bora Bora). ℂ **67.70.51.** Fax 67.77.02. www.hotel-matira.com. 14 units. 21,000CFP–35,500CFP (US$263–US$444/£133–£225). MC, V. **Amenities:** Bike rentals. *In room:* Fridge, coffeemaker, no phone.

Mai Moana Island   More private retreat than hotel, Mai Moana occupies a tiny flat islet on the northwestern side of the reef. It's the home of Stan Wisnieswski, a Polish-born, Paris-based documentary and advertising filmmaker, poet, journalist, sailor, and avid ham-radio operator who speaks Polish, French, and English. Stan and wife Malgorzata have three thatched-roof bungalows near their white-sand beach. Each has a TV, phone, minibar, double bed, ceiling fan, bathroom with solar-heated shower, and porch with lagoon view. They permit only six guests here at any one time, and none of them can be under 12 years old.

B.P. 164, 98730 Vaitape, Bora Bora (on Motu Mute Iti). ℂ/fax **67.62.45.** www.mai-moana-island.com. 3 units. 24,000CFP (US$300/£152) double; 55,800CFP (US$698/£353) entire island. MC, V. Children 11 and under not accepted. **Amenities:** Restaurant; bar; outdoor pool; boat rental; free use of kayaks; laundry service. *In room:* TV, minibar.

Novotel Bora Bora Beach Resort ⓥⓐⓛⓤⓔ   This modest but attractive property is one of the better values on the island. It sports a U-shaped, tropical-style public building and an infinity swimming pool beside a palm-draped section of Matira Beach, where the Novotel shares a wide array of watersports with the Sofitel Bora Bora Marara Resort next-door. On the other side of the round-island road, the motel-style accommodations occupy two-story buildings dressed up in Tahitian thatch and bamboo, which surround a lush courtyard with a lily pond. The medium-size rooms are nicely trimmed with native woods and are comfortably furnished with a queen-size bed, a built-in settee that can double as a single bed, a desk, shower-only bathroom, and sliding doors opening to a patio or balcony. You can dine at the Sofitel Motu but cannot use the other facilities out there.

B.P. 943, 98730 Vaitape, Bora Bora (heart of Matira hotel district). ℂ **800/221-4542** or 60.59.50. Fax 60.59.51. www.accorhotels.pf. 80 units. 16,200CFP–21,600CFP (US$203–US$270/£103–£137) double. AE, MC, V. **Amenities:** Restaurant; bar; outdoor pool; watersports equipment rentals; activities desk; car-rental desk; massage; laundry service. *In room:* A/C, TV, dataport, fridge, coffeemaker, safe.

INEXPENSIVE

Chez Nono   Sitting on the western side of the Point Matira peninsula, this pension is the domain of Noël (Nono) Levard—of *the* Bora Bora Levards, who operate lagoon excursions, safari expeditions, and the Farm black-pearl operation. Since guests here can step from their accommodations right out onto the powdery sands of Matira Beach, this is the most popular beachside pension with French residents of Tahiti (book early). The least expensive units are six simple bedrooms in Nono's house; these all share toilets, hot-water showers, and a kitchen. Two beachside bungalows can accommodate two persons each, while two family-size bungalows are notable for their thatched roofs. All four bungalows have their own bathrooms with hot-water showers, and every unit has an electric fan (much appreciated in the sometimes stuffy house rooms).

B.P. 282, 93730 Vaitape, Bora Bora (Matira Point). ☎ **67.71.38.** Fax 67.74.27. nono.levard@mail.pf. 10 units (6 with shared bathroom). 6,500CFP (US$81/£41) double; 15,000CFP (US$188/£95) bungalow. MC, V. **Amenities:** Communal kitchen; laundry service. *In room:* No phone.

Pension Robert et Tina   This family-run pension consists of three two-story houses right on the southern extremity of Matira Point. One house has six rooms, while the others have three each. You'll share each house's kitchen, toilets, and cold-water showers. If you have a family or group, and don't mind shivering in the shower, Robert and Tina will reduce the rates if you rent an entire house for a week or more. The beach is minimal here, but you can walk across the shallow lagoon to excellent snorkeling near the outer reef. The trade winds can make the point quite breezy and cool during the winter months from June through August.

93730 Vaitape, Bora Bora (Matira Point). ☎ **67.63.55** or 79.22.73. Fax 67.72.92. 15 units (shared bathrooms). 7,700CFP–9,000CFP (US$96–US$113/£49–£57) double. MC, V. **Amenities:** Communal kitchen; laundry service. *In room:* No phone.

Rohutu Fare Lodge ★ Finds   Virtually hidden by botanical gardens on the mountainside overlooking Povai Bay, this little lodge is the creation of Nir Shalev, an Israeli expatriate whom I met shortly after he first arrived on Bora Bora wearing a backpack in 1989. With teak floors and natural thatched roofs, his cleverly designed bungalows are for lovers, definitely not puritans. In addition to suggestive paintings, statues, and other paraphernalia in the sleeping quarters, faucets in the outdoor bathrooms pour water from certain unmentionable parts of nude statues. (After a night here, you may not be up to the 15-min. bike ride to Matira Beach!) Nir's two lagoon-view bungalows are more charming and have better vistas than his mountain-view unit. They all have ceiling fans, kitchens, decks with lounge furniture, and four-poster beds with mosquito nets. You will not have to leave here to enjoy a view of Mount Otemanu's tombstone face.

B.P. 400, 98730 Vaitape, Bora Bora (hillside in Povai Bay). ☎ **70.77.99.** www.boraboralodge.com. 3 units. 14,900CFP (US$186/£94) bungalow. MC, V. **Amenities:** Kayak rentals; free use of bicycles. *In room:* Kitchen, coffeemaker, safe.

Village Temanuata   On a small part of Matira Beach in the hotel district, this few-frills establishment has 11 thatched-roof bungalows ranging from one-room to family-size units with kitchens and sleeping lofts (over their front porches). All have ceiling fans and private bathrooms with hot water but few other amenities. Choice are the two units directly facing the beach. Four better-equipped models (with TVs and complimentary use of bicycles) are on the other side of the point, between the Hotel Maria and Hotel Bora Bora. Matira's restaurants and shops are an easy walk away.

B.P. 544, 98730 Vaitape, Bora Bora (heart of Matira hotel district). ☎ **67.75.61.** Fax 67.78.17. www. temanuata.com. 16 units. 15,000CFP–17,000CFP (US$188–US$213/£95–£108) bungalow. MC, V. **Amenities:** Bike rentals. *In room:* TV (4 units), kitchen (6 units), no phone.

---

8 WHERE TO DINE

Restaurants here primarily are in Matira, on the island's southern end; Povai Bay, on the southwest coast; and in Vaitape village. That's how I have organized them below.

MATIRA

Chez Ben's SNACK BAR/PIZZA   Honeymooners from the nearby Hotel Bora Bora frequently wander to this lean-to across the road from a shady portion of Matira Beach,

Tips **Call for a Ride**

The top restaurants provide free transportation for their dinner guests; always ask when making your reservations.

where Bora Bora–born Ben Teraitepo and his Oklahoma-born wife, Robin, have been serving American-style cooked breakfasts, lunches, and afternoon pick-me-ups since 1988. Ben's fresh tuna-salad sandwiches, pizzas and pastas, unusually spicy *poisson cru,* tacos, and fajitas are homemade and substantial, although Ben's and Robin's company is the main reason to hang out here. They will shoo the dogs and cats away if they bother you.

Matira, between Hotel Bora Bora and Matira Point. ℂ **67.74.54.** Most items 700CFP–1,600CFP (US$8.75–US$20/£4.45–£10). No credit cards. Daily 8am–5pm.

La Bounty ★ Value FRENCH/ITALIAN   This casual restaurant under a thatched roof provides some of the island's best pizza and other reasonably priced Italian (and French) fare. A pie makes an ample meal for one person or can be shared as an appetizer. The spaghetti and tagliatelle are tasty, too, with either smoked salmon, carbonara, Alfredo, Neapolitan, blue cheese, or seafood sauce. Steaks and fish are served under French sauces such as mustard or creamy vanilla. Pizzas are dished up quickly here, but everything else is prepared to order and takes longer. Whatever you choose, it will be excellent quality for the price.

Matira, between Hotel Maitai Polynesia and Bora Bora Beach Resort. ℂ **67.70.43.** Reservations recommended. Pizza and pasta 1,500CFP–1,650CFP (US$19–US$21/£9.50–£10); main courses 1,500CFP–2,800CFP (US$19–US$35/£9.50–£18). MC, V. Tues–Sun 11:30am–2pm and 6:30–9pm.

La Matira Beach Restaurant FRENCH   Literally hanging over the beach, this casual, bistro-style restaurant is an excellent place to have a lagoonside lunch, perhaps a salad under a slice of grilled tuna. Burgers, grilled fish, and pastas also appear at midday. Dinner switches to a somewhat overpriced French menu with local twists, such as roast pork with bananas. It's a beautiful spot on a moonlit night; otherwise, I do lunch here.

Matira, between Hotel Bora Bora and Hotel Matira. ℂ **67.53.79.** Reservations recommended at dinner. Lunch 1,300CFP–1,800CFP (US$16–US$23/£8.20–£11); main courses 3,000CFP–5,100CFP (US$38–US$64/£19–£32). MC, V. Daily 7–10am, 11am–2pm, and 6–9pm.

Restaurant Fare Manuia ★ FRENCH   A thatched roof lends charm to this French restaurant known for large servings, such as huge slabs of prime rib served plain or with a choice of French sauces. The tender beef comes from New Zealand, as do the freshly ground hamburgers served at lunch. Other dinner main courses include mahimahi served on a wood plank with vanilla sauce, rare tuna with wasabi, and a hearty soup with mussels, shrimp, scallops, and fish. In addition to the American-style hamburgers, lunches include fish burgers, salads, pastas, and grilled fish. Breakfast here is strictly continental.

Matira, between InterContinental le Moana Resort and Hotel Maitai Polynesia. ℂ **67.68.08.** Reservations recommended. Breakfast 500CFP–1,600CFP (US$6.25–US$20/£3.15–£10); burgers 1,400CFP–1,900CFP (US$18–US$24/£8.85–£12); main courses 1,900CFP–3,900CFP (US$24–US$49/£12–£25). MC, V. Daily 7–10am, 11:30am–2pm, and 7–10pm.

BORA BORA

9

WHERE TO DINE

Restaurant-Snack Moi Here REGIONAL   Tree limbs hold up the thatched roof covering this little Tahitian restaurant, which almost hangs over Matira Beach. It's less restaurant than permanent *roulotte* (food wagon) with a view. The menu offers local fare such as steaks and fish served with french fries, hamburgers, sashimi, chow mein, and *poisson cru*. My steak was tough, so I always order fish here. Breakfast is continental, while lunch turns to burgers, sandwiches, and omelets. The view is worth more than the price of a meal here.

Matira, between Hotel Bora Bora and Matira Point. ☎ **67.56.46.** Reservations accepted. Most items 500CFP–2,000CFP (US$6.25–US$25/£3.15–£13). MC, V (minimum 2,000CFP). Daily 6am–9pm.

Roulotte Matira (Chez Sam) ★ (**Value**) SNACK BAR   This is one of the best *roulottes* in French Polynesia, especially when owner Samuel Ruver cooks tandoori chicken and curries from recipes handed down by his East Indian father. Otherwise, he works at the gas grill to produce steaks and fish, both served with french fries. Anything with legumes will be a so-so Chinese-style stir-fry. You can get a continental breakfast here. Grab a white plastic table; there's waiter service.

Matira, at the curve. No phone. Main courses 1,500CFP–1,900CFP (US$19–US$24/£9.50–£12). No credit cards. Daily 6am–2pm and 6–10pm.

Snack Matira SNACK BAR   Right on Matira Beach and within hailing distance of Chez Ben's, this open-air snack bar is a favorite lunch and afternoon retreat of Bora Bora's French-speaking expatriates. It offers a *roulotte*-style menu of pizzas, salads, omelets, grilled steaks and fish, juicy burgers, and *casse-croûte* sandwiches, plus ice cream and milkshakes. The company is better at Chez Ben's, but not the lagoon view.

Matira, between Hotel Bora Bora and Matira Point. ☎ **67.77.32.** Reservations not accepted. Most items 300CFP–1,700CFP (US$3.75–US$21/£1.90–£11). No credit cards. Tues–Sun 10am–4pm.

POVAI BAY

Bloody Mary's Restaurant & Bar ★★★ SEAFOOD/STEAKS   Having a few drinks and a slab of barbecued fish at this charming structure is as much a part of the Bora Bora experience as is taking a lagoon excursion. Ceiling fans, colored spotlights, and stalks of dried bamboo dangle from a large thatched roof over a floor of fine white sand (stash your sandals in a foot locker and dine in your bare feet). The butcher-block tables are made of coconut-palm lumber, and the seats are sections of palm trunks cut into stools. Bloody Mary's is essentially an American-style barbecued fish and steak joint—a welcome relief after a diet of lard-laden French sauces. You'll be shown the seafood and beef laid out on a bed of ice. (If it's offered, choose the mouthwatering teriyaki-style wahoo.) The chef will charbroil your selection to order and serve it with a salad, vegetables, and your choice of sauce on the side. Open all day, the cozy bar is cut from a beautifully polished litchi tree and is one of my favorite watering holes. The lunch menu consists of burgers, fish and chips, and salads, which are not served at dinner. Bloody Mary's American owner, Dexter Hewitt, shares the profits with the staff; consequently, the service here is some of the best in French Polynesia. You will have an evening of fun, as have the many famous faces posted on a board out by the road.

Povai Bay, 1km (½ mile) north of Hotel Bora Bora. ☎ **67.72.86.** Reservations strongly recommended. Lunch 950CFP–1,500CFP (US$12–US$19/£6–£9.50); dinner main courses 2,700CFP–3,200CFP (US$34–US$40/£17–£20). AE, MC, V. Restaurant Mon–Wed and cruise-ship days 11am–3pm; Mon–Sat 6–9pm. Bar Mon–Sat 9:30am–11pm. Closed Dec.

> **Fun Facts** **It's a Dog's Life**
>
> Despite several neutering campaigns, dogs seem to be everywhere on Bora Bora. You see them all along the roads and even wandering in and out of some restaurants. Their ancestors arrived in the islands with the first Polynesian settlers more than a millennium ago. Along with pigs and fish, they were a prime source of Polynesian protein back then. No longer on anyone's menu, they roam as they see fit.

La Villa Mahana ★★★ INTERNATIONAL   You will need one night for fun at Bloody Mary's, another for a romantic dinner at this extraordinarily fine little restaurant, the best in all of French Polynesia. Owner Damien Rinaldi Dovio, an accomplished young Corsican-born chef, started my friends and me with tuna *tartare exotique,* a luscious version of *poisson cru* with a sharp wasabi-accented sauce. My friends went on to mahimahi perfectly cooked with a subtle version of coconut curry sauce, while I opted for filet mignon with vanilla cream gnocchi. Both were outstanding. The fixed-price menus for four or five courses will save money. The walls of this Mediterranean-style villa are adorned with the works of noted French Polynesian artist Garrick Yrondi, but Damien has only six tables, so consider calling or e-mailing for a reservation well before you get here.

Povai Bay, behind Boutique Gauguin, 1.5km (1 mile) north of Hotel Bora Bora. ✆ **67.50.63.** damien@villamahana.com. Reservations required. Main courses 5,000CFP–11,000CFP (US$63–US$138/£32–£70); fixed-price dinners 10,500CFP–15,000CFP (US$131–US$188/£66–£95). AE, MC, V. Wed–Thurs 6–8pm.

VAITAPE

Inexpensive *roulottes* roll out near the Vaitape small-boat harbor, some during the day when cruise ships are in port. See "Don't Miss *Les Roulottes*" (p. 140) for details on these inexpensive food wagons. Also in Vaitape, two reasonably priced Chinese restaurants— **Le Panda d'Or** (✆ **67.72.70**) and **Le Cocotier** (✆ **67.74.18**)—can be found north of the small boat harbor.

Aloe Cafe ★ **Value** FRENCH/PASTRIES   I often have breakfast here, for this patisserie bakes very good croissants, tarts, and quiches to go with the strong French coffee. Also on the menu: sandwiches, pizzas by the slice, and a *plat du jour* at lunch. Order at the counter, at a table inside, or on the shopping-center sidewalk. You can use the computer terminal here to check your e-mail (see "Fast Facts: Bora Bora," earlier in this chapter).

North of the Vaitape wharf, in Centre Commercial le Pahia. ✆ **67.78.88.** Most items 500CFP–1,950CFP (US$6.25–US$24/£3.15–£12). No credit cards. Mon–Sat 6am–6pm.

Bora Bora Burger SNACK BAR   You can get salads, *casse-croûte* sandwiches, hot dogs, burgers, and other daytime snacks at this open-air, order-at-the-counter joint next to the post office in Vaitape. The picnic tables and chairs on the veranda make a good place for refreshment while watching the cruise-ship passengers explore the town.

Vaitape, next to post office. No phone. Reservations not accepted. Most items 250CFP–1,300CFP (US$3.15–US$16/£1.60–£8.20). No credit cards. Mon–Sat 8am–5:30pm.

BORA BORA

9

WHERE TO DINE

Restaurant St. James FRENCH Overlooking the lagoon from the Helen's Bay shopping center, north of the small boat harbor, this restaurant provides a picturesque setting for seafood cooked in the French fashion. Tops are parrotfish stuffed with crab under cream sauce, a fricassee of scallops and shrimps in coconut curry sauce, and duck with a blueberry sauce. Have a pre-dinner drink at the thatch-covered bar down by the lagoon. Manta rays expecting a handout often show up here around 7:30pm.

Vaitape, north of small boat harbor, in Centre Helen's Bay. (*C* **67.64.62.** Reservations recommended at dinner. Main courses 2,500CFP–3,200CFP (US$31–US$40/£16–£20). No credit cards. Tues–Sat noon–3pm and 6:30–9:30pm.

9 ISLAND NIGHTS ON BORA BORA

As on all the outer islands, things are really quiet on Bora Bora after dark (this is, after all, one of the world's most romantic honeymoon hideaways, not a place to practice your dance steps). You might want to listen to a Tahitian band playing at sunset or watch the furious hips in a Tahitian dance show, which all the resorts have at least 1 night a week. The schedules change, so call ahead.

You don't have to stay at **Club Med Bora Bora** (*C* **60.46.04**) to dine there and watch the nightclub show staged by its staff. The full meal, wine, and show together cost about 6,500CFP (US$81/£41). Call for reservations.

I found the food to be overpriced at **Monta Restaurant & Lounge Bar,** on the site of the Bora Bora Yacht Club north of Vaitape (*C* **67.68.68**), but on Saturday night the bar was serving finger food to accompany dancing on its sand floor.

The island's sole nightclub is **Le Récife Discothèque,** about 1km (½ mile) north of Vaitape (*C* **67.73.87**), which opens only on Fridays and Saturdays at 11pm (that's right, 11pm) and closes at 3am (or later) the following morning. The young local patrons have been known to throw a few fists at that late hour.

Maupiti

A favorite pastime throughout the Pacific islands is comparing one place to how another place used to be. Locals like to say that Tahiti is like Hawaii used to be, for example, and that Huahine is like Moorea used to be. In the case of French Polynesia's last westward outpost, Maupiti is like Bora Bora used to be.

Just 40km (25 miles) west of Bora Bora, this little jewel even resembles its larger neighbor, in that it consists of an outer barrier reef topped by a horseshoe of sand-edged *motus* enclosing a clear lagoon around a high central island. Here, there is more dry land out on the fringing *motus* than on the main island, which has an area of just 14 sq. km (5¼ sq. miles). The road around the main island is just 9.6km (5¾ miles) long.

Unlike Bora Bora, Maupiti has not a hint of modern tourism. Few visitors come here, and many who do are French residents of Tahiti, who like to spend their weekends relaxing at one of several small pensions, Maupiti's only choice of accommodations. Indeed, Maupiti is definitely a throwback to old Polynesia, when, among other things, very few locals spoke English.

Maupiti reminds me of the Bora Bora of more than 30 years ago, when I camped on a nearly deserted Pointe Matira, now a key part of Bora Bora's booming tourism infrastructure. **Plage Tereia (Tereia Beach),** a gorgeous strip of white-and-pink sand wrapping around a peninsula on the western side of Maupiti's central island, especially reminds me of those bygone days. Fortunately for the preservationists among us, local residents flatly rejected a proposed resort at this lovely location.

Just as Mount Otemanu's tombstone face is Bora Bora's trademark, Maupiti's distinguishing landmark is **Mount Hotu Parata,** a black-basaltic cliff dramatically rising 165m (540 ft.) above **Vaiea,** the island's main village. The cliff is pockmarked with caves that attract throngs of nesting seabirds.

Despite its small size, Maupiti was an important island in pre-European days. Archaeologists have uncovered both *maraes* and petroglyphs on the main island. They have also discovered human remains and other items out on **Motu Paeao,** a small islet separating two shallow passes on Maupiti's north side. Stone axes, whale teeth, and fishhooks have been dated to about A.D. 850, making it one of the oldest settlements in the Society Islands.

Whether you stay on Maupiti or see it as a day trip from Bora Bora, you are in for an authentic old Polynesian treat.

1 GETTING AROUND MAUPITI

Air Tahiti flies to Maupiti from Raiatea about three times a week. Its flights are geared toward Friday-to-Sunday weekend travelers.

The airstrip is on **Motu Tuanai,** the long islet off the northeastern side of the central island. The pensions send boats to pick up guests who have reservations (they usually do not meet the planes in search of travelers without advance bookings), or you can take the Air Tahiti launch to Vaiea.

SOUTH PACIFIC
OCEAN

Motu
Paeao

False Pass

Tearea Pass

Motu Tuanai

Aérodrome
de Maupiti

Pohiva
Point

Farauru

Motu
Auira

Tereia
Point

Mt. Teurafaatiu

Mt. Hotu Parata

Puoro'o
Point

Atipiti
Bay

Vai'ea

Maupiti

SOCIETY ISLANDS

Bora
Bora

Tahaa

Huahine

Raiatea

Moorea

Tahiti

Motu
Tiapaa

Motu
Pitiahe

Passe Onoiau

0   100 mi
0   100 km

Airport

Beach

Reef

0   1 mi
0   1 km

N

ACCOMMODATIONS ■	ATTRACTIONS ●
Fare Pa'eao **1**	Marae Vaiahu **8**
Le Kuriri **14**	Marae Vaiorie **3**
Maupiti Loisirs **4**	Mount Hotu Parata **9**
Pension Maupiti Village **13**	Mount Teurafaatiu **6**
Pension Papahani **12**	Haranaie Petroglyphs **2**
Pension Poe Iti **10**	Plage Tereia **5**
Pension Rose des Isles **11**	
Pension Tautiare Village **7**	

MAUPITI

GETTING AROUND MAUPITI

10

   The fast *Maupiti Express* ferry arrives from Bora Bora three times a week (see "Maupiti as a Day Trip from Bora Bora," below) It docks at the island's only wharf, in Vaiea on the southeastern point of the main island. It and all other vessels must negotiate Onoiau Pass, the only navigable entry into the lagoon. Subject to strong currents and breaking surf, the narrow pass can be treacherous in rough weather, during which the *Maupiti Express* and other boats cannot get into or out of the lagoon. Keep this in mind when making your plans.

   There is no local transportation system on Maupiti. Since the island is so small, most visitors rent bicycles. Mostly crushed coral, the round-island road is flat and follows the coastline except when it climbs over a steep ridge between Plage Tereia and the south coast. When the *Maupiti Express* docks, local residents will be waiting at the wharf to rent bikes for 1,000CFP (US$13/£6.30) a day. At other times, you can contact the **Total** service station at the wharf (© **67.83.46**), **Puanere Locations** (© **67.81.68;** fax 67.80.85), or **Maupiti Loisirs** (© **67.80.95**). The latter is operated by Ui Terihaunui and Simone Chan of the Maupiti Loisirs pension (p. 223).

(*Fast Facts*   **Maupiti**

The following facts apply specifically to Maupiti. For more information, see "Fast Facts: Tahiti & French Polynesia," in appendix A.

Currency Exchange Maupiti does not have a bank, which explains why most pensions here do not accept credit cards. Bring enough cash or traveler's checks to cover your anticipated expenses.

Emergencies & Police The **emergency police** telephone number is © **17.** Maupiti does not have its own gendarmerie (the nearest is on Bora Bora), so ask your pension staff for assistance in case of emergency.

Healthcare The **government infirmary** (© **67.80.18**) is in the *mairie* (town hall) complex in Vaiea village.

Internet Access The Internet is minimally present on Maupiti. There is no cyber-cafe on the island, so ask if your pension has, or can arrange, access if you can't live without e-mail or surfing the Web while here.

Post Office The post office is in the *mairie* (town hall) complex in Vaiea village. Hours are Monday through Thursday from 7:30am to 3pm, Friday from 7am to 2pm.

Visitor Information There is no visitor information office on Maupiti, so be sure to pick up an island map before you get here.

Water Don't drink the tap water on Maupiti. Bottled water is available at the grocery stores.

---

2 EXPLORING MAUPITI

TOURING THE ISLAND

The narrow coastal plain on the east coast is occupied by **Vaiea, Petei,** and **Farauru,** three villages resting at the base of the Mount Hotu Parata cliff. The great majority of Maupiti's 1,200 or so inhabitants live in these villages, which have its only grocery stores and other facilities. They run together, so you won't know when you've left one and entered another, especially when strolling along the picturesque **lagoonside promenade** from the wharf to the island's school. You will see very few older homes here, since a devastating 1997 hurricane destroyed most of Maupiti's houses.

The north coast is notable for the **Haranaie Valley,** site of several **petroglyphs,** including one of a turtle. The petroglyphs are not easy to find, so I recommend a guided tour

(Tips) **Maupiti as a Day Trip from Bora Bora**

You can make a day trip to Maupiti from Bora Bora on the fast ferry *Maupiti Express* ((C) **67.66.69,** 78.27.22, or 72.30.48; www.maupitiexpress.com), which departs Bora Bora Tuesday, Thursday, and Saturday at 8:30am, arriving at Maupiti about 10:15am. It leaves Maupiti at 4pm and returns to Bora Bora about 5:30pm. Fares are 3,000CFP (US$38/£19) one-way, 4,000CFP (US$50/£25) round-trip. *One caveat:* If high waves come up, the *Maupiti Express* may be unable to get out of Maupiti's one pass to return to Bora Bora. In that case, you could be stuck on Maupiti until the sea calms, or until the next Air Tahiti flight with an available seat departs.

(see below). From the road, you'll have fine views of the three *motus* enclosing the north side of the lagoon. The road rounds the base of Mount Hotu, at the northwestern corner, and then follows the west coast, where you'll pass several ancient *maraes,* including **Marae Vaiorie.** This ancient stone structure was built in two parts with a freshwater stream in between.

Go straight when you come to the road junction and follow the sign to the magnificent white-and-pink sands of **Plage Tereia ★★★**. Situated in a coconut grove and facing a shallow lagoon, this is one of French Polynesia's best beaches. There are no changing rooms, water fountains, or other facilities to interrupt its pristine character. Only a few trash cans and the occasional drink can remind you that people even come here. At low tide, you can wade across the waist-deep "Baby Sharks Crossing" to **Motu Auira.** (Yes, you may see small sharks in the shallow lagoon.) Motu Auira, the largest of Maupiti's islets, has melon plantations and a wind-generating facility.

From the beach, you will have to backtrack to the road junction, where the *traversière* (cross-island road) heads up the ridge between the west and south coasts. Push your bike up the hill for a fine view of the west coast and the lagoon from the top.

The descent will take you down to the populated south coast. On the shore about two-thirds of the way back to Vaiea, you'll come to **Marae Vaiahu,** the most important temple on the island. Maupiti's royalty lived in this area during the olden days, and chiefs from Bora Bora and the other islands often joined them at gatherings at Marae Vaiahu. It's notable for its stone fish box, apparently used in ceremonies to bless the fishing fleet.

ORGANIZED TOURS

In addition to the petroglyphs, some other attractions are not easy to find on your own, so I highly recommend taking a half-day guided tour of the island. Every pension can arrange a tour, or you can do it in advance through **Maupiti Loisirs** ((C) **67.80.95**), run by Ui Terihaunui and the English-speaking Simone Chan, who also own Maupiti Loisirs pension (p. 223). Ui and Simone offer two half-day tours. Their regular island tour includes a drive around the central island and a stop for a swim at Plage Tereia (and a wade across to Motu Auira). Their archaeological tour includes stops at the *marae* and a walk to the petroglyphs. The tours cost 2,000CFP (US$25/£13) per person.

3 HIKING, LAGOON EXCURSIONS & SNORKELING

HIKING

Maupiti has two mountain trails that will test your endurance, but reward you with fantastic views. One track begins opposite Snack Tarona (p. 228) and goes to the top of **Mount Teurafaatiu** (also known as Mount Nuupure), Maupiti's tallest peak at 380m (1,247 ft.). It's a hike of about 1¹/₂ hours to the top. The trail is easy to follow going up, but be very careful on the way back down or you can easily lose your way.

Another very steep climb ascends **Mount Hotu Parata,** the cliff looming above Vaiea village. This track is very steep in places, and since the volcanic rock at the top is unstable, you cannot go to the cliff's edge. In places, this trail is more like mountain climbing than hiking. Ask your pension to arrange a guide for the Mount Hotu Parata trail.

LAGOON EXCURSIONS

Although Maupiti's lagoon is not as large or deep as Bora Bora's, getting out on it is an essential ingredient of a visit here. (Getting under it is another matter, since no scuba-diving operator has set up shop on Maupiti.) The excursions pretty much follow the usual script: a boat ride, snorkeling and swimming off a white sand beach, a stop to see the ancient ruins on Motu Paeao, and a picnic on a *motu.* Every pension will arrange an all-day lagoon excursion. Or you can contact **Maupiti Loisirs** (© **67.80.95**), based at Maupiti Loisirs pension on the central island (p. 223), which charges about 3,000CFP (US$38/£19) per person without lunch, 4,000CFP (US$50/£25) if a picnic is included.

SNORKELING

There is very good snorkeling in the lagoon around Motu Paeao, between the two shallow entries into the lagoon: **Tearea (Hiro's) Pass** and **False Pass.** The latter is called False Pass because from the sea, it looks likes a navigable pass, while in reality it is only a few feet deep. You'll find more good snorkeling in the south on the lagoonside Motu Tipaa, but be careful of the strong currents into and out of nearby Onoiau Pass.

---

4 WHERE TO STAY

As mentioned in the introduction to this chapter, Maupiti's residents have rejected proposals to build luxury resorts here. The result: Your choice will be one of the island's

---

> **Fun Facts   A Whaler's Tale**
>
> In 1842, a new American whaling ship named the *Charles W. Morgan* put into Maupiti to refresh its crew. One of them was so refreshed by the daughter of a local chief that he stayed behind and founded a large family. The *Charles W. Morgan* kept on working until 1921. The last 19th-century whaling ship still afloat, it's now berthed at Mystic Seaport in Mystic, Connecticut (www.mysticseaport.org).

MAUPITI

10

WHERE TO STAY

small, family-run establishments. A few are on the main island, but the most appealing are out on the skinny islets surrounding the lagoon.

ON MOTU PAEAO

Fare Pa'eao   Emile and Jeanine Tavaerii's pension sits by itself on Motu Paeao, the flat islet between the two shallow passes at the northern end of the lagoon. They have six of the one-room, government-backed bungalows seen so often in French Polynesia; each has a front porch, a ceiling fan, and a bathroom with cold-water shower. There is very good snorkeling in this part of the lagoon, and Emile and Jeanine provide free kayaks with which to explore (be careful of the currents in and out of the passes through the reef). Rates here include breakfast and dinner; Jeanine will also provide lunch at extra cost.

B.P. 33, 98732 Vaiea, Maupiti (on Motu Paeao). © **67.81.01** or 67.81.92. fare.pae.ao@mail.pf. 6 units. 14,500CFP (US$181/£92) double. Rates include breakfast and dinner. MC, V. **Amenities:** Restaurant; bar; free use of kayaks. In room: No phone.

ON MOTU TIAPAA

Le Kuriri ★★   Beside a white-sand beach on the ocean side of Motu Tiapaa, Le Kuriri is both the most sophisticated and most charming pension here. Kindred spirits of mine, partners Anne-Marie Badolle and Camille Marjorel deserted the corporate life in France to sail around the world, after which they settled on Maupiti and took over this pension. They have added some very nice touches, such as a huge daybed under a thatched roof beside the beach, and an open-air dining room/guest lounge with a crushed-coral floor and library shelves stocked with books left by guests who came here from many countries spanning the globe. Usually featuring fresh seafood, excellent dinners are served family-style in this comfortable setting. Breakfast is taken under its own beachside pavilion. The spacious bungalows have lots of Polynesian accents, including thatched roofs and split-bamboo matting on the walls. They all have ceiling fans, furnished porches, and bathrooms with cold-water showers. Their push-out windows are not screened, but mosquito nets hang over the beds. Anne-Marie and Camille speak English as well as French.

B.P. 23, 98732 Maupiti (on Motu Tiapaa). © **74.54.54.** Fax 67.82.23. www.maupiti-kuriri.com. 4 units (all with bathroom). 12,500CFP (US$156/£79) per person. Rates include breakfast and dinner. MC, V. **Amenities:** Restaurant; bar; complimentary kayaks, snorkeling gear, fishing lines. In room: No phone.

Pension Maupiti Village   Also on the ocean side of Motu Tiapaa, this no-frills pension is one of Maupiti's most basic and least expensive. The buildings consist simply of plywood sides and tin roofs—pretty much what you got before the advent of the more modern government-issued bungalows. Two units are individual bungalows with their

---

 Staying Near a Deserted Beach

I prefer to stay on **Motu Tiapaa,** beside the Onoiau Pass, since it has excellent beaches on both its lagoon and ocean sides. There are four pensions on the island, so if I tire of eating at mine, I can walk over and make a reservation at another. If one side of the *motu* gets too hot, a sea breeze usually cools the other. Skinny-dipping has been known to occur at a deserted beach wrapping around the northern end of the island. The lagoon is very shallow at this gorgeous spot, but the view of the main island is terrific.

own bathrooms (cold-water showers). Two rooms in a house and a dormitory all share outside toilets and cold-water showers. A white-sand beach fronts the property, but the lagoon between here and the fringing reef is too shallow for serious swimming. Owner Audine Colomes prepares meals of fresh seafood and occasionally duck, which guests eat at a long table in a beachside building. Her husband, Alain Colomes, once lived in Canada, and both he and their daughter, Raipoe, speak English as well as French.

98732 Vaiea, Maupiti (on Motu Tiapaa). 🕾/fax **60.15.35.** maupiti.village@mail.pf. 5 units (3 with shared bathroom), 6 dorm beds (shared bathrooms). 12,000CFP (US$150/£76) per person in bungalow; 7,000CFP (US$88/£44) per person in rooms or dormitory. Rates include all meals. No credit cards. **Amenities:** Restaurant; bar; complimentary kayaks and canoes. *In room:* No phone.

Pension Papahani   Friendly Tahitians Denis and Vilna Tuheiava operate this pension beside a lovely white-sand beach on the lagoon side of Motu Tiapaa. Look to the right as you face the lagoon and you will have a fine view of Mount Hotu Paraoa's cliff above Vaiea village. There are three newer, reasonably spacious "family" bungalows; one of these has a front porch that directly faces the beach. Three older bungalows in the garden are smaller and less comfortable. Except for mosquito nets over their double beds, all are rather sparsely furnished, especially the older units. Each has a private bathroom with cold-water shower. Vilna serves home-cooked French and Tahitian fare in an open-air building by the beach. The lagoon next to the pension is shallow, but you can wade out to deeper snorkeling water. Denis and Vilna speak about as much English as I do French, but they bent over backward to make my stay with them an enjoyable one. All meals are included in the rates here.

B.P. 1, 98732 Vaiea, Maupiti (on Motu Tiapaa). 🕾 **60.15.35.** Fax 60.15.36. 5 units. 10,000CFP–13,000CFP (US$125–US$163/£63–£82) per person. Rates include all meals. No credit cards. **Amenities:** Restaurant; bar. *In room:* No phone.

Pension Rose des Isles   Sharing the same beach as Pension Papahani (see above), Rose des Isles has one waterside bungalow built of native materials, making it Maupiti's most authentically Tahitian bungalow. It can accommodate up to five persons and has its own bathroom with cold-water shower. A smaller unit for two persons is back in the garden; its guests share toilets and showers.

B.P. 55, 98732 Vaiea, Maupiti (on Motu Tiapaa). 🕾 **70.50.70.** Fax 67.82.00. 2 units (1 with shared bathroom), 8 tent sites. 8,000CFP–12,000CFP (US$100–US$150/£51–£76) per person room or bungalow (including all meals). No credit cards. **Amenities:** Restaurant; bar; complimentary kayaks and snorkeling gear. *In room:* No phone.

ON MOTU TUANAI

Pension Poe Iti ★   Facing the main island across a white-sand beach on Motu Tuanai, this excellent pension is operated by Gerard and Josephine Sachet, who also own the *Maupiti Express.* Their four units may look like standard government-issued bungalows, but Gerard and Josephine have installed air conditioners, reading lights beside the double beds, hot-water showers, and TVs with DVD players (but no over-the-air reception). All this equipment is powered by both solar panels and two windmill generators, which stand incongruously above the flat island. Although they're located in the gardens rather than beside the beach, the bungalows are the most luxurious I've seen at any pension in French Polynesia. Meals are served family-style in a beachside pavilion, where you will have a fine view of the main island across the lagoon. Breakfast costs 700CFP (US$8.75/£4.45); lunch and dinner, 2,500CFP (US$31/£16) each. Morning and afternoon transfers to the main island are complimentary. Gerard speaks excellent English as well as

French, but it will help if you know some *français* when he's not around. Note that meals are not included in the rates here.

B.P. 39, 98732 Vaiea, Maupiti (on Motu Tuanai). ✆ **67.83.14** or 76.58.76. Fax 67.83.14. maupitiexpress@ mail.pf. 4 units. 8,000CFP (US$100/£51) double. No credit cards. **Amenities:** Restaurant; bar; free use of kayaks, canoes, and snorkeling gear. *In room:* A/C, TV/DVD player, fridge, no phone.

ON THE MAIN ISLAND

Maupiti Loisirs   This really is a traditional pension, since you'll share the home of Ui Terihaunui and Simone Chan, north of Tereia Beach on the western side of the island. Simone speaks English and leads road tours of the island, while Ui is a specialist at boat tours around Maupiti. Their guest rooms have double beds with mosquito nets. The two shared bathrooms have cold-water showers. You can pitch a tent in their yard, or Ui will take you over to a campsite on Motu Auira. They also rent bicycles for touring the island or making the short ride to the beach.

B.P. 66, Vaiea, Maupiti. ✆/fax **67.80.95.** 2 units (shared bathroom). 5,000CFP (US$63/£32) per person in rooms; 4,000CFP (US$50/£25) per person camping. Rates include breakfast and dinner. 1,000CFP (US$13–£6.35) per person camping on Motu Auira (no meals). No credit cards. **Amenities:** Bike rentals; free use of kayaks. *In room:* No phone.

Pension Tautiare Village   On the southern side of the main island, David and Dawn Domingo's pension consists of one modern house with four bedrooms, each with its own hot-water bathroom, plus one more room in their home, which means you both share their bathroom and see island life firsthand.

B.P. 16, 98732 Vaiea, Maupiti. ✆ **67.83.58.** Fax 60.15.91. pension-tautiare@mail.pf. 5 units (1 with shared bathroom). 5,000CFP (US$63/£32) per person. Rates include breakfast and dinner. No credit cards. **Amenities:** Restaurant; bar; bike rentals; free use of kayaks and snorkeling gear. *In room:* No phone.

5 WHERE TO DINE

If meals aren't already included in the room rates, I strongly advise purchasing at least a *demi pension* meal plan (that is, half-board, or breakfast and dinner). This is especially important if you stay out on a *motu,* since you will not be able to go into the village after dark. Even on the main island, there is only one non-pension place to dine, to wit:

Snack Tarona   FRENCH/TAHITIAN   This snack bar is Maupiti's only gathering place for both food and libations. The picnic-style tables and chairs sit on a floor of coral gravel under a thatched-roof pavilion and usually catch the prevailing southeast trade winds, making this a refreshingly breezy location to recover from your bicycle ride around the island. The fare is the typical Polynesian potpourri of grilled steaks with french fries, shrimp with coconut-curry sauce, chow mein, and chicken and shrimp sautéed with vegetables. With freshly caught fish and tomatoes, cucumbers, and beans straight from the garden, the *poisson cru* is among the best I've had anywhere.

Farauru (lagoonside in the village). ✆ **67.82.46.** Reservations not accepted. Main courses 800CFP–1,400CFP (US$10–US$18/£5.05–£8.85). No credit cards. Mon–Sat 10am–1pm and 6–10pm.

The Tuamotu Archipelago

When Paul Woodard and I sailed
our 41-foot yacht *Felicity* from the U.S.
East Coast to Tahiti, our voyage was a relative piece of cake—until we came to the
great line of atolls known as the Tuamotu
Archipelago. Like a fence stretching for
1,159km (720 miles), the Tuamotu islands
block the northeastern approaches to
Tahiti. They are so low—never more than
3m (10 ft.) above sea level, not including
the height of the coconut palms growing
all over them—that hundreds of yachts
and ships have been wrecked on these
reefs, either unable to see them until it was
too late or dragged ashore by tricky currents swarming between the islands and
ripping through the passes into their
lagoons. Those of us who go down to the
sea in yachts well understand why the
Tuamotus were once known as the Dangerous Archipelago.

Needless to say, Paul and I had to be on
our toes when navigating these waters. While
he signaled me from the bow, where he
could more easily see coral heads in the
water, I steered *Felicity* through narrow
Tiputa Pass and into the lagoon at **Rangiroa.** Once safely inside, the calm water
made it seem as if we had sailed into a
monstrous lake in the middle of the South
Pacific Ocean.

Like all atolls, those of the Tuamotus
are necklaces of perfectly flat islets enclosing crystal-clear lagoons. Consequently,
they offer a very different kind of experience than French Polynesia's high, mountainous islands. You will find many
black-pearl farms (most of the country's
orbs are produced here) and small villages
with whitewashed churches, but there is
much less to be seen aboveground than
there is underwater.

Sharks, rays, and more than 400 species
of colorful tropical fish inhabit these
lagoons, making for French Polynesia's finest snorkeling and scuba diving.

Of the 76 atolls, only Rangiroa, **Tikehau, Manihi,** and **Fakarava** have accommodations up to international standards;
accordingly, they are the most visited.
Only yachties and a few other intrepid
travelers go elsewhere.

You will find drier and hotter climes
than in the Society Islands, and sand so
brilliantly white that it alone requires sunglasses in the midday sun. So grab your
hat, your snorkeling gear, and your fins.
Those of us who love the water are in for
a treat up here in the Dangerous Archipelago.

1 RANGIROA ★★

The largest and most often visited of the Tuamotu atolls, Rangiroa lies 312km (194
miles) northeast of Tahiti. Its ring of low, skinny islets encloses one of the world's largest
lagoons. At more than 70km (43 miles) long and 26km (16 miles) wide, it's big enough

Impressions

At Rangiroa you pick up a hundred natives with pigs, guitars, breadfruit and babies.
They sleep on deck, right outside your bunk, and some of them sing all night.
—James A. Michener, *Return to Paradise*, 1951

so that when you stand on one side, you cannot see the other. It's easy to see why it's named Rangiroa, which means "long sky" in the local language. In fact, the lagoon is so large, the entire island of Tahiti could be placed in it, with room to spare.

In the early morning and late afternoon, schools of dolphins usually play in **Avatoru Pass** and **Tiputa Pass,** the two navigable passes into Rangiroa's interior lagoon, both on its north side. Currents of up to 6 knots race through the passes as the tides first fill the lagoon and then empty it during their never-ending cycle.

Most visitors come to Rangiroa primarily for French Polynesia's best scuba diving, snorkeling, and fishing. Others venture across the lagoon to Rangiroa's islets, where they can play Robinson Crusoe at a very remote resort.

Rangiroa's airstrip and all but one of its hotels and pensions are on a perfectly flat, 11km-long (7-mile) stretch of sand and palm trees running between Avatoru and Tiputa passes on the northern side of the lagoon. This main island does not have a name, as it actually consists of seven islets separated by narrow and very shallow reef passes. On the western end, **Avatoru** village is the commercial and governmental center for the northern Tuamotu islands. On the eastern end, Tiputa Pass separates the main island from **Tiputa** village. All but a handful of Rangiroa's 2,500 residents live in Avatoru and Tiputa villages.

GETTING AROUND RANGIROA

Rangiroa's airstrip is on the main island, about equidistant between Avatoru and Tiputa passes. The hotels and pensions send buses or vans to meet their guests. Otherwise, you are on your own, since there is no public transportation on the island.

I usually rent a bicycle, scooter, or car for a day to explore the main island. Its only road crosses six bridges, none of them with guardrails and some of them only one lane wide. The pavement is uneven, adding to the need for constant caution when driving here.

Rangi Rent a Car is the local agent for **Europcar** (© 800/227-7368 or 96.08.28; www.europcar-tahiti.com). It has an agency near Avatoru and desks at the Hotel Kia Ora (p. 235) and Novotel Rangiroa (p. 237). Cars rent for 12,000CFP (US$150/£76) a day. Scooters and open-air "Bugsters" (the most you'll need here) cost about 6,500CFP (US$81/£41) for 8 hours (which is longer than you'll need to see the islet). Bicycles rent for 1,500CFP (US$19/£9.50) for a half-day, 1,800CFP (US$23/£11) for a full day.

Arehahio Locations (© 98.82.45 or 73.92.84) in Avatoru rents cars for 8,400CFP (US$105/£53) per day, scooters for 5,200CFP (US$65/£33) a day, bicycles for 1,600CFP (US$20/£10) a day.

You can cross Tiputa Pass to Tiputa village via **Maurice Navette** (© 96.67.09 or 78.13.25), which operates water taxis daily from 6am to 5pm. Call or check with your hotel staff for schedules and fares.

ISLANDS ●
Fakarava **4**
Manihi **3**
Rangiroa **2**
Tikehau **1**

SOUTH PACIFIC
OCEAN

Fast Facts   Rangiroa

The following facts apply specifically to Rangiroa. For more information, see "Fast Facts: Tahiti & French Polynesia," in appendix A.

Camera & Film **Pata Hoh'a Photo,** near Restaurant Le Kai Kai (☎ **93.12.85**) sells film and will burn your digital photos to CDs. Open Monday to Saturday 9am to noon and 2 to 5:30pm.

Currency Exchange **Banque Socredo** has an agency with an ATM in Avatoru post. It's open Tuesday, Wednesday, and Friday from 8am to noon; Monday and Thursday from 1:30 to 4:30pm. **Banque de Tahiti** also has a branch in Avatoru. It's open Monday and Friday 8am to 4pm, Tuesday and Thursday 8am to 2pm.

Drugstore **Pharmacie de Rangiroa,** in Avatoru (☎ **93.12.35**), is open Monday to Friday 8am to 12:30pm and 3 to 6:30pm, Saturday from 8am to 12:30pm and 4:30 to 6:30pm, Sunday and holidays 10 to 11:30am.

Emergencies & Police The emergency **police** telephone number is ☎ **17.** The phone number of the **gendarmerie** on Rangiroa is ☎ **96.03.61.**

Healthcare There are **infirmaries** at Avatoru (☎ **96.03.75**) and across the pass at Tiputa (☎ **96.03.96**).

Internet Access **Pata Hoh'a Photo,** near Restaurant Le Kai Kai (☎ **93.12.85**), has Internet access for 330CFP (US$4.10/£2.10) for 15 minutes. Open Monday to Saturday 9am to noon and 2 to 5:30pm.

Mail The post office in Avatoru is open Monday to Thursday from 7am to 3pm, Friday 7am to 2pm.

Telephone Public pay phones are at the post office in Avatoru and at the dock on the eastern end of the island. Residents in the Tuamotus tend to write their phone numbers in groups of three digits; that is, 960 375 instead of 96.03.75.

Water Except at the hotels, the tap water is brackish. Don't drink it.

EXPLORING RANGIROA
THE VILLAGES

Avatoru and Tiputa are typical Tuamotuan villages. I consider **Avatoru** to be the more interesting of the two. Not only is it on the main island (you will need to ride a boat across the pass to Tiputa; see "Getting Around Rangiroa," above), but it is also larger and has a bit more to see. When you get into town, follow the main road straight ahead until it makes a right turn at the picturesque Protestant church beside Avatoru Pass. Along the way, you'll see the *mairie* (town hall), post office, banks, and three general stores. The whitewashed stone wall along this part of the road is typical of Tuamotuan villages. You can make a loop by following the main street beyond the church; it circles a large public park before returning to the main road.

LAGOON EXCURSIONS ★★★

Plan to explore this fantastic lagoon. If you're not diving, the best way is on a full-day excursion. The two main attractions are on the eastern and western ends of the lagoon, each at least a 1¹/₂-hour boat ride away from the main island each way. That means you will spend at least 3 hours going and coming, so you will need a full day for each attraction—and a good set of sea legs if a strong wind kicks up choppy waves on the lagoon. The tours do not operate in bad weather or really rough seas, which are more likely to occur during the austral summer months from December through March. In other words, don't be disappointed if the weather washes out your planned excursion.

Les Sables Rose (**Pink Sands**) ★★★, on the eastern end, is a phenomenal beach laden with pink sand. It's one of French Polynesia's most picturesque beaches, and to call it deserted is an understatement. Second on my list is *Lagon Bleu* (**Blue Lagoon**), a small lagoon carved into the reef on the western edge of the big lagoon. Literally a lagoon within a lagoon, this shallow pool is full of colorful corals and plentiful sea life. Thousands of seabirds nest nearby on aptly named *Ile aux Oiseaux* (**Bird Island**). A third day here can be spent at *Ile aux Récifs* (**Reef Island**), on the south side, where erosion has created razor-sharp coral formations (be sure to bring reef shoes on this trip).

(Tips) **Come Up Here First**

There isn't a lot to do in the Tuamotu Islands except snorkeling and scuba diving, which makes them great for resting and recovering from your long flight before tackling Tahiti, Moorea, Bora Bora, and the other Society Islands. I recommend coming here first for a little R & R, then visiting the more developed mountainous islands and their incredible scenery.

THE TUAMOTU ARCHIPELAGO

11 RANGIROA

Tiputa Pass

Tiputa Village

Motu Nuhi Nuhi

SOUTH PACIFIC OCEAN

Lagoon de Rangiroa

Area of detail

Lagoon de Rangiroa

Avatoru Pass

Avatoru Village

Motu Fara

Airport
Beach
Reef

N

0   1 mi
0   1 km

0   10 mi
0   10 km

0   100 mi
0   100 km

TUAMOTU ARCHIPELAGO

Manihi
Fakarava
Rangiroa
Tahiti

ACCOMMODATIONS ■

Hotel Kia Ora **8**
Kia Ora Sauvage **15**
Les Fare de Tiki Hoa **13**
Les Relais de Josephine **11**
Novotel Rangiroa Lagoon Resort **5**
Pension Bounty **9**
Pension Tuanake **3**
Raira Lagon **4**
Île aux Récifs (Reef Island) **14**
Lagon Bleu (Blue Lagoon) **12**
Les Sables Rose (The Pink Sands) **16**

DINING ◆

Restaurant Le Kai Kai **7**
Restaurant Vaimario **6**
Snack-Restaurant Moetua **10**

ATTRACTIONS ●

Cave de Rangiroa **1**
Gauguin's Pearl Farm **2**

> ## (Fun Facts) The Exile Islands
>
> Although the archipelago is now known as the Tuamotu ("many islands"), the chain was once called Puamotu, meaning subservient islands. In the old days, chiefs on Tahiti who did bad things were exiled to the atolls. The indigenous peoples up here refer to the archipelago as Puamotu, its name in those days, and they still speak a distinct Polynesian dialect known in English as Puamotuan.

You will be able to swim and snorkel at these sites, and the boat staff will prepare a beachside lunch. These trips are not inexpensive: Plan on paying 10,000CFP to 12,000CFP (US$125–US$150/£63–£76) or more per person for a full day's outing, including lunch, soft drinks, and use of snorkeling gear. The hotels and pensions either offer their own or can arrange lagoon excursions.

A shorter alternative if you don't have that much time—or that much spare change—is a **glass-bottom boat ride** over the coral heads inside the passes. You'll see lots of fish and, if you're lucky, a shark or two. Most hotels and pensions can arrange these excursions for about 3,000CFP (US$38/£19) per person.

SCUBA DIVING & SNORKELING ★★★

Rangiroa is one of the world's top diving destinations, with an extraordinary array of sea life. Hurricanes have damaged the coral here, so come to see fish, rays, and especially sharks rather than colorful reefs.

Tiputa Pass is the top dive site in French Polynesia. You can see graytip and blacktip sharks all year, but the best time is from December to March, when huge hammerhead sharks gather for their mating season. Another good (and less scary) time is between July and October, when manta rays look for mates. Diving in and out of the pass is for intermediate and advanced divers only, since it is both deep and subject to strong currents. Novices can dive inside the reef near Avatoru Pass and around the small islets sitting just inside both passes. Most other dives here are deep and long compared to American standards, so bring a buddy and be prepared to stretch the limits of the dive tables in order to see the magnificent sea life. Divers must be certified in advance and bring their medical certificates.

Snorkelers as well as scuba divers can **"ride the rip"** tide through Tiputa Pass, one of the most exhilarating waterborne experiences in French Polynesia. You are dropped off just outside the reef and literally drift with the incoming current through the pass, which looks like an underwater valley. These so-called drift snorkeling trips cost about 5,000CFP (US$63/£32) and are worth it—if you've got a strong heart. Book at your hotel activities desk or contact **Snorkeling Rangiroa** (© 96.73.59 or 76.03.31).

While most of its lagoon shoreline consists of pebbly coral, and waves crash directly on the reef over on the ocean side, the main island does have a decent white-sand beach. You'll find it where the island makes a hook on its eastern end—that is, from the Hotel Kia Ora eastward to Tiputa Pass.

Any of the hotels or pensions can arrange scuba dives. The best operators are **Blue Dolphins,** at the Hotel Kia Ora (© 96.03.01; www.bluedolphinsdiving.com), and **TOPdive Rangiroa** (© 72.39.55; www.topdive.com). Other outfitters include the **Six Passengers** (© 96.02.60; www.the6passengers.com), which allows only six divers on its

Rangiroa Paradive (© **96.05.55**). One-tank day dives cost about 7,000CFP (US$88/ £44). Night dives are more expensive.

SHOPPING

You wouldn't expect to be doing any wine-tasting in these atolls, but **Cave de Rangiroa,** near Avarotu (© **96.04.70;** www.vindetahiti.pf), is the display room for Vin de Tahiti (Tahiti Wines), French Polynesia's only vineyard and winery. The Carignan, muscat de Hambourg, and Italia varieties were first planted in a coconut grove out on the *motu* west of the main islet in 1999. You can take a half-day tour to the vineyard for 6,000CFP (US$75/£38) per person, or just stay here in the *cave* and taste the results in air-conditioned comfort for 1,800CFP (US$23/£11). Open Monday through Saturday from 9am to 1pm and 3 to 6pm.

Rangiroa does not produce black pearls in the same quantity as Manihi, but you can visit **Gauguin's Pearl Farm,** west of the airport (© **93.11.30**), and see how it's done. You can buy loose pearls in the shop, which is open Monday to Friday 8:30am to 5:30pm (with demonstrations Mon–Fri at 8:30am, 10:30am, and 2pm), weekends 9am to noon and 3 to 5pm.

You might find good locally produced *pareus,* shell necklaces, or baskets woven of pandanus palm leaves at **Fare Artisant Vaitarip,** the local women's cooperative beside the lake in Avatoru village (no phone). At the east end of the village, **Coconut Boutique** (© **96.85.12**) carries woodcarvings, *pareus,* aloha shirts, French magazines, and toiletries in small sizes. Both are open Monday to Saturday 8am to 5pm.

WHERE TO STAY
EXPENSIVE

Hotel Kia Ora ★★   This romantic establishment in a huge coconut plantation has been Rangiroa's premier hotel for almost 3 decades. Its thatched-roof buildings look like a lagoonside Polynesian village. White sand is hauled over from the ocean side of the island, but the beach still is a bit pebbly; however, a long pier reaches out into deep water for excellent swimming, snorkeling, and sunset watching, and there's a canoe-shaped swimming pool beside the lagoon. Ten bungalows sit over the reef and share the sunsets. Ashore stand two-story beachside bungalows with bedrooms downstairs and up, and one-story models with only the downstairs bedroom. These beach units have Jacuzzi tubs set in their partially covered front decks, but they have not one iota of privacy. Much more luxurious are three deluxe beach units with their own small pools and bathrooms with outdoor tubs. The much smaller original bungalows are back in the gardens; they do not have window screens but some have separate bedrooms. As at most accommodations on Rangiroa, guests here are primarily European and Japanese.

(Moments) Dolphin-Watching

All of Rangiroa's hotels and pensions can arrange dolphin-watching cruises, usually for about 3,000CFP (US$38/£19) per person, but you can ride or walk to the public park at the western side of Tiputa Pass and watch them play for free. The best time is late afternoon, when the playful animals frolic in the pass, often leaping high above the waves churned by the strong currents.

B.P. 1, 98775 Tiputa, Rangiroa (3km/2 miles east of airport, near east end of island). ℂ **96.02.22.** Fax 93.11.17. www.hotelkiaora.com. 58 units. 32,000CFP–68,000CFP (US$407–US$850/£203–£430) double. AE, DC, MC, V. **Amenities:** Restaurant; bar; outdoor pool; tennis court; Jacuzzi; watersports equipment rentals; bike rentals; activities desk; car rentals; massage; babysitting; laundry service. *In room:* A/C, data-port, fridge (stocked on request), coffeemaker, safe.

Kia Ora Sauvage This outpost is one of the South Pacific's most remote Robinson Crusoe–like escapes. Guests are transferred daily by a 1-hour speedboat ride from Hotel Kia Ora, which manages this retreat. Once you're out on tiny, triangle-shaped Avearahi *motu,* you will find a thatch main building, where the Tahitian staff cooks up the day's catch, often caught during the guests' lagoon excursions. Accommodations are in five comfortable bungalows built entirely of native materials. They have their own modern bathrooms, but are not screened, nor do they have electricity. Bring reef shoes, lots of insect repellent, SPF60 sunscreen, and an ample supply of books to read.

B.P. 1, 98775 Tiputa, Rangiroa (hotel is 1-hr. boat ride from airport). ℂ **96.02.22.** Fax 93.11.17. www. hotelkiaora.com. 5 units. 40,000CFP (US$500/£253) double. Meals and drinks 8,500CFP (US$106/£54) per person per day. Round-trip boat transfers cost 12,000CFP (US$150/£76) per person. Minimum 2-night stay required. AE, DC, MC, V. **Amenities:** Restaurant; bar. *In room:* No phone.

MODERATE

Les Fare de Tiki Hoa Like Kia Ora Sauvage but not as rustic, this small hotel provides a get-away-from-it-all experience on a *motu* out on Rangiroa's northwestern side, a half-hour by boat from Avatoru. It's a shorter boat ride from here to Lagon Bleu (Blue Lagoon), but much longer to Les Sables Rose (Pink Sands) on the far side of the lagoon. A nice beach fringes the lagoon side of the islet. The 10 bungalows have natural thatched roofs, ceiling fans, and private bathrooms with cold-water showers. Being able to speak a bit of French will be helpful out here.

B.P. 235, 98775 Avatoru, Rangiroa (hotel is 30-min. boat ride from Avatoru). ℂ **58.45.45** or 73.63.10. Fax 58.45.45. 10 units. www.fare-tikihoa.pf. 13,750CFP (US$172/£87) per person. Rates include all meals. MC, V. **Amenities:** Restaurant; bar; free use of kayaks and snorkeling gear. *In room:* No phone.

Les Relais de Josephine ★ (Value) You can watch the dolphins frolic in Tiputa Pass from this comfortable inn, the creation of the charming Denise Caroggio, an English-speaking Frenchwoman who is like the grande dame of Rangiroa. Her spacious bungalows flank a Mediterranean-style villa with an expansive veranda overlooking the pass.

Readers Comment: Absolutely Alone in a Postcard Setting

Kia Ora Sauvage is truly a magic place, if you allow it to touch you. Due to the lack of electricity, you quickly adapt at living in the sunlight. You get up when the sun is rising and go to bed right after dinner when it is dark (which is around 7:30pm). This place is not for people who need cocktails at the pool bar, deluxe five-course-meals, weekly Polynesian dance performances, and always a dust-free hotel room. But if you enjoy being on your own for a while, unhurriedly reading a good book and lying on a snow-white beach at the lagoon with no one around you, this is your happy place. Being absolutely alone in a postcard setting, accompanied only by hermit crabs, is probably the biggest luxury on earth.

—Christian and Sabrina Rudat, Switzerland

Guests can relax there or in a lounge equipped with a TV, VCR, and CD player. At night, the veranda turns into Le Dolphin Gourmand restaurant, serving excellent three-course French and Mediterranean meals. Furnished with reproductions of French colonial antiques, the bungalows have thatched roofs over solid white walls. Sliding doors open to the porches, outfitted with high-quality wooden patio furniture. Neither the doors nor the prop-up windows are screened, but the queen-size beds are covered by mosquito nets. The substantial bathrooms have double sinks and walk-in showers. Do anything possible to get one of the three units beside the pass.

B.P. 140, 98775 Avatoru, Rangiroa. ©/fax **96.02.00.** http://relaisjosephine.free.fr. 6 units. 14,600CFP (US$183/£92) per person, double occupancy. Rates include breakfast and dinner. AE, MC, V. **Amenities:** Restaurant; bar; bike rentals; laundry service. *In room:* Coffeemaker, safe, no phone.

Novotel Rangiroa Lagoon Resort   This modest but attractive resort sits beside a rocky stretch of lagoon shoreline west of the airport and within walking distance of Restaurant Le Kai Kai and Restaurant Vaimario (see "Where to Dine," below). Brilliant white sand has been brought in to form a sunbathing strip along the property, and you can swim off a pier extending over the lagoon. The 38 bungalows and main building (with French restaurant and bar) are tightly packed on limited land. The units here come either as individual bungalows or as duplex rooms that are narrower than the much more spacious bungalows. Both are tastefully decorated with tropical furniture and fabrics; they also have adequate bathrooms and front porches.

B.P. 17, 98775 Avatoru, Rangiroa. © **800/221-4542** or 93.13.50. Fax 93.13.51. www.novotel.com. 38 units. 19,200CFP (US$240/£122) duplex; 29,300CFP (US$366/£185) bungalow. AE, MC, V. **Amenities:** Restaurant; bar; car and bike rentals; activities desk; massage; laundry service. *In room:* A/C, TV, dataport, fridge, coffeemaker, hair dryer, safe.

Pension Bounty   Although it's not directly beside the lagoon, a sandy path leads from this pension to the main island's best beach. Rooms are in a motel-style building of red cedar and local *kohu* hardwood. Breakfast is included here, but each unit has a kitchen to go along with its ceiling fan, double bed, and private bathroom (with hot-water shower). All of the windows are screened, as are the sliding doors to each unit's large porch. Dinner is available on request. The hosts speak French, English, and Italian.

B.P. 296, 98775 Avatoru, Rangiroa. ©/fax **96.08.22.** www.pension-bounty.com. 4 units. 7,000CFP (US$88/£44) per person. Rates include breakfast. AE, MC, V. **Amenities:** Restaurant; bar; free use of bikes. *In room:* Kitchen, safe, no phone.

INEXPENSIVE

Pension Tuanake ★   This little lagoonside pension sits in a coconut grove on a point of land fringed by pebbly beaches on two sides. Friendly owner Roger Terorotua has six bungalows, all with plywood sides, thatched roofs covered with tin, front porches, mat-lined walls, screened windows, fans, and bathrooms with hot-water showers. They range in size from small units equipped with two single beds to a family-size affair with double and single beds both downstairs and in a loft, which can be entered via its own outdoor stairway. A former leader of Haere Mai, French Polynesia's organization of pensions and small family-run hotels (see "Guesthouses & Family Accommodations," p. 84), Roger and his family speak enough English to make non–French speakers feel welcome here. His is a down-to-earth Tahitian place, so stay somewhere else if you are bothered by chickens and dogs running free around the property.

(Tips)   Expect a Tepid Pension Shower

I once asked the owner of a Tuamotu pension if the bathrooms in his bungalows had hot-water showers. *"Non,"* he replied. Then they must be cold-water? *"Non,"* he said again. I must have looked puzzled. *"Regardez,"* he said, telling me to look at a huge black plastic tank behind the nearest bungalow. As I could see, gutters divert rainwater from the rooftops into tanks, where it bakes in the sun until someone turns on a shower. *"Pas chaude, pas froide,"* he said. "Not hot, not cold." So it is in the atolls, where most fresh water comes not from wells in the ground, but from rainwater, itself a scarce commodity in these semiarid islands. Unless you're staying at a deluxe resort with a desalinization plant, forget lingering in a hot shower.

B.P. 21, 98775 Avatoru, Rangiroa. ℂ/fax **93.11.80.** www.tuanake.fr.st. 6 units. 9,700CFP–14,300CFP (US$121–US$179/£61–£91) double. Add 3,000CFP (US$38/£19) per person per day for breakfast and dinner. MC, V. **Amenities:** Restaurant; bar; bike rentals. *In room:* No phone.

Raira Lagon   Virtually next-door to the Novotel Rangiroa Lagoon Resort, Raira Lagon sits beside a rocky beach equipped with chairs under shade trees. Owners Raumati and Ghislaine Sanford, who speak English as well as French, have 10 small thatched-roof bungalows equipped with double beds, electric fans, bathrooms with hot-water showers, and front porches. Their brightly decorated lagoonside restaurant serves good French fare to both guests and outsiders.

B.P. 87, 98775 Avatoru, Rangiroa. ℂ **99.12.30.** Fax 99.12.31. www.raira-lagon.pf. 10 units. 11,500CFP (US$144/£73) per person. Rates include breakfast and dinner. AE, MC, V. **Amenities:** Restaurant; bar; bike and scooter rentals; free use of snorkeling gear. *In room:* No phone.

WHERE TO DINE

Nonguests are welcome at Les Relais de Josephine's (see above) **Le Dolphin Gourmand** restaurant, where the three-course meals cost 4,100CFP (US$51/£26) per person. Make your reservations before noon. Outsiders are also welcome at the **Hotel Kia Ora, Novotel Rangiroa Lagoon Resort,** and the **Raira Lagon** dining rooms.

The local *roulottes* set up shop after dark at the Tiputa Pass wharf and in Avatoru village, but the best is in the center of the main island near Restaurant Le Kai Kai (it has table service). See "Don't Miss *Les Roulottes*" (p. 140), for details. You'll also find a few inexpensive snack bars in Avatoru.

Snack-Restaurant Moetua   SNACK BAR   You'll be snacking over the lagoon at this simple establishment next to the Tiputa Pass dock. It's a local favorite for burgers, sandwiches, *poisson cru,* and grilled steaks and fish served with fries. In other words, it's like a stationary *roulotte.*

At Ohutu Point (end of the main road at Tiputa Pass). ℂ **28.06.96.** Reservations not accepted. Burgers and sandwiches 400CFP–800CFP (US$5–US$10/£2.55–£5.05); main courses 1,000CFP (US$13/£6.35). No credit cards. Mon–Sat 11am–5pm.

Restaurant Le Kai Kai ★   FRENCH   West of the airstrip and near the Novotel Rangiroa Lagoon Resort, Gaelle Coconnier's open-air restaurant with crushed coral floor and mat-lined ceiling is my favorite spot for a casual lunch or dinner. Midday sees a selection of omelets, salads, and *croques* (toasted sandwiches), while dinner turns to a wide-ranging menu of light French fare. A special prix-fixe dinner menu includes a starter such as beef carpaccio, a main of shrimp in garlic and olive oil, and a dessert (I always opt for a Tahitian sundae with coconut and honey). Reserve for a 7pm pickup from your hotel. Gaelle does all the cooking herself, so don't be in a hurry.

Main road, west of airport. ✆ **96.30.39.** Reservations recommended. Sandwiches and omelets 300CFP–1,000CFP (US$3.75–US$13/£1.90–£6.30); main courses 1,500CFP–2,000CFP (US$19–US$25/£9.50–£13); fixed-price dinner 3,200CFP (US$40/£20). MC, V. Thurs–Tues 11:30am–2pm and 6:30–9pm; Wed 11:30am–2pm.

Restaurant Vaimario FRENCH/ITALIAN   Pizzas are the highlights at this restaurant in a thatched-roof house just west of the airport. You can dine inside, but the preferred tables are on the coral-floor veranda. The best main courses are grilled fresh fish with vanilla, coconut, orange, or ginger sauce. ✆ **96.05.69.**

Main road, opposite Novotel Rangiroa Lagoon Resort. ✆ **96.05.69.** Reservations recommended. Pizza 1,100CFP–1,200CFP (US$14–US$15/£6.95–£7.60); main courses 1,950CFP–2,950CFP (US$24–US$37/£12–£19). MC, V. Wed–Fri and Sun–Mon 11:30am–2pm and 6:30–9pm; Sat 6:30–9pm.

---

2 TIKEHAU ★

Separated from Rangiroa by a deepwater channel, Tikehau is much smaller and less developed than its huge neighbor. Its nearly circular lagoon, 26km (16 miles) across, is no more than 30m (100 ft.) at its deepest. The late Jacques Cousteau found in 1987 that the Tikehau lagoon had more species of fish than any other French Polynesian lagoon. Apparently that's still true, which makes this a great destination for snorkelers and novice divers, as well as providing a substantial income for Tikehau's 400 or so friendly residents, who make more money by trapping and shipping fish to Papeete than from black-pearl farms.

Most local residents live in **Tuherahera,** the only village of any size, on a large *motu* on the southern side of the atoll. It's one of the prettiest Tuamotuan villages; hibiscus, frangipani, bougainvillea, and other colorful flowers seem to grow everywhere. You'll find grocery stores, a post office, and an infirmary in Tuherahera, but **no bank** (bring local currency, especially if your pension does not accept credit cards). The post office sells phone cards, which you can use to make local and international calls at a pay phone outside. As on all the atolls, do not drink the tap water on Tikehau. Bottled water is available at the pensions and from the grocery stores in Tuherahera.

The Tikehau **airport** is on the same island as Tuherahera village; in fact, you can easily walk from the tiny terminal to the village jetty. All of the accommodations will meet you if you have reservations, and all either have, or can arrange, **bicycle rentals** for about 1,500CFP (US$19/£9.50) a day. There are no rental cars here since there is simply no place to drive them!

Tikehau is an excellent place to stay at one of the family-run pensions, for several of them stand beside one of French Polynesia's best beaches—a long, curving beach of both white and pink sand on the eastern side of Tuherahera. Unlike Rangiroa, where you must ride a boat for more than an hour to see a pink-sand beach, here it's actually in the village. The atoll is also home to the **Tikehau Pearl Beach Resort,** an excellent luxury hotel, and the charming **Relais Royal Tikehau,** each on a *motu* of its own (see "Where to Stay & Dine," below).

Tikehau has much better beaches than either Rangiroa or Manihi, and you can wade from them into the lagoon near your accommodations for excellent snorkeling. The Tikehau Pearl Beach Resort, Relais Tikehau, and the pensions can organize boat trips out on the lagoon to little deserted islets such as **Motu Ohihi,** on the eastern edge of the atoll, where you can swim off a pink-sand beach. Out in the lagoon are **Motu Puarua** and **Motu Oeoe,** the so-called Bird Islands, where noddy birds and snowy-white fairy terns nest. These trips often include stops at a black-pearl farm and one of the fish farms, which provide so much of Tikehau's income. In a modern twist on the ancient stone Polynesian fish traps, such as at Maeva on Huahine (p. 174), the locals use bait to lure fish inside the traps and a maze of chicken wire to keep them from escaping. Prices vary from about 7,000CFP (US$88/£44) per person for snorkeling trips to about 11,000CFP (US$138/£70) for a full lagoon excursion, including a picnic on a small islet.

Tikehau's best diving is in and around **Tuheiava Pass,** the one navigable entry into the lagoon. You will see graytip and blacktip sharks and the occasional manta ray, but the appeal here is the enormous population of colorful fish. **Manihi Blue Nui Dive Center,** based at the Tikehau Pearl Beach Resort (*C* 96.23.01; www.bluenui.com), is one of the best in French Polynesia, with top-of-the-line equipment and hard-topped boats with ladders. **Raie Manta Club** (*C* 96.22.53 or 72.89.08; http://raiemantaclub.free.fr) serves the pensions in Tuherahera village. They charge about 6,500CFP (US$81/£41) per one-tank dive and teach PADI certification courses. Raie Manta has snorkeling trips for 2,000CFP (US$25/£13) per person.

WHERE TO STAY & DINE

There are no restaurants or snack bars on Tikehau, and only the **Tikehau Village** pension (see below) welcomes outside guests, so buy a meal plan or pay a room rate that includes at least breakfast and dinner. The pensions listed here have various rates depending on the number of meals provided, so make sure you understand what you're paying for.

EXPENSIVE

Tikehau Pearl Beach Resort ★★★   You may think you have made a horrible mistake as your transfer boat approaches, for rustic Tuamotu-style thatch disguises the luxuries awaiting at this resort, which occupies all of Motu Tiano, a small reef islet a 10-minute boat ride from the village and the airport. Other than a concrete patio separating the lagoonside pool from the conical-roof dining room and bar, everything about it is *très* Polynesian, with lots of thatch, mats, and bamboo. Strong currents in a shallow pass rip in and out beneath some of the overwater bungalows here, which means you can't go swimming from their decks. Consequently, opt for one of the "premium" suites built over quieter water; they do have ladders leading into the lagoon. The beach here has more pink and white sand than you'll find on Rangiroa and Manihi. Every unit is spacious and well-appointed, and the beachside units have large outdoor bathrooms behind high rock walls. The bungalows aren't screened, but the staff closes the windows and turns on the electric mosquito repellents while you're at dinner. Ceiling fans and the trade winds usually provide plenty of ventilation, but opt for a premium overwater or deluxe beach bungalow if air-conditioning is important to you.

B.P. 20, 98778 Tuherahera, Tikehau. *C* **800/657-3275** or 50.84.54 for reservations, or 96.23.00. Fax 43.17.86 for reservations, or 96.23.01. www.pearlresorts.com. 37 units. 43,000CFP–75,000CFP (US$538–US$938/

Tikehau

Manihi

Fakarava

Rangiroa

Tahiti

TUAMOTU ARCHIPELAGO

0   100 mi

0   100 km

0   5 mi

0   5 km

Tuheiava Pass ①

Lagoon de
Tikehau

②

③

④

Area of
Tuherarera
detail

Tuherahera

⑤

⑥

SOUTH
PACIFIC OCEAN

Tuherarera

ATTRACTIONS ●
Motu Oeoe **2**
Motu Ohihi **4**
Motu Puarua **3**
Tuheiava Pass **1**

ACCOMMODATIONS ■
Aito Motel Collette **7**
Chez Justine **10**
Pension Tematie **9**
Relais Royal Tikehau **6**
Tikehau Pearl Beach Resort **5**
Tikehau Village **8**

Lagoon de
Tikehau

Tuherahera

0   1/2 mi

0   0.5 km

SOUTH
PACIFIC OCEAN

7   8   9   10

✈ Airport
🮤 Beach
…… Reef

£272–£475) double. Meals 15,000CFP (US$188/£95) per person per day. AE, DC, MC, V. **Amenities:** Restaurant; bar; outdoor pool; spa; free use of snorkeling gear, canoes, and kayaks; bike rentals; babysitting; laundry service. *In room:* A/C (in premium overwater and deluxe beach units), TV, minibar, coffeemaker, iron (some units), safe.

MODERATE

Relais Royal Tikehau ★★ (Finds)   At low tide, you can walk across the reef and another small islet to the village from this charming little hotel, the creation of the delightful Jean-Claude and Monique Varney. Jean-Claude worked in New Zealand for more than 2 decades, and Monique spent her Papeete career in tourism, so both speak English as well as French. They call this their retirement project, and a fine one it is. Their restaurant-bar building and three of their bungalows stand beside a *hoa,* a shallow pass between theirs and the next *motu.* (I watched from my porch as stingrays trolled for breakfast in the pass just after daybreak.) Four other bungalows are next to a gorgeous beach of white-and-pink sand. The Varneys have four hotel-style rooms upstairs over a monstrous rainwater cistern. Monique decorated each unit with bright, color-matched drapes and *tivaivai* (handmade appliqué quilts). The bungalows and central building are lined with mats and covered with plastic imitation thatch (it lasts five times as long as natural leaves). Every unit has its own bathroom here, but only the bungalows have hot-water showers.

B.P. 15, 98778 Tuherahera, Tikehau. ℂ/fax **96.23.37.** www.royaltikehau.pf. 11 units. 15,750CFP–20,570CFP (US$197–US$257/£100–£130) double; 30,250CFP–42,350CFP (US$378–US$529/£191–£268) bungalow. Rates include breakfast and dinner. 2-night minimum stay required. No credit cards. **Amenities:** Restaurant; bar; laundry service. *In room:* TV (beachside units), no phone.

INEXPENSIVE

The pensions below are all beside the long white-and-pink-sand beach beginning at Tuherahera village and running east to the end of the main *motu.* They are all cut from the same mold—that is, a few bungalows and a main building, where guests can relax and be fed. The island's airstrip is behind them, but don't worry: At worst only a couple of flights arrive and take off each day, only during daylight hours.

Aito Motel Collette   The closest pension to the village, Aito Motel Collette is named both for its owner and the *aito* (ironwood, or Australian pine) trees that shade her property. The beach here is wide, although the lagoon on this western end is shallow, especially at low tide. The clapboard-sided bungalows have high thatched roofs, now covered by tin painted green, and the front porches are trimmed with tree-limb railings, which adds a touch of charm. They come with various bed configurations (two doubles, one double, or a double and a single). Each has its own private bathroom with cold-water shower. Fans and mosquito nets are available. Guests gather in a large living room and on a lagoon-facing veranda, where meals are served. Collette speaks no English, so a knowledge of French will be helpful here.

B.P. 43, 98778 Tuherahera, Tikehau. ℂ/fax **96.23.07.** 5 units. 8,500CFP (US$106/£54) per person. Rates include all meals. No credit cards. **Amenities:** Restaurant; bar. *In room:* No phone.

Chez Justine   Owner Justine Tetua speaks a bit of English, and she allows campers to pitch tents on the sand, which helps to set her pension apart from the others. Her best units are three individual bungalows with private bathrooms by the beach. Two other buildings each have two bedrooms that share a bathroom. All have front porches and screened windows. All showers dispense cold water. Meals are served in the main house.

THE TUAMOTU ARCHIPELAGO

TIKEHAU

> **Fun Facts   Fish, Fish & More Fish**
>
> Given that fish farming is Tikehau's main industry, forget steaks and chicken. Get used to being served fish for lunch and fish for dinner and fish on your *motu* picnic. The locals even eat fish for breakfast.

98778 Tuherahera, Tikehau. ✆/fax **96.22.86.** 5 units (2 with shared bathrooms). 8,000CFP–10,500CFP (US$100–US$131/£51–£66) per person in bungalow, 3,000CFP (US$38/£19) per person camping. Bungalow rates include all meals; camping rates include breakfast. No credit cards. **Amenities:** Restaurant; bar. *In room:* No phone.

Pension Tematie   Midway along the beach, and closest to the airport terminal, this pension has the most unusual architecture here. Two of its octagonal-shaped bungalows are built of coral blocks, which owners Nora and Yves-Marie Dubois scavenged from the reef. The bricklike blocks form the walls of the bungalows and of each unit's outdoor bathroom with cold-water shower. The two smaller *fares* have double and single beds. A larger family-size unit has additional beds in its mezzanine. The pull-back windows here are screened, and electric fans are available. Yves-Marie is a French engineer, and he and Nora lived in many countries before settling on Tikehau, her home island. They serve French- and Tahitian-style meals.

98778 Tuherahera, Tikehau. ✆/fax **96.22.65.** 3 units. 9,000CFP–12,000CFP (US$113–US$150/£57–£76) per person. Rates include all meals. No credit cards. **Amenities:** Restaurant; bar; kayak and bike rentals. *In room:* No phone.

Tikehau Village   Often booked solid by Tahiti residents on vacation, this lively little hotel sits just beyond Aito Motel Collette on the widest part of the beach. The lagoon is relatively shallow here, but a pier provides access to deeper water as well as a diving base for Raie Manta Club (see "Lagoon Excursions, Snorkeling & Scuba Diving," above). The bungalows have more Tuamotuan charm than any others here, with natural thatched roofs and walls trimmed with coconut-palm fronds. Each has a front porch, a ceiling fan, and a private bathroom (cold-water showers in most, hot water in three newer units). Four smaller units are geared for singles and couples, while five larger bungalows attract families. Try to get a beachfront bungalow if you can. Under a big thatched roof to the rear of the property, the moderately priced French and Tahitian restaurant is open to all comers, although reservations are strongly advised.

B.P. 9, 98778 Tuherahera, Tikehau. ✆/fax **96.22.86.** 9 units. 8,500CFP–10,500CFP (US$106–US$131/£54–£66) per person. Rates include all meals. MC, V. **Amenities:** Restaurant; bar; bike rentals. *In room:* No phone.

3   MANIHI

Known for its black-pearl farms, Manihi lies 520km (312 miles) northeast of Tahiti. In fact, French Polynesia's pearl-farming industry began here in the late 1960s, and although many farms are now closed, the 30 or so remaining seem to sit atop nearly every coral head dotting the lagoon. Great lines of buoys float like crab pots atop the blue water, with long strands of pearl oysters suspended below.

Most of the atoll's 800 or so residents live in the only village here, **Paeua,** which sits beside **Tairapa Pass** on Manihi's southern side, the only navigable entry into the lagoon. (Both the village and the pass are also referred to as Turipaoa.) The three pensions here are either very remote or cater primarily to workers at the pearl farms; as a result, in my opinion, Manihi is a one-horse atoll, that horse being the luxurious **Manihi Pearl Beach Resort** (see below). If you can afford its rates, Manihi has very good diving excursions out on its lagoon; otherwise, I would look to another island for my atoll adventure.

From the resort, you can visit Paeua village every day; the hotel launch lands at the jetty inside Tairapa Pass. From there, head inland for 1 block, turn right, and walk to the pass, where there's a grocery store fronted by a huge shade tree. After sipping a soft drink on a bench beside the tree, stroll along the seawall for a sensational view of the outer reef. You'll pass a small, picturesque Catholic church facing the sea.

The **airport** is on the same *motu* as the Manihi Pearl Beach Resort, which sends golf carts to fetch its guests from the terminal. The resort has bicycles for its guests' use, but there are no rental vehicles available here, nor is there public transportation. There is **no bank** on Manihi, so bring local currency if you plan to visit the village. The **post office** (which has pay phones) and the nurse-staffed government **infirmary** (© **96.43.67**) are both in Paeua. Do not drink the tap water; bottled water is available at the resort and from the grocery stores in Paeua.

LAGOON EXCURSIONS, SNORKELING & SCUBA DIVING

At 30km (16 miles) long by 5.6km (4 miles) wide, the clear lagoon is bigger than Tikehau's but not nearly as large—nor as deep—as those in Rangiroa and Fakarava. Like Tikehau, it's better for diving among colorful tropical fish, as opposed to the big rays and sharks that make diving at Rangiroa so exciting. That's not to say there are no sharks here; to the contrary, the lagoon seems infested with the small reef varieties, and rays feed on plankton near Tairapa Pass, which is wider and deeper than those at Rangiroa. Its strong-enough current makes "riding-the-rip" diving and snorkeling trips a highlight here. All dive sites are in or just outside the pass.

As at Tikehau, Gilles Petrie's **Manihi Blue Nui Dive Center,** based at the Manihi Pearl Beach Resort (see below), provides top-of-the-line PADI diving. It charges about 6,700CFP (US$84/£42) per one-tank dive. The resort also allows for fishing (both deepsea and hand-line in the lagoon), snorkeling trips, picnics on deserted islands, and lagoon excursions.

WHERE TO STAY & DINE

Manihi Pearl Beach Resort ★★   This modern resort and the airstrip share a *motu* on the western end of Manihi's lagoon. Like at Rangiroa, the beach here is more pebbly than sandy, but guests can sun themselves on little islets equipped with palm trees and

---

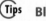 **Black Pearls**

Do not expect to buy the black pearl of your dreams directly from a Manihi farm at a huge discount, for they are all shipped to Papeete to be graded before being sold. Only one farm welcomes guests to see how pearls are produced, and then only on Monday, Wednesday, and Friday. Plan your visit accordingly.

chaise longues, or on a faux beach beside a lagoonside horizon pool. A thatched-roof bar adjacent to the pool is cozy and conducive to meeting your fellow guests. In addition to diving, activities include swimming, snorkeling (you can snorkel outside the pass), canoeing, visiting pearl farms and the village, lagoon and deep-sea fishing, spending a day on a deserted *motu*, and cruising at sunset. The prevailing trade winds can generate a choppy lagoon under the 19 overwater bungalows here. Both the overwater and beachside units have mat-lined walls, natural wood floors, ceiling fans hanging from mat-lined roofs, king-size beds, writing tables, ample shower-only bathrooms, and covered porches with two recliners. Each beachfront unit also has a hammock strung between two palm trees out front, and the beachfront unit bathrooms are outdoors behind high wooden walls. Although a majority of guests here are European couples, the Tahitian staff makes English speakers feel at home.

B.P. 1, 99711 Turipaoa, Manihi. ⓒ **800/657-3275** or 50.84.54 for reservations, or 96.42.73. Fax 43.17.86 for reservations, or 96.42.72. www.pearlresorts.com. 40 units. 28,000CFP–63,000CFP (US$350–US$788/ £177–£399) double. Meals 15,000CFP (US$188/£95) per person per day. AE, MC, V. **Amenities:** Restaurant; bar; outdoor pool; watersports equipment rentals; free bicycles; game room; activities desk; spa; babysitting; laundry service. *In room:* A/C (in premium overwater bungalows), TV, dataport, minibar, coffeemaker, safe.

Pension Vainui   Edmond Buniet moved from France to French Polynesia in 1968, and since 1982 has lived on Motu Marakorako, an islet on the south side of the Manihi lagoon. Edmond dabbles in the pearl business and welcomes travelers to share his little get-away-from-it-all retreat. The simple accommodations are in plywood buildings standing in a proverbial coconut grove. One near the pebbly beach has two narrow units, in which there is just enough room to squeeze double beds. Other buildings away from the beach have larger units; one of these aimed at families has a double bed in one room, over-and-under bunk beds in another. They all have front porches and share toilets and cold-water showers. Edmond serves beer and wine, but bring your own spirits. The 30-minute speedboat ride from the airport can be wet if the trade winds are blowing.

B.P. 51, 99711 Turipaoa, Manihi (on Motu Marakorako). ℂ **96.42.89.** Fax 96.43.30. www.pensionvainui. com. 7 units (none w/bathroom). 12,000CFP (US$150/£76) per person. Rates include all meals. MC, V. **Amenities:** Restaurant; bar (beer and wine only); complimentary snorkeling gear. *In room:* No phone.

4 FAKARAVA ★★

Southeast of Rangiroa and about 490km (300 miles) northeast of Tahiti, Fakarava's rectangular reef encloses French Polynesia's second-largest lagoon. This 60×24km (37×15-mile) aquamarine jewel is filled with such a rich variety of sea life that part of it has been designated a UNESCO nature preserve. Needless to say, there is some very good diving and snorkeling here.

Unlike most Tuamotu atolls, I find Fakarava interesting from a historical standpoint. The airstrip and the main village, **Rotoava,** sit at the atoll's northeastern end, but the first European settlement here was at **Tetamanu,** on the far southern end of the lagoon beside narrow **Tumakohua Pass,** a 1¹/₂- to 2-hour boat ride from the airport. Coupled with fine snorkeling and diving in the pass, seeing the crumbling ruins of a prison and a restored 1834-vintage Catholic church make a visit to the ghostlike Tetamanu one of the more fascinating jaunts in the Tuamotu Archipelago.

The administrative center was moved to Rotoava to take advantage of **Garuae Pass,** the widest in French Polynesia. It's so wide and deep, in fact, that ships as large as the *Queen Elizabeth 2* can safely enter the lagoon and anchor off Rotoava. The cruise ship *Aranui 3* pulls in here on its way to the Marquesas Islands (see "Seeing the Islands by Cruise Ship & Yacht," in chapter 3).

From Rotoava, a road—facetiously dubbed "rue Flosse" because former French Polynesian President Gaston Flosse paved part of it prior to a visit by French President Jacques Chirac in 2003—runs for 30km (18 miles) along French Polynesia's longest *motu.* Extraordinarily beautiful beaches border this skinny strip of land that encloses the northern and eastern side of the lagoon (the western and southern sides consist of reefs dotted with a few small islets). As you ride past these deserted beaches in a boat, you'll wonder how long it will be before Fakarava has more than one international-level resort.

Rotoava has a **post office** (with public phone), **infirmary** (ℂ **98.42.24**), school, whitewashed church, and three general stores, but **no bank.** The island's only resort, the Maitai Dream Fakarava, and most of its pensions accept credit cards, but bring local currency if yours doesn't. Do not drink the tap water on Fakarava; bottled water is available at the resort and the grocery stores in Rotoava.

GETTING AROUND FAKARAVA

The airstrip is on the northern side of the atoll, 4km (3½ miles) from Rotoava. There is no public transportation on the island, so the accommodations meet arriving guests who have reservations. **Relais Marama** (see "Where to Stay," below) rents bikes for 1,000CFP (US$13/£6.30) per day. Other pensions have bicycles for their guests. Anyone can rent a scooter or bike from **Faka Location** (𝄢 **78.03.37**). Scooters cost 5,000CFP (US$63/£32) for a half-day and 8,000CFP (US$100/£51) for 24 hours, while bicycles go for 2,000CFP (US$25/£13) a day. Guests at the Maitai Dream Fakarava resort can charge the rentals to their rooms; everyone else must pay cash.

EXPLORING FAKARAVA
LAGOON EXCURSIONS ★★★

Don't come to Fakarava without spending at least half a day on a lagoon excursion. The pensions will organize these trips. One of the best is **Fakarava Explorer** (𝄢 **98.42.66;**

www.fakarava-divelodge.com), operated by English-speaking Ato Lissant of Pension
Paparara (p. 250). Ato takes dolphin-watching and snorkeling cruises to Garuae Pass,
motu picnics, and fishing trips. He charges 13,000CFP (US$163/£82) per person for
all-day tours to Tetamanu, with a minimum of five persons.

SCUBA DIVING & SNORKELING ★★★

Garuae Pass is one of the most exciting dive sites in French Polynesia. At nearly a kilometer (²/₃ mile) across, it dwarfs all other passes in the Tuamotus and has just about every
kind of fish, shark, and ray you're likely to see in French Polynesia; the coral here is very
good, too. As at Rangiroa, hammerhead sharks gather here from December through
March, manta rays between July and October. July also sees huge schools of marbled
groupers. Most dives are of the drift variety; that is, the dive boat takes you beyond the
reef and you ride the incoming tide through the 15m-deep (50-ft.) pass back into the
lagoon. You had best be an advanced diver to explore Garuae Pass, but those with either
advanced or intermediate credentials can dive the much smaller and less challenging
Tuamakohua Pass, at the southern end of the lagoon. Novice divers can choose from
several sites in the lagoon, much of which is teeming with sea life since it's a protected
marine reserve.

TOPdive Rangiroa is based at the Matai Dream Fakarava (© **98.43.76**; www.topdive.
com), while **Fakarava Diving Center** is at the nearby Pension Paparara (© **98.43.23** or
77.10.00; www.fakarava-diving-center.com). TOPdive charges 7,500CFP (US$94/£47)
for a one-tank dive in or near Garuae Pass, while Fakarava Diving Center charges
6,500CFP (US$81/£41). A full-day's outing to Tetamanu, including a picnic lunch and
diving in Tuamakohua Pass, goes for about 18,500CFP (US$231/£117) per person. The
island's other reputable dive center is **Te Ava Nui Plongé**, in Rotoava (© **98.42.50**;
www.divingfakarava.com).

BLACK-PEARL FARMS

You can spend a few hours wandering around Rotoava, a typical Tuamotuan village of
about 450 residents, and a few more hours looking at black pearls. **Pension Havaiki** (p. 250)
operates a pearl farm on the southern end of the village. **Hinano Pearls,** 3km (2 miles)
north of the Maitai Dream Fakarava (© **98.41.51**), also welcomes visitors and will pick
up resort guests who call ahead. Neither charges admission to visit. You will have a
chance to buy pearls at both, but bear in mind that French Polynesia's wholesalers usually
scarf up the cream of the crop before you get a chance to see them. Before shelling out
any cash, see "Buying Your Black Pearl" (p. 124). I wouldn't buy set pearls here.

WHERE TO STAY

It opened after my visit, but the next time I'm on Fakarava I intend to stay at **Raimiti**
(© **55.05.65**; www.raimiti.com). On a *motu* near the atoll's southeastern corner (a 1¹/₂-hour

boat ride from the airport), it's the creation of Eric Lussiez and Florian Pilloud, who also own Residence Linareva on Moorea (p. 163). They have two simple but charming bungalows, appropriately named "Robinson" and "Crusoe." Eric was the owner-chef of Moorea's excellent Linareva Floating Restaurant, which sank a few years ago, so the food here should be very good. See the website for rates.

EXPENSIVE

Maitai Dream Fakarava   A sister of the Hotel Maitai Polynesia on Bora Bora (p. 214), this unpretentious resort was showing some wear and tear during my recent visit, but is still the top place to stay here. It sits beside the lagoon, a 15-minute ride by *le truck* or boat from the airstrip. A pier extends from the central building out over the multihued lagoon, but there are no overwater bungalows. Instead, the 28 units sit along or facing the pebbly beach, and most of their front porches have lagoon views. Built of timber with peaked shingle roofs, they are spacious and comfortably furnished with king-size and single beds, desks, and ceiling fans, and their ample bathrooms feature open-air showers with their own outside entry. The restaurant serves both indoor and outdoor tables and serves good French fare with Polynesian influences. Tahitians put on a dance show once a week. Kayaks, canoes, and snorkeling gear are free, but you'll pay for excellent lagoon excursions and diving.

B.P. 19, 98764 Fakarava. ℂ **98.43.00.** Fax 98.43.01. www.hotelmaitai.com. 28 units. 27,000CFP–44,000CFP (US$338–US$550/£171–£278). AE, MC, V. **Amenities:** Restaurant; bar; free kayaks, canoes, snorkeling gear; scooter rentals; activities desk; babysitting; laundry service. *In room:* TV, dataport, fridge, coffeemaker, safe.

INEXPENSIVE

Motu Aito Paradise ★★   If you really want to get away from it all, this pension on beach-fringed Motu Aito, on the far southern end of the atoll, is a less expensive version of Rangiroa's Kia Ora Sauvage (p. 236). It's the creation of Manihi and Tila Salmon, a local couple who lived in New Zealand—where they polished their English—before retiring to their remote corner of paradise. Manihi designed and built the thatched-roof bungalows and most of the furniture out of local materials; hence, they have enormous Polynesian charm if not luxurious amenities. Mat walls and tree limbs are everywhere. Each unit has a double bed and a single bed, both on platforms. You can pull mosquito curtains over the large open windows, although the trade winds should keep the pests at bay out here. Manihi and Tila, who are yoga enthusiasts, usually barbecue freshly caught

---

(**Moments**)   **History, Snorkeling & a Robinson Crusoe Picnic**

The most enjoyable lagoon excursion I've ever made in French Polynesia was a full-day excursion to the near ghost village of Tetamanu, on Fakarava's far southern end. After a 1¹⁄₂-hour speedboat ride from the resort, guide Coco Randal landed us at Tetamanu for a look at its early-19th-century prison ruins and restored 1834-vintage Catholic church. After petting a huge grouper and drift-snorkeling with the current inside Tuamakohua Pass, we went out for a picnic on a tiny islet completely surrounded by brilliantly pink sand. Unlike any other lagoon excursion in the Tuamotu Archipelago, this one adds a bit of history to fine snorkeling and swimming.

fish for dinner. They do not have a bar, so bring your own beer, wine, or booze. A 3-night minimum stay is required, understandable since Motu Aito is 1½-hour by truck and boat from the airport.

B.P. 12, 98763 Rotoava, Fakarava (on Motu Aito, south end of the lagoon). ✆ **41.29.00** or 74.26.13. Fax 41.29.00. www.fakarava.org. 6 units. 15,000CFP (US$188/£95) per person. Rates include all meals and airport transfers. 3-night minimum stay required. No credit cards. **Amenities:** Restaurant; free use of snorkeling gear. *In room:* No phone.

Pension Havaiki ★

Set beside the lagoon on the southern end of the village, this is the most popular pension in Rotoava—and with good reason, since most of its bungalows have front porches right on a lovely white-sand beach. Although they have plywood sides and tin roofs, inside they show traditional Polynesian style, with mat walls and ceilings over their double and single beds. The unscreened windows push out, but each bed has a mosquito net. Every unit has a modest private bathroom with cold-water shower. Owner Clotilde "Havaiki" Dariel makes sure all bungalows have fresh flowers, while her husband, Joachim, a Frenchman who speaks fluent English, tends to the family pearl farm at the end of a long pier out over the lagoon. Meals are served family-style in the dining room, and Snack-Restaurant Teanuanua is a short walk away (see "Where to Dine," below).

98763 Rotoava, Fakarava. ✆ **93.40.15.** Fax 93.40.16. www.havaiki.com. 7 units. 18,000CFP–22,000CFP (US$225–US$275/£114–£139) double. Rates include breakfast and dinner. AE, MC, V. **Amenities:** Restaurant; bar; free use of bikes and kayaks. *In room:* No phone.

Pension Paparara

A short walk north of Maitai Dream Fakarava, this is one of the oldest pensions here. Owner Corina Lenior and her English-speaking husband, Ato Lissant, have five A-frame bungalows beside the rocky lagoon shore. Two of these have tiled bathrooms, while the others share toilets and both enclosed and outdoor showers (all showers are cold-water, whether attached to a bungalow or not). If you don't mind walking on a crushed-coral floor, the choice unit has a front porch literally hanging over the lagoon; it also has a second double bed up on a mezzanine. Corina serves meals either in their house or at picnic tables under a thatch pavilion. In addition to owning a pearl farm, Ato operates Fakarava Explorer lagoon tours (see "Exploring Fakarava," above), and Fakarava Diving Center is based here.

B.P. 88, 98763 Rotoava, Fakarava. ✆/fax **98.42.66.** www.fakarava-divelodge.com. 5 units (3 with shared bathroom). 16,000CFP–19,000CFP (US$200–US$238/£101–£120) double. Rates include breakfast and dinner. MC, V. **Amenities:** Restaurant; bar; free use of kayaks; scooter and bike rentals. *In room:* No phone.

Pension Tokerau Village ★

You can see the pier sticking out from the Maitai Dream Fakarava, which is a short walk north of this pension, one of the more comfortable ones here. Owner Flora Borders, who speaks English, has four government-backed bungalows separated from a fine beach by her carefully tended garden. Colorfully decorated with Tahitian fabrics, all have shingle roofs, double beds as well as singles, private bathrooms with cold-water showers, and front porches with lagoon views. Their walls are hung with Borders family photos, including one of Flora with her father when she was 5 years old. Outsiders with reservations are welcome in Flora's open-air restaurant at the rear of the bungalows.

B.P. 53, 98763 Rotoava, Fakarava. ✆/fax **98.41.09.** tokerauvillage@mail.pf. 4 units. 11,000CFP (US$138/£70) per person. Rates include breakfast and dinner. AE, MC, V. **Amenities:** Restaurant; bar; free use of kayaks and bikes. *In room:* No phone.

Pension Vaiama Village   Rustic but charming bungalows built entirely of thatch
and other natural materials distinguish this pension, south of the Maitai Dream Fakarava. Their push-out windows are not screened, but mosquito nets hang over their double
and single beds. Each has a bathroom (with cold-water shower) in outhouse-like buildings. Meals are served at picnic tables under a thatched roof beside the lagoon. The
shoreline here is pebbly, but a lovely white-sand beach is a 5-minute walk away. Friendly
owner Dorita Amaru speaks French but not English.

B.P. 25, 98763 Rotoava, Fakarava. ⒸⒻ/fax **98.41.13.** vaiama.village@mail.pf. 4 units (all with bathroom).
19,000CFP (US$238/£120) double. Rates include breakfast and dinner. No credit cards. **Amenities:** Res-
taurant; complimentary bikes, kayaks, line fishing. *In room:* No phone.

Relais Marama   The French term *relais*, which denotes establishments between a
pension and a hotel, does not really apply to this lodging set in a coconut grove on the
sea side of Rotoava village. The accommodations consist of six small and basic bungalows
with plywood walls and thatched roofs, plus three motel-style rooms. The place is worth
mentioning, however, because you can pitch a tent in the coconut grove next to the ocean
and share toilets, cold-water showers, and the communal kitchen with other guests. The
owners—Frenchman Jacques Sauvage and Tuamotuan Marama Teanuanua—both speak
English.

B.P. 16, 98763 Rotoava, Fakarava. ⒸⒻ/fax **98.42.51.** teavanui@divingfakarava.com. 9 units (shared bathrooms). 7,000CFP–8,000CFP (US$88–US$100/£44–£51) double; 2,000CFP (US$25/£13) per person camp-
ing. No credit cards. **Amenities:** Communal kitchen; bike rentals. *In room:* No phone.

Vahitu Dream   Jacqueline Moeroa's home, on the seaside of Rotoava village, is as
much like a bed-and-breakfast as you will find here. Each of her six rooms has a double
bed with mosquito net and an electric fan, but you will share two toilets, three cold-water
showers, and a TV lounge with your fellow guests. Meals are available on request, but
you can walk to Snack-Restaurant Teanuanua (see "Where to Dine," below). Jacqueline
speaks French but not English.

B.P. 9, 98763 Rotoava, Fakarava. ⒸⒻ/fax **98.42.63.** 6 units (shared bathrooms). 3,800CFP (US$48/£24) per
person. No credit cards. **Amenities:** Restaurant; bike rentals. *In room:* No phone.

Vekeveke Village   Although it lacks charm, this pension does have two guest cottages whose front porches extend out over the lagoon, thus giving them the semblance of
overwater bungalows. They and two smaller beachside units are built of plywood with
tin roofs, and each has a bathroom with cold-water shower. The "overwater" units have
a double bed downstairs and a single bed in a loft. Meals are served in a thatched-roof
building with outdoor seating. You'll need to practice your French here, since owners
Thierry and Lenick Tau do not speak English.

B.P. 149, 98763 Rotoava, Fakarava. ⒸⒻ/fax **98.42.80.** www.pension-fakarava.com. 4 units (all w/bath-
room). 19,000CFP (US$238/£120) double. Rates include breakfast and dinner. MC, V. **Amenities:** Restau-
rant; complimentary bikes and kayaks. *In room:* No phone.

WHERE TO DINE

The **Maitai Dream Fakarava** resort and all the pensions serve meals to their guests. **Pension Havaiki** and **Pension Tokerau Village** welcome outsiders who make advance reservations (that is, before 2pm). As everywhere in the Tuamotu Islands, inquire whether
the hotel rate you're paying includes meals.

Snack-Restaurant Teanuanua FRENCH/ITALIAN   Cecile Casseville's open-air lagoonside restaurant, on the south end of the village and a short walk north of Pension Havaiki, is a fine place for lunch while you're touring Rotoava, or for a sunset drink and early dinner anytime. Cecile, a Frenchwoman who once was a tour guide on Moorea, speaks English fluently. She serves salads, burgers, *casse-croûte* sandwiches, and grilled steak and fish for lunch. Dinner sees both French and Italian preparation of steaks and fish. Like every restaurant out here in the atolls, she serves a daily fresh-fish special. I wear my bathing suit for a sunset drink at a table sitting in the lagoon.

Rotoava, south end of village. © **98.41.58.** Reservations recommended July–Aug. Burgers and sandwiches 700CFP–800CFP (US$8.75–US$10/£4.45–£5.05); main courses 1,300CFP–2,000CFP (US$16–US$25/£8.20–£13). MC, V. Daily 11:30am–2pm; Wed–Sun 6:30–8:30pm.

The Marquesas Islands

Like most sailors navigating down from California or the Panama Canal, I made my first French Polynesian landfall in the Marquesas Islands, at the country's far northeastern edge. These hauntingly beautiful islands were *really* remote 3 decades ago. Air Tahiti made the 3¹/₂-hour flight up here once every 2 weeks, and few cruise-ship passengers ever came close to the Marquesas.

A lot has changed since then. Air Tahiti now flies from Papeete every day to **Nuku Hiva** and **Hiva Oa,** the two main islands; the cruise ship *Aranui 3* comes up here every 2 weeks; and the *Tahitian Princess* and *Paul Gauguin* occasionally ply these waters (see "Seeing the Islands by Cruise Ship & Yacht," in chapter 3). To my mind, the *Aranui 3* is the best way to explore more than one or two islands up here, including **Ua Pou** and **Fatu Hiva,** two of French Polynesia's most dramatically beautiful islands (see "Exploring the Marquesas on the *Aranui 3*," below).

Some things haven't changed, for the Marquesas still seem a world apart from the rest of French Polynesia. They were the first to be settled by Polynesians, who came from Samoa around 150 B.C. and later went on to colonize Hawaii and Easter Island, the northern and eastern outposts of the great Polynesian Triangle. To this day, the Marquesan language is more like Samoan and Hawaiian than Tahitian. Instead of *"Ia orana,"* up here you are as likely to be greeted with *"Ka'oha"*—the origin of the Hawaiian *"Aloha."*

The Marquesans are proud of their ancient culture with its rich heritage of arts and crafts, especially stone sculpture, woodcarving, and tattooing. As in Samoa and Hawaii, their songs are more melodic and their dances are more graceful and not as suggestive as the hip-swinging versions in the Society Islands. Although more Marquesans now live on Tahiti than up here, those who remain are less stressed than their urbanized brethren.

The geography is different here, too. The islands lie between 7¹/₂° and 11° south latitude, placing them much closer to the Equator than Tahiti. The South Equatorial Current brings cool water from South America, however, thus both tempering the climate (it's much drier up here than in the Society Islands) and impeding the growth of coral reefs. As a result, these rugged volcanic islands drop abruptly into the sea. Many of the bays up here have beaches (many infested with biting *no-nos* [sand flies], especially on Nuku Hiva), but with little coral to form lagoons or fringing coastal plains upon which to build round-island roads, getting to them—or anywhere else, for that matter—can be major obstacles in the Marquesas.

In other words, you will be sorely disappointed if you come to the Marquesas expecting a luxurious beach vacation. But adventurous souls who like to shop for exquisite handicrafts, go hiking on spectacular paths, ride the descendants of horses brought here from Chile in the 19th century, and see some phenomenally beautiful scenery will thoroughly enjoy these remote and fascinating islands.

1 INTRODUCING THE MARQUESAS ISLANDS

Known in French as *Isles Marquises* and in the local dialects as *Te Henua Enata* and *Te Henua Enana* (literally, Land of Men), the Marquesas Islands are a 350km-long (214-mile) chain about 1,400km (850 miles) northeast of Tahiti and some 500km (305 miles) beyond the Tuamotu Archipelago. These distances alone make them seem as if you are visiting another country. In fact, they are farther away from Tahiti than the Cook Islands, the neighboring nation to the west.

The 10 main islands are all high, mountainous, and extremely rugged. They are the tops of extinct volcanoes whose ancient craters are clearly visible on topographic maps. The eroding caldera form high plateaus on some islands, and dramatic ridges fan out like spokes from the craters to form steep valleys on all of them. Black basaltic cliffs, buttresses, and stovepipe peaks seem to leap from the sea in many places.

The islands are administratively divided into northern and southern groups. **Nuku Hiva, Ua Pou,** and **Ua Huka** are the inhabited islands of the northern group. A deep ocean channel and about 80km (50 miles) separate them from the inhabited southern islands of **Hiva Oa, Tahuata,** and **Fatu Hiva.**

Nuku Hiva is the administrative center of both the archipelago and the northern group, while Hiva Oa is the capital of the southern islands. They are the only islands that are relatively easy to visit—unless you're on a cruise—and the only two with international-level accommodations.

About 9,000 people live in the Marquesas today. There were many times that number when Europeans first arrived, beginning in 1595 with the Spanish explorer Alvaro de Mendaña, who named the group for Marques Don Garcia Hurtado de Mendoza de Canete, wife of Peru's reigning viceroy. When de Mendaña departed, the population had been reduced by 200 Marquesans killed in a skirmish on Tahuata. English Capt. James Cook dropped by in 1774 and estimated 100,000 people lived on the islands. Thanks to disease, a brief Chilean slave trade, and economic opportunities elsewhere, only 2,225 people lived here in 1926. The population has been increasing thanks to a high birthrate and the Marquesas' awakening to the modern world during the 1990s.

In the absence of coastal plains, more ancient Marquesans lived up in the valleys than down by the ocean. Compared to their seaside relatives in the Society Islands and the Tuamotus, they were mountaineers, and their descendants carry an independent mountaineer streak to this day. Seeing themselves as modern stepchildren of Tahiti, many would like to separate from the rest of French Polynesia and have their own political relationship with France.

Given the steep terrain and no shortage of boulders, the ancients built platforms of stone to make both their *maraes* (*me'aes* up here) and their houses level. Their *me'aes*

Fun Facts   In the Middle of Nowhere

The Marquesas' nearest neighbors to the east are the Galápagos Islands, approximately 3,400 nautical miles away. When you're on a yacht halfway between the two, you are as far away from dry land as you can possibly be on the face of the earth.

dwarfed most *maraes* in the Society Islands and contained even larger *tohuas,* or meeting areas paved with stones. Human sacrifices were made at the *me'aes,* for the Marquesans lived an often violent, brutal life that included frequent wars between tribes followed by cannibalistic rituals. (The last known victim on Nuku Hiva was a 10- or 11-year-old girl eaten in 1924; her skull is in the American Museum of Natural History in New York.)

Stylized stone **tikis** representing ancestors and tribal gods adorned the *me'aes.* (Tiki is spelled and pronounced *ti'i* up here, but I'll keep the *k* in it for simplicity's sake.) The remaining tikis are the largest examples of the Marquesans' extraordinary skills as stone carvers and woodcarvers. Unlike the puritanical 19th-century Protestant missionaries in the Society Islands, who made the Tahitians destroy their idolatrous stone tikis, the Catholic missionaries had more faith in the heathens up here. The priests let them keep most of their tikis, but made them break off the genitalia. The castrated tikis add a delightfully ancient aspect to many Marquesan *me'aes.*

While some *paepaes* (stone housing platforms) are still in use, you will see hundreds of them deserted and overgrown up in the valleys. Coupled with the breadfruit, pandanus, and other trees the ancients planted near their platform homes, these depopulated valleys make the Marquesas Islands seem mysteriously haunted.

Exploring the Marquesas on the *Aranui 3*

Like many folks cursed with wanderlust, I have long dreamed of traveling the South Pacific on a tramp steamer, exploring remote, seldom visited islands while the ship loads and unloads its cargo. The notion has been part of South Seas lore since trading schooners started sailing the islands in the 19th century.

When American archaeologist Dr. Robert Suggs headed to Nuku Hiva to conduct research in 1956, the only way to the Marquesas was by a copra schooner that traded dry goods for dried coconut meat. With a schedule determined largely by which islands had copra ready to trade (closely guarded secrets in those days), it took him 2 weeks to sail from Tahiti to Taiohae Bay. He slept in a cramped cabin.

You can still share a cramped cabin on other interisland freighters from Papeete, but I much prefer the *Aranui 3*, a uniquely designed, 355-foot-long vessel that is half cargo ship and half modern passenger liner. "Seeing the Islands by Cruise Ship & Yacht" on p. 61 has more information.

The *Aranui 3* (the name means "Big Road") is indeed a hybrid. Christened in 2003, it was designed and built in Europe just for this purpose. Its front half carries up to 2,000 tons of cargo, while the rear half accommodates up to 200 passengers. Although not superluxurious, the very comfortable rear has a dining room serving fine French fare, a bar, a boutique, a large guest lounge, a video room, and a small outdoor swimming pool. Accommodations range from two dormitories with eight bunks each to spacious stateroom suites.

An expert accompanies most voyages, and on mine it was Dr. Suggs, who lectured about Marquesan history and culture on the ship and led excursions

GETTING TO & AROUND THE MARQUESAS

The remoteness of the islands and the scarcity of interisland transportation deserve special attention when planning your trip. It's easy to get to Hiva Oa and Nuku Hiva, since **Air Tahiti** flies to both from Papeete almost daily. One of these flights, usually on Saturday, stops in Rangiroa before going on to Hiva Oa and Nuku Hiva (in that order), so you can also fly here after visiting the Tuamotu Archipelago without having to return and connect in Papeete.

Air Tahiti's small planes connect Nuku Hiva, Hiva Oa, Ua Huka, and Ua Pou (no other Marquesan island has an airstrip), so don't be surprised if you are ferried on a smaller plane between Nuku Hiva and Hiva Oa to catch your return flight to Tahiti.

Otherwise, there is no scheduled transportation system among the Marquesas Islands. You will be on your own in tracking down one of the small boats or trading ships that irregularly connect the islands. This is relatively easy between Hiva Oa and nearby Tahuata, but not elsewhere. For this reason, I recommend taking a cruise on the *Aranui 3* or another ship to see more than Nuku Hiva and Hiva Oa in any reasonable amount of time and with as few hassles as possible.

See "Getting Around Tahiti & French Polynesia" and "Seeing the Islands by Cruise Ship & Yacht," in chapter 3, for more information.

to the *me'aes* and other historic sites, some of which he excavated for the American Museum of Natural History in the 1950s. Among his books are *The Archaeology of Nuku Hiva, Marquesas Islands, French Polynesia* (1961). In 2000, he coauthored (with Burgl Lichtenstein) *Manuiota'a: Journal of a Voyage to the Marquesas Islands,* a highly readable account of their cruise on the previous *Aranui.* It's packed with information about the islands.

We left Tahiti on a Saturday morning and arrived at Fakarava the next morning for 2 hours of snorkeling in that great lagoon. After spending the rest of Sunday and all of Monday at sea (the *Aranui 3* rolls a bit on the open ocean, but my scopolamine patch prevented seasickness), we arrived for sunrise behind the phenomenal spires atop Ua Pou, our first Marquesan landfall. The nimble crew unloaded everything, from Toyota pickup trucks to toilet paper, while we explored Hakahau village on foot (comfortable walking shoes are a must) and were treated to a dance show and lunch ashore. That afternoon, the *Aranui 3* moved around to Hakahetau village on Ua Pou's northwest coast, then sailed to Taiohae Bay on Nuku Hiva for the night.

And so it went for 10 more days as we visited Hiva Oa (twice), Fatu Hiva, Tahuata, Ua Huka, and back to Nuku Hiva and Ua Pou prior to returning to Tahiti via a full-day's picnic at Rangiroa.

Thanks to the *Aranui 3* and her marvelous Polynesian crew, I had lived my tramp steamer dream—in anything but a cramped cabin.

VISITOR INFORMATION

Tahiti Tourisme in Papeete distributes information about the Marquesas (see "Visitor Information," in chapter 3). Nuku Hiva and Hiva Oa both have local tourism committees, which have joined together to host a website at **www.marquises.pf**. The committees have visitor information offices on both islands (see the "Fast Facts" sections for Nuku Hiva, below, and Hiva Oa, later in this chapter).

2 NUKU HIVA ★★

Although it appeared on the world's television screens in 2002 as the setting of the fourth *Survivor* series, Nuku Hiva first became famous in the 1840s, when Herman Melville jumped ship and was befriended for several weeks by the otherwise ferocious Taipi tribe in the rugged **Taipivai Valley.** Based on that adventure, Melville's first novel, *Typee,* launched his illustrious writing career.

Then as now, Nuku Hiva is the largest of the Marquesas Islands and the second largest in French Polynesia. It is so rugged that a majority of its 330 sq. km (127 sq. miles) surely go straight up and down. Two volcanoes formed Nuku Hiva. The large central crater has eroded away on one side, leaving in its bottom the high, cool **Toovii Plateau,** now

Be Prepared to Be Flexible

Some of Air Tahiti's flights from Papeete to the Marquesas stop first at Hiva Oa before going on to Nuku Hiva. The airstrip on Hiva Oa sits high up on a ridge and can be closed due to fog or rain, especially from March through August. When that happens, the plane skips Hiva Oa and goes directly to Nuku Hiva. Accordingly, pay close attention to the airline's schedule when planning your trip. And always be prepared to be flexible up here.

devoted to farms and pastureland. On the southern coast, half of another crater fell into the sea, creating deep **Taiohae Bay,** the best harbor in the Marquesas and a favorite port for cruising yachts. On the northern side of the crater, **Mount Muake** abruptly rises for 864m (2,834 ft.), forming an awesome backdrop to the town of **Taiohae,** the capital of the archipelago, and its half-moon harbor. Other than arriving by water, the only way into Taiohae is to descend Mount Mauke's clifflike face.

The central mountains cut off what trade winds blow at this latitude, leaving the western third of Nuku Hiva a desert, known as the **Terre Déserte (Deserted Land).** Rather than being lush and green, the valleys here are dry canyons reminiscent of the American Southwest and the Australian Outback. With the exception of a few cattle ranches and homes near the airport, this area is quite literally deserted.

GETTING AROUND NUKU HIVA

The **Nuku Ataha Airport** is on Nuku Hiva's dry northwestern corner, 48km (29 miles) from Taiohae. A vehicle will be sent from your accommodations to meet you for about 8,000CFP (US$100/£51) per person round-trip. From the airport, it's a tiring ride of about 2 hours on the winding road that climbs up and down two steep mountain ridges and across the Toovii Plateau before descending into Taiohae. (You did not misread me; it takes 2 hours to go 48km/29 miles.) Add that to the 3¹/₂-hour flight from Papeete, and you can easily eat up a day just getting to Taiohae. There is some great scenery along the way, however, so I look at the ride from the airport to Taiohae as just another four-wheel-drive excursion.

Nuku Hiva is the place to get carsick. Although the government is slowly paving them, all of its few roads are narrow, winding, and often treacherous, especially when wet. In places, they are literally blasted into the sides of cliffs. If you miss one of the many 180-degree hairpin curves, you could plunge more than 1,000 feet to your ultimate demise. For this reason, I recommend exploring by guided tour rather than rental vehicle (see "Exploring Nuku Hiva," below). If you insist on taking your life into your own hands, **Europcar** (⟨©⟩/fax **92.04.89;** www.europcar-tahiti.com) and **Pension Moana Nui** (© **92.03.30;** http://pensionmoananui.ifrance.com), both in Taiohae, rent four-wheel-drive vehicles for about 12,500CFP (US$156/£79) per day. I warned you, though, so don't sue me if you drive off a cliff.

There is no regular taxi service on Nuku Hiva as such, but several locals will take you about in their four-wheel-drive vehicles. The arrangements can be made through your accommodations, or contact **Nuku Hiva Transports** (© **92.06.08**), **Huku Tours** (© **92.04.89**), or **Rose Marie Tours** (© **92.05.96**). Fares depend on how far you want to go, so be sure to agree on a price before setting out.

THE MARQUESAS ISLANDS

12 NUKU HIVA

ACCOMMODATIONS ■

He'e Tai Inn **13**
Keikahanui Nuku Hiva
    Pearl Lodge **15**
Paahatea Nui (Chez Julienne) **12**
Pension Mave Mai **10**
Pension Moana Nui **9**

ATTRACTIONS ●

Anaho Bay **2**
CascadeTevaipo **6**
Cathédrale de Notre-Dame
    des Marquises (Notre Dame
    Cathedral of the Marquesas) **8**
Hakaui Valley **7**
Hatiheu **3**
Hatiheu Bay **1**
Hikokua, Kamuihei &
    Teiipoka Me'aes **3**
Hooumi **5**
Monument de Herman Melville
    (Herman Melville Memorial) **11**
Taetae Tupuna He'e Tai
    (Rose Corser's Boutique
    and Museum of Marquesan
    Culture) **14**
Taipivai Valley **4**

Residents of the outlying villages are as likely to travel by **boat** as they are by vehicle. Several individuals rent crewed boats to take you from place to place, such as from Taiohae around to the Hakaui Valley, or from Hatiheu to Anaho on the north shore. Ask at your accommodations to arrange a boat, or contact the local tourism committee for advice (see "Visitor Information" under "Fast Facts: Nuku Hiva," below). The boats moor at the marina on the eastern side of Taiohae Bay.

ⒻFast Facts Nuku Hiva

The following facts apply specifically to Nuku Hiva. For more information, see "Fast Facts: Tahiti & French Polynesia," in appendix A.

Currency Exchange **Banque Socredo** has an office on the waterfront in Taiohae. The ATM is inside the building, so you'll have to come here during banking hours: Monday through Friday from 7:30 to 11:30am and 1:30 to 4pm.

Drugstores **Pharmacie Nuku Hiva,** on the western side of Taiohae (ⓒ **91.00.90**), is open Monday through Friday from 8:30am to noon and 3 to 5pm, Saturday from 9 to 11am.

Emergencies & Police The **emergency police** phone number is ⓒ **17.** The phone number of the **gendarmerie** in Taiohae is ⓒ **92.03.61.**

Healthcare Taiohae has a government **hospital** (ⓒ **91.02.00**), and Haitiheu and Taipivai villages both have **infirmaries.**

Internet Access The island's one hotel and some of its pensions have Internet access for their guests, or you can go to the post and telecommunications office (see below). **Nuku Hiva Yacht Services** (ⓒ **91.01.50;** anneragu@hotmail.com) has access for cruising yachts.

Post Office The post and telecommunications office in Taiohae is uphill between the small boat marina and the cruise-ship port. It's open Monday through Thursday from 7:30 to 11:30am and noon to 3:30pm, Friday to 4:30pm.

Telephone There are *télécarte* phones at the Taiohae post and telecommunications office, at the small boat marina, at the ship dock, on the waterfront near the Kovivi restaurant, and in Hatiheu and Taipivai villages. As in the Tuamotu Archipelago, Nuku Hiva residents are more likely to write their phone numbers in two groups rather than three (for example, 920 000 instead of 92.00.00).

Visitor Information The **Comité du Tourisme de Nuku Hiva,** B.P. 32, 98742 Nuku Hiva (ⓒ **92.03.73;** fax 92.03.25; www.marquises.pf), has a visitor information office near the Taiohae *mairie* (town hall). Its hours are irregular, so call ahead.

Water Don't drink the tap water on Nuku Hiva. The grocery stores sell bottled water.

EXPLORING NUKU HIVA

Given the sometimes dangerous condition of the roads and the difficulty of finding things on Nuku Hiva, I recommend seeing the sights on a guided tour. The best are offered by the **Keikahanui Nuku Hiva Pearl Lodge** (p. 264), which offers a full-day tour to the Taipivai Valley and Hatiheu for about 14,000CFP (US$175/£89) per person, including lunch at Chez Yvonne. It also has a half-day version that goes as far as the Taipivai. The lodge's guides speak English.

Another option is **Pua Excursions** (© **92.06.87**; www.puaexcursions.pf). Owner Georges "Pua" Taupotini will arrange excursions by land as well as on foot and horseback.

TAIOHE

It's easy to explore the town of Taiohae on foot, since its main street follows the curving shoreline of Taiohae Bay for about 3.5km (2 miles).

While most other cruise ships anchor out in the harbor, the *Aranui 3* docks at the main wharf on the eastern side of the bay. The town hall, wharf, post office, visitor information office, and hospital are in the original French settlement on the eastern side of the bay behind **Tu Hiva,** a hill where U.S. Navy Commodore David Porter built a fort in 1813. Porter used Taiohae as a temporary base from which he raided British shipping in the Pacific during the War of 1812. He named this outpost Fort Madison, in honor of then U.S. President James Madison. The French renamed the spot Fort Collette after they took over in 1842. Nothing remains on the hill today except wild goats and a navigation marker.

Most commercial activity is in the middle of town, or just east of where the airport road comes down off the Mount Muake cliff. The junction is marked by a large seaside cross in honor of the first Catholic mission here.

Follow the next road west inland into the Meau Valley and you'll see the *Cathédrale de Notre-Dame des Marquises* (**Notre Dame Cathedral of the Marquesas**). The gate to the compound was part of a wall from the original 19th-century church, but this modern version was built in 1977. Be sure to go inside and see the marvelous stone carvings and woodcarvings that each island donated to the cathedral. The pulpit and Stations of the Cross are elaborately carved from single trunks of *tamanu* (ironwood, or Australian pine). The artists gave the biblical stories a Marquesan touch. St. Paul holds a spear instead of his Sword of Damascus, the breadfruit substitutes as the olive tree, and Hinano beer is depicted as one of the seven deadly sins!

Farther up the valley is a restored *me'ae.*

On the west side of the bay, you'll pass a large park and then the *Monument de Herman Melville* (**Herman Melville Memorial**), a terrific wooden sculpture executed in 1991 by noted local artisan Kahee Taupotini. There's a fine view from here back along the bay. This side of the bay is skirted by a black-sand beach, where locals go swimming and launch their racing canoes. For a bit of refreshment and another excellent view, head up the hill to the Keikahanui Nuku Hiva Pearl Lodge (p. 264).

THE TAIPIVAI VALLEY ★★

My most memorable day on Nuku Hiva was spent traveling to the rugged northeastern side of the island in the company of a tour guide. Although it's hardly more than 25km (15 miles) to the end of the road, this excursion required a full day, a good part of it spent just getting from place to place. This is the top trip for anyone to make, since most of Nuku Hiva's key sites are here, especially Melville's **Taipivai Valley** and the highly picturesque northeast shore village of **Hatiheu.** From Hatiheu, you can hike or take a boat to one of the few coral reefs in the Marquesas, at **Anaho** on the island's northeastern corner.

After climbing up Mount Muake out of Taiohae (there's an unbelievably beautiful view of Taiohae Bay from the top), the road follows a mountain ridge, from which you can see one of the beaches used in *Survivor.* It then steeply descends down to **Taipivai** village, at the head of Controller Bay. From there, another coastal road goes southeast to **Hooumi,** a small village on yet another bay. Since access across Hooumi's white-sand beach is easy, some cruise-ship passengers land here rather than at Taipivai, beside the shallow Taipivai River.

The paved road retraces Herman Melville's footsteps up into the steep **Taipivai Valley.** Your guide will stop about halfway up the valley at restored *paepaes* (stone platforms), the only remnants of the village where Melville reputedly stayed for a few weeks after he deserted an American whaler in 1842. In *Typee,* Melville has his protagonist fall in love with a local beauty, Fayaway, after being captured by the powerful Taipi tribe. Instead of sticking around, he escapes after watching a cannibal ceremony. In reality, the Taipi were friendly and treated Melville well. You'll see several waterfalls off in the distance as you climb higher into the valley.

HATIHEU ★★★

Once out of the valley, you will soon be looking down at **Hatiheu,** one of my favorite villages in all of French Polynesia. It sits in a little bay beside a curving black-sand beach. A Moorea-esque ridge topped by basaltic stovepipes dramatically looms over the western end of the beach, creating a quintessentially South Seas scene. Dating to 1872, a white statute of the Virgin Mary stands atop a cliff overlooking the bay. The best view of the bay is from the stone wharf on the eastern side (follow the dirt road along the shore-line).

Like me, Robert Louis Stevenson was quite fond of Hatiheu and its spectacular setting when he sailed here in 1888. (Great minds do think alike!)

HIKOKUA, KAMUIHEI & TEIIPOKA ME'AES ★★★

Among several restored *me'aes* in the Marquesas, three of the most impressive are **Hikokua, Kamuihei,** and **Teiipoka,** on the Taipivai road above Hatiheu. **Hikokua** is a large open area used for ceremonies, dances, and human sacrifices. Restored for the 1999 Marquesas Festival of the Arts, it has impressive tiki statues. The Kamuihei and Teiipoka sites flank the road higher up in the valley. The expansive Kamuihei part is definitely worth exploring, for it has well-preserved tikis, petroglyphs carved into huge boulders (no one knows what they mean), and a pit under an enormous banyan tree, in which human sacrifices were said to have been restrained prior to being dispatched (it's more likely they were used to store food for feasts or to ferment breadfruit *poi,* one of the

---

(Tips) **Lunch at Yvonne's**

Whether on a tour or on your own, plan to have lunch in Hatiheu at **Restaurant Hinako Nui,** at Yvonne Katupa's **Chez Yvonne** pension across the road from the beach (✆ **92.02.97;** hinakonui@mail.pf). This thatched-roof charmer specializes in fresh seafood, including delicious shrimp beignets and char-grilled tropical lobster. Everything comes with fresh local vegetables and breadfruit fritters, and dessert is often flambéed bananas. Main courses range from 1,500CFP to 3,000CFP (US$19–US$38/£9.50–£19). If you decide to stay overnight, Yvonne has five simple bungalows to rent in the gardens behind the restaurant for 18,000CFP (US$225/£114) double, including all meals. Bring cash, since Yvonne does not accept credit cards.

Ⓕun Facts   **Be Careful Around this Tiki**

If you are thinking of infertility treatments, you can save a bundle by visiting Hikokua, the restored *marae* near Hatiheu village. Hikokua has a carved tiki in the shape of a phallus. Any woman who touches it, legend says, will soon become pregnant.

Polynesians' favorite desserts, which kept well in times of drought). Dr. Robert Suggs, the American archaeologist who often serves as guest lecturer on the *Aranui 3* and the *Paul Gauguin*, discovered human skulls and leg bones in the banyan tree when he excavated the site in 1956 and 1957. The large sizes of these structures are a testament to how many people once lived in this now-deserted valley.

ANAHO ★★

Across a ridge east of Hatiheu, the small village of **Anaho** sits beside a palm-fringed, white-sand beach in yet another bay visited by Robert Louis Stevenson in 1888. Anaho is unusual, however, because it has one of the few coral formations in the Marquesas, a fringing reef off the beach over which you can snorkel. The sand beach has the usual contingent of biting sand flies, so I wear both insect repellent and sunscreen.

Although seldom used by ships these days, **Anaho Bay** is one of the best natural harbors in the Marquesas. In October 1943, an accidental fire severely damaged the cruiser USS *Concord*, which anchored here while carrying Rear Admiral Richard Byrd—of arctic exploration fame—on a mission to find World War II anchorages and potential airfields for the U.S. Navy. Byrd and the *Concord* survived, but 26 American sailors killed in the fire were given seamen's burials in the bay.

You can hire a boat at Chez Yvonne in Hatiheu (see "Lunch at Yvonne's," above) for the 10-minute ride around to Anaho, or hike over the saddle between the two bays. The path starts at a crossroads about 100m (328 ft.) east of the restaurant. The rather strenuous hike takes about 45 minutes each way, but you'll have a nice view of Anaho Bay from atop 218m-high (720-ft.) Teavaimaoaoa Pass.

HAKAUI VALLEY & AHUII WATERFALL

Over Mount Muake to the west of Taiohae, the **Hakaui Valley** is home to the **Cascade Tevaipo**, one of the world's highest waterfalls at 350m (1,159 ft.). The waterfall pours off a high plateau at the head of the valley. This area was a prime set for the *Survivor* television show. The trail from Taiohae into the valley is too dangerous for hiking, but your accommodations can arrange a boat to take you around to Hakaui, from where an ancient stone trail goes upriver to the falls, about a 2-hour walk. Or you can ride horseback from Taiohae (see "Hiking & Horseback Riding," below). Bring food, water, and insect repellent, and wear shoes suitable for fording the river.

HIKING & HORSEBACK RIDING

Nuku Hiva has a number of fine beaches, such as those at Hatiheu and Anaho (see "Exploring Nuku Hiva," above), and there's a black-sand beach on the western side of Taiohae Bay. Unfortunately, they are all infested with biting *no-nos* (sand flies). These nearly invisible pests are particularly aggressive at dusk. If you do go swimming, try to pick a day when the wind is blowing in from offshore, and always lather up with insect repellent.

You will have a pretty good hike just walking along the shoreline of Taiohae village. For something a great deal more strenuous, climb the airport road to the top of Mount Muake for its view down over the bay.

In the old days, Marquesans got around by boat or by trails up and over the mountains. Many of these old tracks still exist. One of them begins at the Taetae Tupuna He'e Tai (see "Rose Corser & Marquesan Art," p. 265), just downhill from the Keikahanui Nuku Hiva Pearl Lodge (p. 264), and goes for 3.5km (2 miles) into **Collette Bay.** The usually deserted beach over there is a fine place for a picnic, but remember to bring—and apply!—your insect repellent.

Marquises Rando (✆ **92.07.13** or 21.08.74; www.marquisesrando.com) provides professional guides for individuals or groups. Its prices range from 6,600CFP (US$83/£42) per person for a 2¹/₂-hour hike to 12,000CFP (US$150/£76) for a 6¹/₂-hour trek, including lunch and transportation to and from the trail heads.

HORSEBACK RIDING

In the 19th century, European whalers and traders brought horses to the Marquesas—plus cattle, pigs, and goats—which soon became wild and had a serious impact on native flora and fauna. You are unlikely to encounter a wild pig on Nuku Hiva these days, and most cattle are confined to ranches on the Toovii Plateau, but you will see horses along the roads and goats prowling the rocky mountainsides.

The strong, capable Marquesas horses are prized throughout French Polynesia, and you horse devotees will have rode their cousins on Moorea and Huahine. You can ride them here on many of the ancient trails, such as to Hakaui Valley and the Ahuii waterfall.

Up on the plateau just north of Taiohae, Patrice Tamarii of **Le Ranch** (✆ **92.06.35;** danigo@mail.pf) rents horses, leads trail rides, and has 1- to 3-night horseback trips to the north shore, where you camp on beaches. **Alphonse and Sabine Teikiteetini** (✆ **92. 01.52** or 21.24.15; tourisme@marquises.pf) lead half- and full-day rides; contact them for reservations and prices.

WHERE TO STAY & DINE

During my recent visit, Rose Corser was in the process of building **He'e Tai Inn** (✆ **91. 03.00;** rose.corser@mail.pf), an eight-unit hotel next to her museum on the western side of Taiohae Bay (see "Rose Corser & Marquesan Art," p. 265). The motel-style rooms will be air-conditioned, and the inn will have a restaurant and bar—the latter with daily happy hours for cruising yachties and other visitors. Rose said she plans to charge about 10,000CFP (US$125/£63) for a double, including continental breakfast, and will accept MasterCard and Visa credit cards.

You can stay away from Taiohae at **Chez Yvonne,** in Hatiheu village, home of the charming Restaurant Hinako Nui (see "Lunch at Yvonne's," p. 262).

All accommodations here have meal plans. The restaurants at **Keikahanui Nuku Hiva Pearl Lodge** and **Pension Moana Nui** are open to the public, but reservations are advised.

For inexpensive fare, a *roulotte* sets up on the waterfront next to Magasin Kamake (look for the big "Lotto" sign). See "Don't Miss *Les Roulottes*" (p. 140) for more information.

EXPENSIVE

Keikahanui Nuku Hiva Pearl Lodge ★ Sitting on a hill with a fine view of Taiohe Bay, this is one of the two international-level hotels in the Marquesas Islands, its sister on Hiva Oa being the other. The entire complex blends so well into its natural setting that

Rose Corser & Marquesan Art

Rose Corser and her late husband, Frank, sailed their yacht from California to Nuku Hiva in 1972 to study Marquesan art and culture for a master's degree Rose had in the works. It was a great subject to study, since the islands are justly famous for both their unique culture and their long history of extraordinary art and handicrafts.

More than any other South Pacific islanders, the ancient Marquesans were masters at carving tikis from stone and wooden war clubs and spears from local hardwoods, adorning the latter with the same intricate geometric designs used in their tattoos (which covered most of their bodies) and on the tapa cloth they made from the bark of the paper mulberry tree. Their carving skill was evident even in everyday items such as bowls, axes, pestles, and fishhooks.

The old crafts have been preserved to a remarkable degree, especially carvings made of stone, wood, and bone. The Cathédrale de Notre-Dame des Marquises and the Monument de Herman Melville in Taiohae both are terrific examples (see "Exploring Nuku Hiva," above).

You will come across artisans carving away in their shops in both Taiohae on Nuku Hiva and Atuona on Hiva Oa, and many villages have *centres artisanal* (artisan centers) where the crafts are for sale, especially when cruise ships are in port. The best items are often sold in Papeete, however, especially during the *Heiva Nui* festival in July and at special Marquesan art exhibitions.

Rose and Frank Corser went back to the United States after their 1972 voyage, but they returned for good in 1979. Rose never finished her master's degree, but she founded the marvelous **Taetae Tupuna He'e Tai ★★★ (© 92.03.82** or 91.03.00), also known as Rose Corser's Boutique and Museum of Marquesan Culture, just downhill from the Keikahanui Nuku Hiva Pearl Lodge in Taiohae. Not only is it the best place to buy Marquesan art, but it's also a terrific museum. Here you will see artifacts dating from the Polynesian settlement period of about a.d. 150 to the 1800s. Many of the ancient pieces are on loan from Marquesan families, who have owned them since the dawn of Polynesian time. The carvings, tapa-cloth paintings, grain-seed necklaces, and *kumu hei* (a local lei made of fragrant plants) and other items on sale are all unique pieces of art, not handicrafts. Indeed, Rose's museum is a required stop on your visit to the Marquesas Islands.

you hardly notice the shingle roofs when looking this way from Taiohae Bay. Local artisans contributed woodcarvings and tapa cloth to the central building and to each of the 20 bungalows, thus giving the entire property a distinctly Marquesan character. The high-ceiling central building with restaurant, bar, and swimming pool overlooks the bay, as do most of the bungalows (room rates here vary by the quality of each unit's view). Each bungalow has a full picture window in front to take advantage of the bay or garden view, plus a covered porch with wooden lounge chairs. All are equipped with king-size beds and bathrooms with tiled showers. The restaurant, understandably, is the best on the island.

B.P. 53, 98742 Taiohae, Nuku Hiva (western side of Taiohae town). ☎ **800/657-3275** or 92.07.10. Fax 92.07.11. www.pearlresorts.com. 20 units. 28,000CFP–39,500CFP (US$350–US$494/£177–£250) bungalow. AE, DC, MC, V. **Amenities:** Restaurant; bar; outdoor pool; activities desk; bicycle rentals; limited room service; laundry service. *In room:* A/C, TV, dataport, minibar, coffeemaker, hair dryer, safe.

INEXPENSIVE

Paahatea Nui (Chez Julienne)   Also opposite the black-sand beach on the western side of Taiohae, Julienne and Justin Mahiatapu rent three rooms in their house and have six shingled-roof bungalows in their tropical gardens. All of the bungalows and one of the rooms have private bathrooms with hot-water showers, while two in-house rooms share toilets and showers. One family-size bungalow has a kitchen. Guests here are served breakfast, but no other meals.

B.P. 201, 98742 Taiohae, Nuku Hiva. ☎/fax **92.00.97.** paahateanui@mail.pf. 9 units (2 with shared bathroom). 8,000CFP (US$100/£51) double room; 10,000CFP (US$125/£63) bungalow. No credit cards. *In room:* Kitchen (1 unit); no phone.

Pension Mave Mai   On a hillside between the boat docks and the center of Taiohae, Régina and Jean-Claude Tata's pension boasts some of the better-equipped rooms here, with air-conditioning, ceiling fans, balconies or patios, and small private bathrooms with hot-water showers. They occupy a modern, two-story motel-like building, with half the units upstairs, half down. Two units have kitchens. Guests can lounge and have meals on a large patio overlooking the bay.

B.P. 378, 98742 Taiohae, Nuku Hiva. ☎/fax **92.08.10.** pension-mavemai@mail.pf. 6 units. 8,000CFP (US$100/£51) double. AE, MC, V. *In room:* A/C; kitchen (2 units); no phone.

Pension Moana Nui   Across the main drag from the bay in the center of Taiohae, this pension is sometimes called the Hôtel Moana Nui, and with good reason, since it doubles as Nuku Hiva's commercial hotel for business types who can't afford the Keikahanui Nuku Hiva Pearl Lodge. The upstairs rooms have televisions (a rarity here), narrow balconies, and private bathrooms with hot-water showers. Four of them are air-conditioned. The owners also rent an air-conditioned bungalow. The pleasant, open-air restaurant serves good pizzas and French fare, but I was not impressed with the island-style dishes such as shrimp in coconut-curry sauce.

B.P. 33, 98742 Taiohae, Nuku Hiva. ☎/fax **92.03.30.** http://pensionmoananui.ifrance.com. 8 units. 6,500CFP (US$81/£41) double. MC, V. **Amenities:** Restaurant; bar; car rental. *In room:* A/C (5 units), TV, no phone.

3 UA HUKA ★★

Sitting 42km (26 miles) due east of Nuku Hiva and one-quarter its size, Ua Huka may be the least visually appealing of the major Marquesas Islands, but to my mind it is one of the more interesting from both artistic and cultural standpoints. Some of the most talented woodcarvers and sculptors in French Polynesia live and work on Ua Huka, and the island's 600 or so local residents are so proud to be Marquesan that they have established not one but *four* museums explaining their indigenous culture. They also have planted the territory's only botanical garden beyond Tahiti.

The success of its carvers and sculptors has made Ua Huka one of the most prosperous islands in the Marquesas. An acquaintance of mine told me of her sculptor brother

Centre Artisanal de Hane (Art Center of Hane) **3**
Jardin Botanique Communal de Vaipaee
 (Community Botanical Garden of Vaipaee) **2**
Me'ae Meiaiaute **4**
Musée Communal de Ua Huka
 (Community Museum of Ua Huka) **1**
Musée de la Mer (Museum of the Sea) **3**
Oho'au ke'a Ha'atiki (House of Petroglyphs) **5**

coming from Ua Huka to Tahiti to buy a new vehicle. When he and the dealer had agreed on a price, he opened his backpack and counted out the purchase price—in cash! Despite its not having a bank in which he could deposit his money, Ua Huka has three times more motor vehicles per capita than any other Marquesan island—and its only road is fully paved.

Ua Huka is the top of an extinct volcano, whose southern half either exploded or fell into the sea, leaving two-thirds of a small crater and half of a large one. Only the tops of the mountains along the craters' rims get reliable rainfall, and only their upper slopes and the river- and stream-fed valleys are green. It wasn't like this in 1813, when American Admiral David Porter described lush vegetation and fertile, populated valleys.

All of the island's inhabitants live along the desertlike southern shore, which is made even more brown and barren than it would naturally be by wild horses and feral goats. Together they have destroyed much of the native vegetation outside the valleys. (The flip side of that coin is that horseback riding is easy to arrange, and some of the goats wind up in a decent local curry.)

(Fun Facts) **An Offshore Ruckus**

One way ancient Polynesian navigators discovered islands in the vast Pacific Ocean was to follow birds to their land-based nests. This must have been true of Ua Huka, for millions of sooty terns (*kaveka* in the local language) nest on **Teuaua** and **Hemini,** small islands just off its southwestern coast. These huge avian flocks create such a ruckus that you can hear them from ships as you pass nearby—and if the wind is right, you can smell them, too! Locals have installed a rope ladder up Teuaua's clifflike sides so they can collect *kaveka* eggs, which reportedly taste like sardines, from nests on the flat top. Cone-shaped Hemini, however, is off-limits.

EXPLORING UA HUKA

Ua Huka's three villages and all of its points of interest are on or near its south shore. A paved road runs the 13km (8 miles) from **Vaipaee** village in the west through **Hane** to **Hokatu** in the east. Vaipaee is the administrative center, although Hane is the larger of the villages. The post office and main infirmary are at Vaipaee, but I repeat: There is no bank on Ua Pou.

Nor is there public transportation, although many locals will gladly take you around the island in their ubiquitous vehicles. The **Ua Huka Airport** sits elevated above sea level on a plateau about halfway between Vaipaee and Hane. Your pension will arrange to meet your flight if you have reservations.

Your pension will arrange horseback riding, or you can contact **Alexis Fournier** (© 92. 660.05) or **Edmond Lichtlé** (© 92.60.87).

VAIPAEE

Ua Huka's only safe harbor is at Vaipaee, and quite a harbor it is. A narrow fjord leads from the sea, and virtually hides the village and its black-sand beach at the head of a small bay. The bay is so shallow that the *Aranui 3*—but not larger vessels—must pivot completely around and moor out in the fjord with its bow facing back out to sea. There is barely enough room for the ship to turn around without hitting the cliffs on either side of the fjord. We all got up early on the *Aranui 3* to watch this remarkable maneuver, a testament to the skipper's ability with the helm and throttle.

A short walk inland leads to the island's post office and administrative offices, behind which is the small but exceptional **Musée Communal de Ua Huka (Community Museum of Ua Huka)** ★★★ (© 92.60.13). Here is a remarkable collection of artifacts such as *adzes* (primitive stone axes), fishhooks, drums, war clubs, earrings, and necklaces. Be sure to go to the back, where one exhibit displays a prehistoric Polynesian kitchen and another re-creates a remote burial cave complete with an original canoe (which held the deceased's bones) and a wooden vase (which held the skull). The seashell collection is notable. Best of all are several tikis carved by Joseph Tehau Vaatete, the museum's custodian and Ua Huka's most noted carver. Since many of the best original tikis were removed from the island by collectors or traders, Joseph painstakingly re-created them based on photographs taken during a 1920s expedition by the Bishop Museum in Hawaii. Some of those photos are on display, too. An adjacent handicrafts shop sells some of the best woodcarvings I have seen in the Marquesas. The museum and shop are always open when cruise ships are here; at other times, ask at your pension about arranging a visit. Admission is free, but donations are accepted.

At Papuakeikaha, between Vaipaee and the airstrip, **Jardin Botanique Communal de Vaipaee (Community Botanical Garden of Vaipaee; ✆ 92.61.51)** was created in 1974 in an effort to protect and preserve the native flora, which was quickly disappearing into the mouths of Ua Huka's wild goats. The collection has steadily grown to include exotic plants from elsewhere, plus groves of citrus trees. Unfortunately, the examples are not labeled. There's a small aviary here, and this is a good place to watch for several native species of birds. The garden is open Monday to Friday from 6:30am to 4:30pm, on weekends by request. Admission is free.

HANE

The attractive village of Hane begins at a beach and climbs into a valley created by its own volcanic crater. Archaeologists have dated pottery fragments found in a sand dune near the beach to about 150 b.c., making this one of the earliest examples of human habitation in French Polynesia. A paved road and shady parks now skirt the shore of this picturesque half-moon bay. The beach fringing the bay here is good for swimming and snorkeling, or just sitting back and watching local men carry heavy bags of copra out to whale boats sent ashore by other trading boats.

At the T-intersection near the center of the bayside promenade, the **Musée de la Mer (Museum of the Sea; ✆ 92.60.13)** displays ancient canoes, fishhooks, and nets, plus re-created examples of canoe prows. It shares a building and phone number with the **Centre Artisanal de Hane (Art Center of Hane),** where you can buy excellent woodcarvings and stone carvings as well as *tivaivai,* the handmade appliqué quilts local women have been making since missionaries taught them how to sew in the 19th century. Both the museum and crafts shop are open when cruise ships are here; otherwise by appointment. Admission is free.

Super carver and community museum custodian Joseph Tehau Vaatete has his open-air studio on the paved road heading inland from the museum (✆ **92.60.13**). Joseph accepts commissions and will ship your piece to you.

Keep walking about 30 minutes uphill on the paved road, a dirt path, and then concrete stairs to **Me'ae Meiaiaute,** the most important ancient temple on Ua Huka. Although its stone platforms have not been restored, and some of its four tikis are damaged, the site commands a splendid view back down over the coastline.

HOKATU

From Hane, the main road reduces to one paved lane and climbs around a steep headland (if one vehicle meets another on this stretch, one must either back up or fall off a cliff!) before descending into another small bay and picturesque little Hokatu. The village's main street is lined with hibiscus, bougainvillea, and other flowers, but the beach consists entirely of black rocks and gravel. Rather than trying to swim, spend your time at the local handicrafts shop known as **Huau Ote Papatuhuna** (no phone), which has a wide selection, and observing the remarkable plaster re-creations of ancient petroglyphs found on Ua Huka in **Oho'au ke'a Ha'atiki (House of Petroglyphs; ✆ 92.60.55).** Explanatory labels under the petroglyphs are written in both French and English. The shop and petroglyphs museum are open when cruise ships are in port; otherwise by appointment. Admission is free to both.

Ua Huka has no hotels, only four family-run pensions. All serve meals, but none accepts credit cards, nor do they have post office boxes. Write to them simply at 98744 Vaipaee, Ua Huka, or you can make reservations at www.haere-mai.pf.

Le Réve Marquisien (©/fax **92.61.84;** revemarquisien@mail.pf) is in Pahataua Valley about 1km (a half-mile) from Vaipaee. Owners Marie-France and Charles Aunoa have four bungalows with private bathrooms and TVs. They charge about 12,000CFP (US$150/£76) double for these luxuries.

Karen Taiaapu-Fournier's **Pension Mana Tupuna Village** (©/fax **92.60.08;** mana tupuna@mail.pf), on a hillside overlooking Vaipaee, has three bungalows with private bathrooms (hot-water showers). Karen charges about 14,000CFP (US$175/£89) double, including breakfast and dinner.

Auberge Hitikau (©/fax **92.61.74**), in Hane village, is more like a motel than the others. It has three rooms (with shared bathrooms) adjacent to the open-air **Restaurant Chez Fournier,** where Celine Fournier serves lunch to cruise-ship passengers, including goat curry and an unusual *poisson cru* made with mayonnaise instead of coconut milk. Rates are about 3,500CFP (US$44/£22) double.

In Hakatu village, Maurice and Delphine Rootuehine have five bungalows with private bathrooms at their **Chez Maurice et Delphine** (©/fax **92.60.55**). Their tin-roof bungalows have fine views from their porches down over Hakatu's narrow valley and small bay. They charge 3,000CFP (US$38/£19) per person.

4 UA POU ★★★

About 40km (25 miles) south of Nuku Hiva, Ua Pou is one of the most dramatically beautiful islands in French Polynesia. I was awe-struck when I first saw it from the deck of the *Aranui 3* as we approached at dawn from the southwest. Before us, the triangular, cloud-topped peak of **Mount Oave** stood 1,203m (4,042 ft.) high in the middle of Ua Pou, but most spectacular were a dozen basaltic thumbs protruding from ridges descending from the peak. This jagged outline of Moorea-esque spires justifiably appears in many promotional photographs, and it led Jacques Brel to write his song, "La Cathédrale." The first Marquesans also must have been impressed, for the name Ua Pou means "the Columns."

The volcano that created Ua Pou, the third largest Marquesan island, was different from others in the group, for it created both phonolite, a hard rock that was excellent for flaking into cutting tools, and so-called **flower stones,** or pebbles whose imbedded crystals create flowerlike designs in the dark rock. Found only on Ua Pou, flower stones are excellent, easy-to-carry souvenirs.

EXPLORING UA POU

Although a rough dirt road circles the island, most of Ua Pou's population of some 2,200 lives on the northern coast in and between the villages of **Hakahau** and **Hakahetau.** Hakahau is the administrative center, with a gendarmerie, infirmary, post office, and Banque Socredo branch (both the post office and bank have ATMs).

There is no public transportation system on Ua Pou. The pensions pick up guests who have reservations at **Aneou Airstrip,** on the north shore about equidistant between the two villages. With the sea at one end of the airstrip and a mountain at the other, Air

ACCOMMODATIONS ■
Chez Dora **2**
Pension Pukue'e **5**
Pension Vehine Hou **4**

ATTRACTIONS ●
Tenai Paepae **3**
Eglise Saint-Etienne
 (St. Etienne Catholic Church) **1**
Anahoa Beach **7**
White Cross **6**

0 0.25 mi
0 0.25 km

N

To Airport

Point
Matahiva

Hakahau
Harbor

Main
Wharf

✉

Gendarmerie

Kopuaeu River

5 ● **6**

3

1

4

2

To
Hohoi

N

area of
map

Hakahetau

Hakahau

Ua Pou

Hakamoui

Mt. Te Ana One Maui

Hakamaii

Hohoi

0 5 mi
0 5 km

Tahiti's small planes land uphill headed inland and take off downhill in the opposite direction, regardless of which way the wind is blowing.

HAKAHAU

Ua Pou's basaltic spires form a picturesque backdrop to Hakahau, which sits beside a black-sand beach in a gorgeous half-moon bay on the northeast coast. A breakwater protruding halfway across the bay protects the local dock from the sea swells and makes it possible for the *Aranui 3* (but not larger vessels) to come alongside here. From the dock, a paved street runs along the bay past a large, thatched-roof pavilion—under which locals sell handicrafts when ships are in port—to the town hall, post office, bank, and island school.

The street beside the school leads inland to **Tenai Paepae,** the ancient gathering place restored for an arts festival in 1995. Locals stage dance shows on the *paepae* for cruise-ship passengers.

Facing the *paepae* is **Eglise Saint-Etienne (St. Etienne Catholic Church),** a stone structure erected in 1981 on the site of the first church in the Marquesas. In addition to spectacular woodcarvings, the church is worth visiting for the view of the mountainous spires framed by a triangular window above its southern nave. Carved from a single tree trunk, the pulpit symbolizes the bow of God's ship splitting the stormy seas of life.

A partially paved, partially dirt road leads through dry scrub brush from the eastern side of the bay across a ridge to **Anahoa Bay,** site of a lovely beach. It's good for swimming in the surf, but cover yourself with insect repellent to ward off the *no-nos,* and be on the lookout for jellyfish in June and July. It's worth the 20-minute hike up to the large **white cross** standing atop the ridge, where you will have a marvelous view down over Hakahau.

HAKAHETAU

Unlike arid Hakahau, which sits in the dry rain shadow of Mount Oave, the charming little village of **Hakahetau** is green and lush. Its little bay is unprotected from the sea swells, and the village dock—at the base of a sheer cliff—is often buffeted by waves. The eroding beach has been replenished with black stones. Although the bay is picturesque, Hakahetau's charm is along the paved street following a stream inland. It passes a small **Catholic church** built of river stones in 1859. One of the oldest in the Marquesas, its roof is supported by posts carved with likenesses of the Apostles and the Polynesian transliterations of their names. Cross the bridge farther upstream to a pavilion where **stone carvers** work and sell their handicrafts.

Keep going past the pavement to a natural, open-air copra-drying platform, where locals lay out coconut meat to dry in the sun. It commands an excellent view of the village and bay. On the way up, you will pass a sign for the **Manfred Cascade,** a waterfall about a 30-minute walk upstream via a track best negotiated on foot or in a four-wheel-drive vehicle. The cascade is like a swimming hole in the jungle, but lather up with insect repellent against the hordes of mosquitoes living up here.

WHERE TO STAY & DINE ON UA POU

There is no international-standard hotel on Ua Pou, but only pensions run by local families.

The best view and most attractive digs are at **Pension Pukue'e,** B.P. 31, 98745 Haka-hau, Ua Pou (©/fax **92.50.83;** http://chez.mana.pf/~pukuee), on the road to Anahoa Bay. Owner Hélène Kautai has five rooms sharing two bathrooms (both with hot-water showers) in her modern home overlooking Hakahau. Hélène also has an outdoor swimming pool.

Pension Vehine Hou, B.P. 54, 98745 Hakahau, Ua Pou (©/fax **92.53.21;** heato@ mail.pf), is down in Hakahau village. Owner Marie-Claire Teikiehuupoko has two rooms in her house with shared bathrooms and two bungalows with private bathrooms (and hot-water showers).

At **Chez Dora,** 98745 Hakahau, Ua Pou (©/fax **92.53.69**), up in the valley south of Hakahau village, Dora Teikiehuupolo has three bedrooms in her two-story house, one of which has a private bathroom.

All charge about 8,500CFP (US$106/£54) per person including meals. None accepts credit cards.

The restaurants at Pension Pukue'e and Pension Vehine Hou both are open to outsiders who make reservations. Rosalie Tata, who makes a delicious *poisson cru,* opens her **Restaurant Chez Rosalie** (no phone) only when cruise ships are in port.

---

5 HIVA OA ★★★

Just as Nuku Hiva has had its famous guests in Herman Melville and the sand-fly-bitten cast of television's *Survivor,* so has Hiva Oa, for here lie the remains of French artist Paul Gauguin and Belgian singer-poet Jacques Brel. Gauguin arrived in 1901 to escape what he saw as harassment by French colonial officials on Tahiti. He died here in 1903. Brel sailed his yacht here in 1975 and just plain fell under the spell of Hiva Oa's beauty and serenity. Brel was planning to build a spectacular home here when he died in 1978.

The second largest of the Marquesas Islands, Hiva Oa is indeed a place of beauty and serenity. Its rugged scenery was created by a series of volcanoes on an east-west line. One of the craters partially fell into the sea, forming huge **Taaoa Bay** on the south shore and leaving the fishhook-shaped island we see on today's maps. Another crater dominates the center of the island, while a third, on the northeastern coast, also partially collapsed to form **Puamau Bay,** upon whose banks sit one of French Polynesia's most important archaeological sites. In fact, Hiva Oa is pockmarked with the remains of ancient *me'aes,* many of them restored.

Gauguin and Brel both lived in **Atuona,** the island's only town—and my first landfall when I sailed to French Polynesia in 1977. Their graves and an excellent museum dedicated to both of them are highlights of any visit to Hiva Oa. Atuona isn't as physically impressive as Taiohae on Nuku Hiva, but it retains more of a French colonial ambience, with some buildings still standing from Gauguin's day.

GETTING AROUND HIVA OA

The **airport** is at an altitude of 500m (1,650 ft.) up on the Tepuna Plateau, 13km (8 miles) northeast of Atuona. Fog or rain can unexpectedly close the airstrip here, so be prepared to enjoy an extra night or two on Hiva Oa. *Always* plan to fly back to Papeete a few days before your international flight home.

Your accommodations will arrange to pick you up if they know you're coming, or look for **Vaite Transport (Ida Clark Taxi;** © 92.71.33 or 72.34.73). Despite her *anglais* name, Ida Clark speaks scant English, but she will take you into Atuona for 1,500CFP (US$19/£9.50).

Atuona Rent a Car (©/fax **92.67.07** or 72.17.17), **Hiva Oa Location** (© **91.70.60** or 72.83.83), and **David Location** (© **92.72.87;** davidkmk@mail.pf) all rent four-wheel-drive vehicles for about 12,000CFP (US$150/£76) a day. The main road is paved from Atuona past the airport going northeast, but be extremely careful when driving here. The north-shore road is so dangerous that I strongly recommend taking an organized tour to see Puamau (see "Exploring Hiva Oa," below).

(Fast Facts) Hiva Oa

The following facts apply specifically to Hiva Oa. For more information, see "Fast Facts: Tahiti & French Polynesia," in appendix A.

Currency Exchange **Banque Socredo** has an office on the main road in Atuona. The ATM on the side of the building is open only during banking hours: Monday through Friday from 7 to 11:30am and 1 to 4pm.

Drugstores **Pharmacie Atuona** (© 91.71.65) is in the Taiohae *mairie* (town hall) complex in the center of town. It's open Monday through Friday from 8am to noon and 2 to 5:30pm, Saturday from 8:30 to 11:30am.

Emergencies/Police The **emergency police** phone number is © **17.** The **gendarmerie** in Atuona (© 92.73.61) is a major landmark in the middle of town.

Healthcare The Atuona government **infirmary** (© 92.73.75) and **dental clinic** (© **92.73.58**) are in the Taiohae *mairie* (town hall) complex in the center of town.

Internet Access The island's one hotel and some of its pensions have Internet access for their guests. The post and telecommunications office has two computers for public use (see below).

Laundry If your accommodations won't wash your dirty clothes, contact **Atuona Yacht Services** (© 92.79.85) or **Marie-Jo** (© 92.73.43 or 26.14.59), both of whom do a booming business during the cruising yacht season from April to September. They will wash, dry, and fold a kilogram (2¼ lb.) of clothes for about 400CFP (US$5/£2.55).

Post Office Like most things official in Atuona, the post and telecommunications office is in the *mairie* (town hall) complex. It's open Monday through Thursday from 7:30 to noon and 12:30 to 4:30pm, Friday to 2pm. Puamau village also has a post office.

Telephone There are *télécarte* phones at the Atuona and Puamau post and telecommunications offices, as well as at Tahauku harbor in Atuona. As in the Tuamotu Archipelago, Hiva Oa residents are as likely to write their phone numbers in two groups as in three (for example, 910 000 instead of 91.00.00).

Visitor Information The **Comité du Tourisme de Hiva Oa,** B.P. 273, 98741 Atuona, Hiva Oa (©/fax **92.78.73;** www.marquises-hivaoa.org.pf), has a visitor information office in a small building near the Gauguin museum. It's open Monday through Friday from 8 to noon and 1 to 3pm.

Water Don't drink the tap water on Hiva Oa. The grocery stores sell bottled water. The town of Atuona can run short of water, so don't be surprised if the tap water is suddenly shut off at 8pm.

Atuona

SOUTH PACIFIC OCEAN

Bordelais Channel

Hanamoenoa Bay

Tahuata

Hiva Oa

Cape Matafenua

Natue Bay

Puamau

Motuua

Hanapaaoa

Mt. Ootua

Hanapanoa Bay

Hanaiapa

Hanaiapa Bay

Matatepai Point

Mt. Feani

Mt. Temetiu

Hanatenu Bay

Kiukiu Point

Taaoa

Taaoa Bay

Teachoa Point

Motopu

Vaitahu

Hapatoni

Hana Tetena

Hana Teio

Tahauku Bay

Ship Dock

✈ Airport
🏖 Beach

5 mi
5 km
0

1/8 mile
200 meters
0

MARQUESAS ISLANDS

Eiao, Motu One, Hatutu

Nuku Hiva

Ua Pou, Ua Huka

Fatu Huku

Hiva Oa

Motane

Tahuata

Fatu Hiva

100 mi
100 km
0

ATTRACTIONS ●

Cimetière du Calvaire
(Calvary Cemetery) **5**

Gendarmerie **6**

Espace Jacques Brel
(Jacques Brel Cultural Center) **7**

Puamau and Iiopona Me'ae **1**

Stele Jacques Brel
(Jacques Brel Memorial) **3**

Taaoa Valley **4**

Tehueto Petroglyphs **2**

Tohua Papa Nui
(Paul Gauguin Cultural Center) **7**

ACCOMMODATIONS ■

Hanakee Hiva Oa Pearl Lodge **12**

Pension Gauguin **9**

Pension Kanahau **8**

Relais Moehau **11**

Temetiu Village **10**

A rocky headland divides the town of **Atuona,** on the northern shore of **Traitors Bay,** into two parts. Cargo ships and cruising yachts put into **Tahauku Bay,** a narrow cove on the east of the headland. Other than the black-sand beach and a freshwater faucet emerging from a cliff, there was little there when I sailed into the harbor back in 1977. Today, a man-made breakwater protects the concrete town dock and small boat marina. From the black-sand beach, the **Faakua Valley** goes off to the northeast.

On the western side of the headland, the original village borders another curving black-sand beach and follows the Vaioa River up into a valley. Unlike Taiohae on Nuku Hiva, where the main road follows the shoreline, here the main street is a block inland, separated from the beach by houses, churches, and parks. Sunset comes early to Atuona, for to the west looms the pointed peak of **Mount Temetiu,** tallest in the Marquesas at 1,190m (3,927 ft.). Atuona's other key landmark is the **gendarmerie,** at the center of town. Two blocks west on the main road is the town's **Tohua Pepeu,** a restored ancient meeting ground where locals stage dance shows and sell handicrafts to visiting cruise-ship passengers.

ATUONA'S TOP ATTRACTIONS

Cimetière du Calvaire (Calvary Cemetery) ★★   Paul Gauguin and Jacques Brel are both buried in this cemetery, on a hill overlooking Atuona. On the way up, you'll pass Brel's home, to the left when the road bends. The large basaltic tombstone above his grave bears a plaque with Brel's likeness and that of his mistress and companion, Maddly Bamy (she and Brel's family reportedly are in a constant struggle over the plaque!). I am always amazed at the number of flowers and shell necklaces left on the grave by Brel's fans. Gauguin's tomb is two rows up to the right. You'll recognize it by the sign at his feet and the replica of his *Oviri* statue standing over his head. Frangipani trees constantly deposit their fragrant flowers on the grave. Stop for a few minutes before the cemetery's tall white crucifix and take in the fine view over Atuona and Taaroa Bay.

Atuona, uphill from gendarmerie. Free admission. Daily 8am–sunset. From gendarmerie, follow the signs and climb the inland road uphill.

Espace Jacques Brel (Jacques Brel Cultural Center)   Behind Tohua Papa Nui (the Gauguin Cultural Center; see below), this hangarlike museum recounts the singer's life. From the rafters is suspended his Beechcraft Twin Bonanza airplane, *Jojo,* which he used to go back and forth to Tahiti, often on missions of mercy. You will see displays of traditional Marquesan arts and crafts as well. The shop sells CDs and tapes of his albums. The Brel and Gauguin cultural centers share a ticket office.

Atuona, 1 block west of gendarmerie. Admission 500CFP (US$6.25/£3.15) adults, 250CFP (US$3.10/£1.60) children 12–18. Mon–Fri 8–11am and 2–5pm; Sat 8–11am.

Stele Jacques Brel (Jacques Brel Memorial)   Brel had intended to build a home on a ridge near the airport, in a spectacular overlook of Tahauku and Taaroa bays. Construction had not begun when illness cut his life short in 1978 at age 49, but the site is marked by this black rock bearing his portrait and a line from his song "Marquesas." It's not easy to find, so see it on a tour or ask directions from one of the locals.

Atuona, 5km/3 miles northeast of town on airport road. Free admission. Daily 24 hr.

Tohua Papa Nui (Paul Gauguin Cultural Center) ★★★   A block west of the gendarmerie is this fine museum, located on the site of Gauguin's last residence. It was opened in 2003 on the 100th anniversary of his death, so discount earlier reports about it not being open or not being very good. Start by watching a 2-minute video about Gauguin's life and then take plenty of time to see the reproductions of his paintings by the wife-and-husband team of Viera and Claude-Charles Farina (who could make an illegal fortune as forgers!). Instead of using old copra bags made of jute, as did Gauguin, the Farinas executed these stunningly accurate replicas on real canvas. The exhibition starts with his self-portraits and then follows chronologically. His French Polynesian works, therefore, are near the rear of the building.

Out back is a replica of Gauguin's last residence, which he called his **Maison du Jouir (House of Pleasure)**—an apt name, apparently, since he painted *Barbaric Tales,* one of his best nudes, while living here.

Be sure to shop for Marquesan handicrafts in the boutique, which the center shares with *Espace Jacques Brel* (see above).

Autuona, 1 block west of gendarmerie. Admission 600CFP (US$7.50/£3.80) adults, 300CFP (US$3.75/£1.90) children 12–18. Mon–Fri 8–11am and 2–5pm; Sat 8–11am.

TEHUETO PETROGLYPHS
Reaching northeastward from Traitors Bay, the Faakua Valley is known for its **Tehueto Petroglyphs,** or stone carvings in basaltic rock. Done eons ago, these figures depict human beings with their arms in the air. The site is within hiking distance of Atuona, but the road is so rough that I do not recommend the walk. You can see it on a tour (see "Organized Tours," below), but your time will be better spent at Puamau.

PUAMAU & TE ME'AE TEIIPONA ★★★
Like an excursion to Hatiheu on Nuku Hiva, seeing **Puamau** and its archaeological site is the top trip to make on Hiva Oa. Be prepared for a long day, for it takes 2¹/₂ hours to get here from Atuona. The road is paved from town past the airport onto the Tepuna plateau, a cool region with ferns and pines and wild orchids, but it soon turns to gravel and gradually descends to the north shore, where it is literally blasted into cliffs above the serrated coastline. The views are spectacular on this winding road, but it is the most dangerous stretch on Hiva Oa, especially during or just after rain. For this reason, I highly recommend taking an organized tour to Puamau.

On the northeastern side of the island, picturesque Puamau village sits beside a black-sand beach and is surrounded on three sides by the steep walls of an extinct volcanic crater. The beach is good for swimming on its eastern side.

You may meet some of Paul Gauguin's descendants here, but Puamau's highlight is the restored **Te Me'ae Teiipona.** One of the most significant ancient temples in French Polynesia, it is famous for the largest stone tiki in all of Polynesia other than the mysterious

---

Fun Facts   A Debt Left Unpaid

Magasin Gauguin, an old clapboard general store beside a huge mango tree near the Gauguin Cultural Center on Atuona's main street, is a relic of the days when Paul Gauguin lived here. In those days it was owned by American merchant Ben Varney, himself the founder of a large mixed-race family. The painter bought his supplies here, including bottles of liquor that he kept cool in a well beside his house (he would fetch them with a long bamboo pole). It is said that when Gauguin died on May 8, 1903, he owed Varney a considerable debt.

(Fun Facts) Lunch with Marie-Antoinette

Most tours stop for lunch in Puamau village at **Pension Peheku'a (Chez Marie-Antoinette; (C) 92.72.27)**, which has two simple rooms to rent. On the grounds is **Tohua Pehe Kua,** the grave of Puamau's last Polynesian queen before the French took over in 1842. She lived until the early 20th century. A popular but unfounded legend says she's buried here with her two bicycles. For sure, Marie-Antoinette's family-style lunches are pure Polynesian: *poisson cru,* goat roasted with onions in coconut milk, boiled mountain bananas, deep-fried breadfruit, and sugary *po'e* (the local version of Hawaiian poi). Lunch is often included in the price of a tour; if not, expect to pay about 2,000CFP (US$25/£13) for a full meal—in cash. You can stay overnight for 7,000CFP (US$88/£44) per person, including all the *po'e* you can eat.

figures on Easter Island, far off in the eastern South Pacific between here and Chile. In fact, some anthropologists believe the Polynesians who first settled Easter Island came from Puamau. The tallest figure here, a rendition of a Polynesian chief named Taka'i'i, is much smaller than those on Easter Island, but still stands 2.4m (8 ft.) tall. The most unusual is of a woman lying on her stomach with her hands lifted skyward behind her back, said to be the likeness of a woman giving birth.

TAAOA VALLEY

About 7km (4¼ miles) by dirt road southwest of Atuona, the **Taaoa Valley** has the largest concentration of ceremonial sites in all of French Polynesia. Some of the more than 1,000 *paepaes* (stone platforms) have been restored, but many more still lie in the jungle. Archaeologists believe one of the stone tikis here was used to prepare humans to be sacrificed. Although you can find your way to Taaoa easily enough, the remains occupy most of the valley, so a tour is the best way to see it all.

HANAIAPA

The paved cross-island road from Atuona descends through the narrow Vaipeehia River valley and terminates at the beach in the pleasant north coast village of **Hanaiapa.** You can swim in the bay off the canoe shed near the river's mouth, and if the sea is calm, snorkel off the concrete dock (bring your own gear). Residents of Atuona like to escape to Hanaiapa on the weekends, for in addition to the beach, a plethora of fruit trees and flowers make this one of the more attractive villages in the Marquesas. There are no restaurants or other facilities, but a handicrafts shop opens when cruise ships are here.

ORGANIZED TOURS

The best tours with English-speaking guides are organized by the **Hanakee Hiva Oa Pearl Lodge** ((C) 92.75.87), the island's only international-level hotel (p. 280). It charges about 12,500CFP (US$156/£79) per person for an all-day excursion to Puamau, including lunch at Pension Chez Marie-Antoinette. Half-day trips to Taaoa cost about 4,000CFP (US$50/£25) per person. One of its guides will take you to the *Stele Jacques Brel* (Jacques Brel Memorial) or to see the Tehueto Petroglyphs for about 2,500CFP (US$31/£16) each.

DIVING, FISHING, HIKING, HORSEBACK RIDING & MOUNTAIN BIKING

When you've had enough of Paul Gauguin, Jacques Brel, and ancient archaeological sites, you can hit the great outdoors on Hiva Oa.

DIVING

With cliffs plunging into the sea and no fringing coral reefs, the waters off Nuku Hiva present a very different diving experience from that found anywhere else in French Polynesia. The cool South Equatorial Current makes these waters rife with plankton, while limiting visibility to 10 to 20m (33–66 ft.). On the other hand, you may well encounter scalloped hammerhead sharks, melon-headed whales, and other creatures not seen elsewhere in the islands. And even novice divers can enter caves, one of which has a sandy floor populated by stingrays.

At this writing, Eric Le Lyonnais' **SubAtuona** (✆ **92.70.88** or 27.05.24; eric.le lyonnais@wanadoo.fr), is the only dive operator in the Marquesas. Bring you own mask, flipper, full wet suit, underwater flashlight, and diving computer. Book well in advance. He charges about 6,000CFP (US$75/£38) for a one-tank dive.

FISHING

There's some pretty good hunting for tuna, mahimahi, and other deep-sea game fish in these waters. A charter boat can be arranged through your accommodations, or you can contact Gabriel "Gaby" Heitaa, owner of the **Pua O Te Tai** (✆ **91.70.60;** heitaagaby@mail.pf). His is one of the boats that also provides transportation between Hiva Oa and Tahuata.

HIKING

You can hike from Atuona to the Tehueto Petroglyphs and to Taaoa, but I think it's best to go with a guide. The **Hanakee Hiva Oa Pearl Lodge** (✆ **92.75.87**) organizes hiking excursions, or you can contact Bonno Henry of **Hiva Oa Rando-Trek** (✆ **92.74.44**) or **Hiva Oa Trek** (✆ **20.40.90**).

HORSEBACK RIDING

Another way to see the Tehueto Petroglyphs or Jacques Brel's intended home site is on the back of a strong Marquesan horse. Up on the plateau near the airport, **Maui Ranch Tahauku** (✆ **92.47.92**) leads excursions to both sites for about 7,000CFP (US$88/£44) and 14,000CFP (US$175/£89), respectively.

MOUNTAIN BIKING

In addition to horseback rides, the **Hanakee Hiva Oa Pearl Lodge** (✆ **92.75.87**) also organizes mountain-bike excursions to various points in and near Atuona. Contact the hotel for particulars and prices.

SHOPPING

You will see several "Sculpture Traditionnelle" signs around Atuona and Puamau directing you to the workshops of local carvers who are here and at work. The **Comité du Tourisme de Hiva Oa** knows where they are (see "Visitor Information" under "Fast Facts: Hiva Oa," p. 274). The boutique at the **Tohua Papa Nui (Paul Gauguin Cultural Center)** usually has some top-quality pieces and is well worth exploring (p. 276). There's another good handicrafts shop across the road from the center.

All of Hiva Oa's hotels and pensions offer various meal plans. If available, I would opt for a rate that includes breakfast only. You will likely have lunch on an excursion or at a "snack" in town while seeing the sights, so there is little point in paying for that in advance. I also like to dine out while here, so I don't pay for dinner, either.

The most remote place to stay is **Pension Peheku'a (Chez Marie-Antoinette),** in Puamau village on the far northeastern shore, at least 2¹/₂ hours by road away from Atuona (see "Lunch with Marie-Antoinette," p. 278).

EXPENSIVE

Hanakee Hiva Oa Pearl Lodge ★   With a stupendous view out to sea from its perch on a ridge above the eastern side of Tahauku Bay, this is the island's top place to stay—and along with its sister, the Keikahanui Nuku Hiva Pearl Lodge, it's one of the two international-level hotels in the Marquesas. You will be welcomed into the main building by a large and quite immodest Marquesan tiki. It and other carvings throughout the complex will not let you forget where you are. The main building opens to a small infinity-edge pool with a 200-degree view up the Tahauku Valley all the way around to the Bordelais Channel and (on a clear day) Tahuata island in the distance. Virtually identical to those at Keikahanui Nuku Hiva Pearl Lodge (p. 264), the guest bungalows step downhill below the pool. The most expensive are those with sea views, while the least expensive face the valley (*Tip:* Bungalow no. 7 looks toward both the sea and the valley.) Each unit was decorated by a Marquesan woodcarver and has a king-size bed, a porch, and a tiled bathroom with shower. The dining room shares the view and serves very good French fare—it's far and away the best restaurant on Hiva Oa. The hotel offers its guests a wide range of activities (see "Organized Tours" and "Diving, Fishing, Hiking, Horseback Riding & Mountain Biking," above).

B.P. 80, 97742 Atuona, Hiva Oa (on airport road 3.5km/2 miles northeast of town). ⓒ **800/657-3275** or 92.75.87. Fax 92.75.95. www.pearlresorts.com. 14 units. 22,400CFP–39,200CFP (US$280–US$490/£142–£248) bungalow. AE, DC, MC, V. **Amenities:** Restaurant; bar; outdoor pool; complimentary bicycles; activities desk; limited room service; laundry service. *In room:* A/C, TV, dataport, minibar, coffeemaker, hair dryer, safe.

INEXPENSIVE

Pension Gauguin   The most convenient pension to Atuona's prime attractions, this two-story building sits on a hill behind Snack Make Make (p. 282). It's a bit like an old-fashioned B&B, since the six clean bedrooms share four bathrooms with hot-water showers. The units are equipped with either a double bed or two singles. Guests share a common lounge, dining room, and wide terrace with a view of Taaoa Bay.

B.P. 34, 98741 Atuona, Hiva Oa (in the old village). ⓒ/fax **91.73.51.** pens.gauguin@mail.pf. 6 units (shared bathrooms). 4,000CFP (US$50/£25) per person. MC, V. **Amenities:** Restaurant; bar; free use of washers and dryers. *In room:* No phone.

Pension Kanahau ★★   One of the better pensions in French Polynesia, this fine little inn sits on the ridge between Atuona town and Faakua valley. Marquesan-born owner Tania Dubreuil learned English while dealing with all the yachties who put in at Atuona, and she got the idea of building a restaurant where they could come and have dinner overlooking the small boat harbor in Tahauku (Traitors) Bay. Later she installed four standard government-backed bungalows and decorated them in island style, with *tivaivai* (handmade appliqué quilts) on the beds and colorful fabrics on the windows. They also have televisions, ceiling fans, mosquito nets over queen-size beds, sofas that convert to single beds, writing tables, and private bathrooms with hot-water showers. Two of the front porches look across Tahauku Bay to the sea, while the other two face the valley. Most meals are taken under a large shade tree on a patio beside the main house, which has a television lounge. Guests with children can use the kitchen inside. Tania's is a relaxed, friendly establishment that can become quite lively when the yachties are in town from April through September.

B.P. 101, 98741 Atuona, Hiva Oa (Tahauku valley, 2km/1¹/₄ mile east of town). © 91.71.31 or 70.16.26. Fax 91.71.32. http://pensionkanahau.ifrance.com. 4 units. 12,500CFP (US$156/£79) double. No credit cards. **Amenities:** Restaurant; bar; massage; free use of washers and dryers. *In room:* TV, coffeemaker, no phone.

Relais Moehau ★   This modern, two-story white building with a green-tile roof is the best choice within easy walking distance of Atuona's top attractions. It sits up on a hillside overlooking the black-sand beach of old Atuona. The rooms are all upstairs and open to a veranda that wraps around the building, so you can sit out and admire the view. Although not extravagant, the units are clean and comfortable, each with a ceiling fan, a double or two single beds, and a private bathroom with hot-water shower. Open to all comers, the downstairs restaurant specializes in wood-fired pizzas as well as French fare. Owners Georges and Gisèle Gramont are originally from the Tuamotu Archipelago. A bit of French will come in handy here.

B.P. 50, 98741 Atuona, Hiva Oa (east side of town). © 92.72.69. Fax 92.77.62. www.relaismoehau.pf. 8 units. 12,000CFP (US$150/£76) double. Rates include breakfast. MC, V. **Amenities:** Restaurant; bar. *In room:* TV, kitchen (2 units), fridge, no phone.

Temetiu Village ★   Like Pension Kanahau, this is a good establishment on the eastern side of the ridge separating the town from the harbor. Friendly owner Gabriel "Gaby" Heitaa operates the Pua O Te Tai fishing boat (see "Diving, Fishing, Hiking, Horseback Riding & Mountain Biking," above), while his equally friendly wife Feli speaks English. Their seven hillside bungalows all have a view of the bay. Three of them have two bedrooms with three single beds in each. All have televisions and private bathrooms with hot-water showers.

B.P. 52, 98741 Atuona, Hiva Oa (east side of town). © 91.70.60. Fax 91.70.61. heitaagabyfeli@mail.pf. 7 units. 8,200CFP (US$103/£52) double. AE, MC, V. **Amenities:** Restaurant. *In room:* TV, no phone.

WHERE TO DINE

The **Hanakee Hiva Oa Pearl Lodge** has the best restaurant on the island and a fine view to go with its excellent French and Continental fare. The best pension dining rooms—with the best views—are at **Relais Moehau** (especially if the pizza oven is lit) and **Temetiu Village.** Reservations are essential at both.

Restaurant Hoa Nui MARQUESAN   You will have a Marquesan feast at this large restaurant, across the road from the Vaioa River. As at Chez Marie-Antoinette in Puamau, the chow is deliciously local, with the likes of goat with onions and coconut milk, fried breadfruit, and sweet banana *po'e*. You can get breakfast and lunch here without a reservation, but bookings are required a day in advance for dinner.

Atuona (in Vaioa Valley). © 92.73.63. Dinner reservations required 1 day in advance. Full dinner 2,700CFP (US$34/£17). No credit cards. Daily 6am–10pm.

Snack Kaupe REGIONAL   You can get an American-style hot dog at this "snack" next to historic Magasin Gauguin; it's the nearest restaurant to the Gauguin Cultural

Center. Otherwise, it serves the usual local collection of burgers, Chinese stir-fries, steak and french fries, and *poisson cru.*

Atuona, center of town behind Magasin Gauguin. ✆ **92.70.62.** Reservations not accepted. Snacks and meals 750CFP–1,650CFP (US$9.40–US$21/£4.75–£10). No credit cards. Fri–Wed 11:30am–8pm.

Snack Make Make REGIONAL   East of the gendarmerie, this gaudy green building is another landmark in old Atuona. The menu is typically Tahitian, with burgers, grilled steak or chicken with french fries, *poisson cru,* chow mein, and shrimp in coconut curry sauce. You can order to go. The hours can vary here.

Atuona, east of gendarmerie. ✆ **92.74.26.** Reservations not accepted. Snacks and meals 600CFP–2,500CFP (US$7.50–US$32/£3.80–£16). No credit cards. Mon–Fri 11am–2pm and 6–9pm; Sat 6–9pm.

6 TAHUATA ★★

Lying less than 4km (2¹⁄₂ miles) south of Hiva Oa across the Bordelais Channel, lush and lovely Tahuata is the smallest inhabited island in the Marquesas. Most of its creating volcano dropped into the sea, leaving only the northwestern rim of its crater still standing. The old caldera wall forms Tahuata's steep southeastern coastline, while sharp ridges fan out and create beautiful valleys to the north and west.

Although Fatu Hiva was first to be sighted, Tahuata was the first of all Polynesian islands to be visited by Europeans. Spanish explorer Alvaro de Mendaña "discovered" it in 1595 and sailed into the little bay at **Vaitahu,** then and now the island's main village. He named it *Madre De Dios* (Mother of God). Capt. James Cook stopped here in 1774. Admiral Dupetit-Thouars claimed the island for France in 1842, but a local chief named Iotete resisted. Several French sailors were killed in the ensuing skirmish and are buried on a hill above Vaitahu. The admiral built a fort overlooking the valley; although overgrown, it's still here, too. The French prevailed, but the Tahuatuans are still fiercely independent.

They also are the best bone carvers in French Polynesia, making this the best place to shop for scrimshaw and other such items.

EXPLORING TAHUATA

Vaitahu has a post office, but there is neither a bank nor an airport on Tahuata. Access is strictly by boat from Tahauku Bay on Hiva Oa. The Hanakee Hiva Oa Pearl Lodge (p. 280) and other accommodations on Hiva Oa will organize day trips to Tahuata, and the island's lone pension arranges transfers for its guests. There are no car rentals; in fact, there are few vehicles on Tahuata since its only road (linking Vaitahu to Motopu in the north and Hapatoni to the south) is barely more than a dirt track. Most folks get around here by boat.

You will definitely need a boat or yacht to reach the beautiful white-sand beaches skirting **Hanamoenoa** and **Ivaiva bays** north of Vaitahu. Unfortunately, both of these idyllic spots have *no-nos.*

VAITAHU

Midway on the island's west coast, historic **Vaitahu** sits in a narrow valley. There is no harbor here, only a wharf on the north side of the bay, where boats from the cruise ships land their passengers (it's a sight to see a big yellow backhoe removing cargo from barges sent ashore by the *Aranui 3*). From there a paved road runs around the bay past a small, wooden Protestant church to the town hall, post office, school, and a large thatched-roof pavilion used for meetings and the sale of handicrafts to cruise-ship passengers. Definitely worth examining are museum-quality bone carvings by **Teike Barinas** (☎ 92. 93.24).

In front of the town hall stands a monument declaring, in French, that after 1995 the Marquesas Islands shall be known to the world by their original name, *Fenua Enata* (Land of Men). Another commemorates Chief Iotete's rebellion against the French in 1842. As I said, the Tahuatans are independent-minded.

In the school, the small **Musée de Vaitahu (Vaitahu Museum;** ☎ **92.92.19)** tells of expeditions in the valleys and displays fishhooks, *adzes* (primitive stone axes), and other items discovered during the digs in the 1990s. Organized by archaeologist Barry Rolett of the University of Hawaii, the captions are in French, English, and Marquesan. The museum is open Monday to Friday and on cruise-ship days from 8am to 4pm. Admission is 150CFP (US$1.90/95p).

Facing the bay from a large open space stands the impressive **Eglise Sainte Mère de Dieu (Holy Mother of God Catholic Church),** built of stone with Vatican backing in 1988, the anniversary of the arrival of the first Catholic priests in 1838. The name also evokes Mendaña's visit in 1595. Look up at the church steeple, where a woodcarving by noted sculptor Damien Haturau depicts the Virgin Mary holding the baby Jesus, as does an impressive stained-glass window inside the church.

A paved street follows an often-dry streambed inland from the beach. You will pass a number of wood-frame houses dating from the early 20th century. Across a bridge is the studio of **Felix Fii** (no phone), one of the best tattoo artists in French Polynesia.

HAPATONI

About 15 minutes by boat south of Vaitahu, **Hapatoni** is one of the most pleasant and friendliest villages in the Marquesas. Enormous *temanu* trees and the **Royal Road** skirt the little bay, making for an picturesque stroll. The middle of the village is dominated by the restored **Me'ae Anapara** and **Me'ae Eia,** two large meeting and worshiping sites. Next to them, a gray stone Catholic church and cemetery offer a contrast of ancient and modern worshiping methods.

Hapatoni seldom sees foreign visitors except when the *Aranui 3* pulls in every third Sunday. Then the entire village turns out to offer fresh fruits, a meal of Marquesan cuisine, and handicrafts for sale.

WHERE TO STAY & DINE ON TAHUATU

The only place to stay is **Pension Amatea,** 98743 Vaitahu, Tahuata (☎/fax **92.92.84),** where Marguerite Kokauani rents five rooms in her house. Guests share a bathroom and shower. Marguerite charges about 4,500CFP (US$56/£28) per person. She also serves meals and will arrange horseback riding and other excursions. Book well in advance, for Marguerite must also arrange your boat transfer from Hiva Oa.

7 FATU HIVA ★★★

Lying 56km (34 miles) southeast of Tahuata, remote Fatu Hiva is one of the most dramatically beautiful islands in French Polynesia. Like Moorea, it's half a bowl formed by the remaining third of a volcanic crater that rises steeply from the sea, resulting in many

THE MARQUESAS ISLANDS

12

FATU HIVA

cliffs plunging precipitously into the surf. Rising from the middle of the original crater's floor, rugged **Mount Teamotua** is flanked on either side by narrow valleys in which the island's 560 residents live. On the south side, **Omoa** is the administrative center, while to the north, **Hanavave** is the most unusual valley in the Marquesas.

The island came to the world's attention in 1938 when Thor Heyerdahl published *Fatu Hiva: Back to Nature,* describing the year he and his bride, Liv, spent here trying to live a totally natural life. It didn't work. Nearly emaciated, he and Liv were evacuated by local missionaries. While here, Heyerdahl developed the theory that the Polynesians came originally from South America, which led to his sailing the balsa raft *Kon Tiki* from Peru to the Tuamotu Archipelago in the late 1940s.

Today Fatu Hiva (whose name is sometimes spelled Fatu Iva) is French Polynesia's leading producer of **tapa,** the natural cloth made from the bark of paper mulberry, banyan, and other trees. Geometric designs were tattooed on the bodies of the wearers in ancient times, not on the cloth, but the modern version is decorated with a multitude of designs. Local women show cruise-ship passengers how bark is beaten into cloth and then painted. Fatu Hiva is the best place in the territory to buy tapa.

EXPLORING FATU HIVA

There is no airstrip on Fatu Hiva, and the only sensible way of getting here is on the *Aranui 3,* which anchors first at picturesque **Omoa** village beside a small bay. Omoa has a post office and an infirmary. There is no bank on Fatu Hiva; hence, credit cards are useless here.

Omoa's prime attractions are large, back-to-back tikis standing at the waterfront and **Musée Grelet (Grelet Museum;** no phone), on the first level of a colonial-era house built by François Grelet. A Swiss man, he settled here in the 19th century, married a local woman, and began collecting Marquesan art. Carried on by his descendants, the museum contains war clubs and spears, *adzes,* tikis, and stone pestles used to pound breadfruit into poi. Most impressive are intricately carved wooden *koka'a* bowls, from which poi is served. Many modern items are very much for sale. The museum is open on cruise-ship days, other times by appointment. Admission is free.

From Omoa, a 17km (11-mile) dirt road scales the central mountain and down into **Hanavave.** It's much faster and easier to go between the two villages by boat, but four-wheel-drive vehicles occasionally use this road, which was built to service the electric power lines linking the two settlements. It's a popular 4- to 5-hour hike, especially for *Aranui 3* passengers since they rejoin the ship at Hanavave. Although usually passable, the track has sections of slippery mud that can stick to the bottom of shoes and hiking boots. It can be a hot walk, too, so bring ample supplies of water, snacks, and sunscreen. You should be in good health before making this hike.

The road gradually climbs out of Omoa Valley, crosses the central mountain, then descends very steeply into Hanavave. The views from the switchbacks are awesome; at one point, it seems as if you are looking straight down into the **Baie des Vierges (Bay of Virgins)** at Hanavave. The valley itself is punctuated with tiki-shaped spires protruding from sharp ridges descending from the old crater wall. No other place in French Polynesia is this ephemeral.

Hanavave village sits on a small flat plain beside a beach of black rocks and boulders. Its backdrop consists of huge black pillars standing like the posts of a giant gate between it and the valley. The phallus shape of these posts has given rise to humorous conjecture that the 19th-century French missionaries added an "i" to *Baie des Verges* (Bay of Phalli, let us say), thus renaming it *Baie des Vierges* (Bay of Virgins). The Marquesan name means "Surf Bay."

Hanavave attracts scores of cruising yachts, in part because the setting sun invariably paints this gorgeous valley with an enormous variety of changing colors.

WHERE TO STAY & DINE ON FATU HIVA

You must be an intrepid traveler to get to Fatu Hiva on your own, but you can stay at Bernadette Cantois' **Chez Lionel,** B.P. 1, 98740 Omoa, Fatu Hiva ((✆/fax **92.81.84;** chezlionel@mail.pf), about 1.5km (1 mile) inland from the Omoa wharf. Bernadette has a kitchen-equipped bungalow whose private bathroom has a hot-water shower, plus two rooms in her house (with shared facilities). She charges about 9,000CFP (US$113/£57) double for a bungalow, 7,000CFP (US$88/£44) double for a room, including breakfast, but she does not accept credit cards. Bernadette will arrange horseback riding, fishing, and excursions. You can book through www.haere-mail.pf.

Appendix A: Fast Facts Tahiti & French Polynesia

The following facts apply to French Polynesia in general. For more specific information, see the "Fast Facts" sections in the specific island chapters.

AMERICAN EXPRESS The American Express representative is **Tahiti Tours,** on rue Jeanne-d'Arc (© **54.02.50;** fax 42.25.15), across from the Centre Vaima in downtown Papeete. The mailing address is B.P. 627, 98713 Papeete, Tahiti, French Polynesia.

AREA CODES French Polynesia does not have domestic area codes. The country code for calling into French Polynesia is **689.**

ATM NETWORKS & CASHPOINTS See "Money & Costs," p. 42.

BUSINESS HOURS Although many shops in downtown Papeete stay open over the lunch period, general shopping and business hours are from 7:30 to 11:30am and from 2 to 5pm Monday to Friday, 8am to noon on Saturday. In addition to regular hours, most grocery stores also are open from 2 to 6pm on Saturday and from 6 to 8am on Sunday.

CAMERA & FILM Photographic film and color-print processing are widely available. Digital camera batteries are available in Papeete.

CASHPOINTS See "Money & Costs," p. 42.

CURRENCY See "Money & Costs," p. 42.

CLIMATE See "When to Go," p. 46.

CLOTHING Evening attire for men is usually a shirt and slacks; women typically wear a long, brightly colored dress (slacks or long skirts help to keep biting sand flies away from your ankles). Women sunbathe topless at most beaches (although I saw more exposed bums than breasts during my recent visit). Shorts are acceptable during the day almost everywhere. Outside Papeete, the standard attire for women is the colorful wraparound sarong known in Tahitian as a *pareu,* which can be tied in a multitude of ways into dresses, blouses, or skirts.

CUSTOMS Customs allowances are 200 cigarettes or 100 cigarillos or 50 cigars; 2 liters of liquor, champagne, or wine; 50 grams of perfume, .25 liter of eau de toilette; 500 grams of coffee and 100 grams of tea; and 30,000CFP (US$375/£190) worth of other goods. Narcotics, dangerous drugs, weapons, ammunition, and copyright infringements (that is, pirated videotapes and audiotapes) are prohibited. Pets and plants are subject to stringent regulations (don't even think of bringing your pet).

DRINKING LAWS The legal drinking age is 21. Most grocery stores sell beer, spirits, and French wines. Hinano beer is brewed locally and is less expensive than imported brands, which are taxed heavily. I bring a bottle of duty-free liquor with me.

DRIVING RULES See "Getting Around Tahiti & French Polynesia," p. 57.

DRUG LAWS Plenty of pot may be grown up in the hills, but possession and use of dangerous drugs and narcotics are subject to long jail terms.

DRUGSTORES The main towns have reasonably well-stocked pharmacies, or chemists. Their medicines are likely to be from France.

ELECTRICITY Electrical power is 220 volts, 50 cycles, and the plugs are the French kind with two round, skinny prongs. Most hotels have 110-volt outlets for shavers only, so you will need a converter and adapter plugs for other appliances. Some hotels, especially those on the outer islands, have their own generators, so ask at the reception desk what voltage is supplied.

EMBASSIES & CONSULATES The **United States** has a consular agent on Tahiti in Centre Tamanu Iti in Pauaauia (✆ **42.65.35;** fax 50.80.96; usconsular@ mail.pf), whose main function is to facilitate local residents in applying for visas from the U.S. embassy in Suva, Fiji. Australia, Austria, Belgium, Chile, Denmark, Finland, Germany, Italy, Monaco, New Zealand, Norway, the Netherlands, South Korea, Sweden, and the United Kingdom have honorary consulates in Papeete. Tahiti Tourisme has their phone numbers; see "Visitor Information," p. 39.

EMERGENCIES If you are in a hotel, contact the staff. Otherwise, the emergency **police** phone number is ✆ **17** throughout the territory.

ETIQUETTE & CUSTOMS Even though many women go topless and wear the skimpiest of bikini bottoms at the beach, the Tahitians have a sense of propriety similar to what you find in any Western nation. Don't offend them by engaging in behavior that would not be permissible at home.

FIREARMS French Polynesians can own shotguns for hunting, but handguns are illegal.

GAMBLING There are no casinos in French Polynesia, but you can play "Lotto," the French national lottery.

HEALTHCARE Highly qualified specialists practice on Tahiti, where some clinics possess state-of-the-art diagnostic and treatment equipment; nevertheless, public hospitals tend to be crowded with local residents, who get free care. Most visitors use private doctors or clinics. English-speaking physicians are on call by larger hotels. Each of the smaller islands has at least one infirmary (see "Fast Facts" in chapters 9–11). American health insurance plans are not recognized, so remember to get receipts at the time of treatment.

HITCHHIKING Hitchhiking is possible in the rural parts of Tahiti and on the outer islands, but women traveling alone should be extremely cautious.

HOLIDAYS For more information on holidays, see "When to Go," p. 46.

INSECTS There are no dangerous insects in French Polynesia. The only real nuisances are mosquitoes and tiny, nearly invisible sand flies known locally as *no-nos,* elsewhere as *no-seeums.* They appear at dusk on most beaches here. Wear trousers or long skirts and plenty of insect repellent (especially on the feet and ankles) to ward off the *no-nos.* If you forget to bring insect repellent along, look for the Off or Dolmix Pic brands at the pharmacies.

INSURANCE Medical Insurance Most U.S. health plans (including Medicare and Medicaid) do not provide coverage in French Polynesia, and the ones that do often require you to pay for services upfront and reimburse you only after you return home.

As a safety net, you may want to buy travel medical insurance, particularly if you're traveling to a remote or high-risk area where emergency evacuation might be necessary. If you require additional medical insurance, try **MEDEX Assistance**

(© 410/453-6300; www.medexassist.com) or **Travel Assistance International** (© 800/821-2828; www.travelassistance.com; for general information on services, call the company's **Worldwide Assistance Services, Inc.,** at © 800/777-8710).

Canadians should check with their provincial health plan offices or call **Health Canada** (© 866/225-0709; www.hc-sc. gc.ca) to find out the extent of their coverage and what documentation and receipts they must take home in case they are treated overseas.

Travelers from the U.K. should carry their European Health Insurance Card (EHIC), which replaced the E111 form as proof of entitlement to free/reduced-cost medical treatment abroad (© 0845 606 2030; www.ehic.org.uk). Note, however, that the EHIC only covers "necessary medical treatment," and for repatriation costs, lost money or baggage, and cancellations; travel insurance from a reputable company should always be sought (www.travelinsuranceweb.com).

Travel Insurance The cost of travel insurance varies widely, depending on the destination, the cost and length of your trip, your age and health, and the type of trip you're taking, but expect to pay between 5% and 8% of the vacation itself. You can get estimates from various providers through **InsureMyTrip.com.** Enter your trip cost and dates, your age, and other information, for prices from more than a dozen companies.

U.K. citizens and their families who make more than one trip abroad per year may find an annual travel insurance policy works out cheaper. Check **www.money supermarket.com**, which compares prices across a wide range of providers for single- and multi-trip policies.

Most big travel agents offer their own insurance and will probably try to sell you their package when you book a holiday. Think before you sign. Britain's **Consumers' Association** recommends that you insist on seeing the policy and reading the fine print before buying travel insurance. The **Association of British Insurers** (© 020/7600-3333; www.abi.org.uk) gives advice by phone and publishes *Holiday Insurance,* a free guide to policy provisions and prices. You might also shop around for better deals: Try **Columbus Direct** (© 0870/033-9988; www.columbus direct.net).

Trip Cancellation Insurance Trip-cancellation insurance will help retrieve your money if you have to back out of a trip or depart early, or if your travel supplier goes bankrupt. Trip cancellation traditionally covers such events as sickness, natural disasters, and U.S. State Department advisories. The latest news in trip-cancellation insurance is the availability of **expanded hurricane coverage** and the **"any-reason"** cancellation coverage—which costs more, but covers cancellations made for any reason. You won't get back 100% of your prepaid trip cost, but you'll be refunded a substantial portion. **TravelSafe** (© 888/885-7233; www.travelsafe.com) has both types of coverage. Expedia also offers any-reason cancellation coverage for its air-hotel packages. For details, contact one of the following recommended insurers: **Access America** (© 866/807-3982; www. accessamerica.com); **Travel Guard International** (© 800/826-4919; www.travel guard.com); **Travel Insured International** (© 800/243-3174; www.travelinsured. com); and **Travelex Insurance Services** (© 888/457-4602; www.travelex-insurance. com).

INTERNET ACCESS See "Staying Connected," p. 80.

LANGUAGE French is the official language (see appendix B). Most residents also speak Tahitian, and English is widely spoken among hotel and restaurant staffers.

LIQUOR LAWS Regulations about where and when you can drink are liberal. Anyone who is age 21 or over can purchase alcoholic beverages at bars and grocery stores, which sell wine, beer, and spirits. Official *conventionné* restaurants and hotels pay reduced duty on imported alcoholic beverages, which will cost less there than at local bars and nightclubs.

LOST & FOUND   Be sure to tell all of your credit card companies the minute you discover your wallet has been lost or stolen and file a report at the nearest police precinct. Your credit card company or insurer may require a police report number or record of the loss. Most credit card companies have an emergency toll-free number to call if your card is lost or stolen; they may be able to wire you a cash advance immediately or deliver an emergency credit card in a day or two.

MEASUREMENTS   French Polynesia is on the metric system. Metric measurements in this guide are listed first, followed by non-metric conversions in parentheses. Conversions for metric to non-metric, and vice versa, are available online at www.onlineconversion.com.

MAIL   All the main towns and many Papeete suburbs have post offices. Letters usually take about a week to 10 days to reach overseas destinations in either direction. Mailing addresses in French Polynesia consist of post office boxes (*boîtes postales* in French, or B.P. for short) but no street numbers or names. Local addresses have postal codes, which are written in front of the city or town. (If you send a letter to French Polynesia from the U.S., do *not* put the postal code behind the name of the town; otherwise the U.S. Postal Service may dispatch it to a zip code within the United States.)

NEWSPAPERS & MAGAZINES   The *Tahiti Beach Press,* an English-language weekly devoted to news of Tahiti's tourist industry, runs features of interest to tourists and advertisements for hotels, restaurants, real estate agents, car-rental firms, and other businesses that cater to tourists.

Establishments that buy ads in it give away copies free. The daily newspapers, *La Dépêche de Tahiti* and *Les Nouvelles,* are in French. **Le Kiosk** in front of the Vaima Centre on boulevard Pomare in Papeete sells some international newspapers and magazines.

PASSPORTS   All visitors to French Polynesia must have a passport that will be valid for 6 months beyond their stay here. Allow plenty of time before your trip to apply for a passport; processing normally takes 3 weeks, but can take longer during busy periods (especially spring). And keep in mind that if you need a passport in a hurry, you'll pay a higher processing fee.

For Residents of Australia: You can pick up an application from your local post office or any branch of Passports Australia, but you must schedule an interview at the passport office to present your application materials. Call the **Australian Passport Information Service** at ✆ **131-232,** or visit the government website at www.passports.gov.au.

For Residents of Canada: Passport applications are available at travel agencies throughout Canada or from the central **Passport Office,** Department of Foreign Affairs and International Trade, Ottawa, ON K1A 0G3 (✆ **800/567-6868;** www.ppt.gc.ca).

For Residents of Ireland: You can apply for a 10-year passport at the **Passport Office,** Setanta Centre, Molesworth Street, Dublin 2 (✆ **01/671-1633;** www.irlgov.ie/iveagh). Those under age 18 and over 65 must apply for a 3-year passport. You can also apply at 1A South Mall, Cork (✆ **021/272-525**) or at most main post offices.

For Residents of New Zealand: You can pick up a passport application at any New Zealand Passports Office or download it from their website. Contact the **Passports Office** at ✆ **0800/225-050** in New Zealand or 04/474-8100, or log on to www. passports.govt.nz.

For Residents of the United Kingdom: To pick up an application for a standard 10-year passport (5-year passport for children under 16), visit your nearest passport office, major post office, or travel agency or contact the **United Kingdom Passport Service** at (C) **0870/521-0410** or search its website at www.ukpa.gov.uk.

For Residents of the United States: Whether you're applying in person or by mail, you can download passport applications from the U.S. State Department website at **http://travel.state.gov**. To find your regional passport office, either check the U.S. State Department website or call the **National Passport Information Center** toll-free number ((C) **877/487-2778**) for automated information.

POLICE The emergency **police** phone number is (C) **17** throughout French Polynesia. The territory has two types of police: French *gendarmes* and local *commune* police. Both enforce traffic laws.

RADIO & TV French Polynesia has government-operated AM radio stations with programming in French and Tahitian. Several private AM and FM stations in Papeete play mostly American and British musical numbers in English; the announcers, however, speak French. Two government-owned television stations broadcast in French. Most hotels pick up a local satellite service, which carries CNN International in English. The government-owned radio and TV stations can be received throughout the territory via satellite. Moorea has an American-style cable system with CNN International and HBO, both in English.

SAFETY Do not leave valuables in your hotel room or unattended anywhere. Street crimes against tourists are rare, and you should be safe after dark in the busy parks along boulevard Pomare on Papeete's waterfront. Friends of mine who live here,

however, don't stroll away from the boulevard after dark. For that matter, stay alert everywhere after dusk. Women should not wander alone on deserted beaches any time, since some Polynesian men may still consider such behavior to be an invitation for instant amorous activity.

SMOKING Although antismoking campaigns and hefty tobacco taxes have reduced the practice to a large extent, cigarette smoking is still more common in French Polynesia than in Western countries. Most office buildings and the airlines are smoke-free, and you will find nonsmoking sections in some restaurants (the French law against smoking in bars and restaurants had not taken effect here as I write). Not all hotels have nonsmoking rooms, so be sure to ask for one.

TAXES Local residents do not pay income taxes; instead, the government imposes stiff duties on most imported goods, and a value-added tax (VAT, or *TVA* in French) is included in the price of most goods and services. Only the TVA on set pearls is refundable in the European fashion (see "Buying Your Black Pearl," p. 124). Another 12% tax will be tacked onto your hotel bills (including restaurant and bar expenses) and another 50CFP to 200CFP (US65¢–$2.50/30p–£1.25) per night for the Tahiti, Moorea, and Bora Bora communities.

TELEPHONE See "Staying Connected," (p. 80).

TELEGRAPH, TELEX & FAX See "Staying Connected," (p. 80).

TIME Local time in the most-visited islands is 11 hours behind Greenwich Mean Time. That is 5 hours behind U.S. Eastern Standard Time or 2 hours behind Pacific Standard Time. Add 1 hour to the Tahiti time during daylight saving time in the U.S.

The Marquesas Islands are 30 minutes ahead of the rest of the territory.

Since French Polynesia is on the east side of the international date line, Tahiti has the same date as the United States, the U.K., and Europe, and is 1 day behind Australia and New Zealand.

TIPPING   Although tipping is considered contrary to the Polynesian custom of hospitality, it's a widespread practice here, especially in Papeete's restaurants (credit card forms now have a "tip" line here). Nevertheless, tipping is not expected unless the service has been beyond the call of duty. Some hotels accept contributions to the staff Christmas fund.

USEFUL PHONE NUMBERS   See "Toll-Free Numbers & Websites," below, for useful international numbers.

Air France ✆ 47.47.47

Air Moorea ✆ 86.41.41

Air New Zealand ✆ 54.07.47

Air Tahiti ✆ 86.42.42

Air Tahiti Nui ✆ 46.03.03

Airport flight information ✆ 86.60.60

Arimiti Ferry ✆ 50.57.57 in Papeete, 56.31.10 on Moorea.

Hawaiian Airlines ✆ 42.15.00

Lan Airlines ✆ 50.30.10

Moorea Express Ferry ✆ 45.00.30 in Papeete, 56.43.43 on Moorea.

Tahiti Tourisme ✆ 50.57.12

U.S. Centers for Disease Control International Traveler's Hotline: ✆ 404/332-4559

U.S. Dept. of State Travel Advisory ✆ 202/647-5225 (staffed 24 hr.)

U.S. Passport Agency ✆ 202/647-0518

WATER   Tap water is consistently safe to drink only in Papeete and on Bora Bora. Well water in the Tuamotu islands tends to be brackish; rainwater is used there for drinking. You can buy bottled water at every grocery store. The local brands Vaimato and Eau Royal are much less expensive than imported French waters.

Appendix B: Useful French Terms & Phrases

It's amazing how a word or two of halting French will often change your hosts' disposition. In my experience, this is especially true of the islanders, who genuinely appreciate your attempts to communicate with them in a language they understand. To be frank, many independence-minded Tahitians are not particularly fond of French people, but they quickly warm to us non-French visitors when they hear us speaking less than perfect *français*. It's a quick tip-off that we are from someplace other than France.

At the very least, try to learn a few numbers, basic greetings, and—above all—the life-raft phrase, *Parlez-vous anglais?* (Do you speak English?). Many islanders do speak passable English and will use it liberally, if you demonstrate the basic courtesy of greeting them in their language.

Go out, try our glossary, and don't be bashful. *Bonne chance!* (Good luck!)

1 BASIC FRENCH VOCABULARY & PHRASES

English	French	Pronunciation
Yes/No	**Oui/Non**	Wee/Nohn
Okay	**D'accord**	*Dah*-core
Please	**S'il vous plaît**	Seel voo *play*
Thank you	**Merci**	*Mair*-see
You're welcome	**De rien**	Duh ree-*ehn*
Hello (during daylight)	**Bonjour**	Bohn-*jhoor*
Good evening	**Bonsoir**	Bohn-*swahr*
Goodbye	**Au revoir**	O ruh-*vwahr*
What's your name?	**Comment vous appellez-vous?**	Ko-*mahn* voo za-pell-ay-*voo?*
My name is	**Je m'appelle**	*Jhuh* ma-pell
How are you?	**Comment allez-vous?**	Kuh-mahn tahl-ay-*voo?*
So-so	**Comme ci, comme ça**	Kum *see,* kum *sah*
I'm sorry/excuse me	**Pardon**	Pahr-*dohn*

English	French	Pronunciation
Do you speak English?	**Parlez-vous anglais?**	Par-lay-voo ahn-*glay*?
I don't speak French	**Je ne parle pas français**	Jhuh ne parl pah frahn-*say*
I don't understand	**Je ne comprends pas**	Jhuh ne kohm-*prahn* pas
Could you speak more loudly/ more slowly?	**Pouvez-vous parler plus fort/plus lentement?**	Poo-*vay*-voo par-lay ploo for/ ploo lan-te-*ment*?
What is it?	**Qu'est-ce que c'est?**	Kess-kuh-*say*?
What time is it?	**Qu'elle heure est-il?**	Kel uhr eh-*teel*?
What?	**Quoi?**	Kwah?
How? or What did you say?	**Comment?**	Ko-*mahn*?
When?	**Quand?**	Kahn?
Where is?	**Où est?**	Oo *eh*?
Who?	**Qui?**	Kee?
Why?	**Pourquoi?**	Poor-*kwah*?
here/there	**ici/là**	ee-*see*/lah
left/right	**à gauche/à droite**	a goash/a drwaht
straight ahead	**tout droit**	too-*drwah*
Fill the tank (of a car), please	**Le plein, s'il vous plaît**	Luh plan, seel voo *play*
I want to get off at	**Je voudrais descendre à**	Jhe voo-*dray* day-*son*-drah ah
airport	**l'aéroport**	lair-o-*por*
bank	**la banque**	lah *bahnk*
bridge	**le pont**	luh *pohn*
bus station	**la gare routière**	lah *gar* roo-tee-*air*
bus stop	**l'arrêt de bus**	lah-*ray* duh boohss
by means of a car	**en voiture**	ahn vwa-*toor*
cashier	**la caisse**	lah *kess*
church	**l'église**	lay-*gleez*
driver's license	**le permis de conduire**	luh per-*mee* duh con-*dweer*
elevator	**l'ascenseur**	lah-sahn-*seuhr*
entrance (to a building or a city)	**une porte**	ewn *port*
exit (from a building or a freeway)	**une sortie**	ewn sor-*tee*
gasoline	**du pétrol/de l'essence**	duh pay-*trol*/de lay-*sahns*
hospital	**l'hôpital**	low-pee-*tahl*
luggage storage	**la consigne**	lah kohn-*seen*-yuh
museum	**le musée**	luh mew-*zay*
no smoking	**défense de fumer**	day-*fahns* de fu-may

English	French	Pronunciation
one-day pass	**le ticket journalier**	luh tee-*kay* jhoor-nall-ee-*ay*
one-way ticket	**l'aller simple**	lah-*lay* sam-pluh
police	**la police**	lah po-*lees*
round-trip ticket	**l'aller-retour**	lah-*lay*-re-*toor*
second floor	**le premier étage**	luh prem-ee-*ehr* ay-*taj*
slow down	**ralentir**	rah-lahn-*teer*
store	**le magasin**	luh ma-ga-*zehn*
street	**la rue**	lah *roo*
telephone	**le téléphone**	luh tay-lay-*phone*
ticket	**un billet**	uh *bee*-yay
toilets	**les toilettes/les WC**	lay twa-*lets*/les vay-*say*

NECESSITIES

English	French	Pronunciation
I'd like	**Je voudrais**	Jhe voo-*dray*
a room	**une chambre**	ewn *shahm*-bruh
the key	**la clé (la clef)**	la *clay*
How much does it cost?	**C'est combien?/ Ça coûte combien?**	Say comb-bee-*ehn*?/ Sah coot comb-bee-*ehn*?
That's expensive	**C'est cher/chère**	Say *share*
Do you take credit cards?	**Est-ce que vous acceptez les cartes de credit?**	Es kuh voo zak-sep-*tay* lay kart duh creh-*dee*?
I'd like to buy	**Je voudrais acheter**	Jhe voo-*dray* ahsh-*tay*
aspirin	**des aspirines/ des aspros**	deyz ahs-peer-*een*/ deyz ahs-*proh*
condoms	**des préservatifs**	day pray-ser-va-*teef*
a dress	**une robe**	ewn robe
envelopes	**des envelopes**	days ahn-veh-*lope*
a gift	**un cadeau**	uh kah-*doe*
a handbag	**un sac**	uh sahk
a hat	**un chapeau**	uh shah-*poh*
a map of the city	**un plan de ville**	uh plahn de *veel*
a newspaper	**un journal**	uh zhoor-*nahl*
a phone card	**une carte téléphonique**	ewn cart tay-lay-fone-*eek*
a postcard	**une carte postale**	ewn cart pos-*tahl*
a road map	**une carte routière**	ewn cart roo-tee-*air*
shoes	**des chaussures**	day show-*suhr*
soap	**du savon**	dew sah-*vohn*
a stamp	**un timbre**	uh *tam*-bruh
writing paper	**du papier è lettres**	dew pap-pee-*ay* a *let*-ruh

English	French	Pronunciation
Are taxes included?	**Est-ce que les taxes sont comprises?**	Ess kuh lay taks son com-*preez*?
Is breakfast included?	**Petit déjeuner inclus?**	Peh-*tee* day-jheun-*ay* ehn-*klu*?
We're staying for . . . days	**On reste pour . . . jours**	Ohn *rest* poor . . . jhoor
balcony	**un balcon**	uh *bahl*-cohn
bathtub	**une baignoire**	ewn bayn-*nwar*
hot and cold water	**l'eau chaude et froide**	low *showed* ay fwad
room	**une chambre**	ewn *shawm*-bruh
shower	**une douche**	ewn *doosh*
sink	**un lavabo**	uh la-va-*bow*
suite	**une suite**	ewn *sweet*

NUMBERS & ORDINALS

English	French	Pronunciation
zero	**zéro**	*zare*-oh
one	**un**	oon
two	**deux**	duh
three	**trois**	twah
four	**quatre**	*kaht*-ruh
five	**cinq**	sank
six	**six**	seess
seven	**sept**	set
eight	**huit**	wheat
nine	**neuf**	noof
ten	**dix**	deess
eleven	**onze**	ohnz
twelve	**douze**	dooz
thirteen	**treize**	trehz
fourteen	**quatorze**	kah-*torz*
fifteen	**quinze**	kanz
sixteen	**seize**	sez
seventeen	**dix-sept**	deez-*set*
eighteen	**dix-huit**	deez-*wheat*
nineteen	**dix-neuf**	deez-*noof*
twenty	**vingt**	vehn
thirty	**trente**	trahnt
forty	**quarante**	ka-*rahnt*
fifty	**cinquante**	sang-*kahnt*

English	French	Pronunciation
one hundred	cent	sahn
one thousand	mille	meel
first	premier	*preh*-mee-ay
second	deuxième	*duhz*-zee-em
third	troisième	*twa*-zee-em
fourth	quatrième	*kaht*-ree-em
fifth	cinquième	*sank*-ee-em
sixth	sixième	*sees*-ee-em
seventh	septième	*set*-ee-em
eighth	huitième	*wheat*-ee-em
ninth	neuvième	*neuv*-ee-em
tenth	dixième	*dees*-ee-em

THE CALENDAR

English	French	Pronunciation
Sunday	dimanche	dee-*mahnsh*
Monday	lundi	luhn-*dee*
Tuesday	mardi	mahr-*dee*
Wednesday	mercredi	mair-kruh-*dee*
Thursday	jeudi	jheu-*dee*
Friday	vendredi	vawn-druh-*dee*
Saturday	samedi	sahm-*dee*
yesterday	hier	ee-*air*
today	aujour d'hui	o-jhord *dwee*
this morning/ this afternoon	ce matin/ cet après-midi	suh ma-*tan*/ set ah-preh-mee-*dee*
tonight	ce soir	suh *swahr*
tomorrow	demain	de-*man*

2 FOOD/MENU TERMS

English	French	Pronunciation
I would like to eat	Je voudrais manger	Jhe voo-*dray* mahn-*jhay*
Please give me	Donnez-moi, s'il vous plaît	Doe-nay-*mwah*, seel voo *play*
a bottle of	une bouteille de	ewn boo-*tay* duh
a cup of	une tasse de	ewn *tass* duh
a glass of	un verre de	uh *vair* duh
a plate of breakfast	une assiette de le petit-déjeuner	ewn ass-ee-*et* duh luh puh-*tee*-day-zhuh-*nay*

English	French	Pronunciation
a cocktail	**un apéritif**	uh ah-pay-ree-*teef*
the check/bill	**l'addition/la note**	la-dee-see-*ohn*/la *noat*
dinner	**le dîner**	luh dee-*nay*
a knife	**un couteau**	uh koo-*toe*
a napkin	**une serviette**	ewn sair-vee-*et*
a spoon	**une cuillère**	ewn kwee-*air*
a fork	**une fourchette**	ewn four-*shet*
Cheers!	**A votre santé!**	Ah vo-truh sahn-*tay*!
Waiter!/Waitress!	**Monsieur!/ Mademoiselle!**	Muh-*syuh*/Mad-mwa-*zel*
appetizer	**une entrée**	ewn ahn-*tray*
fixed-price menu	**un menu**	uh may-*new*
main course	**un plat principal**	uh plah pran-see-*pahl*
tasting menu	**menu dégustation**	may-*new* day-gus-ta-see-*on*
tip included	**service compris**	sehr-*vees* com-*pree*
wine list	**une carte des vins**	ewn cart day *van*

MEATS

English	French	Pronunciation
beef stew	**du pot au feu**	dew poht o *fhe*
chicken	**du poulet**	*dew poo*-lay
chicken, stewed with mushrooms and wine	**du coq au vin**	dew cock o *vhin*
frogs' legs	**des cuisses de grenouilles**	day cweess duh gre-*noo*-wee
ham	**du jambon**	dew jham-*bon*
lamb	**de l'agneau**	duh lahn-*nyo*
rabbit	**du lapin**	dew *lah*-pan
rolls of pounded and baked chicken, veal, or fish (often pike), usually served warm	**des quenelles**	day ke-*nelle*
sirloin	**de l'aloyau**	duh lahl-why-*yo*
steak	**du bifteck**	dew beef-*tek*
veal	**du veau**	dew *voh*

FISH

English	French	Pronunciation
fish (freshwater)	**du poisson de rivière,** or **du poisson d'eau douce**	dew pwah-*sson* duh ree-vee-*aire*, dew pwah-sson d'o *dooss*
fish (saltwater)	**du poisson de mer**	dew pwah-*sson* duh *mehr*

English	French	Pronunciation
lobster	du homard	dew oh-*mahr*
Mediterranean fish soup or stew made with tomatoes, garlic, saffron, and olive oil	de la bouillabaisse	duh lah booh-ya-*besse*
mussels	des moules	day *moohl*
oysters	des huîtres	dayz *hwee*-truhs
shrimp	des crevettes	day kreh-*vet*
smoked salmon	du saumon fumé	dew sow-*mohn* fu-*may*
tuna	du thon	dew *tohn*
trout	de la truite	duh lah tru-*eet*

SIDES/APPETIZERS/CONDIMENTS

English	French	Pronunciation
butter	du beurre	dew *bhuhr*
bread	du pain	dew *pan*
gooseliver	du foie gras	dew fwah *grah*
mustard	de la moutarde	duh lah moo-*tard*-uh
pepper	du poivre	dew *pwah*-vruh
potted and minced pork products, prepared as a roughly chopped pâté	des rillettes	day ree-*yett*
rice	du riz	dew *ree*
salt	du sel	dew *sel*
sugar	du sucre	dew *sooh*-kruh

FRUITS/VEGETABLES

English	French	Pronunciation
cabbage	du choux	dew *shoe*
eggplant	de l'aubergine	duh loh-ber-*jheen*
french fries	des pommes frites	day puhm *freet*
fruit salad	une salade de fruit/ une macédoine de fruits	ewn sah-lahd duh *fwee*/ ewn mah-*say*-doine duh fwee
grapes	du raisin	dew ray-*zhan*
green beans	des haricots verts	day *ahr*-ee-coh *vaire*
green salad	une salade verte	ewn sah-lahd *vairt*
lemon/lime	du citron/du citron vert	dew cee-*tron*/dew cee-tron *vaire*

English	French	Pronunciation
lettuce salad	**une salade de laitue**	ewn sah-lahd duh lay-*tew*
pineapple	**de l'ananas**	duh lah-na-*nas*
potatoes	**des pommes de terre**	day puhm duh *tehr*
potatoes au gratin	**des pommes de terre dauphinois**	day puhm duh *tehr* doh-feen-*wah*
spinach	**des épinards**	dayz ay-pin-*ards*
strawberries	**des fraises**	day *frez*

BEVERAGES

English	French	Pronunciation
beer	**de la bière**	duh lah bee-*aire*
coffee (black)	**un café noir**	uh ka-fay *nwahr*
coffee (with cream)	**un café crème**	uh ka-fay *krem*
coffee (with milk)	**un café au lait**	uh ka-fay o *lay*
coffee (decaf)	**un café décaféiné** (slang: **un déca**)	un ka-fay day-kah-fay-nay (uh day-kah)
coffee (espresso)	**un café espresso** (**un express**)	uh ka-fay e-*sprehss*-o (un ek-*sprehss*)
milk	**du lait**	dew *lay*
orange juice	**du jus d'orange**	dew joo d'or-*ahn*-jhe
tea	**du thé**	dew *tay*
tea (herbal)	**une tisane**	ewn tee-*zahn*
water	**de l'eau**	duh *lo*
wine (red)	**du vin rouge**	dew vhin *rooj*
wine (white)	**du vin blanc**	dew vhin *blahn*

DESSERTS

English	French	Pronunciation
cake	**du gâteau**	dew *gha*-tow
caramelized upside-down apple pie	**une tarte tatin**	ewn tart tah-*tihn*
cheese	**du fromage**	dew fro-*mahj*
fruit, especially cherries, cooked in batter	**du clafoutis** **une tarte**	dew kla-foo-*tee* ewn *tart*
thick custard dessert with a caramelized topping	**de la crème brûlée**	duh lah *krem* bruh-*lay*
vanilla ice cream	**de la glace à la vanille**	duh lah *glass* a lah vah-*nee*-yuh

INDEX

See also Accommodations and Restaurant indexes, below.

RESTAURANTS

FROMMER'S® COMPLETE TRAVEL GUIDES

Alaska
Amalfi Coast
American Southwest
Amsterdam
Argentina
Arizona
Atlanta
Australia
Austria
Bahamas
Barcelona
Beijing
Belgium, Holland & Luxembourg
Belize
Bermuda
Boston
Brazil
British Columbia & the Canadian Rockies
Brussels & Bruges
Budapest & the Best of Hungary
Buenos Aires
Calgary
California
Canada
Cancún, Cozumel & the Yucatán
Cape Cod, Nantucket & Martha's Vineyard
Caribbean
Caribbean Ports of Call
Carolinas & Georgia
Chicago
Chile & Easter Island
China
Colorado
Costa Rica
Croatia
Cuba
Denmark
Denver, Boulder & Colorado Springs
Eastern Europe
Ecuador & the Galapagos Islands
Edinburgh & Glasgow
England
Europe
Europe by Rail

Florence, Tuscany & Umbria
Florida
France
Germany
Greece
Greek Islands
Guatemala
Hawaii
Hong Kong
Honolulu, Waikiki & Oahu
India
Ireland
Israel
Italy
Jamaica
Japan
Kauai
Las Vegas
London
Los Angeles
Los Cabos & Baja
Madrid
Maine Coast
Maryland & Delaware
Maui
Mexico
Montana & Wyoming
Montréal & Québec City
Morocco
Moscow & St. Petersburg
Munich & the Bavarian Alps
Nashville & Memphis
New England
Newfoundland & Labrador
New Mexico
New Orleans
New York City
New York State
New Zealand
Northern Italy
Norway
Nova Scotia, New Brunswick & Prince Edward Island
Oregon
Paris
Peru

Philadelphia & the Amish Country
Portugal
Prague & the Best of the Czech Republic
Provence & the Riviera
Puerto Rico
Rome
San Antonio & Austin
San Diego
San Francisco
Santa Fe, Taos & Albuquerque
Scandinavia
Scotland
Seattle
Seville, Granada & the Best of Andalusia
Shanghai
Sicily
Singapore & Malaysia
South Africa
South America
South Florida
South Korea
South Pacific
Southeast Asia
Spain
Sweden
Switzerland
Tahiti & French Polynesia
Texas
Thailand
Tokyo
Toronto
Turkey
USA
Utah
Vancouver & Victoria
Vermont, New Hampshire & Maine
Vienna & the Danube Valley
Vietnam
Virgin Islands
Virginia
Walt Disney World® & Orlando
Washington, D.C.
Washington State

FROMMER'S® DAY BY DAY GUIDES

Amsterdam
Barcelona
Beijing
Boston
Cancun & the Yucatan
Chicago
Florence & Tuscany

Hong Kong
Honolulu & Oahu
London
Maui
Montréal
Napa & Sonoma
New York City

Paris
Provence & the Riviera
Rome
San Francisco
Venice
Washington D.C.

PAULINE FROMMER'S GUIDES: SEE MORE. SPEND LESS.

Alaska
Hawaii
Italy

Las Vegas
London
New York City

Paris
Walt Disney World®
Washington D.C.

FROMMER'S® PORTABLE GUIDES

Acapulco, Ixtapa & Zihuatanejo
Amsterdam
Aruba, Bonaire & Curacao
Australia's Great Barrier Reef
Bahamas
Big Island of Hawaii
Boston
California Wine Country
Cancún
Cayman Islands
Charleston
Chicago
Dominican Republic

Florence
Las Vegas
Las Vegas for Non-Gamblers
London
Maui
Nantucket & Martha's Vineyard
New Orleans
New York City
Paris
Portland
Puerto Rico
Puerto Vallarta, Manzanillo &
    Guadalajara

Rio de Janeiro
San Diego
San Francisco
Savannah
St. Martin, Sint Maarten, Anguila &
    St. Bart's
Turks & Caicos
Vancouver
Venice
Virgin Islands
Washington, D.C.
Whistler

FROMMER'S® CRUISE GUIDES

Alaska Cruises & Ports of Call

Cruises & Ports of Call

European Cruises & Ports of Call

FROMMER'S® NATIONAL PARK GUIDES

Algonquin Provincial Park
Banff & Jasper
Grand Canyon

National Parks of the American West
Rocky Mountain
Yellowstone & Grand Teton

Yosemite and Sequoia & Kings
    Canyon
Zion & Bryce Canyon

FROMMER'S® WITH KIDS GUIDES

Chicago
Hawaii
Las Vegas
London

National Parks
New York City
San Francisco

Toronto
Walt Disney World® & Orlando
Washington, D.C.

FROMMER'S® PHRASEFINDER DICTIONARY GUIDES

Chinese
French

German
Italian

Japanese
Spanish

SUZY GERSHMAN'S BORN TO SHOP GUIDES

France
Hong Kong, Shanghai & Beijing
Italy

London
New York
Paris

San Francisco
Where to Buy the Best of Everything

FROMMER'S® BEST-LOVED DRIVING TOURS

Britain
California
France
Germany

Ireland
Italy
New England
Northern Italy

Scotland
Spain
Tuscany & Umbria

THE UNOFFICIAL GUIDES®

Adventure Travel in Alaska
Beyond Disney
California with Kids
Central Italy
Chicago
Cruises
Disneyland®
England
Hawaii

Ireland
Las Vegas
London
Maui
Mexico's Best Beach Resorts
Mini Mickey
New Orleans
New York City
Paris

San Francisco
South Florida including Miami &
    the Keys
Walt Disney World®
Walt Disney World® for
    Grown-ups
Walt Disney World® with Kids
Washington, D.C.

SPECIAL-INTEREST TITLES

Athens Past & Present
Best Places to Raise Your Family
Cities Ranked & Rated
500 Places to Take Your Kids Before They Grow Up
Frommer's Best Day Trips from London
Frommer's Best RV & Tent Campgrounds in the U.S.A.

Frommer's Exploring America by RV
Frommer's NYC Free & Dirt Cheap
Frommer's Road Atlas Europe
Frommer's Road Atlas Ireland
Retirement Places Rated